HOLLYWOOD BE THY NAME

HOLLYWOOD BE THY NAME

African American Religion in American Film,
1929–1949

JUDITH WEISENFELD

University of California Press

Berkeley   Los Angeles   London

The publisher gratefully acknowledges the generous
contribution to this book provided by the African
American Studies Endowment Fund of the University
of California Press Foundation, which is supported by
a major gift from the George Gund Foundation.

University of California Press, one of the most distinguished university presses in the United States, enriches
lives around the world by advancing scholarship in the
humanities, social sciences, and natural sciences. Its
activities are supported by the UC Press Foundation
and by philanthropic contributions from individuals
and institutions. For more information, visit
www.ucpress.edu.

University of California Press
Berkeley and Los Angeles, California

University of California Press, Ltd.
London, England

Library of Congress Cataloging-in-Publication Data

Weisenfeld, Judith.
  Hollywood be thy name : African American religion
in American film, 1929–1949 / Judith Weisenfeld.
      p.   cm.
  Includes bibliographical references and index.
  ISBN 978-0-520-22774-3 (cloth : alk. paper).—ISBN
978-0-520-25100-7 (pbk. : alk. paper)
  1. African Americans in motion pictures.
2. Religion in motion pictures.   3. Motion pictures—
United States. I. Title.
PN1995.9.N4W45   2007
791.43′652996073—dc22   2006037488

Manufactured in the United States of America

16 15 14 13 12 11 10 09 08 07
10 9 8 7 6 5 4 3 2 1

This book is printed on New Leaf EcoBook 50, a 100%
recycled fiber of which 50% is de-inked post-consumer
waste, processed chlorine-free. EcoBook 50 is acid-free
and meets the minimum requirements of ANSI/ASTM
D5634–01 (Permanence of Paper).

For Timea

CONTENTS

ILLUSTRATIONS

ACKNOWLEDGMENTS

I am truly fortunate to have had the support of family, friends, and colleagues in the course of what has been a much longer and more difficult journey than I had imagined when I began this project. Lisa Collins, David Gerstner, Paula Massood, Colleen McDannell, MacDonald Moore, Barbara Savage, Jacqueline Stewart, Timea Széll, Terry Todd, and David Wills read part or all of the manuscript and contributed to my work through their extraordinarily thoughtful and careful evaluation of the work-in-progress. The project also benefited from the questions and comments of students and faculty at colleges and universities that were generous enough to invite me to discuss my work, and I am especially grateful to participants in the working group on African American religion in the 1930s that David Wills organized at Amherst College.

Many other colleagues and friends provided direct and indirect support along the way, including Mark Cladis, Marc Epstein, Rick Jarow, Margaret Leeming, Lynn LiDonnici, Larry Mamiya, Deborah Dash Moore, Michael Walsh, Tova Weitzman, my valued colleagues in the Department of Religion at Vassar, and Wendy Borden, our department secretary. Joan Bailey, Lee Bernstein, Joan Bryant, Andy Bush, Anthea Butler, Elizabeth Castelli, Celia Deutsch, Heather Hendershot, Kathryn Jay, Martha Jones, Laurie Maffly-Kipp, Mary McGee, Charles Musser, Ann Pellegrini, Caryl Phillips, Albert Raboteau, Jana Riess, Susan Shapiro, Valerie Smith, and Jeffrey Stout have also offered valuable wisdom and encouragement. Writing group members Karen van Dyck, Linda Green, Zita Nunes, Maggie Sale, Priscilla Wald, and Angela Zito helped me define the project in its early stages, as did R. Marie Griffith, James Hudnut-Beumler, Colleen McDannell, Robert Orsi, Daniel Sack, Leigh Schmidt, David Harrington Watt, and Diane Winston in the Material History of American Religion Project. Chaya Deitsch's friendship and hospitality made research trips to Los Angeles a pleasure, and she has also been a generous reader of the work-in-progress. The project took an unexpected turn during my year as a fellow-in-residence at the Institute for the Advanced Study of Religion at Yale; fellows Cheryl Townsend Gilkes and Nick Salvatore offered much helpful advice as I set out in new directions, and I also thank them for their mentorship during a period of professional transition. I am indebted to Jon Butler and Harry Stout for the opportunity of time, space, and fellowship that the year at the institute afforded and to Kenneth Minkema and the staff for their administrative assistance. The late Richard Newman was a wonderful mentor who always made time to talk about my work and provide suggestions for new research resources and avenues. I try to keep his enthusiasm for research and his humor with me, and I hope he would have enjoyed the final version of this project. I thank my research assistants at Vassar, especially Josh Boydstun, Rashaad Chowdhury, and Emily Vezina, for putting in much hard work on the project and Kaile Shilling from Loyola Marymount University for additional assistance.

Grants from a number of projects, foundations, and institutions helped with travel to archives and provided time for research and writing. I am grateful for the support of the National Endowment for the Humanities Summer Stipend, the Material History of American Religion Project, the Institute for the Advanced Study of Religion at Yale, and the Robert R. Woodruff Library at Emory University for their generous financial support. I also wish to acknowledge the Vassar College Brink Fund for assistance with the publication of the book. The librarians and archivists at the Margaret Herrick Library at the Academy of Motion Picture Arts and Sciences and the Cinema-Television Library at the University of Southern California offered invaluable assistance, as did Randy Roberts in the Axe Library Special Collections at Pittsburg State University and Randall K. Burkett in the Robert R. Woodruff Library at Emory University. I am tremendously grateful for John Kisch's generosity in providing a large number of the images reproduced in the book. His Separate Cinema Archive is extraordinary, and this project is greatly enhanced by these illustrations.

The opportunity to publish some of the work-in-progress helped me to develop the project in ways that have certainly improved it, and I thank the editors of the volumes for their support. Earlier versions of parts of the work have appeared in

"Projecting Blackness: African-American Religion in the Hollywood Imagination," in *Race, Nation and Religion in the Americas*, ed. Henry Goldschmidt and Elizabeth McAlister (Oxford University Press, 2004), 305–27; "Saturday Sinners and Sunday Saints: The Nightclub as Urban Menace in 1940s Race Movies," in *Faith in the Market: Religion and The Rise of Urban Commercial Culture*, ed. John Giggie and Diane Winston (Rutgers University Press, 2002); "Teaching Morality in Race Movies," in *Religions of the United States in Practice*, ed. Colleen McDannell (Princeton University Press, 2001), 2:131–40; "For the Cause of Mankind: The Bible, Racial Uplift, and Early Race Movies," in *African Americans and the Bible: Sacred Texts and Social Textures*, ed. Vincent Wimbush (Continuum, 2000), 728–42; and "For Rent: 'Cabin in the Sky': Race, Religion, and Representational Quagmires in American Film," *Semeia* 74 (1996): 147–65.

Reed Malcolm, my editor at the University of California Press, has been enthusiastic, supportive, warm, and extraordinarily patient, and I am grateful for his thoughtful comments on the manuscript and his wisdom in guiding me through the process of bringing this project to completion. Mary Severance and the production staff were wonderful to work with as well.

My greatest thanks go to Timea Széll, whose love, generosity, humor, intellectual rigor, and unfailing confidence mean more than I can say. I have dedicated this work to her as a small offering for everything she has given me.

Introduction

In November and December of 1928, *The King of Kings*, Cecil B. DeMille's silent film about the life of Christ, played at the Royal Theatre in Baltimore, one of eleven theaters in the city that catered exclusively to black audiences. The movie proved so popular that the theater booked it for a return engagement and enhanced the show by adding "special religious music by a choir of trained voices as well as special orchestral effects by the Royal Symphonic Orchestra."[1] In addition to announcing that the film had been held over, Baltimore's black weekly, the *Afro-American*, published an item recounting an event at a late November screening under the headline "Women Get Happy, Shout at Moving Picture Show." The paper presented the ecstatic, emotional, and embodied response of audience members Alice Harris and Hattie Hutchins to the movie as humorous, hinting strongly that their behavior was inappropriate for the modern urban environment. "'Old time religion' was felt at a picture show performance here recently," the brief account began, "when two women, becoming happy, were injured when they fell shouting down the steps of the Royal theatre during the showing of 'King of Kings.'" The item noted that the women, both in their sixties, were overcome by religious ecstasy and, while heading downstairs from the balcony, "fell down the stairs shouting." One fractured an arm and the other received lacerations on her face.[2]

What is remarkable about this account, probably included in the *Afro-American* simply for its entertainment value, is what it reveals about how some African Americans engaged film in the early twentieth century. The stage was set for this partic-

ular encounter by the fact that the film was self-consciously religious. White director DeMille saw great potential in the cinema as a vehicle for religious instruction
and directed many religious spectacles and biblical epics in the 1920s and 1930s and
again in the 1950s.[3] Black audiences clearly appreciated *The King of Kings,* and it is
possible that the theater added a choir performance not only in response to audiences' enthusiastic support for the film as entertainment but also in recognition of
some general sense among its patrons that the event was a religious one. DeMille's
popularity with African American audiences continued when, in 1933, *The Sign of
the Cross* opened at the Tivoli Theater in Los Angeles. On this occasion, the black
weekly the *California Eagle* commented, "It is remarkable the effect the stirring and
frequently deeply pathetic scenes had on the audience. Tears were frequently seen
in the eyes of the patrons as the perfect screen and sound brought the ancient scenes
to life again."[4] For Harris and Hutchins and perhaps many others who sat in the darkened Royal Theatre and watched the life of Christ play before their eyes, the exhibition of DeMille's *The King of Kings* rendered the movie theater an appropriate
place for religious expression, and these women fashioned their own religious meaning from the movie experience with particular enthusiasm. Had they not been injured,
the account of their religious ecstasy, an experience enabled by viewing a film, would
never have been preserved.

In the case of this particular biblical epic featuring white actors, spectatorship facilitated an exuberant religious experience for some African Americans, but typically
the appearance of African and African American religious practices on movie screens
elicited a very different response from black audiences. Writing in *The Crisis* in 1934,
Loren Miller, a black Los Angeles–based civil rights attorney, bemoaned the troubling presence of "Uncle Tom in Hollywood." Miller decried an industry whose
products encouraged black audiences to cheer for the white hero who rescues the
blonde heroine from "savage" Africans and to consume newsreels that "poke fun
at Negro revivals or baptisings."[5] He argued forcefully that African Americans
should take very seriously the impact of media on American political and social life.
"The cumulative effect of constant picturization of this kind is tremendously effective in shaping racial attitudes. Hollywood products are seen in every nook and corner of the world. Millions of non-residents of the United States depend almost
entirely on the movies for their knowledge of Negro life, as those who have been
abroad can testify. Other millions of white Americans of all ages confirm their beliefs
about Negroes at the neighborhood theaters while Negroes themselves fortify their
inferiority complex by seeing themselves always cast as the underdog to be laughed
at or despised." Miller's focus on religion in both examples of representations that

concerned him—scenes of heathen Africans practicing human sacrifice and of emotional and overwrought African American revivals—emphasizes the contribution that portrayals of black religion have made to the production of ideas about race in general and about African Americans in particular.

This book traces the contours of cinematic representations of African American religion in American film from the late 1920s through the late 1940s, addressing some of the concerns Loren Miller raised in his discussion of the racial implications of Hollywood productions. Examining movies produced in a variety of arenas and for a range of audiences, including films by white directors from Hollywood and "Poverty Row"[6] and by independent and semi-independent black filmmakers, I argue that religion was central to American film's representations of African Americans in this period. To be sure, black religious practices had appeared in American films by both black and white directors from the industry's earliest years. The presence of such images and themes in American popular culture reflected the long-standing importance of religion for many members of African American communities both as an expression of an individually held spiritual commitment and, institutionally, as a route to forming communal identity, exercising corporate political and social influence, and fostering economic development. In the absence of access to certain kinds of freedom and power, the formation of black religious community gave many people the experience of other sorts of economic and spiritual liberty. It is no wonder, then, that significant institutional, ritual, and cultural expressions of black religiosity would prove appealing to filmmakers who were interested in representing black life and characters. The prominence of black church denominations like the National Baptist Convention, the African Methodist Episcopal Church, and the Church of God in Christ, for example, and the influence of black religious cultural forms, particularly musical expression, in twentieth-century black life made religious themes natural subject matter for the movies.[7]

At the same time that the power of religious institutions and expressions in black life contributed to filmmakers' desire to include representations of black religion in the movies, this subject matter, when projected by Hollywood, served broader ideological functions. It may have been natural for Hollywood filmmakers to look to religion when they told stories about or stories that included African Americans, but we must think further about the varied motivations for doing so. The American film industry's portrayal of black religion contributed powerfully to the medium's function as one of many cultural means of formulating and promoting ideas about race in twentieth-century America. Articulating racial and ethnic categories in conjunction with discourses about Americanness has been an integral part of American film from the earliest years of moviemaking in the United States. As Daniel Bernardi notes in his collection on race and early film, "[C]inema's invention and early development coincided with the rise in power and prestige of biological determinism, with increased immigration and immigrant restriction laws, and with the United States' imperialist practices in the Caribbean and Asia." He further argues that these "sociopolitical practices" so profoundly affected the development of early cinema that processes of racializing can be seen across "studios, authors, genres, and styles."[8] Exploring, defining, and projecting concepts of race, then, were woven into the fabric of this industry that would become such an influential part of American popular culture. By the 1930s, when the Hollywood studio system had solidified what scholars refer to as the classical Hollywood style, race had become a central and unremarked component of silver screen images of Americanness.[9]

As much as scholars of American film have identified and examined the ideological functions of the cinema with regard to the production and maintenance of racial categories and racial hierarchy, none have addressed the profound connections between ideas and representations of religion and those of race in the history or the filmic presentation of African Americans. Similarly, scholars of African American religion have not attended to complicated and significant cultural approaches to the creation of religious and racialized meaning in American history. The production and maintenance of racial categories require "technologies"—legitimating mechanisms that help structure our lives in public and material ways as well as in more subtle and veiled ways of which we are sometimes hardly aware. These technologies consist of the set of elaborated discourses, "implemented through pedagogy, medicine, demography, . . . [and] economics," for example, that produce, reproduce, and seek to regulate race.[10] Film, as a significant contributor to the discursive production of race, gender, and sexuality in America, deserves an important place in any discussion of the technology of race.

My broadest concern in this book is with the ways American films have represented religion, specifically African American religion, through the technology of race. The involvement of representations of religion in particular ways of racializing characters in film (that is, using the power and the privileged gaze of the camera to invest skin color with moral meaning) is striking even in any brief survey of American movies. The coupling of religion and race at certain moments in film authorizes and naturalizes American racial categories and works to describe and prescribe the boundaries of the category of religion. In many cases, mobilizing race in relation to religion helps train the spectator with regard to what is and is not to be considered appropriate religion for the American context. The drive to define insider and outsider categories of religion, common in so many social contexts, has often coincided with the power exercised in the United States by some racialized groups over others. We must understand the contest for the right to define what constitutes religion as situated in a field of other categories in process, including those of "modern," "primitive," "American," "foreign," "man," "woman," "black," and "white." Lillian Smith, in reflecting on growing up white in the Jim Crow American South, has described the impossibility of disaggregating the elements that have contributed to the formation of American identities and of understanding these categories in isolation from one another. "Religion . . . sex . . . race . . . avoidance rites . . . —no part of these can be looked at and clearly seen without looking at the whole of them. For, as a painter mixes colors and makes them new colors, so religion is turned into something different by race, and segregation is colored as much by sex as by skin pigment."[11] Film has functioned as an important arena in which this mixing has taken place.

Hollywood Be Thy Name examines the complicated ways filmmakers and their films engaged in the ongoing process of articulating race and religion in America in the early twentieth century. The migration and increasing urbanization of African Americans over the first decades of the twentieth century, the religious, artistic, and literary creativity that emerged from burgeoning urban centers, and the development in the 1920s of technology to produce sound film fostered conditions that made the representation of African American subject matter appealing. Demographic shifts in America's black population from rural to urban captured artistic imaginations, as did the potential consequences of this transformation for African American claims to modernity and to citizenship. Black and white filmmakers were particularly drawn to the possibilities that black religious music offered for the new sound technology, and Hollywood and independent studios recognized the aesthetic power of African American religious expression, so often grounded in using the body's sound and motion as conduits to the divine. Many actors brought to the productions I consider in the book their experiences with and commitment to a religious way of being that emphasized modes of worship developed in African American social contexts and that valued oral and embodied performances of the Word. Attempts to translate these religious commitments to the artistic medium of film often generated debate in African American communities over the appropriateness of literalizing complex theological ideas and of commodifying them in popular culture. The major Hollywood films of the period generally mobilized black religious aesthetics in service of an essentialized understanding of African American religion, presenting something the filmmakers understood to be the fundamental religious and racial nature of "the Negro race." In this view, African Americans do not experience the true power of the divine in their lives but simply imagine—through childish, emotional, and musical displays, devoid of theological inquiry—that they do. But as consistently as Hollywood promoted this essentialized view, there were significant variations in the approaches that different filmmakers took to their explorations, as well as important changes over time in relation to changing religious, social, and political contexts. African American religion proved to be a flexible trope, tool, and lens. I argue that filmmakers' explorations of religion spoke to broader issues about American identity and citizenship and projected ways of understanding African Americans' location in relation to both.

Although representations of African and African-derived religious traditions in the Americas and Caribbean played an important part in how Hollywood film in particular imagined black religion, my work focuses specifically on filmic interpretations of Christianity in African American contexts. My intention is neither to underestimate the power of film images of African and African-derived religious traditions in shaping American racial discourse nor to conflate "religion" and "Christianity" but rather to chart the large portion of the discussion about and images of African American religion in American film that posits Christian practices as critical terrain for understanding African American identity. In some instances, the rendering of African American religion is explicitly Christian and tied to particular denominational contexts, and in others it is more generally biblically oriented. Exploring under what circumstances and to what ends the films I examine in this work make such distinctions is useful for understanding the films' construction of relationships between religion, race, and American identity.

The study also explores how black audiences and critics engaged these white mainstream entertainment products as having profound religious, political, and social consequences and, in some cases, produced their own films to narrate themselves religiously and politically. Alice Harris and Hattie Hutchins's ecstatic response to viewing a movie provides evidence of a religious approach to the filmgoing experience, and part of this work is devoted to examining how black filmmakers sought to make film an accepted and productive part of the religious lives of African Americans by creating films for black audiences with the intention of producing religious affect in viewers and motivating a commitment to Christian standards of behavior. Relatively few examples of such films survive, but these significant pieces of black religious art are crucial for understanding the broad sweep of representational practices with regard to black religion in the period. I am also concerned with how taking films seriously as religious texts reshapes our understanding of twentieth-century

African American religion. While African Americans' access to explicitly religious black films was occasional at best, the existence of these films—as well as accounts of their emotional impact and commercial success—calls on us to think expansively about what constitutes the stuff of black religious life, including various visual arts, commercial or otherwise, alongside the well-mined textual and musical sources.

Studying the varied approaches of Hollywood and Poverty Row studios, as well as independent and semi-independent black filmmakers, to representing African American religion in the first half of the twentieth century requires attention to a number of contexts, some of which are considered in this book and others of which open up areas beyond its scope. It is important to begin with brief discussions of religious and moral influences on the Hollywood studio system; the theatrical precedents for Hollywood representations of African American religion and the dialogue between plays and films; and the complicated and varied responses of black religious leaders to American popular culture and to movies in particular. Together, these general contexts set the stage for the specific cases I examine in individual chapters.

The Hollywood studio system, which standardized the narrative style of film that has come to dominate American moviemaking, has been a profoundly influential arena for the production of representations of African American religion in American culture. The control that Hollywood studios exercised over the vast majority of film images of African Americans meant not only that the studios' box-office and broader economic concerns set the terms for how black religion made its way into the movies but also that the industry's investments in the construction of particular understandings of American identity helped shape Hollywood products. Various modes of censorship, through which the studios and religious critics of the movies policed the moral content of films that were released by major studios, functioned as central mechanisms for envisioning and projecting religion and race, always powerful components of constructions of Americanness.[12] Thomas Doherty reminds us that "to think of classical Hollywood cinema is to think not solely of a means of production and film style, silent or sound, but to conjure a moral universe with known visual and ethical outlines. . . . What makes Hollywood's classic age 'classical' is not just the film style or the studio system but the moral stakes."[13] The ways in which censorship, formal and informal, worked to project and police understandings of religion as fundamentally racialized unquestionably upped the moral stakes, for Hollywood could not run the political or economic risk of contravening the nation's long-standing religious and racial hierarchies, nor did it generally desire to do so. Understanding the context in which studios, filmmakers, censors, and viewers mapped this moral landscape with regard to representations of religion and race generally and African American religion specifically is a central concern of this book.

In the early 1930s, seeking to offset mounting criticism of their products and avoid the imposition of federal censorship, the studios agreed to submit to a system of self-censorship. The standards for the projection of Hollywood's moral universe became codified in the Production Code, a set of guidelines written by Father Daniel J. Lord, S.J.; Martin Quigley, a Catholic layman; and Will Hays, a Presbyterian elder. After 1934, the code was administered by the Production Code Administration (PCA) of the Motion Picture Producers and Distributors Association (MPPDA), with another Catholic layman, Joseph Breen, overseeing the PCA's work. The code, whose animating principle was that consumption of any film should not "lower the moral standards of those who view it," marked an expansion of an earlier list of "Don'ts and Be Carefuls." Although the MPPDA adopted the code in 1930, the association did not administer it with vigor until 1934, and from that point on the PCA and the code became central agents in defining the bounds of Hollywood's moral universe. Under the Production Code, Hollywood studios submitted their products for review by the PCA, which then attempted to ensure that art and entertainment would not glorify "evil" or "sin." The review began at the earliest stages of production, in accordance with the insistence of some white religious film reformers that "we cannot cut the devil out of a picture with a pair of scissors; we must go back to the source of a production."[14] The code's requirements, though concerned primarily with sex and crime, stipulated as well that Hollywood films must not "throw *ridicule* on any religious faith," that "*ministers of religion* in their character as ministers of religion" should not be used for humorous purposes or be cast as villains, and that any presentation of a religious ritual should be done respectfully and with attention to accuracy. Its provisions regarding the handling of sex included the expected prohibitions for its era, such as adultery, prostitution, rape, and homosexuality, but also explicitly forbade the representation of "miscegenation," which the code's authors defined specifically as a "sex relationship between the white and black race." In addition, the code included a prohibition against any unfair representation of "the history, institutions, prominent people and citizenry of other nations" but failed to ban offensive representations of "any race," as had been the case in the "Don'ts and Be Carefuls," a provision of the earlier guidelines that had made African American observers hopeful for the film industry's future.[15]

Many of the white religious reformers who advocated federal censorship or who helped to shape the self-censorship system of the Production Code wanted to accomplish more than simply shielding viewers from images of sex and crime. They also envisioned the possibilities the movies held for transforming American society in positive ways. At the same time, these white Christian reformers' investment in the progressive possibilities of film often relied on and promoted narrow and exclusionary constructions of Americanness. Throughout the 1920s and 1930s a good deal of the discourse about the dangers that movies posed to American society blamed the predominance of American Jews in positions of power in Hollywood.[16] Even when white Protestant and Catholic reformers did not interpret what they saw as the morally degrading state of the motion picture industry to be the result of a Jewish conspiracy, concern about the moral content of movies often took the shape of fear about how the movies might sap the ability of a white Christian America to lead the world.[17] Thus, for many reformers, the campaign to protect American morals from the dangers of the movies was necessarily a project of policing and enforcing American identity, at home and abroad, as white and Christian.[18] Some commentators who were opposed to any mechanism of formal censorship, whether state censor boards, a federally controlled process, or self-censorship, understood the code and its antecedents as attempting to provide a protected space for Christianity in the movies and as participating in the production and maintenance of racial hierarchy, goals that often proved inextricably intertwined.[19]

While the censors pursued an agenda that helped set the moral terms for Hollywood, their work necessarily began with the projects the studios already had under way and was limited in many regards by the studios' particular interests and goals in representing religion and race. The exclusion of African American actors, writers, and directors from positions of power within the Hollywood studio system ensured that, when Hollywood did present black religion on film, African Americans could do little to help shape those representations. Greater opportunities in this period for black artistic agency were provided in the arena of theater, where religious themes appeared frequently. Black artists and audiences nevertheless had to contend with fetishizing and demeaning constructions of African and African American religious practices in theater just as they did in their consumption of film. An understanding of the interactions between theater and film in the representation of African American religion, while outside the scope of this project in its full detail, provides important background for an examination of film.

Hollywood's interest in African American religion as potential subject matter for the movies grew, in part, from the success of black-themed plays on Broadway and in theaters in other cities, particularly in the 1920s and 1930s. An important early entrant in this group of plays was the white playwright Ridgley Torrence's *Three Plays for a Negro Theatre*, which opened in New York in 1917 and included the one-act play *Simon the Cyrenian* and a setting of Jesus's crucifixion in an all-black context.[20] Other white playwrights followed suit, producing all-black-cast dramas and frequently using religious themes, characters, and settings. Nan Bagby Stephens's successful *Roseanne* (1923) featured Paul Robeson playing a greedy and manipulative black minister who wreaks havoc on his congregation, and Em Jo Basshe's poorly received *Earth* (1927) revolved around a struggle between a church congregation and "the voodoistic rites" of a "witch doctor."[21] Marc Connelly's wildly successful Pulitzer Prize–winning *The Green Pastures* opened on Broadway in 1930 and in many ways set the standard for judging every play thereafter that engaged black religion, whether written by black or white playwrights.

It was, no doubt, the sense that plays about black religion were "in" that led to the strangest and most controversial entrant in black-subject plays with religious themes—Ethel Barrymore's dramatization of *Scarlet Sister Mary*, a Pulitzer Prize–winning novel by the white author Julia Peterkin. Opening in Columbus and then moving to Broadway, the play starred Barrymore in blackface makeup as Sister Mary or Si May-e, a Gullah woman who moves between the church and conjure practices. Theater critics were united in their negative response to the production, which apparently made it to Broadway only because Barrymore was able to stage it at her own theater.[22] The black critic Theophilus Lewis panned the show and mused that "the ineptitude of the play is accompanied by gaucheries of a production that reminded me of a performance given in the basement of the Fourth Baptist Church by members of the Ladies' Auxiliary to raise money to buy the pastor a new overcoat."[23] The play closed after only twenty-four performances. Despite its failure and the ridicule of Barrymore by black and white critics alike, *Scarlet Sister Mary* was, as Langston Hughes noted years later, a significant marker of the era when "the Negro was in vogue."[24]

During that era, a group of black playwrights who were interested in religious questions were able to see their works produced on the New York stage. Garland Anderson, the first African American to have a play produced on Broadway, promoted his work, which featured a hotel bellhop who heals through "a combination of new thought and faith healing," as delivering a spiritual message "to prove to everyone who sees it that they can accomplish much bigger things if they will but believe and trust in their own divine self."[25] Anderson had been working as a bellhop at a San Francisco hotel when he wrote *Judge Not by Appearances* after laboring over the Bible and praying for God to help him deliver his message. He sent it around to several producers and critics, who responded positively and eventually forwarded it to Al Jolson. Jolson liked the play so much that he paid Anderson's way east, and New Yorkers raised money to get it produced.[26] Although some New Yorkers were clearly taken with the idea of seeing a former bellhop's play on Broadway, *Appearances* opened in October of 1923 to negative reviews, with one critic describing it as "a strange potpourri of not ineffective melodrama and Pollyannaish preaching."[27] Despite the negative critical response from white critics, Anderson's play provided an opening for black playwrights to capitalize on the commercial popularity of black religious subjects in theater, and even though they were not entirely successful in exercising complete control in shaping these representations the opportunities were important.[28] As uneven as the quality of these black-cast productions with religious themes proved to be, the cycle of plays had an influence on Hollywood and on the race movie industry, prompting the production of a set of films that elicited strong responses from African Americans. In addition, portrayals of African American religious thought and practices in theater and film generated considerable debate within black church communities about the relationship between religion and entertainment.

Throughout the first half of the twentieth century, many black civil rights activists, film critics, and artists argued that attentiveness to filmic representations of African American religion would be critical for the progress of the race. For example, in an important 1944 survey on the place of the media in improving race relations, the reporter and activist L. D. Reddick identified "the superstitious church-goer" as one of the "principal stereotypes of the Negro in the American mind" that was widely promoted in American film. Real progress in race relations, he argued, depended on recognizing the propagandistic power of the media and putting an end to "the stream of anti-Negro propaganda" issuing from them.[29] Many African Americans interested in the function of black churches as major political voices bemoaned the failure of religious leaders to engage the movies and other popular entertainments, calling on them not only to protest potentially damaging images but to adopt a more productive attitude toward the movies. Simply characterizing worldly entertainments as sinful and to be avoided, these activists argued, would not address the problem of racist film images. By the time Hollywood turned its attention to all-black-cast films in the early sound era, white Protestant and Catholic leaders had established themselves, through the emerging mechanisms of film censorship, as the most significant arbiters of the moral content of films.[30] Importantly, many white Protestant clergy had also looked to bring "both secular and religious film into the church as an aid to evangelism, entertainment, education, and the sermon."[31] Black film commentators noted with disappointment that black church leaders had neither attempted to shape the moral valence of the movies nor embraced the religious potential of cinema. While this was not entirely accurate—there are several examples of involvement of clergy in attempts to create black film production companies in the industry's early years—these critics of churches argued that the consequences of such inaction could be profound, both for the churches and for African Americans in general.[32]

In many cases, these discussions were framed by broad questions about entertainment culture and about whether and how African Americans should seek pleasure, both inside and outside the church. Not only did film critics and other black intellectuals chastise black religious leaders for failing to engage film in a productive way, but they spared no ink in lambasting ministers for their public campaigns against moviegoing. They charged that churches opposed the movies simply because moviegoing represented a threat to their cultural dominance and siphoned money from church projects. "The Investigator" penned a piece for the *Half-Century Magazine* that highlighted the inconsistency of ministers who condemned their congregants for going to the movies and spending money on entertainments while they themselves presented plays in church to raise funds. "The fact that the minister will not only urge the members to attend the play given in the church, but enjoys it heartily is proof enough that he approves of plays and musicals as a form of entertainment. His only reason for condemning his members for attending a show in a regular playhouse is because the price of admission to the show will be going into the coffers of the playhouse instead of into the pockets of the minister and the trustees of the church."[33] Ministers readily bracketed the dictates of conservative theology when financial issues came into play, the writer argued.

Jean Voltaire Smith also made a plea in the *Half-Century Magazine* for ministers to stop campaigning against movies. She wrote, "Like many other forms of amusement, the cinema had been condemned by many of our religious leaders for various reasons. In many sections the war between the church and the motion picture theater has been a very bitter one." She reported that a survey of teachers and students at a school in a large city revealed a high level of attendance at the movies—"as many as nine shows a week"—indicating a profound shift in attention from the church to the movies. "This means," she concluded, "that an enormous amount of money is spent in the motion picture theaters, much of which would reach the church, if the movies were less popular." Smith predicted that ministers would preach to "tiny audience[s] in despair" as movie audiences grew unless they could develop a more nuanced attitude toward the increasingly powerful cinema. Educational, historical, and biblical films were both entertaining and worthwhile, she insisted, and ministers should encourage attendance at such movies, as well as support the production of wholesome, educational fare that could promote racial uplift. In short, she concluded that the church's "prejudice against stage folks is like the prejudice of most white people against Colored—they judge the whole race by a few miscreants."[34]

From within church contexts, several commentators took up the question of the relationship between entertainments and religious life and the possibilities for pleasure in the life of the church and its members. For example, in 1936 the *Georgia Baptist*, the organ of the General Missionary Baptist Convention of Georgia, presented a two-part series entitled "The Church and Recreation," addressing the issue as it related to "the conservative Negro Churchman and the laity." The unattributed essay argued that neither the view "that any kind of social or entertainment given by the church or otherwise is inherently evil" nor the view "that all socials given and attended exclusively by the church people are good" could address adequately the place of entertainment in African American life.[35] The author concluded that the church should not abdicate responsibility for recreation, arguing that Christians and their institutions should be active in all aspects of social life and that they should seek varied ways to do so. "Here is an entirely new field for the work of the S. S. [Sunday School] and B.Y.P.U. [Baptist Young People's Union] Convention in the future. Here is something the church might do in order that all of us might get a new picture of how Christians may engage in amusements of our future churches and 'go by unharmed.'"[36] Entertainment need not be socially or morally damaging simply because it brought pleasure, the piece argued. Writing in the January 1932 issue of the *A.M.E. Church Review*, Dennis A. Bethea, a medical doctor from Indiana, also took the church to task for not taking seriously the current "era of leisure" (brought about in part through technological advances as well as profound unemployment). "In the past," Bethea wrote, "the church has been the Negro's old reliable, and it has never proved false to him; so I feel that we must call it into service at this junction. The church has meant a great deal to the race. Of course at the present time, its influence is on the wane. There has been a decided letting down from the spiritual fervor of the past. Folk treat the church now just about as they would a step-child or a third-hand automobile."[37] Bethea proposed that churches focus on the primary function of offering religious services (leaving recreation to the YWCA and YMCA) and that these services be shortened and "pepped up." For Bethea, religion was an essential part of human life, but it should be simply one part of a varied social and political life, with leisure and entertainment valued as well. He concluded, "I think a mistake has been made by the church in denouncing all kinds of amusements. Now, it is good for anyone to have fun or sport, for it lightens up your being like yeast in bread. It would be advantageous for even the minister to occasionally go to a good 'movie' or to the theatre for a good play, or to the ball game. We should condemn vile amusements, but encourage those that are clean, providing our people do not go amusement crazy."[38]

While church members like Bethea and the writer in the *Georgia Baptist* felt that black Christian clergy should not denounce entertainments categorically but insisted that entertainment remain outside the realm of the church, other ministers and laypeople sought to foster a more engaged relationship between the two arenas. In his work on mid-twentieth-century black churches in Brooklyn, Clarence Taylor notes that "as mass culture took on greater significance, churches decided to adopt it, in part, to attract and hold on to members. Many churches made a decision that they could reconcile mass cultural activities with Christian principles. . . . Church leaders were also attempting to challenge the growing preoccupation with secular mass culture by offering their own brand of popular entertainment, remaining moral leaders of the community as they attempted to adopt mass forms within the boundaries of Christian principles."[39] Thus, even while sometimes engaged in a battle with popular entertainments over the hearts and souls of their congregants, many black Christian leaders took a more pragmatic approach to the relationship between the church and worldly entertainments.

The perspective that sought to reconcile religion and entertainments and incorporate popular culture into the churches did not always sit easily with some black Christians, as an exchange in the Chicago-based *Half-Century Magazine* makes clear. Langston L. Davis, who contributed articles on a variety of religious topics, on one occasion criticized churches for incorporating social activities like concerts, plays, and bazaars into congregational life. "The church edifice is a place of worship and should be used as such," he wrote. "If we used it for no other purpose and permitted nothing outside the sphere of the church to enter therein, the general public would have more respect for churches and things clerical." The success of movie theaters could be attributed to the devotion of "their undivided time and attention to giving the public just what it wants," Davis insisted, and he proposed that the church adopt the same approach.[40] Some readers, like Eileen Jones of Cleveland, registered their support for Davis's opinion that it was inappropriate for churches to host entertainments, but others wrote in to challenge him. Zechariah Johnson of Natchez, Mississippi, objected to Davis's proposal to "forbid entertainments in the church, thus depriving Christians of innocent diversions." "I suppose he would have them attend shows and dance halls with sinners," Johnson continued, concluding, "I believe the church is the place for Christians to seek their pleasure."[41]

Indeed, many black Christians pursued this course of action, attempting to make churches places that could satisfy desire for pleasure and entertainment in ways similar to those made possible in the movie house. For the most part, the movie fare offered in churches remained limited to films with religious themes and stories deemed appropriate for the particular venue. The *California Eagle* reported in 1936 that Los Angeles's Hamilton Methodist Episcopal Church would show a film on the life of Christ featuring scenes from the Oberammergau and Freiburg passion plays. In the same period, the People's Independent Church of Christ in Los Angeles began showing movies in 1937, inaugurating the practice with a Palm Sunday screening of Cecil B. DeMille's *The King of Kings*. In 1938 the People's Independent Church began exhibiting sound films with a free screening of DeMille's *The Sign of the Cross* (1932), accompanied by a performance by the church's choir under the direction of Mrs. A. C. Bilbrew, who was well known for her work as the chorus director for Fox's 1929 film *Hearts in Dixie*.[42] In these cases, popular culture made its way into churches in the form of religious-subject films, probably the most common mode of interaction between the two realms of life in black communities. Black church members also encountered other film genres and forms through exhibitions in churches such as those by the Memphis minister Rev. L. O. Taylor, who made films, which he dubbed "Taylor-Made Pictures," of his trips to National Baptist Convention meetings, as well as documentaries as of local religious, social, and sporting events. His documentary *The Negro in Church Life*, which he billed as "a moving picture show that puts the Church on the screen," featured hand-drawn intertitles that described the action. Years later, members of Taylor's congregation at Olivet Baptist Church recalled that he would screen his films before audiences of seven to eight hundred people and that viewers were greatly moved and entertained by the experience of what some characterized as "sacred" pictures.[43] Black churches in Baltimore exhibited an educational film starring the boxer Joe Louis and based on his life story—probably the 1938 film *The Spirit of Youth*.[44] Also in the late 1940s, the New York City–based Royal Gospel Productions offered black churches a variety of options for embracing film, including sponsoring exhibitions of its black-audience religious films in local theaters, schools, and auditoriums as well as churches.[45]

In some cases, black exhibitors of film sought to encourage churches and other religious groups to participate in cooperative endeavors that used film for moral education. As early as 1917, African Americans in Louisville, Kentucky, developed a "Help One 'Nother Club" through the city's black-owned Palace Picture Parlor, which was housed in the Masonic Lodge Hall.[46] The cooperative plan that the operators of the Palace Picture Parlor proposed involved donating 50 percent of the proceeds of each Tuesday's and Thursday's receipts to a church, club, lodge, hospital, or other "race organization."[47] As an added attraction for each of these screenings, the club arranged for ten-minute "race talks by race men" preceding the picture, as well as music appropriate to a program of racial uplift, all designed to create an atmosphere that would "teem with race grit and backbone." The first exhibition benefited the St. James Old Folks Home. In promoting the "Help One 'Nother Club," its officers emphasized the democratic nature of such a club, insisting that it had no "passwords or secret grips," thus participating in a discourse about the democratic nature of film itself as well as providing a critique of the exclusivity of the fraternal organizations so popular in black communities.[48] Instead of situating themselves as competing for the attentions and souls of members of black communities, the leaders of such enterprises promoted their work as functioning in conjunction with that of churches and benevolent societies. Moreover, the programs of such groups as the "Help One 'Nother Club" worked against the image of the movie theater as a morally dangerous environment, a characterization common in American culture in the early days of film.[49]

This struggle among religious and secular African Americans over how to approach popular entertainments reflected broader cultural issues in the period. Black churches, which had long functioned as umbrella arenas for a broad range of black social, educational, economic, and political activities, were in the midst of a cultural shift that involved the separation of many of these activities from their purview, and their leaders felt the potential for churches' cultural influence to decrease. Beginning in the early twentieth century, African Americans experienced a dramatic expansion of consumer opportunities as they encountered more of the growing variety of popular entertainments such as film, theater, nightclubs, professional sports, and radio as well as consumer items like beauty products, records, literature, newspapers, magazines, and toys marketed specifically to their communities. Many religious African Americans embraced this diversification, but many church leaders resisted it because they felt it undermined the authority and unique standing of religious institutions in black communities.

Understanding the varied representations of African American religion in early sound films requires examining these films in light of the commercial and artistic interests of Hollywood studios, the moral concerns of the censors, the presence of black religious themes in theater and popular culture in the period, and the debates within black religious communities about film and popular culture. *Hollywood Be Thy Name* explores various engagements between African American religion and

American film, charting contestation over representations of religion and cooperative endeavors to use film in the service of religious experience. By exploring a range of films from Hollywood studio productions to Poverty Row productions and independent black films, it opens up new approaches to addressing the multiple questions raised by Loren Miller's critical evaluation of black religious tropes in American film and Alice Harris and Hattie Hutchins's religiously enthusiastic film spectatorship.

Chapters 1 and 2 examine early Hollywood studio films—Metro-Goldwyn-Mayer's *Hallelujah* (1929) and Warner Bros.' *The Green Pastures* (1936)—that featured entirely black casts and set their narratives in African American Christian contexts. These chapters show how the Hollywood studio system projected and policed understandings of religion as fundamentally racialized and constructed African American religion as alternately childlike, hypersexual, or horrifying. Chapters 3 and 4 focus on "race movies," films produced for exhibition before African American audiences, and on the uses of religion in broader discussions about changes in black political and social life brought on by the Great Migration, urbanization, and the broadening scope of commercial possibilities for African Americans. Chapter 3 is concerned with a body of films by African American directors that were produced with explicitly religious goals, and Chapter 4 with genre films (comedies, musicals, dramas) in which religious individuals and institutions appear as part of the broader narrative. Chapters 5 and 6 consider various attempts to transform representations of African American Christianity in the context of World War II and postwar discussions of civil rights. Chapter 5 addresses Hollywood's return to black-cast films during the war, as well as an attempt by the U.S. Army, in the orientation film *The Negro Soldier* (1944), to project an American faith in which African Americans participate, in part, through military service. The chapter also considers the similar approach taken in the black-audience film *We've Come a Long, Long Way* (1944). Chapter 6 examines the function of white liberal religious discourse in the effort of *Lost Boundaries* (1949), one of a number of films of the period that take racial passing as their subject, to explore the moral meaning of race in postwar America.

In the period under consideration in this study, when the movies exerted such great cultural influence in America and elsewhere and when religious institutions were so powerful in African American communities, exchanges between the two realms were inevitable. One night in Georgia, Langston Hughes recognized with delight the possibilities of such interaction. In a brief note to his friend Carl Van Vechten in the summer of 1927, Hughes reported that he had run into Zora Neale Hurston while they were both traveling in the South. Having decided to return together to New York City in Hurston's car, the two took the opportunity to visit with the parents of mutual friends, then living in Georgia. Hughes described the activities of an evening:

> Tonight we went out into the country to a backwoods church entertainment given by a magician. It closed with his playing on a large harp and singing the Lord's Prayer in a very lively fashion. And his version began like this:
>
> > Our Father who art in heaven,
> > *Hollywood* be Thy name![50]

Hughes provided no further comment on the performance, certain that Van Vechten would appreciate the wonderful combination of magic, entertainment, and religious spectacle involved in the event.

ONE **"'Taint What You Was,
It's What You Is Today"**

Hallelujah *and the Politics of
Racial Authenticity*

In 1928 King Vidor, one of Metro-Goldwyn-Mayer's most successful directors, finding himself between projects, decided to spend some time in Europe. Having directed a number of important and successful silent films for the studio—most notably *The Big Parade* (1925), a tremendously popular World War I epic, and *The Crowd* (1928), a study of the life of an average man in the large urban environment of New York City—Vidor returned home when the studio asked him to direct his first sound film. Despite his initial predictions that "sound pictures [would] do away entirely with the art of motion pictures," Vidor soon began to see the possibilities that the new technology presented and was especially excited that sound would make it possible for him to direct a film that he had long wanted to make.[1] Synchronous sound, in which the dialogue or singing corresponds with the movements of the actors' lips, had only begun to make its way into American feature films since the 1927 release of Warner Bros.' landmark film *The Jazz Singer,* itself very much about complex processes of racializing religion in America.[2] Just as the projection of constructions of race had been part of the development of the silent motion picture, as D. W. Griffith's 1915 *The Birth of a Nation* had ably demonstrated, so the addition of sound had been bound up in conjunctions of religion and race from the outset. Vidor had in mind something that would contribute both to the new "talkie" technology and to the portrayal of racialized religion. He recalled in a memoir years later that the idea for this movie had been with him for a long time: "For several years I had nurtured a secret hope. I wanted to make a film about Negroes, using only Negroes in the cast. The sincerity and fervor of their religious expression intrigued me, as did the honest simplicity of their sexual drives. In many instances the intermingling of these two activities seemed to offer strikingly dramatic content."[3] Having been unable to convince MGM to permit him to do such a film in past years, Vidor was excited that the availability of the new sound technology would strengthen his argument, and he began making concrete plans. Aboard ship returning to the United States he drew up a list for the studio of elements "suitable for an all-Negro sound film," foregrounding religion: "river baptisms, prayer-meetings accompanied by spirituals, Negro preaching, banjo playing, dancing, and the blues."[4] Vidor's desire to make this film was so great that, in attempting to overcome the resistance of the studio to the idea of an "all-Negro-cast" film, he pledged to defer receiving his salary in order to defray the film's production expenses; in exchange he would receive a percentage of the film's net profit.[5] Once Vidor received permission to go ahead with the film, the studio allowed him to exercise a large measure of control over all phases of production. Consequently, the final product was largely the result of Vidor's wishes and decisions, with a few significant exceptions of intervention from the studio and the censors.[6] The studio's willingness to allow Vidor to proceed paid off: the film received many favorable reviews, earned a spot on the *Film Daily* and *National Board of Review*'s lists of the ten best pictures of 1929, and garnered an Academy Award nomination for Best Director for Vidor.[7] When interviewed almost thirty years later, Vidor listed *Hallelujah* and *The Crowd* as his two favorite films.[8]

The story that Vidor chose for his first sound film focuses on Zeke, the eldest son in a large family of sharecroppers, his rise to renown as an itinerant revivalist, and his fall resulting from the seductive lures of a woman he converts and baptizes after she indirectly brings about his brother's death. Despite the attempts of his parents, both devoutly religious, to keep him from falling prey to temptation in the city, Zeke succumbs. After considerable tragedy, Zeke returns to his family and to the idyllic life of the rural South. Although *Hallelujah* would differ in scale and in subject matter from his earlier works, Vidor presented himself as uniquely suited to write and direct such a film precisely because he considered himself an authority on "the negro." In interviews leading up to the film's release Vidor insisted that he had created the story from his own observations of southern black life, and he argued forcefully for its authenticity. He told a reporter, "I used to watch the Negroes in the South, which was my home. I studied their music, and I used to wonder at the pent-up romance in them. . . . The story is based on events with which

I was familiar as a boy at home in Texas."[9] When the picture was finally released, the studio's promotional material also emphasized Vidor's qualifications to direct this "authentic" rendering of black life, asserting, "Mr. King Vidor, who was chosen by Metro-Goldwyn-Mayer to direct this film, is a native of a Southern State, and from his childhood, his background has been that of the cultured Old South in its days of glory. Knowing the negro, he has chosen a simple theme for 'Hallelujah,' a theme centered upon an humble negro farmer and his family, their lives and joys and sorrows. He has caught the rhythm of their existence and has reproduced for the first time, a section of humanity so little understood by those who do not know this colorful race."[10] For his writer, Vidor selected the white screenwriter Wanda Tuchock,[11] and Ransom Rideout, a black playwright and studio writer, added dialogue at the studio's request.[12] The studio also listed Harold Garrison as assistant director on the film. Vidor described him as "a Negro bootblack at the studio. He had a stand set up and we called him Slickum. We made him second assistant director in charge of the Negro cast." Garrison's role seems to have been to act as an intermediary between Vidor and the large numbers of local extras engaged on location and perhaps to oversee the travel of the lead cast members on Jim Crow railroad cars to the location shoot in Memphis, Tennessee.[13] And while Vidor insisted that the film's story was grounded in his experiences, it should be noted that it recapitulated the familiar tale of a child moving away from family ties to pursue his or her own path and then returning to a newly defined relationship with the family. Warner Bros. had made particularly productive use of this formula in its 1927 film *The Jazz Singer.*[14]

Vidor understood that the studio feared that white southerners would interpret the release of an all-colored-cast film as a political statement. In numerous comments to the press during the production period the director attempted to dismiss any connection between his film and campaigns for civil rights for African Americans by articulating a set of small goals and insisting that he had no intention of having an impact on American politics. Nevertheless, Vidor saw himself as providing some sort of service to African Americans by making them the subject of his movie and rendering them as "real." Louella Parsons, a Hollywood gossip columnist for the Hearst newspapers, reported that "Mr. Vidor hopes to make a race picture just as 'Nanook of the North' was a race picture, and above all, he wants to show Negro life as it really is and without a mission or problem to solve."[15] Vidor insisted that the film would be a small, focused, emotional study in contrast to the large-scale pictures he had done in the silent cinema, and he reassured the studio and potential white viewers that such a "factual" representation need not involve any statement for social change.[16]

Just as Vidor claimed to have no interest in politics in producing this film, he asserted that he did not intend to make a religious statement, although he did understand the medium of film to be, in many ways, a mode of spiritual expression. "All my life I have been interested in the science of being: ontology," Vidor said many years later. "And this fascination has kept pace with my professional dedication: film making." He continued,

> Perhaps films can help us learn about life and living. Does the chance to watch shadows of ourselves in the speaking dark of a movie house explain cinema's great attraction? . . . Must I, as a director, continue to see films and life as an antinomy? Why must I painfully shuttle back and forth between the real and the unreal? Life is one. I must try to meld the science of being and the aesthetics of cinema. Only by doing this can I hope to evolve a comprehensive and viable philosophy of film making. . . . How else are we to express our humanness? How else are we to express God?[17]

Although Vidor did not put this discourse into play during the production and publicity phases of the film, his perspective on film as an expression of the divine must certainly have informed his approach to *Hallelujah,* one of the few films in his body of work to take on religious issues.

It seems clear that, from Vidor's perspective, multiple authenticating mechanisms combined to support and justify this production. First, he relied upon his belief that the cinema affords the filmmaker privileged access to profound ontological questions, to the very nature of being. In *Hallelujah,* Vidor explored the ontological contours of "the Negro," relying on what he understood to be the fundamentally racialized nature of being. Second, he emphasized the importance of his own specialized knowledge of African American life, acquired through his empowered position as a white male observer, in ensuring the authenticity of the production. The question of the authenticity of the film's representation of black religiosity would surface time and again as the censors evaluated the film, as various publics viewed and commented on it, and as many African Americans objected to its rendering of "Negro life as it really is"—that is, to the imaginings of a southern white man who insisted that "the Negro" was a singular entity and that he had privileged insight into something essentially "Negro."

The black press devoted considerable attention to the progress of the production of Vidor's new "talkie," to the director himself, and to the actors who would appear in the film. The *New York Amsterdam News* was particularly interested in the film's progress because it was in New York that Vidor concluded his national search for "new" talent for this film about southern black life. Indeed, in October of 1928 the *Amsterdam News* reported that the former slave Harry Gray, a member of its own janitorial staff, had been selected to play the part of Zeke's father in the film. Three other lead members of the cast—Daniel L. Haynes, a well-known stage actor who played Zeke, Honey Brown, a dancer at the Club Harlem who was to play Chick, and Victoria Spivey, a popular blues singer who played Missy Rose—were also signed in New York.[18] All of the black press coverage during the production period made clear the tremendous hope of many African Americans that the film might reshape screen images of blacks and thereby influence their social and political possibilities, indicating a profound faith and investment in visual culture despite the history of uses of film in support of white supremacy.

Two aspects of the production stood out as particularly heartening for many black commentators and as indicative of film's potential to help reshape American life and culture: first, that it was to be a sound picture and, second, that its story would focus on black religious life. In some cases the press linked the two issues, as in the *Amsterdam News*' conjecture that, "since Hallelujah is to have dialogue and vocal sequences, it is quite likely that the actors will sing all the well known spirituals."[19] The coming of sound, many black observers thought, would finally allow black actors to appear on the screen in dignified ways. Attention to the vocal skills of black actors, one line of argument proposed, would necessarily shift focus from the physical, aggressively embodied, and often comedic approach to representing blackness in the silent cinema. Eva Jessye, a writer at the *Baltimore Afro-American* and *Hallelujah*'s musical director, emphasized the film's shift from the stereotypical characterizations of blacks exclusively as "joker, comedian, servant, fool" to more complex characterizations, in part because of its reliance on a range of black musical styles.[20] Ruby Berkley Goodwin, an entertainment writer for the *Pittsburgh Courier*, opined, "Much depends upon the Negro pioneers in this field of art. Interviewing some of them, we are convinced that the race will be well represented. Their voices blend perfectly in the spirituals and folk songs of the Negro. Their voices, soft and intonating[,] are suited perfectly for screen-sound reproduction."[21] Reviewing *Hearts in Dixie*, Fox's 1929 all-colored-cast film that also had a religious story, Robert Benchley evaluated the film in the context of imagining the possibilities of sound films, which before the release of this movie he had considered uncertain. "With the opening of 'Hearts in Dixie,'" he wrote, "the future of the talking-movie has taken on a rosier hue. Voices *can* be found which are ideal for this medium. It may be that the talking-movies must be participated in exclusively by Negroes, but, if so, then so be it. In the Negro, the sound-picture has found its ideal protagonist."[22]

Those critics who focused on the ability of the talking pictures to provide a showcase for African American culture also hoped that the new technology would necessitate the end of blackface performances in film, imagining that "black voices" would require actual black people, even though cases like the radio show *Amos 'n' Andy* proved otherwise.[23] But many commentators, though investing tremendous hope in sound technology, were also realistic about the prospects for change and seemed prepared for the possible continuation of traditional patterns. Not long after the release of *The Jazz Singer*, the *Pittsburgh Courier* predicted that silent films would soon be a thing of the past and wondered whether sound would portend a change for black actors. The piece continued with what was, perhaps, an apocryphal story about race, class, region, and American speech:

> A humorous story is told of how the "talkies" are playing havoc with the old actors. It is said that Farina [Allen Hoskins of Hal Roach's *Our Gang* comedies] was tried out in the "talkies" with the expectation that he would use the broken English suitable to the characters he portrays in the silent drama. However, Farina was born in Boston and has had the best of tutors, so when he opened his mouth his English did credit to Fifth Avenue's most polite social circles. On the other hand, it is said that when Adolph Menjou, the evening clothes idol, was tried out in the "talkies" his English was so atrocious it was suggested that Farina be allowed to do his talking while Menjou acted and Menjou be allowed to do Farina's talking while Farina acted. Such is the upset the "talkies" have caused in the cinema world.[24]

What the outcome of this "upset" would be was not clear in 1929 when Vidor began production of *Hallelujah*, but the adding of sound and the possibility that spirituals—widely taken to represent African Americans' most profound contribution to American culture—would have a prominent place on the sound track augured well.

Appearing in the context of the large-scale urbanization of southern blacks and the tremendous expansion of vibrant black cultures in Chicago, Detroit, New York, and other cities as a result of migration, *Hallelujah* touched on issues of concern to African Americans, most particularly the religious meaning of urbanization and modernization.[25] Vidor seems to have understood that a great deal was at stake—not just for African Americans but for all Americans—in the shifts of population, ideology, and sense of self brought on by the Great Migration of the early twentieth century. The North, figured as it had been during slavery days as the promised land in which African Americans might finally experience the benefits of citizenship, held an exalted place in the imagination of African Americans in this period. Almost two million African Americans fled the hardships of the rural South, some opting for urban areas in the South and others moving to major cities in the North. Although the majority of African Americans remained in the South, the symbolic importance of the migration north was profound. It was in the context of these thriving urban environments that new religious, social, political, and artistic movements developed in the years following the First World War.[26]

Framed by rapid demographic changes and by the emergence of "the New Negro," *Hallelujah*'s representation of southern black religious life could not help bearing the burden of intense scrutiny. Those black intellectuals who were part of the New Negro movement saw themselves as heralding the arrival of a new race spirit. Alain Locke, professor of philosophy at Howard University and the chronicler of the movement, wrote in 1925:

> With this renewed self-respect and self-dependence, the life of the Negro community is bound to enter a new dynamic phase, the buoyancy from within compensating for whatever pressure there may be of conditions from without. The migrant masses, shifting from countryside to city, hurdle several generations of experience at a leap, but more important, the same thing happens spiritually in the life-attitudes and self-expression of the Young Negro, in his poetry, his art, his education and his new outlook, with the additional advantage, of course, of the poise and greater certainty of knowing what it is all about. From this comes the promise and warrant of a new leadership.[27]

While elitist in many regards, Locke's project did not facilely relegate African American folk culture to the dustbins of history with the emergence of the New Negro. Instead, he saw black culture as inevitably benefiting from these developments and undergoing an attendant liberation. Locke compared what he took to be the emotional and psychological development of African Americans in this migration period to the stages of transformation of black religious music: "Recall how suddenly the Negro spirituals revealed themselves; suppressed for generations under the stereotypes of Wesleyan hymn harmony, secretive, half-ashamed, until the courage of being natural brought them out—and behold, there was folk-music. Similarly the mind of the Negro seems suddenly to have slipped from under the tyranny of social intimidation and to be shaking off the psychology of imitation and implied inferiority."[28] And he further argued that this gradual and insistent emancipation amounted to a spiritual release.

Where the New Negro movement emphasized and facilitated self-representation and agency in picturing African Americans, however complicated and contested this process might be, the marginal status of blacks in these early Hollywood films necessarily meant that the images produced were largely out of their control. The way African American religious leaders, expressions, and institutions would appear in the Hollywood imaginary would be largely the result of a series of negotiations between white men in Hollywood and in the various agencies that managed the products of the industry. Vidor seems to have understood himself as working against the progressive political stance embodied by the urban "New Negro," and in talking about the film he positioned himself with what he imagined to be the authentic—and necessarily southern—folk Negro. In comments on "race psychology," Vidor asserted that "[t]he Negro of the North always wants to see himself as a poet. He is not content to see himself as he is pictured in 'Hallelujah.' Even the polished Negro of Carl Van Vechten possesses, under the surface, the rhythm and abandon, the love song and laughter of those in a primitive state."[29] Clearly, for Vidor, African Americans had little agency in formulating their culture and identities and instead were the products and property of white men like the author and photographer Carl Van Vechten and himself. In Vidor's view whites were more authorized than blacks to adjudicate the authenticity of blackness, and his insistence on this point would become central to the evaluation of *Hallelujah* by many interested parties.

The Motion Picture Producers and Distributors Association (MPPDA), the body responsible for regulating the content of Hollywood films, found much of Vidor's story proposal far too explicit in its portrayal of the fall of a preacher. At this point in its history the MPPDA operated under the guidelines of the "Don'ts and Be Carefuls," which prohibited, among other things, "willful offense to any nation, race, or creed" and "ridicule of the clergy" in any film produced by members of the association, "irrespective of the manner in which they are treated."[30] Colonel Jason Joy, the head of the MPPDA's Studio Relations Department at this time,[31] wrote to his staff that he had informed Vidor and the MGM producer Irving G. Thalberg that the story raised a number of problems in relation to the "Don'ts and Be Careful's." Joy's initial discomfort with the scenario also had to do with Vidor's plans to include a scene of a crap game and the use of the word *nigger*.[32] The MPPDA's caution about using the term *nigger* in the script did not, apparently, have an impact on Vidor or Thalberg. It fell to the film's black actors to force the issue. *Hallelujah*'s musical director, Eva Jessye, wrote an exposé published in many black newspapers shortly after the film had been released in which she addressed the question of the script's language. She wrote, "[S]ince the 'Hallelujah' cast was all Negro, it is difficult to understand why it was necessary to use any references whatever to race. Yet, it was done, and what is more, with utter disregard for the feelings of the cast, they were handed scripts that any worthy Negro would resent."[33] Jessye noted that the term was used in the script to describe various characters, as well as in dialogue to be delivered by the actors, and that the terms *darky* and *pickaninny* also appeared throughout. Jessye was incredulous that the actors were to expected to deliver lines like "I'm a bad nigger" and reported that the members of the cast "were solid on the stand to do nothing by word or action that could be taken as a reflection on the black race."[34] They were successful in resisting the use of such terms in their dialogue, and the final print of the film contains no such language.

Although the MPPDA did not appear to have pressed the issue of derogatory language in the script, other questions arose about the film's content that concerned the censors. Once the film had been completed and Jason Joy sat down with Thalberg to screen it, he began to feel uncomfortable with other issues regarding the representation of blackness as fundamentally connected to sexuality and religion. He was particularly nervous about the film's explicit representation of "a strong negro [Zeke] exhibiting passion," which he was sure whites would find objectionable. Joy understood this to be a problem in particularly gendered ways, explaining in a memo that "the passion shown by Chick, a small negress, will not be deleted because of its treatment."[35] Joy feared that the image of a black man expressing desire would encourage such expressions in actuality and necessarily lead to the rape of white women. Negresses, however, (and particularly small ones) could justifiably be portrayed as sexual agents in this view. Images of black women as hypersexual were readily available in popular culture and worked against any factual evidence of sexual assault of black women by white men. Images of black male hypersexuality, on the other hand, while also readily available and often invoked to sanction lynching, could not be usefully deployed in this particular instance, according to Joy. For Vidor, however, sexuality was a constituent and necessary component of any representation of black religion, an understanding that Joy obviously did not share.

Joy also found the film's uses of religion discomfiting. That the film associated Zeke's work as a revivalist with that of "real" ministers might offend "the religious people of the country," he thought. This association was made clear, according to Joy, in a scene in which Zeke preaches at a revival and begins by saying, "The text of my sermon will be . . . " In addition, in the first scene in which we see Zeke as a preacher, he and his family arrive in a small town to conduct a revival. They disembark from a railroad car that has the words "Ezekiel The Prophet" painted on the side (see figure 1). Zeke, wearing a silk robe, rides on a donkey at the rear of a parade of children waving small American flags and singing "Great Day, the Righteous Marching." Joy found this image particularly disturbing, since it could easily be read as "emulat[ing] Christ's journey into Jerusalem."[36] Joy did, however, hold out the possibility that the story could be made acceptable to "the religious people of the country" and that, in contrast to the main thrust of Vidor's story, black religion could be presented as "real" religion. He told his staff:

> I advised them [MGM] it might be less objectionable if the negro preacher and evangelist was not portrayed as a weak character, succumbing to temptations in various forms. The story as now written makes the preacher's son the weak character and I have advised MGM that I believe too much prominence is now given to the religious importance of the son; that this criticism may be avoided by making it evident in the picture that the father is the real leader and minister and that the son is merely a zealous convert used by the parson as part of his shown [sic].[37]

Although Vidor never modified the story to displace Zeke as the central character, Joy would soon be appeased on a number of counts: Vidor revised the synopsis, emphasizing to Joy's satisfaction that the father remained an appropriate clerical model (at least, as we shall see, for a black preacher) and later removing references to Zeke as "the black Jedus" [sic].[38]

Other people at the MPPDA who evaluated the script and the completed film asserted that African American religion had at best a tenuous connection to real Christianity and expressed discomfort with the possibility that the film might leave a more positive impression of it with viewers. Vidor's representation of black religiosity used available stereotypes enough to make sense to and placate the censors, however. Although the MPPDA required minor changes in the script, the association ultimately approved the project on the grounds that it provided a "realistic" portrayal of African American life. Lamar Trotti, one of the MPPDA censors, made authenticity the focus of his evaluation of the project in a letter he wrote summarizing his initial impressions. Trotti wrote:

> I hardly know what to say about "Hallelujah" by King Vidor. If the characters were whites, I would think very definitely that Vidor was treading on very

FIGURE 1.

"Ezekiel the Prophet" in *Hallelujah*. Courtesy John Kisch, Separate Cinema Archive.

dangerous grounds—that of a renegade parson running off with a strumpet, seeing her die, brutally murdering her lover. But such is the influence of my rearing in the South. I can't get excited about this in the lives of negroes. We think such things happen, everyone seems to accept them as natural and no one bothers about them. Religion for negroes is regarded as a joke in the South. Baptizings in the rivers are circuses, and people go for miles to see them. They aren't taken seriously at all by whites. There is an old saying down there that *a negro with hair in the palm of his hand has religion*. Apparently the others haven't. So I am a bad judge of what the effect of the picture would be. The story seems real enough. If the characters were white it might be likened to Elmer Gantry, but there is no thought that Zeke is a hypocrite. He is just a weak nigger in the toils of a black Deborah.[39]

Despite the initial resistance from the censors, as well as some from the studio, Vidor was permitted to proceed, and by many accounts he succeeded in his attempt to produce a "realistic" story about black life and religion in the South. An evaluator for the MPPDA who saw the film at its premiere at the Embassy Theater in New York City wrote, "This film is full of the religious customs of the uneducated negroes, camp meetings where they roll on the floor and wave their arms and do all sorts of crazy things, baptisms in the river, where they act like crazy people; and many other curious performances which although true to life will not be understood by anyone who doesn't know negro customs fairly well."[40] In many cases, the alleged realism of the film's portrayal of African American religious display served as the most potent justification of its racism. When, for example, the Canadian province of British Columbia rejected the film for distribution on the basis of its conjunction of religion and sexuality, a studio representative suggested that the MPPDA argue in the film's favor on its merits as a "sincere portrayal of negro religious rituals."[41] One of *Variety*'s reviewers argued that the film presented "a camera reproduction of the typical southland with its wide open cotton spaces, where the good natured, singing negro continues to eke out a bare existence. . . . It brings realistically to the screen how he lives in nondescript surroundings with continual evidence of illiteracy that even remains unpolished when becoming hysterically religious."[42]

In *Hallelujah* Vidor sought to provide a definitive statement on the black race, its psychology and its religious practices. His approach incorporated existing traditions of representations in popular culture of black religion as simple and instinctive and therefore appropriate for the childlike Negro. For Vidor, a focus on religion was fundamental to his portrayal of black life. In addition to using commonplace images of black religion, Vidor amplified these images by insisting on the connection between religion, race, and sexuality, presenting black religion as extraordinarily embodied, fundamentally sexual, and available as a spectacle.

Hallelujah is a gorgeous film that provides viewers with vivid landscape sequences. Vidor's commitment to preserving the art of cinema while incorporating the new sound technology that so often in its early years limited camera movement (because the equipment had to be encased to muffle the sound) produced an extraordinary example of what sound film could become. His interest in using many sequences of outdoor location shots led him to begin production before having finished casting the film or having worked out all the technical issues of how to record the sound for these shots. The available cast set out for Memphis so that Vidor could film scenes that included black farmers bringing in the cotton crop, a river baptism, and one of the final segments that involved an elaborate chase through a swamp. In many ways, then, the visual elements remained of primary concern in this important early sound film. While the postproduction dialogue sound may seem poorly rendered from our perspective, one of the film's greatest achievements was its ability to maintain the visual richness of silent film while taking advantage of the various vocal talents of its actors.

Vidor's insistence on the need to include outdoor scenes had a great deal to do with the particular story he was telling. It seems clear that for him any representation of "the Negro" required deliberate attention to the natural world. Black people are inextricably connected to the land in this view, and Vidor frames the film with two segments in which farm families pick cotton in the fields. He follows the first of these with a scene in which the Johnson family, having brought in their annual crop (to the tune of "Cotton, Cotton, Cotton, Cotton"), prepares to send Zeke (Daniel L. Haynes) and his younger brother Spunk (Everett McGarrity) off to the cotton gin and then to the city to sell the crop (see figure 2). Each member of the family makes sure that Zeke knows what items they would like him to bring home— all small things like candy, chewing gum, a dress, and spectacles.[43] Zeke's family is close knit, and family members seem to have little care for the world beyond their small community. In beautifully filmed shots Vidor begins the film by creating a strong sense of connection among the members of the family and between the people and the land. The studio's publicity for the film prepared viewers to understand the story in this way: as one piece of promotional literature asserted, "American life has changed, has become a standardized industrial spectacle; but the negro of the Southern United States, though no longer a slave, is unchanged. He is still a part of the moist earth and growing crops, one who sings for joy when the sun shines and the sky is blue."[44] In the world of this film, tragedy strikes when one of these simple, unchanging people leaves his or her natural habitat of the rural South.

After introducing the viewer to the family, Vidor establishes a nexus of religion, race, and sexuality and draws the film's main characters in relation to this complex construction. Early in the film we see Zeke, his parents, and his siblings gathered for dinner after a day's labor during which they have completed bringing in the cotton crop. Gathered around a rough-hewn table in the yard, Mammy (Fanny Belle DeKnight) and Pappy (Harry Gray) listen to one of their six children read aloud from Exodus 20—the Ten Commandments. In opening the scene in this way, Vidor situates the Bible as the standard of conduct, one that viewers should easily recognize, allowing them to identify with this family in important ways. Soon enough, however, the characters' actions complicate and dismantle the relationship Vidor has established between the members of this family and a strict interpretation of biblical precepts. Similarly, subsequent events in the film's story will undermine the moral authority of Pappy and Zeke, the film's two central male characters. As the scene

FIGURE 2.

Zeke and Spunk in the foreground, taking the family's cotton to the gin in *Hallelujah*. From the author's collection.

proceeds, we come to see how little Pappy can assist others in holding to the standards of the Ten Commandments. Shortly after dinner the family receives visitors. Adam and Eve and their children approach, and Adam asks Pappy whether he is available to perform a wedding ceremony.

> PAPPY: To marry you? Ain't these eleven children yourn?
>
> ADAM: That's right. We thought it was about time for us to make it more permament [*sic*].
>
> EVE: That's right. (giggle)
>
> PAPPY: Seems like you made it mighty late to get round here to get married. The damage is all done.
>
> ADAM: But could you fix us up anyhow?
>
> PAPPY: Well, it's never too late to do the will of the Lord.
>
> EVE [bowing]: That's right, that's right.[45]

When Mammy congratulates them on finally getting around to "doing the right thing," Eve ties the decision to marry to her sense of herself as a respectable woman, insisting that she has always been respectable and wants to avoid any implication otherwise. Pappy and Mammy give some indication of discomfort with Adam and Eve's perspective on marriage, and Pappy agrees to assist them in doing God's will, but there is no sense during this exchange that the couple have recommitted themselves to upholding the Ten Commandments or that they intend to raise their children according to its standards. While this scene incorporates these rural black folk into the grand Christian narrative of human sin and redemption, the film's racial essentialism locates this particular Adam and Eve in a local context in which black sexual desire and expression seem to overcome rational religious understandings.

Vidor appears to be particularly interested in whether what he takes to be the essential moral character of blackness can be accommodated to American national identity. Zeke, Mammy, and Pappy become central to his exploration of this issue, and his conclusion requires the characters to remain located in the strangely utopic cotton fields of the deep South, laboring happily as sharecroppers but having no contact with whites. In this view, urbanization and cultural transformations that move blacks away from the countryside can only be damaging because these processes might lead African Americans to imagine themselves as other than a primitive subculture within American society. Even though Mammy's remark, in response to Eve's situation, that "'[t]aint what you was, it's what you is today" implies the possibility of progressive development and transformation, the film's overall thrust contradicts this perspective. *Hallelujah*'s central argument is that the character of blacks is fixed and irredeemable despite their best efforts to act in ways contrary to that fundamental racialized nature. With the initial exchange between the couples and Mammy and Pappy's easy acquiescence to Adam and Eve's request, Vidor makes clear the relative and compromised nature of Pappy and Mammy's moral standards, quickly undercutting the earlier reading of the Ten Commandments. Nevertheless, the parents remain at the top of the film's moral hierarchy, and Pappy stands as a strong model of the kind of man that Zeke could become.

We soon witness Zeke's moral descent resulting from his conflation of religion and sexuality, another of the film's significant themes. As Adam, Eve, Mammy, and Pappy prepare for the wedding, Zeke follows Rose (Victoria Spivey) into the living room. By this time the viewer has already learned that Mammy and Pappy adopted Rose with the hope that she would eventually marry Zeke. This is all we know of Rose, who remains a cipher in the film, as Vidor gives the audience little access to her character through dialogue. The visual presentation sets her against the vivacious Chick, casting her as simple and plain (see figure 3). When Zeke enters the room, Rose, who is sitting at a small organ, begins to play the wedding march. We see Rose from behind as she sways from left to right on the stool, clearly enjoying the music and delighting in the occasion. As Zeke advances toward her, Rose, unaware that Zeke is behind her, completes the song and leans toward the window to listen to Pappy performing the ceremony. Vidor cuts to a close-up of Zeke's face as he approaches Rose from behind. He breathes heavily, and the expression on his face is clearly one of desire. We see Rose listening, still unaware that Zeke is in the room. Then, in a particularly intense sequence, Vidor shoots from Zeke's point of view and we see his hand reaching out to Rose's shoulder. Innocently, Rose turns around and looks in the direction of Zeke's face (which we still do not see). At first she seems happy to see him, but alarm soon registers on her face. As Vidor cuts to a wider shot of Rose sitting and Zeke standing, we hear Pappy outside explaining to the bride and groom that marriage is like the mystical union between Christ and his church. Just then Zeke insists that Rose kiss him, and as she stands up and begins to back away he grabs her and draws her to him. As Rose begs Zeke to let her go, he pulls her close and kisses her, and, while she is clearly uncomfortable, she does not struggle. Zeke suddenly backs away from Rose and clutches his chest, looking shocked at what he has done. When they are called to come outside to celebrate the conclusion of the wedding ceremony, Zeke apologizes to Rose, saying, "It looks like the devil's in me here tonight." Rose readily forgives him.

The scene is characterized by a number of powerful juxtapositions between marriage understood as a sacred institution and the desire for illicit sex. As we have already seen, Vidor introduces the encounter between Zeke and Rose with Adam and Eve's announced desire for a wedding ceremony despite their having been together long enough to have produced many children. Pappy conducts the ceremony under a tree in the backyard, no doubt a reference to the tree in the Garden of Eden, given the deliberate selection of the names Adam and Eve. The sanctification of the couple's relationship, one already marred by illicit sex, takes place in the shadow of the symbol of the fall of humanity. Vidor may also have been subtly referring to the ascendancy of sexual desire over the sanctity of marriage in his positioning of Zeke and Rose in relation to one another. When Rose sits at the organ with her back to Zeke, an inverted broom leaning against the wall divides the frame, with Rose to its left and Zeke to its right.[46] The broom is a potent symbol in African American history. Denied legally recognized marriage ceremonies, enslaved African American men and women frequently conducted a ritual to mark their commitment to one another that involved jumping over a broomstick. Vidor's use of an inverted

FIGURE 3.
Victoria Spivey as Missy
Rose in *Hallelujah*. From
the author's collection.

broom in the frame emphasizes his view that sexuality compromises these characters' religious commitment.[47]

The viewer cannot help continuing to question Zeke's faith even as he undergoes a transformative experience in the aftermath of the death of his brother, Spunk. In setting out this part of the narrative, Vidor emphasizes his sense of the simplistic and literal nature of black religiosity and its conjunction with the relentless pull of sexuality, placed in the context of the inevitable sinfulness of the urban context. When Zeke takes the family's crop to town to sell, he sees Chick (Nina Mae McKinney) singing and dancing for a group of men and is immediately attracted to her. Also called "High Yella," a reference to her "high yellow" or light skin color, Chick recognizes Zeke as an easy mark and, in the tradition of the stereotype of the treacherous "black Jezebel" and the treacherous mulatta, sets in motion the events that lead to Spunk's death.[48] In an effort to impress Chick, Zeke begins to flash the money he made from selling the crop, and Chick and "Hot Shot" (William E. Fountaine), her partner in crime, draw him into a game of craps in a local saloon. Zeke soon loses the money. Zeke and Hot Shot begin to argue over the money, and when Zeke takes out a switchblade Hot Shot counters with a pistol. In the struggle that ensues, the gun discharges, killing Spunk, who has just entered the saloon in search of Zeke. Zeke brings Spunk's body home to his inconsolable parents, and the family and neighbors gather for a wake.

During the wake Zeke has a profoundly moving religious experience that opens up the possibility of genuine spiritual and moral transformation for this central character. He cannot bring himself to mourn with the others and instead lies on the ground outside, weeping. His father joins him and tries to console him, insisting that he has not come to judge Zeke and reminding him that God forgives. Zeke asks his father for help, and Pappy, telling him that God has sent an angel to show him the way, points to the sky and describes the angel's snow white robe and chariot. When Zeke looks up to the sky, Vidor cuts to a shot of clouds with rays of light streaming through. Then, as the light from the sky illuminates the two standing with their arms outstretched, Zeke preaches a spontaneous sermon about God's love and forgiveness:

> The Lord done showed me the light.
> The Lord done revealed the truth of his creation.
> I done laid my brethren down in the ground but the ground can't hold my brother.
> No, Pappy, the ground can't hold him.
> The Lord is stronger than the ground. The Lord is the ground.
> The Lord is the sky and the heaven and the moon and the sun. The Lord is the earth and all the living things of the earth.
> The Lord in [*sic*] his Kingdom.
> There ain't no more pain. There ain't no more sorrow. And there ain't no more death.
> So why do we wail and grieve?
> Oh my brethren . . . I give you back to the Lord.
> The Lord is the beginning as well as the end.
> Come with your sorrows and leave in his joy.
> Come with your defeat and leave with his victory.
> Come, oh come with your sinfulness and leave in the goodness of his joy.
> Come, oh come, oh Lord.
> Come to that land of green pastures and clean waters. Come to the Lord.
> Amen.

Zeke's sermon demonstrates a deep understanding of Pappy's teaching about God's forgiveness and has the potential to set the stage for a profound transformation in the character.

In many ways, this scene in which Zeke experiences God's power is extraordinarily potent. Daniel L. Haynes delivers a compelling sermon in a traditional black preaching style, with great emphasis on rhythm and tone in chanting, and the performance is emotional and sensual in ways that mark it as genuinely felt. Indeed, Vidor signals the power of the sermon by intercutting shots of mourners who, sensing that something deeply religious is occurring, come out of the wake and gather around Zeke. At the same time, Vidor chose to film the scene from a distance using no close-ups, thereby limiting the viewer's ability to use the main characters' facial expressions to evaluate their emotional tenor. He takes the same approach to the two other scenes in which Zeke preaches, at once allowing an unadulterated moment of thoughtful religious expression and diminishing its potential power through what is perhaps a deliberate distancing of the viewer. Vidor uses close-ups most often in *Hallelujah* to indicate sexual desire, showing the characters as wildly overcome and animalistic in their passions, and rarely to facilitate access to other aspects of the characters' interior emotional lives.[49]

In addition to emphasizing a view of black religion as simplistic and emotional, the film insists upon the blending of religion and sexuality in the scenes where we see the characters participating in religious ritual, leading the viewer to conclude that, for African Americans, these two are inextricably linked. When Chick is baptized after being converted under Zeke's preaching at a revival, for example, she interprets her religious experience in sexualized terms and in terms of her relationship to Zeke rather than to God or Jesus. As she is being dunked in the river, she cries out, "I have been a wicked woman. Oh, I've been a wicked woman but I'm sanctified now. Hallelujah. All because of you, brother Zekiel. Keep me good, keep me good, don't let me sin no more." And later, when Hot Shot ridicules her conversion, she tells him that her soul has been "washed in the spring of the Lamb," to which he responds that she's been "washed in fires of the devil." Chick objects to Hot Shot's attempt to convince her to continue in the con game with him and insists that no one will "keep [her] from the protecting arms of Brother Zekiel." At her baptism Chick becomes completely lost in religious ecstasy, and, to the dismay of his family and followers, Zeke carries her out of the water and into a nearby tent. He is clearly affected by his proximity to Chick and by her sexualized moans. Vidor cuts to the interior of the tent as Mammy enters. We cannot see Zeke and Chick, but we can hear her persistent moaning. The camera cuts to Chick lying on a cot, moaning in religious and/or sexual ecstasy, and Zeke embracing her and wildly kissing her neck. Mammy sends Zeke off, now ashamed of himself, and chastises Chick, calling her a hypocrite and telling her that she's got more religion than is good for her. From this point on, neither Zeke nor Chick can seem to separate sexual expression from religious experience when they are in each other's presence.

Irving G. Thalberg, MGM's production head, understood how important Chick's unrestrained sexuality was to the narrative and did not agree with Vidor's initial choice of Honey Brown, a dancer from New York's Club Harlem, for the part. When the cast and crew left hastily for location shooting in Memphis, Tennessee, in October of 1928 to get footage of the cotton in the fields, Vidor had no doubts about having cast Honey Brown, who, he said, "stood out like a sore thumb" from all those he had seen in his national search.[50] But when Thalberg saw the first rushes—prints of each day's takes—he became convinced that Brown was not sexy enough to carry off the part. He telegrammed Vidor immediately, writing, "Terribly disappointed in Honey Brown. She has lots of pep but very little if any sex. Great for first part with comedy scenes but am afraid audience would laugh at her in sex scenes and question whether they should believe sincerity of story which is strong sex attraction between Chicky and boy." Vidor defended his choice and argued that he found Brown to be beautiful, sexy, and talented enough to handle the part. Thalberg, who had the authority to overrule Vidor's decisions, wired back to explain his reaction, asserting that "my chief objection to Honey Brown is certain ugliness particularly around her mouth, her flat chestedness, and her upper lip has very outstanding hair line."[51] Thalberg's decision stood, and the substitution of Nina Mae McKinney satisfied him with regard to her ability to engage the viewer with her sexuality (see figure 4). He voiced concerns about the fact that McKinney's hair was straight but remained satisfied that this "problem" could be easily fixed.[52] Clearly, Thalberg had in mind not only a particular image of female sexuality but also a racialized one that required that McKinney not to appear too white—that is, not to have straight hair or skin that was too light. At the same time, however, the film locates sexual desirability in the lighter-skinned Chick as opposed to the darker Missy Rose.

The most interesting and profoundly articulated section of the film in which Vidor weds African American religion to sexuality takes place at the evening Jubilee revival following the baptism (see figure 5). The set for the revival is a large, open barnlike structure with a stage at the front on which Zeke and his family stand. The room is darkened, but the available light casts shadows on the walls. Zeke preaches a short sermon promising to fight the devil on behalf of his people. Following the sermon the people begin to sing "I Belong to the Band." They form a circle and move slowly around the room counterclockwise in a fashion reminiscent of a ring shout, a southern African American ritual of communal worship. We hear the sound of women wailing as it becomes clear that Chick is standing at the center of the crowd, deeply involved

FIGURE 4.
Nina Mae McKinney as Chick in
Hallelujah. From the author's
collection.

in the emotion and physicality of the worship. Chick thrusts in time to the music with
her arms raised, moving up and down, bending her knees. Following a close-up of
Chick dancing ecstatically, Vidor cuts to a medium close-up of Zeke looking down at
Chick from his position on the stage, his eyes wide with desire. Vidor then repeats this
exchange, following with a close-up of Rose, and later one of Mammy and then of
Pappy, all clearly suspicious of Chick's intentions (these are the only close-up shots
in the film that do not indicate sexual desire). Chick moves toward Zeke, stands directly
in front of him, and grasps his leg as he attempts to control himself. Chick motions
with her head for Zeke to join her, and he steps down from the platform, bobbing up
and down in the same manner that Chick has been. Zeke and Chick are now at the
center of the circle, bending their knees in time to the music and moving in a clearly
sexual manner. At one point, Chick looks at Zeke intensely, takes his hand, and puts
the base of his thumb in her mouth, emphasizing the sexual nature of this worship.
Eventually, Chick leaves the building with Zeke following close behind, and the two
run off into the woods. This scene serves as the culmination of a number of scenes in
which Zeke and Chick commit themselves to resisting sexual temptation but find that
religious experience leads them, inevitably, to sexual expression.

FIGURE 5.
The Jubilee revival scene with Missy Rose at the center, flanked by Mammy and Pappy, in *Hallelujah*. Courtesy John Kisch, Separate Cinema Archive.

Through the character of Chick, Vidor provides a relentless pull on Zeke that draws him away from his home and family. From the first moment he sees her wearing a dress with a pair of dice on them, singing "Shuffle Along" and dancing before a crowd of entranced men, he sets off on a path that moves him to risk everything he has to be with her. Zeke is drawn to Chick from the start, but the attraction becomes irresistible once she embodies a sexualized religiosity as well. Missy Rose, chosen by Zeke's parents as an appropriate wife for him and never dressed in anything other than what appears to be a burlap sack, can never compete with Chick's lures. Indeed, Zeke proposes to Rose simply in an attempt to "get the devil off him," and after she declares her love he abandons her. Vidor and Wanda Tuchock, one of the film's writers, emphasized the dramatic differences between these two women in their continuity synopsis draft, writing of the baptism scene, "Chick is in Zeke's line, and he feels a strange thrill when his arms support her and her arms cling about his neck. *These* arms are soft yaller [*sic*], while Missy's arms are black. Chick's soft body seems to cling to Zeke, and her lips are very red, and her breath is warm upon his cheek. He tries to release himself and finds the girl is holding him fast—and then he doesn't *try* to get away."[53] After her conversion and baptism Chick does sing religious music instead of the show tunes of her earlier performances, indicating an attempt to reform, but delivers a decidedly sensual version of "Give Me That Old Time Religion" as she prepares to attend the Jubilee revival. She is available and open to the devil's work in accordance with the conventional gendering of sin, but her racial location, which sexualizes her in unique ways, amplifies this and makers her profoundly dangerous for Zeke.

Music is an integral part of the film's insistence upon African Americans' conflation of religion and sex in ways that marginalize them in the American context. Music inaugurates and accompanies much of the religious frenzy and, outside the religious contexts in the film, helps to present the characters as carefree children. At the same time, however, the film's music is often extremely compelling and enriches the high-quality visual elements. As a folk musical, *Hallelujah* seamlessly integrates music into the story, relying on contexts in which people might naturally sing—at work in the fields, performing household chores, at religious services, and so on.[54] With the exception of "At the End of the Road," written by Irving Berlin, most of the film's music comes from African American contexts, particularly traditional spirituals, blues, and folk music, arranged and conducted by Eva Jessye. In an article published some months before the film's release, Jessye argued that music would be central to the film's power and took special pride in the variety of "Negro music" included and in her work as arranger and conductor for Baltimore's Dixie Jubilee Singers, featured on the sound track.[55] The sound track also contains a segment in which Chick sings W. C. Handy's "St. Louis Blues." Many black commentators on the film noted the effective use of spirituals. W. E. B. Du Bois, in his review in the NAACP's *The Crisis*, longed for even more traditional music instead of the Irving Berlin "theme-song" but conceded that "the world is not as crazy about Negro folk songs as I am."[56] Berlin's song, "At the End of the Road," which tells of happiness and redemption in the future, anchors the film's presentation of music, and in some ways the film positions Berlin's interpretation of "jazz" or of black music as equally if not more authentically black than the spirituals.[57]

Spirituals and the blues function in expected ways in the film to draw a contrast between religious life and worldliness, as well as to authenticate *Hallelujah*'s portrayal of black life. The film contains extremely moving moments in which Mammy sings traditional folk songs or sings extemporaneously, underscoring the potential of the folk musical to tap "the transforming power of memory."[58] Early on, Mammy sings "All the Pretty Little Horses" while rocking each of her small children to sleep in turn. Later in the film, Mammy vocalizes her distress as she senses something amiss (she will soon learn of the death of her son), chanting, "Lord, have mercy on my soul."[59] At the same time that folk songs and spirituals lend an air of dignity to some of the characters, the coupling of the spirituals with "tom-tom" drums signals the danger of sexuality. Indeed, the first sound one hears as the film begins—even as the screen remains black—is that of a distant drum, marking the characters and narrative to follow as primitive and likely unable to be redeemed or elevated.

At the film's conclusion, Zeke returns to his family, having served time on a chain gang for murdering Hot Shot, Chick's former partner. This conclusion sees Zeke through a variety of transformations and reinstates him in his former role in the family, albeit in a more mature and more responsible form. After running off from the revival, Zeke and Chick spend months living together while Zeke works as a hand in a sawmill. Chick becomes extremely bored with her life by the time Hot Shot appears and offers her escape. When Zeke finds out that Chick has left with Hot Shot, he pursues them, bringing about Chick's death as she falls from a carriage and then strangling Hot Shot. In the final version of the film, the scene in which Zeke works on the chain gang is brief, meant to indicate that he has been punished and paroled in preparation for reintegration into the family. When he arrives back at the cotton farm, singing "Goin' Home," his parents welcome him, Rose forgives him, and his mother immediately offers him chitterlings and spare ribs.[60]

Over the course of the film Vidor moves Zeke from his life as an artless farm laborer who has little access to the outside world, through the dangers of the urban environment, and back to the simplicity of the farm. Along with these geographic shifts, his religious life is transformed from a home-based experience that seeks to adhere to biblical moral standards, to the revival in which he is particularly interested in his public persona, to a return to his rural roots. The film insists that Zeke's life as a revivalist is inappropriate for him and for his family because it moves them beyond their social and theological capacities, and Vidor signals the discrepancy largely through costuming. When we first see the family in their appropriate context they are dressed simply and seem comfortable in their clothing, but when Zeke becomes an itinerant revivalist he and the other members of the family wear new formal clothes that do not seem to fit them, just as Zeke cannot conform to the role of "Ezekiel the Prophet." Given Vidor's understanding of the limited possibilities for character development for African Americans, it is not surprising that he used class markers in his costuming of the characters to assist the audience in evaluating Zeke's odyssey.

The original story outline and script drafts contain a much longer and complex sequence charting Zeke's redemption in which the members of the chain gang work on a levee in a flooded river under the watchful eyes of the black prison guards. As the water rises the prisoners' lives become endangered and Zeke pleads for a guard to release them from their chains so that they can get to safety. The guard refuses, but eventually Zeke wrestles the keys away and, after taking a moment to rescue a small dog, helps the men find refuge on a mound in the river. In a story synopsis, Vidor and Tuchock described Zeke's emotions at this point, asserting that "[h]is sense of leadership returns and, lifting his arms aloft, he voices fervent prayer to the Lord. The others are fired with Zeke's spirit and join the praying, and presently the waters cease to rise! They are saved!"[61] In this version of the story, Zeke would have regained a strong sense of himself as a religious leader and would have returned home with more than simply a song on his lips. It seems that Vidor filmed this sequence but chose not to include it in the final cut, leaving the completed film without this more complicated version of Zeke's transformations as a result of his encounters with Chick.[62]

The visual, musical, narrative, and ideological elements of *Hallelujah* combine to create a powerful result. Vidor interpreted all of these elements featured in the film—a racially compromised moral sensibility, sexualized religious expression, and emotional musical display devoid of deeper theological content—as fundamentally part of the nature of "the negro race." This emphasis on a fixed racial nature and on racial psychology allowed little room for transformation or progress. Vidor emphasized his vision of the unyielding and invariable simplicity of blackness and of African American religion in many of his statements to the black and white press prior to the film's release. In one interview he described how easy it was to work with the cast because "[i]n the emotional scenes the players lived through the episodes; they truly didn't act them. They felt them. . . . A Negro is a natural actor, singer, and a born mimic. Any group of them naturally can sing and dance in harmony. They are born that way."[63] In another interview in which he again described the cast as not acting but simply experiencing the emotions of the scene and "pray[ing] themselves into a sort of frenzy," Vidor emphasized the danger this presented to the largely white crew, who risked "infection" and the loss of reason when surrounded by black people who could not, in his reckoning, discern the difference between drama and reality. The crew tried to maintain its critical distance, he assured readers, but he concluded that "[o]f course, the fact that they [the black actors] are speaking and singing all the time makes this influence even more potent than otherwise."[64]

After the film was released, Eva Jessye countered Vidor's claim of the set as dominated by the true religious frenzy of the black cast members. In her accounts of the film's production published in the black press, Jessye wrote of the intense preparation the cast members undertook for various scenes and interpreted their strong responses when being filmed as the result of their professionalism and preparation. "Surely no cast ever fell more heartily into their respective roles," she wrote. "Haynes would brood for hours in order to get himself into the solemn mood required for the religious scenes."[65] She also asserted that her own training and dedication to the job contributed to the realistic sense of the film's religious scenes, as well as easing Vidor's job. She wrote that in the wake scene, for example, she had instructed the members of her choir and the extras who appeared in the scene how to move and to interject prayers and songs at various points. "It required exactly twenty minutes for a perfect take, instead of the entire day, as had been anticipated. An amusing thing in connection with this was the fact that the director thought the individual singing bits were accidental. They were done so easily and naturally that he did not realize that these bits had been carefully planned for dramatic effect."[66]

Vidor's assessment of the actors as essentially untrained, naturally emotional and religious, and unselfconscious about their performances also stood in marked contrast to their biographies and to the coverage of their careers in much of the black press. From the initial announcement that Daniel L. Haynes would have a major role in the film, the *Amsterdam News* emphasized his experience in the New York theater as understudy to Charles Gilpin, one of the best-known actors in America at the time, and to Jules Bledsoe in the Florence Ziegfeld production of *Show Boat*. In addition, the fact that Haynes had earned a degree from Morris Brown University in Atlanta and had taken courses toward a master's degree at the University of Chicago was an important part of the black press's presentation of this new film star.[67] In the *Baltimore Afro-American*, Eva Jessye, the film's musical director, chronicled Victoria Spivey's rise from poverty in Houston, Texas, to a career as an Okeh Records recording artist, emphasizing the financial sacrifices her mother had made for her daughter's music lessons. Spivey's self-presentation focused on the amount of work she had put into her career up to this point, telling Jessye that "[g]rit, pure grit is the thing that counts in trying to get ahead. Whatever you want, if you want it bad enough to work hard enough and wait long enough, you will surely get. Spend your time trying to improve rather than envying and talking about somebody else. Luck? I don't believe a word of it. There is a Power that keeps watch and knows our worth to the last inch. There is no withholding of just deserts or overpaying. We get just what we deserve."[68] Harry Gray was not a professional performer, so the papers could not focus on his acting or singing experience as they did with Spivey and Haynes, for example. A profile by Ruby Berkley Goodwin in the *Pittsburgh Courier* highlighted the harsh conditions and hard work of his early life under slavery, his career as a preacher, and his philosophical bent. Goodwin wrote that she asked him "about his English, for he spoke as a scholar, with the wisdom of the old masters."[69] According to Gray, he had met "an intellectual bum," and, in exchange for drinks, the man taught him about "science, art, history, and anthropology."[70] Such interviews in the black press with members of the cast of *Hallelujah* offset some of the impact of Vidor's statements prior to the film's release and permitted African Americans to continue to invest their hopes in the film.

In many ways *Hallelujah* lived up to the expectations of a variety of black commentators on film, religion, and politics, and many of them praised the film as art and as a moving and vivid portrayal of aspects of black life. In his review in the NAACP's journal *The Crisis*, W. E. B. Du Bois hailed the film as "a great drama" and argued that the kind of African American religiosity portrayed—the faith of "a deeply superstitious people"—must be understood as having developed as a universal human response to tragedy and disaster.[71] Du Bois also emphasized the universal human appeal of the story and noted the potentially positive consequence of the film's effective use of documentary-style sequences of black laborers. For Du Bois, this kind of attention to the daily reality of black life was of great importance, and he was not alone in his evaluation of *Hallelujah*'s significance.[72] Illinois Congressman Oscar DePriest, speaking to a Harlem audience after the film's segregated premiere—at the Lafayette Theatre in Harlem and the Embassy Theatre downtown simultaneously (see figures 6 and 7)—announced, "We are standing on the threshold of civil and cultural emancipation in America. Tonight we have seen how far our race has progressed culturally and artistically since the Emancipation Proclamation."[73] Daniel L. Haynes, one of the film's stars, wrote, "I cannot say what our race owes King Vidor and Metro-Goldwyn-Mayer—there are not words forceful enough for that. 'Hallelujah' will, as Moses led his people from the wilderness, lead ours from the wilderness of misunderstanding and apathy."[74] Other reviewers emphasized that, whatever the shortcomings of *Hallelujah*, it was a significant advance over earlier representations of African Americans in film. A *New York Age* editorial declared that because the film seemed "to present the Negro as more of a human being, with a full assortment of human frailties and a few simple virtues, it may be accepted as a distinct advance over the former conception of him as a butt and a jest, a role that was growing a trifle threadbare."[75] Most of the praise from African American quarters emphasized the talents the actors displayed rather than the film's story or direction. In a

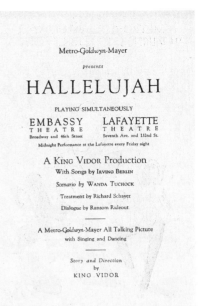

FIGURES 6/7.
Program for the New York premiere of *Hallelujah*. From the author's collection.

marked contrast to Vidor's insistence that the members of the cast did little more than *be* their raced selves, black and white critics, whether reviewing the film favorably or not, lauded the performances as thoughtful and sophisticated.[76]

Many of the white reviewers recognized the quality of the performances but also discerned the film's attempt to delineate the fundamental nature of blackness through an exploration of religiosity. A reviewer for *Variety* provided an extensive psychological analysis of the film's story, grounded in and fully accepting of racist stereotypes:

Simple emotions, primitive situations of love, lust, jealousy and remorse. . . . To these credulous children of cotton the devil is a real person, ever present, and violation of God's edicts brings bad fortune.

Students of Freud will read into the revival shindig a close affinity between religious frenzy and sex impulses. This is intelligently presented when the hot mamma in a fever of sudden repentance for her former sins is, all unconscious to herself, consumed with desire for the strong, manly preacher.

Vidor has poured himself into this picture, designed as an epic of the negro. He has packed in a lot of glamor and action and humanity. If the picture is limited, its boundaries are inherent to the subject.[77]

The *New York World*'s reviewer characterized the film as "a fine and simple record of the most emotional race on earth," and Creighton Peet of the *New York Evening Post* concluded, "Instead of looking at 'Hallelujah' as an exposé of a quaint aspect of this our America, I think we should settle down to the fact that the Negro is as different from the rest of us as we are from the Russians, the Germans or the French."[78] In interpreting the film in this way, the reviewers took the cue of the studio's promotional material that declared, "Because this epic of the screen, which you are about to witness, concerns a people almost buried within another people, it is necessary that certain things be understood. This picture concerns a simple folk, whose standards and emotion, though of this era, are based upon those of their savage ancestors."[79] Such responses to the film understood Vidor's exploration of black religion to support the view of African Americans as unfit and unable to ever join the ranks of "us"—Americans.

Despite the widespread acknowledgment that Vidor had accomplished a great deal with his first sound film and that the release of an "all-colored-cast" film produced by a major studio was a historic event, many commentators and reviewers—black and white—remained deeply uncomfortable with what they understood to be the broader implications of this particular rendering of black religiosity. Earl A. Ballard, "a race writer," commented that "[w]hile the photoplay has served to give vent to the innate ability as actors to the principal characters who have won favorable comments from the critics of the daily press, it is a flagrant and misleading mockery of the race's religion. Some say it is blasphemous and had any other race been involved, never would have passed the Board of Censors."[80] John T. Sherman of the *New York News* insisted that "[w]hile 'Hallelujah' gives great opportunity for the race artistry, it undeniably pictures the group as moral morons and religious barbarians."[81] One black New Yorker who attended the film's segregated premiere objected to the *Amsterdam News*' support for Vidor's work and emphasized the disjuncture between the self-representation of many African Americans in the period and Vidor's representation:

After the picture was well under way on its opening night, it was clearly to be seen that the superb acting of the cast was being overshadowed by the amount of spirituals, meaning weeping and wailing, and the weak, the low [in] spirit were dominating the picture. When one sees "Hallelujah," stripped to the bone and laid bare it is not hard to imagine why Harlem is the largest Negro City in America, why Chicago, Philadelphia, and Baltimore and the others are increasing in Negro populations. "Hallelujah" is the answer. Of course the good editor of *The Amsterdam News* might not wholly approve of the above statements, but from close observation from the sixth row [, . . .] the applause given only when the cast was acting is proof enough of just what Harlem in general thinks of this picture.[82]

"Progressive Harlem," this writer insisted, did not respond favorably to this film, which he took to be merely southern racist propaganda. A *Cincinnati Union* editorial summed up the sentiment of some African Americans about the film, noting that the paper had "received many criticisms concerning the picture 'Hallelujah' from colored people who have wondered how any intelligent Negro could advocate its being exhibited."[83]

Eva Jessye, who criticized many elements of the film publicly after its release, defended the presentation of religious enthusiasm as realistic and as simply one of a variety of expressions of human excitement about life. She wrote:

There has been a lot of bitter comment on the part of Negroes concerning this "shouting" scene. Many foolishly contend that it was exaggerated. Many say that it is a reflection upon the race. Opinions may differ, but facts are facts. That shouting scene is a mild duplication of what takes place nightly in many Negro churches. I was raised up among shouters and have seen that very thing in my hometown, Coffeyville, Kansas, with my own relatives leading the gyrations. You can see shouting equally uncontrolled in certain churches in New York City—so why pretend?[84]

Significantly, Jessye's defense sought to counter the sense, commonly expressed in criticism of the film, that, while uneducated, backward black southerners might accept *Hallelujah*'s representation of African American religion without question, educated, modern, northern urbanites would not. For Jessye, "shouting" was but one way some African Americans expressed their religious fervor, and neither region nor educational background had an impact on the "temporary abandon to the power of religion." Clearly, she was interested in preserving the variety of African American religious expression even in the context of urbanization, and she wrote that she refused to be ashamed of this aspect of black culture.[85]

Many African Americans were not sure that they wanted the attention to their religious cultures or the imaginings about their religious practices that Hollywood devoted in this period. A reviewer from the Chicago-based Associated Negro Press (ANP) pondered the exigencies of commercial culture and the uses to which images of African Americans had long been put, comparing the situation in Hollywood to a slave economy. "It is understood that Mr. Vidor feels bad about the Negro's reaction to his picture. He should not. He has made a picture that is expected to sell. He should be willing to understand if the Negro is a bit sensitive about going on the block."[86] This commentary on what African Americans understood to be the high stakes involved in filmic representations of black people and black life cuts to the core of the concerns of African Americans at the time about the treatment of African American religion in the Hollywood imaginary. The ANP reviewer's discomfort with Vidor's film did not stem entirely from a belief that it presented inaccurate images. Indeed, the author conceded that some of the content was "true to life," but he objected to the commodification of a particular rendering of blackness in service of an argument for white superiority and black inferiority. Many African American public figures in this period—W. E. B. Du Bois, James Weldon Johnson, Alain Locke, and others—were also contending with what to do with various "true-to-life" but, for them, problematic aspects of black culture. A major component of the projects of many black intellectuals in the early twentieth century involved positioning black folk culture (and many traditional black religious practices that are a part of that folk culture) as a valued part of the African American past that should be carried into the future as history and tradition rather than as the primary cultural orientation of a new, modern and more urbanized culture. Zora Neale Hurston, who often disagreed with Du Bois and Locke about precisely how to value black folk culture, was also attentive to Hollywood's uses of African American religion. She criticized black leaders for what she took to be their unqualified gratitude for the increased presence of black characters in the movies. Such praise, she argued, so "flattered [white authors and producers] that they actually believed they were authorities on Negro religion."[87] Hollywood imaginings of African American religion, along with representations in literature and music, became especially contested ground as black intellectuals negotiated their varied relationships to black folk cultures and did so in relation to mainstream popular culture's commodification and re-presentation of elements of that culture.

White reviewers who accepted the film as "a camera reproduction of the typical southland"[88] and black reviewers who found it difficult to understand the objections of many African Americans to the film frequently emphasized what they understood to be unreasonable expectations on the part of black audiences. One white film critic saw the protests as characteristic of "certain racial groups" to "squawk" whenever what they saw on the screen did not conform to their image of themselves. He continued, "One of the hardships in picture making is the certainty that race sensitiveness will result in uproar if any of the many peoples is presented in any save flattering colors. The latest of these manifestations comes from certain uppity Negroes who write letters to newspapers protesting that 'Hallelujah,' the very excellent picture made by King Vidor for M.G.M., is unfair to the black race." He concluded that the protesters were "merely emulating the Latins, the Irish, and certain of the Chinese."[89] Romeo Doughtery, the *New York Amsterdam News*'s entertainment editor, defended the film to black viewers who preferred films whose stories focused on the black elite, such as those produced by the independent black film director Oscar Micheaux. Doughtery chided such people for desiring what he took to be false images. "Like in some of the productions of Oscar Micheaux they would have us arriving at Villa Navarra in the Rolls-Royce we do not own, and there until the wee hours of the morning trip the light fantastic and in our spare moments doing our durndest to act like Mr. Eddie for whom we must crawl out the next morning with rag and duster."[90]

Regardless of the position that African Americans took on this film, it seemed clear to all those who entered the public debate that more than just the assessment of a movie was at stake and that any representation of African Americans on film could have social and political consequences. In the North, white exhibitors feared that large numbers of African Americans who wished to see the "all-colored-cast" films would go to theaters in areas outside "their own neighborhood houses," mingle with whites, and inflame racial tensions in cities newly bursting with southern black migrants. In the wake of the film's release, a convention of film exhibitors in the Southeast voted to forego showing any Negro pictures, and participants devoted special attention to MGM for its production of *Hallelujah* and its plans to release other films with black characters.[91]

The template that *Hallelujah* set for representing African American religion in Hollywood sound films involved insisting on a fundamentally simplistic and imitative theology, a relentless association between the imagined hypersexuality of blacks and their religious expression, and the deployment of religion to characterize African Americans as essentially carefree, morally irresponsible, and apolitical. Music, an essential component of the template, often allowed for the most complex moments of expression in the film but also often served to signal the carefree laziness of southern black life. All of the "all-colored-cast" films produced from the late 1920s through the mid-1940s that use religious contexts avail themselves of many of these elements set forward in King Vidor's work. For the most part, the intense focus on sexuality found in *Hallelujah* drops out, and the films emphasize instead religion as a window on the fundamental incapacity and permanent childlike status of African Americans. The filmic techniques the studios employed to promote this perspective did not, in general, follow the style of *Hallelujah*'s hyper-realistic, ethnographic approach but turned instead to very stylized, fantastical settings that relied on dreams and dreamlike contexts for their narratives. We turn next to examine this stylistic shift in Hollywood's presentation of African American religion in the 1936 Warner Bros. film of Marc Connelly's 1930 play *The Green Pastures*.

TWO   "'De Lawd' a Natchel Man"

The Green Pastures *in the American Cultural Imagination*

The stage and screen page headlines of the March 14, 1936, issues of both the *New York Amsterdam News* and the *Chicago Defender* trumpeted scandal in the life of Rex Ingram, the actor who had been selected after a long search and much deliberation to play the part of "De Lawd," the God character in Warner Bros.' film version of Marc Connelly's play *The Green Pastures*.[1] The *Chicago Defender*'s report conjectured that the studio might fire Ingram from the film, then in production, as a result of the negative publicity arising from lawsuits that had recently been filed against him. He faced a suit filed by the parents of his deceased wife for $3,000 to compensate them for caring for his child, another by a woman who claimed that she had loaned Ingram more than $650 that he had failed to repay, another by a former landlord for unpaid rent, and a divorce suit by his current wife.[2] Despite the black press's prurient interest in Ingram's personal life and speculation that his exploits would undermine his career, its writers did not gain satisfaction. Warner Bros. did not pull Ingram from the film, and the studio's production files give little evidence that his difficulties concerned Connelly or William Keighley, the film's co-directors, or Hal Wallis, the film's producer, except insofar as the "bad news" that Ingram received in February of 1936 "upset him," causing the production to wrap ten days behind schedule.[3] When compared with other problems that caused production delays on *The Green Pastures*, as well as with production schedules for other films at the time, wrapping ten days late was not out of the ordinary. Not only did the scandal not appear of particular concern to the studio, but, shortly after production wrapped, studio head Jack Warner presented Ingram with a bonus check to pay for a planned vacation down South. According to the *Chicago Defender*, "Ingram promptly purchased a handsome trailer, a shining 'land yacht'" that Connelly christened the "Silver Cloud," referring to the large, fluffy clouds featured in the film's sets of heaven.[4]

In the distance between the black press's extravagant coverage and rather obvious joy at "De Lawd's" vulnerability and the studio's failure to note the exposure of its actor's moral failings with any dismay lies much of the story of the impact of the film version of *The Green Pastures* in American and indeed world culture. Over the years, the responses to this most enduring of the "all-colored-cast" Hollywood films and to the play on which it was based have been varied, ranging from extreme adulation to calls for boycott. The responses of both the black press and the studio to the controversy over events in Ingram's personal life involved differing estimations of the authenticity of Connelly's work. Taking a different approach from King Vidor's claims to ethnographic authority with *Hallelujah*, Connelly offered his work as authentic African American Protestant theology, a view from the inside. Was Connelly's story a "humble, reverent conception" of the Bible from the mind of the simple Negro, as some parties were deeply invested in proving, or was it pure artifice—"a white-washed burlesque of the religious thought of the Negro" waiting to be exposed by African American artists, as others insisted? Even when the response was somewhere between these poles, this film and its dramatic source frequently became a lightning rod for discussions of African American religion in popular culture and, more broadly, on the American political and social scene.

The black press was certainly justified in wondering about the potential for the scandals and the negative press coverage to undermine the production, which was based on one of the most successful Broadway plays of the era. *The Green Pastures*, which premiered on Broadway in February of 1930 and for which Connelly won the Pulitzer Prize for drama, had shone a bright spotlight on the African American actors in the production and on the subject matter—Connelly's fantasy of a black version of the Hebrew Scriptures. Because the film was the first feature-length Hollywood production to use an all-black cast since MGM's 1929 *Hallelujah* and because it claimed to present the core of African American Protestant theology, it was intensely scrutinized by African American commentators.

The Green Pastures was evaluated not only by African American audiences regarding its claims to *black* authenticity but also by black and white viewers regarding its claims to *religious* authenticity. In telling how he came to write *The Green Pastures* and how it made its way to Broadway, Marc Connelly often emphasized how potentially explosive it was for white Americans to come to terms with this play in which he had depicted God as a black man. This vision, he insisted, was faithful to the Bible, and the only significant change from the scriptural sources was its black context. He believed that only the courage of a producer new to the Broadway scene and willing to take a risk made it possible for the play to be mounted.[5] For Connelly, the success of the play with regard to its faithfulness to the Bible rested on the casting of "De Lawd" because, as theater critic Brooks Atkinson insisted, "No suave performer or artful elocutionist could carry a part that has so many sacred implications."[6] As a result, in casting the part both for the Broadway production and for the film, Connelly insisted on finding a man to play God who could bring to the production the appropriate solemnity and who, in his view, was spiritually sound. Connelly's commitment to these criteria led him to seek an African American leader of high stature with a major public profile. Among those Connelly approached for the play were Rev. Adam Clayton Powell Sr. of New York's Abyssinian Baptist Church and, for the film, Dr. Robert Russa Moton, the recently retired president of the Tuskeegee Normal Institute and Booker T. Washington's successor. Both men declined to leave their careers to take up acting, forcing Connelly to turn to professionals. When the time came to cast the film he was extremely pleased with Rex Ingram (see figure 8), whose screen test he found "magnificent."[7]

The seemingly endless disclosures of Ingram's personal weaknesses—the revelation that "'De Lawd' a natchel man," as one newspaper described his difficulties—seriously threatened the ability of the studio to market the movie as a religiously grounded work. The black press seemed to enjoy reporting on "De Lawd's" problems because its writers understood that Connelly's claim to authenticity, based in part on the insistence that Negroes visualize God as black, was not as uncomplicated as Connelly seemed to believe. Writing in the National Urban League's magazine *Opportunity*, Randolph Edmonds, a professor of English at Morgan College and a pioneering African American theater critic, noted that "Negroes who have never seen the play criticize it sharply. They cannot see how a fish fry could represent the Negro's idea of heaven when they have been told all their lives about pearly gates and golden stairs. God being black is something they have never heard, except as a humorous part of the Garvey movement."[8] While Edmonds gave the play a favorable review, his sympathy for the objections that many African Americans voiced highlights the political import of both the play and the response to it, particularly in his likening the idea of a black God to Marcus Garvey's black nationalist ideology. At stake here was not just a frivolous piece of popular culture or a profit-seeking enterprise on the part of the studio. For many African American viewers of this film, the consequences of Connelly's vision involved a public assertion of the

FIGURE 8.
Rex Ingram as "De Lawd" in *The Green Pastures*. Courtesy John Kisch, Separate Cinema Archive.

marginal and ever-unassimilable status of black people in the American body—marked by the insistence that they understood the divine in a narrow and parochial way. For white Americans, whiteness, as unmarked and unremarked, is necessarily universal. While African Americans' traditions of envisioning themselves in the likeness of God in all ways, including race, date back before Marcus Garvey arrived on the American scene, these approaches were not without controversy.[9] Most important for some black viewers of Connelly's play, the work's insistence that southern African Americans imagined God in the way he put forward made them uncomfortable.

From the start, Connelly presented his play both as authentically African American and as a reverent portrayal of African Americans' understanding of the Bible. At the same time, the Warner Bros. film of the play retreated in a variety of ways from Connelly's emphasis on authenticity in relation to the Bible—for reasons intimately connected with the fact that the setting was an all-black world—and ultimately presented the story as the fantastical imaginings of childlike minds. *The Green Pastures* followed *Hallelujah* as the next film produced in a series of Hollywood's "all-colored-cast" films that rely on religion and would eventually overshadow it and come to dominate white Americans' imaginings about black religion well into the twentieth century. In this regard it proved a much more resilient part of American popular culture than most other representations of African American religion, in part because it purported to be a self-representation. Likewise, *The Green Pastures* would come to represent for many African Americans the risks attendant upon Hollywood uses of African American religion precisely because so many white

Americans accepted Connelly's work as an authentic rendering of the theology of African American Christians and accepted his assertions about the simplicity of black theology and the unchanging nature of black thought.

It is impossible to evaluate the 1936 Warner Bros. film *The Green Pastures* without gauging the impact of the earlier theatrical productions. Marc Connelly wrote the play that would fix conclusively the future course of his career, as well as those of many others involved, after having read Roark Bradford's collection of stories, *Ol' Man Adam an' His Chillun* (1928).[10] A white journalist and fiction writer from Tennessee and a resident of New Orleans, Bradford sought to present a southern black version of the Bible and relied on his lifelong observations and evaluations of African Americans to determine the work's sensibility. Bradford was a regular contributor to *Collier's*, *Saturday Evening Post*, *Harper's*, and the *Forum*, among others, and had written about African Americans and about black religion prior to the publication of *Ol' Man Adam*. In his "Notes on the Negro," which supplemented the publication of the short story "The River Witch" in the November 1927 issue of the *Forum*, Bradford outlined the perspective that informed his writing:

> For my own personal study of the black race, I have divided its members into three groups. . . . The first group I call the "nigger." He is the shiftless, ignorant laborer type, the steamboat rouster, and the field hand. . . . . The nigger took [his master's] religion and adapted it into a simple, childlike game between two very human, rather likeable beings called God and Satan. . . .
>
> The second classification of mine I call the "colored person." He is, so to speak, the next step up on the ladder of civilization. He is neither fish nor fowl, but because of his atavistic tendencies that can so readily send him back to the "nigger" classification, or his unsatisfied longings that may send him still further up the ladder, he is pretty fair red herring. . . .
>
> My third classification is the Negro,—capital "N." The specimen is all too rare. He is, so to speak, the real thing. He is not ashamed of being black. . . . He knows that his race has done pretty well, all things considered, in the past two hundred years. He hopes it will do better in the future. . . . The Negro can imitate the white man, but at best, it is an imitation. The white man has a convenient thing called "dignity" that estops [*sic*] him from leading a mule or carrying *flambeaux* in a Mardi Gras parade.[11]

Bradford's *Ol' Man Adam* follows his understanding of the religious life of shiftless, ignorant "nigger," in which he claimed he also recognized genuine emotion and productive religious expression in the "ceremonial" elements of music and movement.

Marc Connelly, a native of western Pennsylvania, member of the Algonquin Round Table, and sometime collaborator of George S. Kaufman, had no personal experience in the South but was moved by Bradford's version of the Bible after a friend insisted that he read it.[12] As a young child he had met the black composer Will Marion Cook and entertainers Bert Williams and George Walker when they were guests at his father's hotel, but, when interviewed years later, Connelly declined to draw any connection between his father's progressive stance on race and his own interest in the material that had led him to write *The Green Pastures*.[13] Just as he did not have social or political goals in taking up Bradford's work, Connelly denied any personal religious commitment or desire to promote religion. "I am not a religionist," he asserted. "To me, any creed that has lasted more than five hundred years has merit in it somewhere, but I have never been able to accept insistences by hierarchies or sectarian policing. As an agnostic, I recognized that I must at all times respect the faith of the black fundamentalists."[14] At the center of the work, he insisted, was tremendous respect for African American religious creativity. Connelly wrote, "I had found rich promise in the vision of Negroes uprooted from their African culture, ties broken with animistic theology, looking with hope and reverence to Jehovah and Christ. My play, then, would try to interpret a spiritual phase of the Old Testament. The search of God for man, and man's search for God."[15] In addition, Connelly saw in African American religious adaptation a significant moment in the history of Western drama. "The Western theater begins with the satyr plays of the pre-Athenic Greeks. The altar was part of the setting for the vernal theatricals that invoked the favor of the deity. The Bacchic festivals also were attempts by God's creatures to relate themselves to Him. It seemed to me that in embracing Christianity the slave was making a similar attempt to find divinity within himself."[16] For Connelly, then, religion was good drama, and the specific case of African American religion, as he understood it, provided insight into universal human desires. In important ways, Connelly's public statements about his goals for the work had a very different emphasis from King Vidor's in *Hallelujah* in that Connelly gestured toward broad religious and cultural issues. In contrast, Vidor understood his project as engaging a racially specific religious context. At the same time that he wanted to explore broad religious questions, Connelly's rendering of southern black theology made it difficult for many critics to acknowledge universal themes in the play.

While Connelly relied heavily on the general frame established by Bradford's book, he made a critical shift in perspective that paradoxically proved the source of both the unabashed praise and the biting criticism the play received. Bradford focused on the human characters of the Hebrew Scriptures, but Connelly's script made God the play's central character as a means to explore "man's ancient, intensive search for his own soul" and "attempt to find divinity within himself."[17] It is God's search for connection with humanity that drives the drama of Connelly's play, and, in choosing to make God the central character in this drama of humanity's search for their own divine qualities, Connelly increased the probability that some viewers would find the play blasphemous.

Like King Vidor, Connelly was concerned with providing an "authentic" rendering of both black Protestant theology and southern black dialect and insisted that he did not, under any circumstances, wish to "[impose] any humorous concept not racially proper."[18] Just who would be the arbiter of said humor, besides himself, was not clear. To ensure authenticity in adapting *Ol' Man Adam*, Connelly visited Bradford in New Orleans and spent the summer in black churches and "barrelhouse dives" while reworking the first draft of the play. He recalled that he came away from that summer with a sense of some variety of theological orientation within what he called "fundamentalist Negro churches," "indicating differences as definite as the deepwater and the sprinkling forms of baptism."[19] Connelly was particularly interested in the differences among black Christians in their attitudes toward dancing and other forms of movement, both socially and in the context of worship. After observing a range of churches, he was most impressed with those that prohibited social dancing, since he felt their songs and movement in worship were much more energetic and affecting. Before he returned to New York, he tested the dialect in his work before groups of servants in the homes of various wealthy whites, "mindful of Robert Burns's habit of reading his poems in dialect to peasants for criticisms of their authenticity," and reported that their responses to the language were favorable.[20] It is important to note that Connelly's choice of a single view of African American religious life—the more theologically conservative—effectively erased the reality of religious diversity among black Americans in his representation. Moreover, he valorized a theological approach that sometimes rejected a broad social life that included both the secular and the religious. Even as he grounded his claim to authenticity in broad research, his insistence that this one view represented the authentic perspective of black Christians would inevitably bring criticism from some African American commentators.

Despite Connelly's initial difficulties in securing a producer who would brave the risks of mounting a Broadway production that depicted God as black, the play, which he directed, was an enormous success, garnering the Pulitzer Prize for Drama in

1930 and running on Broadway for a year and a half despite the harsh financial climate of the Depression. Reviews of the play were extravagant, with one critic asserting that *The Green Pastures* "reaches moments which are for me more stirring than anything I have ever seen in the theatre"[21] and another calling it "simply and briefly one of the finest things that the theatre of our generation has seen."[22] Following the Broadway run, Connelly took the cast on record-breaking national and international tours and then returned for another Broadway run in 1935.[23] The longevity of the production prompted at least one observer to wonder wryly whether some changes in the cast, many of whom were children when the play premiered, might be necessary. Langston Hughes saw *The Green Pastures* in San Francisco in May of 1932 and commented that "old man Harrison [as "De Lawd"] is still as great as ever, but the cherubims are almost as tall as the angels now."[24] In addition to the various Broadway and touring productions and the 1936 Warner Bros. film version, Connelly's creation would be performed on the radio, on television, and by all-white casts in blackface makeup in Sweden and Denmark.[25] It also spawned imitations, most unsuccessful, as in the case of the 1932 Broadway production of *Ol' Man Satan*, by the African American composer and conductor Donald Heywood, and the Los Angeles theater production of *Cabin Echoes*, a.k.a. *Mammy's Boy*, by the African American playwright and actor Thaddeus Jones.[26]

Judging from the responses to the Broadway production, Connelly was correct in seeing the casting of an appropriately dignified actor in the part of "De Lawd" as key to the play's success. Indeed, the appeal of the play was attributed, in large measure, to the performance of Richard Berry Harrison as God. Harrison, a devout Episcopalian and the son of slaves who had escaped and settled in Canada after spending time in London and Haiti, resisted taking the part because he objected to the literal vision of God rendered in Connelly's play. The playwright eventually convinced him to sign on, in part through the intervention of Connelly's friend the Episcopal suffragan bishop of New York.[27] By all accounts, Harrison, whom Connelly described as having a speaking voice "like a cello," handled the difficulties both of playing God and of the unfamiliar southern folk context skillfully. One reviewer wrote, "It is possible that there might be somewhere throughout the realm another person who could portray the Lord as well as he, but it is difficult to imagine anyone doing it better."[28] Harrison was lauded by African American communities, entertained by mayors and college presidents during the tours, and awarded the NAACP's Spingarn Medal for distinguished achievement in 1931.[29] T. Thomas Fletcher, who published a poem in the *New York Amsterdam News* in 1930 dedicated to Harrison, was so profoundly affected by the actor that he credited the performance (but not necessarily the play itself) with transforming his theology:

> He is no more
> The stern-eyed, pale faced God
> Of childhood days,
> To whom I nightly prayed,
> Yet so often wondered why
> A God so coldly white as He
> Should care if black men
> Lived or died.
> But now that I know
> He is not white
> My heart's unburdened, free;
> No longer do I fear
> His cold pale face, for
> He is brown like me![30]

Thomas's paean to Harrison not only underscores the power of the actor's performance in the production but also gives some indication, contrary to Connelly's claims, of the complicated and fraught relationship that some African Americans had to the question of racializing God.

When Harrison died in March 1935, an estimated 16,000 people viewed his body and 7,500 gathered for his funeral service at St. Edmund's Episcopal Church in Chicago.[31] The *Amsterdam News* published comments from "prominent pastors of all denominations," including Rev. Adam Clayton Powell Jr. of New York's Abyssinian Baptist Church, who called "De Lawd" "a genius, a gentleman and a Christian." George Edmund Haynes of the Federal Council of Churches lauded Harrison for his contributions to bettering race relations and for "the vision he gave the world of the deep spiritual and mental resources of Negro life and character." Rabbi W. A. Matthew of the Commandment Keepers congregation of black Jews proposed that "the spirit of Richard Harrison shall soon be accounted worthy of reincarnation."[32] Clearly, Connelly was not alone in feeling regret that he would not be able to introduce Harrison to a filmgoing audience. The dramatically different reception that Rex Ingram, the film version's God, received is striking.

Another central component of the play's success, and one on which Connelly could rely for the film, was the music, which he understood to be an indispensable part of any attempt to represent African American religious life. While in New

Orleans conducting research, Connelly chose the "Negro melodies" he would include in the play, and later in the film, in consultation with Roark Bradford and Alma Lillie Hubbard, an African American concert performer of spirituals and faculty member at New Orleans University.[33] The music was realized by Hall Johnson and the Hall Johnson Choir, whose work anchors the film's narrative and enlivens the often stilted presentation of the dramatic narrative immeasurably. Johnson, the son of an African Methodist Episcopal minister, a graduate of Atlanta University who also studied music at the University of Pennsylvania, the Hahn School of Music, and the Institute of Musical Art (Julliard's predecessor), arranged the selected spirituals, and his choir performed them in an engaging and moving manner.[34] The combination of Connelly's excellent choices and the choir's complex and spirited renditions make the music one of the most effective, affecting, and memorable parts of the film. Johnson's spirituals would become so closely associated with representations of black religion in American film that he would go on to do the vocal arrangements for many of the most significant iterations of the film's pattern throughout the 1940s, including *Tales of Manhattan* (1942) and *Cabin in the Sky* (1943).[35] His work on the play and the film of *The Green Pastures* would become one of the most important legitimating markers of the work as culturally African American, and his career would be irrevocably shaped by his participation in the project in its various incarnations. But over time Johnson would come to repudiate the work as "a whitewashed burlesque of the religious thought of the Negro," insisting that he and the other participants only suffered the production for the opportunity to work on Broadway and in film.[36]

Throughout the process of rehearsing and performing the play, as well as while making the movie, Connelly engaged in a discourse about authenticity and the "natural qualities" of African Americans that was similar to King Vidor's discussions during the production of *Hallelujah*. In the press coverage preceding the opening of the play and later the film, he emphasized the natural acting abilities of African Americans, intimating that what viewers would see would be "real" blackness, not artifice, and emphasizing that the large cast contained many who were not professional actors. In 1930 he told a reporter, "I believe almost every Negro is a good actor. There are only a few in this play who have ever been on the stage before, yet they all know how to act."[37] In fact, he continued, he had lost a friend because he enticed her maid to join the cast. Connelly went on to describe an unnamed casting agency in Harlem that maintained no files but simply sent its representatives out on the street to find the right type for the particular part in question. In 1936, shortly before the film was released, a reporter wrote that according to Connelly "the whole art of acting is based on poise, on a sort of non-self-conscious frenzy which projects one into something he is not. Warming to his subject, Connelly said, 'Negroes can throw themselves into imaginary surroundings more easily and wholeheartedly than any actors I have ever seen.'"[38] Theater critics and other commentators on the play would emphasize this sense of the childlike abandon of the play's actors and of African American religiosity in general, and most white reviewers of the play took it, therefore, to be an authentic presentation of the religious "mind of the Negro."[39]

As in the discussions surrounding the cast of King Vidor's *Hallelujah*, those on the cast of *The Green Pastures* illustrated a contrast between the black press's emphasis on the acting experience and impressive personal histories of the actors and the director's insistence on their performances as the natural result of inborn acting talents of black people. The contrast points to the profoundly different ways in which the various camps of commentators and participants in the project understood the significance of the film event. Although Connelly tended to talk about Richard B. Harrison, who played "De Lawd" on Broadway, as an amateur who dabbled in "readings of Shakespeare and Dunbar in schools,"[40] many African American commentators saw his work as an actor and dramatic reader as critical to the history and development of black theatrical arts.[41] Other members of the original Broadway cast of *The Green Pastures* included Daniel L. Haynes, who was known to audiences from his performance as Zeke in *Hallelujah* and who had since appeared in numerous plays and in the film *The Last Mile*. The film version would also feature Frank Wilson as Moses, known to theater audiences from Paul Green's 1926 Pulitzer Prize–winning play, *In Abraham's Bosom* (also a white playwright's foray into black life), and Eddie Anderson, who had already appeared in four films by major studios, as Noah.[42] Although Connelly used many untrained actors, especially children, to great effect in the play and later the film, the cast also included well-known and highly regarded African American actors. As was the case with *Hallelujah*, the insistence that the film would give white viewers special insight into the religious mind of the Negro seemed to require a denial of the training and skills that the black participants brought to the project. In the case of *The Green Pastures*, the fact that the cast included many children and that the film presented the Bible stories in the context of a Sunday school lesson influenced and often infiltrated the evaluation of the adult actors. In the film, because of Connelly's visual association between the children who hear the stories and the adults who tell and hear the stories, all of the cast members in effect become children, and the enduring appeal of the work for many viewers lies in the blurring of these lines.

Although some African Americans objected to the implication that Connelly's writing represented black Christian theology realistically, the positive response to the production often had to do with the sense that the members of the cast were doing important social and political work through their success on stage. In 1931 the Associated Negro Press ranked *The Green Pastures* number twelve in its list of the year's "most important race achievements," telling readers that "the production brought to public notice the possibilities of the Negro as a dramatic actor and opened new potential fields for him."[43] The arrival of the touring production of *The Green Pastures* had an impact on local black communities in important ways. Black communities across the country received and entertained cast members at a range of events connected to local political and religious concerns. African Americans in the Young Women's Christian Association in Omaha, Nebraska, held a banquet for the company; the Hallie Quinn Brown Club of St. Paul, Minnesota, entertained the cast at its community house; and the Milwaukee Urban League welcomed the cast to the city. In Boston, the St. Charles African Methodist Episcopal Church hosted some members of the cast who performed a concert, and in Los Angeles Harold "Slick" Garrison, the MGM studio bootblack who had worked as production assistant on *Hallelujah*, and his wife hosted the cast at a party on their Sunday off. In each of these cases, African American communities small and large were able to show their support for members of the cast and to enlist them on behalf of local causes during their stay, in addition to simply gaining the benefits of association with this renowned Broadway production.[44]

The practical issues of hosting the cast members and of mounting the production in racially segregated towns and cities often provided an opportunity for African Americans to challenge Jim Crow. When the group was on tour in 1934, for example, the local branch of the NAACP in Cumberland, Maryland, joined with the white clergy of the Cumberland Ministerial Alliance to effect a suspension of segregated seating at the play's performance by threatening a boycott of the theater. Although the ad hoc coalition was not as successful in addressing the question of accommodations for the cast, it is clear from the press coverage how significant the community took to be both the actions of those involved in protesting segregation and the limited erasure of the color line in the social lives of Cumberland's residents.[45] The issue of separate performances of *The Green Pastures* for black and white audiences at Washington, D.C.'s National Theatre in February 1933 proved much more controversial, however, and the community and its leaders could not come to easy agreement about how best to approach the problem. Carter G. Woodson, a number of prominent black clergy, and the local branch of the NAACP called for a boycott of the play. The controversy became so intense that Richard B. Harrison was assigned a police escort in response to a rumor that opponents of the segregated performances planned to kidnap the lead actor. On the other side, Kelly Miller, dean of the College of Arts and Sciences at Howard University, argued that although a "Jim Crow" performance was not preferable the community should support the play because of the important work the cast had done to end racial discrimination.[46] In this regard, Miller's views were in line with those of many in the public and in the black press. As one press report emphasized, "*The Green Pastures* is gaining for the Negro the respect and understanding for which the group has striven so many years, and its members are trying to crumble the walls of prejudice which surround the group."[47] While African Americans in communities across the country could support the members of the cast and enlist them on behalf of local causes during their stay, the film version of the play provided no such possibilities, accounting, in part, for the tepid response by black audiences and in the black press.

Anticipating interest by film studios in Connelly's work when *The Green Pastures* opened on Broadway to rave reviews in 1930, the Studio Relations Committee of the Motion Picture Producers and Distributors Association (MPPDA) solicited its own evaluations of the play in order to assess its handling of the delicate issue of a "black version" of the Bible. Daniel J. Lord, a Jesuit priest and one of the authors of the Production Code, presented a very positive assessment of the play for the MPPDA as "the most original piece of drama I have seen in ages."[48] While lauding its originality, Lord also reveled in its familiarity, comparing it to medieval mystery plays. He reported that he found the play generally moving and humorous but always respectful, never approaching blasphemy. Most important for Hollywood, Lord saw no potential violations of the code with regard to the representation of religion. He did caution, however, that, "[i]n America your small town audience would probably miss [the point] badly. The same group that resented the Negroes as an actor [*sic*] in 'Hallelujah' and Fox's 'Hearts in Dixie' would resent the negroes in this—which is thoroughly stupid."[49] Lamar Trotti, the MPPDA staffer who had been so vocal about *Hallelujah*'s story striking him as a truthful representation of southern black religion, also evaluated the Broadway production of Connelly's play. He too found it an enjoyable experience, thought it would make a wonderful movie, and foresaw no difficulties with the Production Code since the play was, for him, simply "the story of the Bible as understood by primitive negroes in the South who interpret it in terms of their own experiences."[50] Although the MPPDA was aware of the interest of Paramount, Universal, and MGM in the property, all these studios declined to proceed at the time because they did not think that national and international audience response would be sufficient to make a film of *The Green Pastures* financially viable.[51] It was not until six years later, after a long Broadway run, national and international tours, and a return run on Broadway, that Warner Bros. took up the project. Nevertheless, these early evaluations by the film censors identified critical areas of potential controversy—the discomfort that "small town" white Americans might feel regarding a film with an all-black cast and the implications, for many black Americans, of the assertion that the play represented the theological understandings of their "primitive minds."

When Warner Bros. acquired the property some years later, the studio signed Marc Connelly to direct the film despite his never having directed a movie before, a decision that ultimately endangered the production and reflected what many black critics felt was Connelly's investment in his own ego at the expense of African American dignity. Although he was not a neophyte in Hollywood, having written and acted in a number of short films, his inexperience soon became a major issue on the set.[52] A few days into production, Hal Wallis, Warner's production executive, and Henry Blanke, the film's supervisor, began to realize the gravity of the situation in terms of both delays and the quality of the footage they were screening in the daily rushes. Wallis was extremely disappointed to find that Connelly's direction involved "two people standing up in front of the camera, in straight-on shots, and speaking their lines in close-up, as they do on the stage."[53] In addition, Wallis received reports of considerable chaos on the set, resulting largely from Connelly's indecision and inexperience, which created a working environment that inevitably led to production delays.[54] The black press also reported on the slow start to the production as well as on some complaints by cast members about delays.[55] Eventually, Wallis assigned William Keighley as co-director. Keighley was a seasoned director who had turned out a number of films in Warner Bros.' trademark gangster film style, including *'G' Men*, starring James Cagney, and *Special Agent*, starring Bette Davis, both released in 1935.[56] According to reports from the set, the situation improved slightly when Keighley joined the production, and the film wrapped shooting only ten days behind schedule.[57]

Other issues in addition to Connelly's inexperience hampered the film's production and led to concern among African Americans about the quality of the final product and the potential negative reception of a film that purported to represent a black interpretation of the Bible. Chief among these was the problem of casting the part of "De Lawd"; Richard B. Harrison had played the part in the Broadway production, but he had died by the time Connelly turned his attention to transforming the play into a film. Once Warner Bros. decided to go ahead with the production, the controversy attendant upon presenting a black God came to the fore for African American observers of the film industry as well as for sympathetic whites, and a rumor spread among African American Angelenos that Warner Bros. would cast the white performer Al Jolson, famous for performing in blackface makeup, as "De Lawd," presumably to play the part in blackface.[58] Elizabeth St. Charles Edwards, president of the Movie Fan Club of Los Angeles, working in cooperation with the Southern California Federation of Church Women, wrote to Joseph Breen at the MPPDA to address the rumors. Emphasizing the impact of negative representations in the movies on interactions between black and white Americans, Edwards commended Warner Bros. for taking up the challenge of filming Connelly's play, a project she felt to be a wonderful tribute to the late Richard B. Harrison. The rumor that the lead part would "be done by a non-Negro actor, who, perhaps, will assume a racial identity by the art of make-up," alarmed her and the club's members, however, and they felt compelled to lodge a complaint.[59] Floyd C. Covington, executive secretary of the Los Angeles Branch of the National Urban League, also directed a letter to Breen indicating that he too had heard rumors that a white man (neither he nor Edwards named Jolson specifically) would be cast in the part that Harrison had played on Broadway. Covington insisted that "we know of no actor of any race more prepared to play the part of 'De Lawd' than one of the flesh and blood of the race."[60] Breen forwarded the letters to Jack Warner, quipping, "I take it that hereafter the Lord must be a coloured man." Warner replied that the studio had every intention of proceeding in "the same good taste and spirit as it was done on the stage."[61] But while Breen made light of the rumors and Warner seemed unworried, Elizabeth Edwards's letter pointed to a much broader concern that motivated this level of scrutiny by African Americans of the production—that "the type of pictures which do include racial artists can be either helpful or harmful to more than twelve million American citizens" and even more so because the production involved a representation of God.[62]

The issue of representing the divine on stage and film had long been controversial, both in America and abroad, and white religious leaders and filmmakers struggled over film portrayals of the life of Christ. These disputes were heated in early film history, but controversies over actors portraying Jesus on the American stage dated back to the nineteenth century, when many white Protestant ministers evaluated American versions of the passion play as sacrilegious. American clergy generally found American passion plays inferior when compared to European passion plays like Oberammergau, or even the popular stereopticon and magic lantern lectures on Oberammergau, but found that film presented additional complications.[63]

Discomfort over representing the story of the passion of Jesus in the movies turned on the ability of film to shape narrative in unique ways. Charles Keil writes: "While significant debate was emerging within religious and academic institutions regarding approaches to the Bible as text, little disagreement existed within the North American Christian populace as a whole with regard to the proper status of Jesus as a religious figure. And certainly the representation of Christ within popular entertainment, particularly in a form so consistently linked with technologically perfected powers of mimesis and verisimilitude as cinema, could only be executed with due recognition of the sacred nature of Christ's existence. Hence, the principal watchword for any photographically-based rendering of Christ as character was 'reverence.'"[64] Christian leaders exhibited great anxiety about the power of filmmakers to present sacred text using techniques of "trick photography," such as the superimposition of one image over another, to represent miraculous events. Perhaps fearing the loss of control of the religious imagination of Christians to the movies and a demeaning of the miraculous by photographic techniques, some ministers sought to reassert their authority by seeking to bar such representations. Nevertheless, Bible films had proved popular in the silent film era, and by the time *The Green Pastures* premiered on Broadway film audiences had recently seen a variety of such films, including Cecil B. DeMille's first version of *The Ten Commandments* (Paramount, 1923) and *The King of Kings* (Producers Distributing Corporation, 1927), Michael Curtiz's *Noah's Ark* (Warner Bros., 1928), and Fred Niblo and Ferdinand P. Earle's *Ben-Hur* (Metro-Goldwyn-Mayer, 1925). Given how controversial numerous attempts to represent the divine on film using white actors had been, Connelly's setting of stories from the Hebrew Scriptures in an entirely black context was potentially explosive.[65]

Understanding, as he did when he cast the Broadway play, that the casting of the part of God was central to the project's success, Connelly returned to his original idea of casting a widely respected public figure instead of a professional actor. The production team began the casting process by conferring with several people, including Roark Bradford, author of the book from which Connolly had drawn the idea for the play. After speaking with Bishop Robert E. Jones of the Methodist Episcopal Church, Bradford recommended Dr. Robert Russa Moton, who had recently completed a long term as president of the Tuskegee Normal and Industrial Institute (as Booker T. Washington's successor), as the "best man in America, mentally, physically and spiritually."[66] Jones also noted that Dr. Stanley Grunnum, president of Sam Houston College in Austin, Texas, might do a good job with the part. Connelly tracked Moton down in his retirement and wrote to him, reminding him that they had met after a performance of the play when it was on Broadway. He continued, "I regretted that you were not an actor. Now I am wondering if you would entertain the idea of becoming one."[67] When Moton declined, Connelly approached Noble Johnson, a veteran film actor and producer of "race movies," who also declined to participate.[68] Like Connelly's attempt to cast Rev. Adam Clayton Powell Sr. for the Broadway play, his pursuit of Robert Russa Moton and consideration of Grunnum reflects a combination of respect for these prominent African American men and a patronizing confidence that they would set aside their careers to be in a film. In addition, the attempt to secure a political or educational leader rather than an actor for the lead role reveals Connelly's deeply rooted sense that the authentic black religious sensibility he believed he had captured in the play did not require a trained actor.

Eventually Warner Bros. tested the veteran film actor Rex Ingram for the part, and Connelly was thrilled with him. Ingram had begun his career with a bit part in the first *Tarzan* film in 1918. Under the names Cliff and Clifford Ingram he appeared in the black-audience film *Tenderfeet* (1928), directed by Spencer Williams, in Fox's all-black cast *Hearts in Dixie* (1929), and as a warrior in the RKO picture *King Kong* (1933). He also worked on Broadway before being cast in the parts of God, Adam, and Hezdrel in the film version of *The Green Pastures*.[69] Despite Ingram's excellent credentials and a sense among black theater and film critics that he would do a good job with the part, the black press, as we have seen, did not hesitate to cover the scandals in his personal life or to ridicule the claim that the film would be an authentic portrayal of black religious thought, a status that necessitated a morally upright leading man. This negative attention given to the production in the black press certainly compounded the skepticism of those who expected that the film would not reflect well on African Americans and saw another occasion in which they would be "on the block" for the entertainment of whites.

Coverage in some quarters of the black press of the film's progress made clear that observers worried that *The Green Pastures* would be a low-budget production and that, as a result, the quality would suffer, as would the actors involved. Jack Gracia, the movie columnist for the *New York Amsterdam News*, predicted that the film would be a success ("you know how popular is this illiterate-Negro-conception-of-things")[70] and that the studio would certainly realize a profit on the endeavor, since it had cast Rex Ingram in three of the leading roles and, according to reports, used local extras at very low pay. Gracia concluded his piece by commenting on the disparity of pay and opportunity between white and black actors in Hollywood. No matter how much it seemed that Ingram was being paid in comparison to his previous acting jobs, Gracia noted, white actors with long-term studio contracts made considerably more and had year-round employment.[71] Another item in the *Amsterdam News* disclosed a Motion Picture Actors' Guild protest of the low salaries and blamed Connelly, who, the article noted, had reportedly paid the actors in the Broadway production very little.[72] The sense that the production might be a cheap, low-quality one may also have been influenced by the fact that the Warner Bros. studio, unlike MGM, which produced *Hallelujah*, was known more for its "B" productions (low-budget second films on double bills) than for large-budget, high-quality movies.[73]

Even though the claim that the black actors in *The Green Pastures* were being treated poorly when compared with most other actors in Hollywood had some merit, in many regards the studio spent a typical amount on production and salaries for the film. Warner Bros. budgeted $539,000 for the film, a standard amount for a midlevel production in the mid-1930s, with "above-the-line" costs of $63,000 for Connelly— $30,000 for story and script and $33,000 for directing—also typical for such a production. The addition of Keighley as co-director increased these costs, but the overall production costs remained moderate.[74] The veteran actors Rex Ingram and Eddie Anderson, who played Noah, received the highest salaries, with Ingram being paid $550 per week for his three parts and Anderson $500 per week. Oscar Polk received $325 per week for three weeks for playing the part of Gabriel. Less well-known actors or ones with smaller parts were paid anywhere from $150 to $325 per week (with some working for only one or two weeks), and all the actors were subject to a rider on their contracts stipulating that the studio would provide "period clothing" and the performers would furnish "modern wardrobe," an unusual provision for a major studio. Almost half of the talent for the film came from the New York theater, and Warner Bros. was concerned about travel expenses adding to the film's cost, particularly as negotiations with Hall Johnson over how many members of the choir would travel west for the production dragged on. In the end, Warner Bros. made a commitment to a moderately expensive production—foregoing Henry Blanke's suggestion that they use technicolor, which he thought would "help making your colored people ten times more attractive than in black and white"[75] Although Gracia was correct to note that few of these actors could count on long-term studio contracts or careers that would provide them with parts other than as servants, Warner Bros.' expenditures for *The Green Pastures* were quite typical for its midrange features of the period. Ultimately, all of these questions about the actors' salaries and the budget would fade in light of the release of the film itself and evaluations of the film's content and of its portrayal of the Bible.

The most striking aspect of *The Green Pastures* is its presentation of stories from the Hebrew Scriptures in a contemporary and racialized setting. In his memoirs Connelly wrote that he was attracted to Bradford's idea because it captured so well his sense of African Americans' encounter with "the white man's Bible." For him, that encounter necessarily entailed a re-envisioning of the Scriptures' context. "The five Books of Moses came to life for the invariably illiterate slaves," he wrote, "when early black preachers, ordained only by their personal faith and popularity as speakers, placed the biblical occurrences in familiar neighborhoods."[76] In his author's note in the published play, Connelly outlined his impressions of African American theology: "Unburdened by the differences of more educated theologians they accept the Old Testament as a chronicle of wonders which happened to people like themselves in vague but actual places, and of rules of conduct, true acceptance of which will lead them to a tangible, three-dimensional Heaven."[77] In choosing this literalizing approach, Connelly exploited an element that was prominent in the religious thought of enslaved African American Christians in which they indeed interpreted biblical stories and the broader theological significance of Christianity in terms of their own experiences. This method of interpretation, however, involved more than a simplistic imagining of heaven as a plantation owned by a kindly master, instead positing a theology that insisted on God's commitment to the liberation of his people. Through identification with biblical stories like the Exodus and with characters like Daniel who experienced liberation in his lifetime and was not required to wait for heaven, enslaved African American Christians lived in expectation of their own liberation as a people.[78] Connelly's characterization of African American Protestant theology as simplistic, unchanging, and oriented exclusively toward future benefits narrows the scope and complexity of early-twentieth-century black theology. In addition, in a period of ongoing struggle between fundamentalist and modernist Protestants over how to interpret the Bible, with fundamentalists insisting on the infallible divine authority of Scripture and modernists embracing a historical-critical approach, Connelly assigned to African American Christians a third position—believing the text to be literally true but also unable to understand the original context, an intellectual failing that required them to translate and modernize.

In light of Connelly's emphasis on literalism in biblical interpretation, it is surprising that the film version does not attempt to marshal viewers' expected familiarity with the Bible stories it contains or to mobilize the authority of the Bible itself to gain the viewer's sympathy. Indeed, the film opens with a disclaimer that provides an escape from any clear association between the Bible as Scripture and the interpretation of the Bible imagined by Connelly. As the Hall Johnson Choir sings a medley of spirituals, including "Won't You Get the Children to the Promised Land" and "Certainly Lord," we see a title with the Warner Bros. logo in the background that reads, "Warner Bros. Pictures Inc. Have the Honor to Present." With a dissolve, we move to a shot of a large book propped upright on a table on which also sits a candle. On the front of the book large letters spell out "The Green Pastures." The title frame that follows the image of the book identifies the story that we will see as "a fable by Marc Connelly" and notes that it was "suggested by" Bradford's book. The production credits, displayed on worn parchment, follow, and the presentation of the titles is punctuated by short scenes of clouds floating through the frame. Finally, Connelly and Keighley present us with a foreword that scrolls across a background of clouds and reads, "God appears in many forms to those who believe in Him. Thousands of Negroes in the Deep South visualize God and Heaven in terms of people and things they know in their everyday life. 'The Green Pastures' is an attempt to portray that humble, reverent conception."[79]

In the course of this very short opening title sequence, Connelly and Keighley engage in multiple strategies of distancing their work from the Bible, a very different approach from the majority of biblical epics (in both the 1920s and the 1950s) that insisted upon their faithfulness to the texts and attentiveness to historical context.[80] The film's very title begins the distancing process. It does not indicate that the movie is a telling of "the Bible" or of particular Bible stories (Adam and Eve, Cain and Abel, the life of Moses, etc.). Instead it points to a persistent fantasy among white writers who use African American religion in their work, that blacks envision heaven in terms of the pastures of southern plantation life, a belief underscored in Connelly and Keighley's foreword to the film. Connelly's method of charting the genealogy of the work stands as another strategy of distancing in these opening titles. He removes the work multiply from the biblical source by emphasizing the story's origins in the minds of humble Negroes in the South, tracing it through Bradford's book, which "suggested" the story to him, and then designating his own product as "a fable." Finally, Connelly's decision to have his characters refer to the God character in the play and in the film most frequently as "De Lawd" also provides the opportunity for viewers to distance themselves from fully imagining the God of the Bible as a black man. This character becomes, instead, simply the God of black people.

Aesthetic choices for the production also make it difficult for audiences to form a clear association between the Bible and the story contained in the film. In *Hallelujah* King Vidor employed a documentary style that entailed considerable location shooting to emphasize the "reality" of the story and to impress upon viewers the timelessness of the primitive nature of the Negro. While Connelly was, like Vidor, concerned with giving audiences a window into what he understood to be an enduring culture, resistant to the forces of modernization, his aesthetic approach could not have been more different from Vidor's. The settings for the fable *The Green Pastures* take the viewer into a highly artificial environment in which angels sport wings that clearly are attached to the backs of the white robes they wear and in which they float on fluffy white clouds that hang from visible wires. It is not simply that a theatrical production serves as the film's source or that heaven serves as the setting for a portion of the film. The artifice of *The Green Pastures* points us to an imagined, fantastic world and highlights the distance between the Bible as most viewers would understand it and what they see in the film's black version. The telling of the Bible stories is mediated through images reminiscent of the world of black collectibles, the romanticized images of black mammies, uncles, and "pickaninnies" preserved in ceramic kitchen items that seek to reassure whites by domesticating blacks.[81]

In addition to distancing the film from the Bible at the very beginning, Connelly and Keighley introduce an important narrative and ideological theme in the opening frame by locating the telling of biblical stories in the context of a Sunday school class. Mr. Deshee (George Reed), the minister, escorts young Carlisle (Phillip Hurlic) to the church after having had Sunday dinner at the boy's house. Along the way, they encounter other children also bound for Sunday school, and the group proceeds together. Here Connelly retreats for a moment from his repeated differentiation between the stories of the film and the text of the Bible when Myrtle asks Mr. Deshee what "story" they will hear that day. He replies, "Ain't gonna tell no story today. We're going right to the good book itself. You're going to hear about Genesis." But Connelly quickly begins to undermine the minister's abilities as a teacher when one of the children asks, "What's Genesis, Mr. Deshee?"[82] The minister, clearly embarrassed that the child does not know the first book of the Bible, tells him to stop asking questions because they are all late for Sunday school. The scene then dissolves to the interior of the church as the children listen to Deshee recite the ages of the Patriarchs, and they do not hide their boredom and confusion. After Myrtle admits she does not understand what the minister is talking about, she and the other children begin to ask questions about the nature of Creation and, with this, Deshee abandons his first attempt to go "right to the good book" and goes back

FIGURE 9.
Mr. Deshee and Carlisle discuss clouds in *The Green Pastures*. From the author's
collection.

to his general approach of talking about religious issues by using images familiar to
the children and with which he seems much more comfortable himself.

The audience has already been introduced to Mr. Deshee's easy reliance on children's imagery in an exchange between the minister and Carlisle while on their way
to Sunday school in a sequence intended to foreshadow the film's version of the story
of Noah's ark. As the two discuss the weather and Carlisle wonders if it will rain
again and cause the river to rise, Mr. Deshee explains that the clouds they see are
not rain clouds (see figure 9). Carlisle asks him what good clouds are to people if
they don't carry rain, and Deshee ventures, "Maybe the Lord uses them as sofa pillows." "What does he do," Carlisle asks, "lay his head on them?" "Maybe so," says
Deshee.[83] Connelly couples the minister's easy, playful, and productive use of such
images in this bit of dialogue with a pointed reference to his ignorance in the next,
making it difficult for the audience to determine whether Deshee tells the stories simply for the children's benefit or whether he himself imagines God reclining on sofa
pillows made of clouds. Immediately following the exchange about clouds, Deshee

and Carlisle meet the other children who eventually accompany them to Sunday school. The children stand before a large billboard advertising a circus and compare the images of animals on the billboard with those in their illustrated ABC book. One child asks another what a tiger is, and another answers that a tiger is a lion's wife. Yet another child notes that the poster does not show anything like the aardvark he finds in the book. When the children turn to Deshee and ask if there will be an aardvark in the circus, he replies, incredulous that such a thing exists, that if there is one at the circus he surely wants to see it.

The opening frame that uses the Sunday school to locate the film's religious vision in the minds of the children accomplishes two important things. First, despite the association between the film's story and a child's view of the Bible, Connelly implicates in the acceptance of this vision the two adult men who are present and participating in the telling of the story. As already noted, Mr. Deshee is comfortable with fanciful religious images, and the sexton (Frank H. Wilson) listens to Deshee's stories every bit as rapt as the children. Indeed, just as the dissolve to the first scene set in heaven begins with a close-up of a girl's smiling face, the final return to the Sunday school and the conclusion of the film uses a medium shot of the sexton, lost in thought, to lead into the end title. As much as this seems to be a story for children, it is difficult to avoid the conclusion that all those involved are, in some way, children. The opening frame also establishes thematic and visual elements that will appear when the scene shifts from the Sunday school to the timeless period of the Bible and to heaven. For example, the ukelele that a young woman plays will appear in a scene shortly just before the Flood, the circus advertisement foreshadows the tale of Noah's ark, the homes we see as Mr. Deshee and the children walk to church will be called to mind when we see Noah's house, and a banner in the church appears in Pharaoh's court.[84]

The visual foreshadowing of the setting for the Bible stories, combined with Deshee's approach to answering the children's questions, guides the viewer to Connelly's image of a black vision of heaven. In an attempt to shift the lesson from a boring recitation of the generations of humanity, one girl asks about God's appearance. Rev. Deshee thinks for a moment and tells the children that when he was young he thought God must look like his pastor, Reverend Dubois, who was very wise and fine looking. The children then ask what life in heaven is like and how God decided to create the world. As the minister continues to describe heaven, the camera cuts to close-up shots of various children listening intently, and when he tells them that the heavenly choir had the special assignment of singing the songs that the Lord liked to hear, the camera pans in closer on the face of a small girl. The scene dis-

FIGURE 10.
Fish fry in heaven in *The Green Pastures.* From the author's collection.

solves from her face to clouds in the sky. The viewer is then transported to a fish fry picnic in heaven where the angels in attendance are wearing long white robes and sporting large wings (see figure 10). By the time Deshee has arrived at the point of describing life in heaven, he has dispensed with relying exclusively on "the good book" and has reverted to "telling stories," clearly a much more satisfying approach not just to the children but also to the sexton and the minister himself. From this point on, the majority of the film's action follows "De Lawd" in heaven and on earth in biblical times as he oversees his two domains, both troublesome and disappointing to him in significant ways.

While clearly powerful, the God of *The Green Pastures* is neither omnipotent nor omniscient. He feels his way and improvises as he goes along, rather than proceeding in a thoughtful, considered manner, a characterization that for many viewers proved problematic. For example, "De Lawd" creates the earth as a result of his dissatisfaction with the amount of firmament in the custard an angel serves him at the fish fry. In "passing a miracle" to make more firmament, God is overzealous and makes so much that the cherubs become drenched in the moisture of the firmament. Rather than break up the fish fry by sending the cherubs home, De Lawd decides to create the earth to have a place to drain off the excess firmament. The angel Gabriel (Oscar Polk) comments that the new earth has a beautiful south forty acres that will make nice farming land and notes that De Lawd should not let the nice garden nearby go to waste. And so, seemingly on a whim, God creates Adam (also played by Rex Ingram without the beard and gray hair). Throughout the rest of the film humanity confuses and irritates God, who alternates between complete neglect of his creations and hurling thunderbolts at them. De Lawd concocts various "schemes" to subdue humanity, but none are successful, and he finally renounces his creation. The black God of Connelly's film seems, at times, far less mature than the humans on earth, and it takes repeated prodding from various angels to remind De Lawd of his responsibilities to humanity.

In representing on film his sense of African Americans' understanding of divine power, Connelly uses images that resonate with the practice of conjure and other African American magical traditions, as well as with the theatricality of freemasonry. Pharaoh's throne room is decorated as a lodge room or a Universal Negro Improvement Association meeting hall, with banners that read, "Enchanted and Invisible Cadets of Egypt Boys Brigade" and "Supreme Magicians and Wizards of the Universe." Because of Pharaoh's love of "tricks," God teaches Moses magic so that he can obtain an audience with Pharaoh. While the outlines of the narrative do not differ from those of the biblical text, the film does little to convey a sense of an awesome divine power pitted against the inept flailings of believers in a false god. God's magical powers are superior to the gri-gri (African-derived magical charms) of Pharaoh's head "tricker," but the equation the film makes between De Lawd's power and that of the magicians leads the viewer to conclude, along with the head magician, that Moses's tricks are new but that his magic does not represent a radically different order of power. Thomas Cripps notes that Connelly and Keighley's choices for framing the shots in this scene work to underscore this leveling of types of power: "Pharaoh in *his* court is seen in as many tilted-up close-ups as God is in *his* court."[85]

In the end, Connelly's God loses all agency in this recounting of biblical history. Having renounced his creations and put them from his mind, God finds himself tormented by the faithful prayers of Hezdrel, a character of Connelly's creation (also played by Rex Ingram), from the midst of a battle on earth and cannot resist returning to investigate why they have such an effect on him.[86] In Hezdrel, De Lawd finds a man deeply confident that the God of mercy will help him liberate his people from

Herod. Surprised by this description of God as merciful rather than wrathful (because he has so clearly given himself over to wrath), De Lawd, posing as a preacher, asks Hezdrel how human beings learned about mercy. Hezdrel tells him that suffering is the only way to understand mercy and explains that people no longer see God as wrathful because they "jes' got tired of God's appearance dat ol' way." Enlightened, De Lawd replies, "So that's what faith is" and thanks Hezdrel for educating him on things he missed while remaining distant from humanity. In the filmed version of Connelly's play, God learns about humanity's capacity for faith and is somewhat surprised by Hezdrel's ability to understand the divine as merciful and caring, even in the face of evidence of wrath or neglect. While De Lawd seems quite confused and "way behind de times" in the filmed version, in an earlier draft of the script, Connelly presented De Lawd as frightened and troubled by Hezdrel's implication that there might be more than one God—the God of wrath (as De Lawd understands himself to be) *and* the God of mercy (the one in whom Hezdrel places his confidence). "But ain't dey only one God?" De Lawd asks Hezdrel, "terrified" of the answer. In this version, Hezdrel does not provide a definitive answer for De Lawd but simply insists that he is no longer afraid of God.[87] In the final filmed version, De Lawd is no longer terrified that there might be a competing God but does not seem entirely certain that he is alone among divinities.

Not only does Connelly's God require a human to demonstrate the concept of faith for him, but he does not seem to be the author of the plan for humanity's salvation or to be responsible for effecting it. Upon returning to heaven after his encounter with Hezdrel, God considers the implications of what he has learned about mercy through suffering, and, in the film's penultimate scene, De Lawd and the angels in heaven become aware of "someone else on earth" who is being nailed to a cross. We get the sense that De Lawd had nothing to do with the appearance of or sacrifice by Jesus on humanity's behalf in this version of the Christian story. As Martha Denise Green writes, "Connelly veers from the Christian account in which an omniscient, omnipotent God sends Jesus as the fulfillment of his plan and instead creates a human character . . . to shame God into developing a measure of compassion."[88] The implications of this redirection are profound for the film's portrait of African American theology and undermine any claims to universality. This representation of God as childish and lacking in agency with regard to the salvation of humanity, coupled with the film's various strategies for distancing itself from sacred Scriptures, renders black theology parochial, limited, and childish. In the author's note for the play in which he introduced his understanding of African American theology, Connelly emphasized the limited nature of this God as simply "the summation of all of the virtues His follower has observed in the human beings around him."[89] In the context of Connelly's play, it seems that the most that black people can ask of God is to be a good master. This aspect of the God character in Connelly's work would become a major focus of reviews and responses to the film and a major source of dissatisfaction for many black reviewers.

While earth and its people present innumerable irritations and frustrations for "De Lawd," heaven also has its problems. Living on a plantation that features weeping willow trees and a gated entrance, heaven's angels are more like stereotypes of house and field servants than supernatural beings. They are supervised by God, who is the "big boss," and by the Archangel Gabriel, De Lawd's "working boss." Many black viewers found this element of Connelly's story to be especially inauthentic. Zora Neale Hurston, for example, commented that "if there is anything that is not in the Negro's conception of Heaven, it is work. . . . This is the white man's idea of Heaven palmed off to perpetuate the belief that the Negro's status, even in eternity, will be that of a menial."[90] While they work hard for "De Lawd," the angels seem especially interested in entertainments during their spare time, including dancing around the moon on Saturday nights, an activity that causes it to begin to melt and "De Lawd" to ban the activity. The angels of *The Green Pastures* do not create the kind of serious trouble that God's human creations make but seem little more than another burden to "De Lawd," who pours over the account books and reviews the status of every angel with Gabriel on a regular basis. It is ultimately these angels who provide the template for a black theology based on the good old days of plantation life.

Many of God's troubles with humanity derive from the same sources as those in stories related in the Hebrew Scriptures and with which viewers would likely be familiar—Cain's murder of Abel and the enslavement of the Israelites by the Egyptians, for example—but the context in which the film sets the majority of humanity's misbehavior is distinctive and aimed specifically at diagnosing contemporary African American life. Whereas heaven is a rural plantation where the big boss manages to keep his workers productive, cares for their needs, and regulates their leisure, the character of earth after the expulsion from the Garden of Eden is decidedly urban. As the film proceeds and humans become ever more annoying to God, we see their surroundings become increasingly urbanized. In the scenes leading up to the Flood, for example, God walks along a country road that eventually leads to town. Coming upon Zeba (Edna Mae Harris) sitting against a tree and strumming a ukelele, De Lawd soon finds himself ridiculed as a "country boy" when he chastises her for profaning the Sabbath. The nearby town in which he meets Noah is relatively small, but its inhabitants are engaged in the kind of "loose living" typically associated with urban life, and the film's Babylon, where humanity's behavior moves God to renounce them, is set in a New Orleans nightclub. Significantly, the film's heroic characters, especially Moses, Noah, and Hezdrel, all function to valorize the rural. Moses, for example, encounters De Lawd while herding sheep, and the scene in which De Lawd meets Hezdrel takes place outside the city's walls as he and his forces attempt to retake the city.

The urban environment, a reality for an increasing number of African Americans in 1930 when the play premiered, emerges as an important element in Connelly's understanding of African American religious life. Although he attempted to assert a fundamentally timeless and unchanging core to African American religion, the urbanization of life for many African Americans had indeed wrought changes that were of interest to Connelly and, perhaps finally, his primary concern. The use of New Orleans as the setting for the opening and closing framing segments, coupled with the explicit narrative throughout the course of the film that locates sin in urban contexts, leaves the viewer with a strong message about the transformations in contemporary black life and the dangers these present to the nation as a whole. African Americans can remain truer to accepted moral standards, the film insists, when contained in rural environments; they become a threat to American morality when unrestrained in the city.[91]

Some contemporary reflections on the film understood the degree to which the anxiety of white Americans about urban black culture lay at the heart of Connelly's story. Warner Bros. cartoonist Isadore "Friz" Freleng's version, *Clean Pastures* (1937), foregoes any discussion of the rural context and places the contest between heaven and hell firmly in an urban environment.[92] Bypassing the potential problem of a black God, the cartoon instead focuses on St. Peter's administration of "Pair-O-Dice" and on his frustration at reports of the falling value of Pair-O-Dice preferred stock while that of Hades, Inc., rises. The domain of Hades, Inc. is Harlem, where we see African Americans dancing, drinking, and gambling in nightclubs, the sole activities of the neighborhood's residents in the white imaginary. St. Peter sends Gabriel, a caricature of the black film comedian Stepin Fetchit, to earth to drum up business.[93] Gabriel takes a traditional recruiting approach, standing on a platform with lettering on the bottom that reads, "Come to Pair-O-Dice." Next to him is a sign, clearly modeled on James Montgomery Flagg's World War I Army recruiting poster, with an image of St. Peter pointing at the viewer and declaring, "Pair-O-Dice Needs You! Opportunity, Travel, Good Food, Watermelon, Clean Living,

Music." Gabriel's languid approach, tied to stereotypes of southern black life, falls flat, as does his description of what heaven offers when compared with Harlem. As if to underscore the failures of Gabriel's old-fashioned campaign, two men—one of them a caricature of Bill "Bojangles" Robinson and the other of Al Jolson in black-face makeup— pass his platform, sing minstrel songs, and then decide to abandon their performances for the fun of the Kotton Klub nightclub. "I'se supposed to keep you out of those darn places," Gabriel whines. Freleng's decision to use a caricature of Stepin Fetchit for the Gabriel character referenced Oscar Polk's laconic performance as Gabriel in Connelly's film but, more important, located the recruiting campaign firmly in the rural past. Rather than attempt to argue that the rural is necessarily the appropriate context for African Americans, or that their salvation can be carried out through the traditional approaches, the cartoon embraces the fact of the urban in African American life. In the face of Gabriel's complete failure to sell Pair-O-Dice in ways associated with the rural South, a number of angels—caricatures of Fats Waller, Cab Calloway, and Louis Armstrong—approach St. Peter and argue that they will have to take a more modern approach, with rhythm. A big-band performance of "I've Got Swing for Sale" brings the residents of Harlem dancing into Pair-O-Dice, making it such a hot commodity that even the devil seeks to gain entrance.[94] This pared-down version of *The Green Pastures*' story, which sets aside any attempt to engage theology or biblical narratives, cut to the heart of concerns among many African Americans about the impact of Connelly's work on public discourse—that is, that their theology seemed less important than whether the dangers they were imagined to present to American culture could be contained. On one level, *Clean Pastures* tells the story of the fading of one generation of black entertainers (Bill "Bojangles" Robinson, Stepin Fetchit) and the rise of a new one (Fats Waller, Cab Calloway, and Louis Armstrong), but it also highlights the social concerns in *The Green Pastures* by focusing on the politics of urbanization. Although no more complex than *The Green Pastures* in its rendering of black life or theology, *Clean Pastures* proceeds from the premise that Connelly's fish fry in the sky represents an older African American understanding of heaven and that African Americans would be looking for the modern entertainments of the urban North in the afterlife. At the same time that the cartoon participates in producing a discourse about the dangers of black urban culture, its critique of the outmoded approach of *The Green Pastures* to black life and culture is significant. Commentators in the black press who wrote about the play and the film did not devote attention to *Clean Pastures*, perhaps because they dismissed animation as artistically and politically inconsequential. Nevertheless, the cartoon remains an important commentary on and revision of *The Green Pastures* and highlights the centrality of images of black urban life to some viewers' impressions of the film.[95]

In the preface to his book *The Negro's God as Reflected in His Literature* (1938), Benjamin E. Mays felt compelled to address the long-term cultural impact of *The Green Pastures* in American life before he could move on to the book's true scholarly project. "It has been taken for granted that the Negro is over-emotional and super-religious," he wrote. "It has been assumed by many people that the ideas of God expressed in Green Pastures are wholly representative of what the Negro thinks of God. Although the author did not set out in this study to disprove anything presented in Green Pastures, the data themselves show that the Negro's idea of God is *not* now and has never been what Green Pastures may lead some people to believe."[96] In his own work, Mays used literature to explore African American theology from the eighteenth through the early twentieth centuries, focusing on relationships between theology and social context. No unchanging, childlike view of the divine or of the relationship between humans and God characterizes this body of literature, Mays concluded, but rather a series of critical engagements between text and context, some of which he found productive and some problematic. But *The Green Pastures* had cast a long shadow, as Mays's discomfort reveals some two years after the film's release, and contemporary responses to the play and the movie understood Connelly's attempt to render an African American version of God to be the central element for evaluation.

Gilbert Seldes's review of the play focused on the problems of Connelly's God character, noting, "God is weary of his chosen people and forsakes them, but their cries unnerve and bewilder him, he is dragged down to earth again, and although he does not save them again from Herod, we have the intimation that the burden of the earth is too great and that the Savior comes as much to take the burden from God as to save mankind."[97] Theophilus Lewis of the *New York Age* concurred with Seldes's evaluation, writing of De Lawd, "He is portrayed as an apotheosized Negro preacher, kindly and tolerant and with a somewhat rural point of view. He falls short in both omniscience and omnipotence, and the way the world gets out of hand suggests that He would not make a success of building up a church. This kindly old Deity has a great deal of trouble with a world that won't behave and in His effort to prevent his recalcitrant creation from going to the pot the best He earns is a draw."[98] Both Seldes and Lewis concluded that, in this characterization, Connelly's play struck a false note. But Seldes, who was white, attributed the falseness to Connelly's addition of a theology beyond the capacity of African Americans, reasoning, "The theology is too complicated for what has gone before; one doubts whether it is the work of the igno-rant Negro." The African American critic Lewis, on the other hand, found De Lawd somewhat ridiculous and questioned whether this could be "the Negro's" vision of God. He wrote, "A faithful presentation of a religion in the terms of its believers must include their attitude toward their deity and their faith. I do not believe that the Negroes of the type Mr. Connelly describes see their deity and his works in a humor-ous light. In many instances they would express his ideas in the same words used by Mr. Connelly. But the meaning would be different. To them God's efforts to keep the world sinless would appear to be a heroic and solemn struggle"[99]

For the most part, white reviewers of the play took every opportunity to empha-size their understanding of this work as reflective of the childlike and "primitive" psychology of African Americans. The *New York Telegram*'s reviewer praised the drama for making connections to universal human themes such as the struggle of mercy to overcome hate. He hastened to assure his readers that his evaluation of blacks as human and even as "play[ing] a vital part in bringing back to current Chris-tianity its kindliness" did not mean that he advocated social equality. The review continued, "[The Negro] belongs, if you will, to an inferior race, but that does not block him off from purity of heart. To be sure, hell has been thundered out from many a wayside camp meeting, but mostly the Negro has been enraptured by the vision of the Lamb of God. The Christ who suffered little children would surely have made room on that bench for members of an inferior race."[100] The *Motion Pic-ture Herald*'s review of the film assured exhibitors that it was very amusing and not at all sacrilegious, concluding, "It is the living but primitive Negroes' conception of De Lawd, heaven and familiar incidents in the Bible."[101] *Motion Picture Review* saw the film as providing "a real feeling of religion and a deeper understanding of a simple, childlike race," and the *Commonweal* reviewer felt that it "set out to depict the rare, sincere, at times childish intimacy with which the illiterate, primitive Negro imagines his relationship with heaven and its constituents."[102]

Reviews in the black press were mixed, and in general the papers devoted con-siderably less attention to the release of the film than they had to the play's Broad-way run and subsequent tours, with the exception of the interest in Rex Ingram's personal life. Responses ranged from those who considered the production the best picture of the year or certainly worthy of high praise to those who found it insult-ing or simply poorly produced. Almena Davis in the *California Eagle* and J. Cullen Fentress of the Associated Negro Press both proclaimed it the year's best film and rated Rex Ingram's performance as outstanding. The New York lawyer and jour-nalist Roi Ottley declared, "Green Pastures is Punk" and joked that, having played three parts in the film, Ingram had three chances to give a good performance but failed. Only Hall Johnson's arrangements of spirituals had any merit as far as he was concerned. In a later comment about the film, Ottley chastised black newspapers for their habit of praising any production, no matter how poorly done, that featured black actors.[103]

Despite the highly mediated representation of the Bible and the explicit work the film does to attempt to domesticate and contain African Americans in a childlike and primitive state, various people involved in the production anticipated objections to the representation of God as a black man and opposition to exhibitions of the film. Will Hays of the MPPDA cautioned Joseph Breen, his top staffer, to "watch 'The Green Pastures' very closely from the viewpoint of Southern opinion and ideals and the viewpoint of the Evangelistic churches," but no significant protest materialized.[104] The expected opposition never emerged. It seems likely that the various strategies within the film of distancing it from the Bible were successful and, in the United States, exhibitors and viewers took the film to be a window into the "mind of the Negro" rather than an attempt to present a biblical epic. In addition, the studio's publicity campaign seems to have consciously avoided any reference to the all-black cast. The posters contain no images of cast members—something typical in film advertising— and the lobby cards only a few. The pressbook that exhibitors received with suggestions for marketing and for such things as lobby displays contains drawings that would easily lead theater owners and ticket buyers to think that the actors were white were it not for a few references to "dusky angels" and "pickaninnies."[105]

Even though Warner Bros. did not face opposition to its release of *The Green Pastures* in the United States, the studio found itself unable to distribute the film in a number of other countries. Here it encountered difficulties similar to those that Connelly faced when he took his stage play on an international tour and found that England and other countries prohibited any representation of "the Deity" on stage or film, considering it blasphemy.[106] The United Kingdom banned the film, prompting protest on the film's behalf from some clergy. The Lord Bishop of Norwich entered the fray, writing in an editorial for the *Sunday Dispatch* that the censors had been far too rigid in their approach to this film. Because the story was set in the context of a children's Sunday school, he argued, the film had great potential to teach both children and adult Christians who might be "hardened by familiarity" with the Bible. The film, he wrote, "puts before us the intuitions of a primitive race who do not reflect as we do, but react like children to the words of the Bible. . . . And we can learn much when we observe the way unsophisticated minds respond to the things of God. . . . [I]n far lands we see the power of God when it first touches native races.

The virgin soil responds unmistakably. If the natives take up a western infection with disastrous results, they take up the Gospel just as strikingly, and its power holds them."[107] England's film censor finally lifted the ban on *The Green Pastures* in 1936 after determining that the act "forbidding the impersonation of the Deity" applied only to the stage and not to the screen.[108]

In addition to England, Australia, Finland, Palestine, China, Barbados, British Malaya, Latvia, and the Straits Settlements (the British colonies of Singapore, Malacca, and Penang) rejected the film. Other countries went beyond a prohibition of any representations of the divine and rejected the film precisely because its God was black. For the Hungarian censor board, "The story of this film is apt to mislead the great masses with respect to the dogmatics of the Christian religion. But in other respects, too, this picture is quite incomprehensible, as the negro mentality is very remote and foreign to us." The Dutch East Indies censor board similarly justified a ban on the film "[b]ecause the Deity is represented in it as a negro and allegedly in a disrespectful manner."[109] The premier of the province of Ontario in Canada supported a ban by declaring the film "an insult to the Christian religion."[110]

The studio, the MPPDA, and supportive outsiders attempted to overturn or circumvent these restrictions on exhibiting the film in various countries. Warner Bros. considered a variety of options in consultation with the American censors. Joseph Breen of the MPPDA apparently told Hal Wallis at Warner Bros. "that Paramount had encountered difficulties similar to what we are experiencing now with 'GREEN PASTURES' when they tried to show [DeMille's] 'THE KING OF KINGS' in England. . . . According to Breen, they overcame this by running the pictures in auditoriums and halls that were not classified as theatres."[111] In addition to attempting to get around the restrictions, the studio had the benefit of groups of concerned clergy who rallied around the film. In response to the Ontario censor's ban, a group of priests, rabbis, and ministers met in New York for a special screening, after which they declared it "a sermon in itself, conducive to religion." Here, again, the clergy relied on the sense that the film presented "a simple interpretation" from a simple people.[112] The ban was lifted in response to the protests of these and other clergy in the United States and Canada.

Despite the resistance to the exhibition of *The Green Pastures* outside the United States, the film did reasonably well in its domestic release in 1936.[113] In later years, however, as opportunities for more varied representations of African American religious thought and life became available, the general public proved less interested in Connelly's vision of an unchanging African American theology. When the play was revived on Broadway in 1951, Rev. Decatur Ward Nichols, bishop of the Fifth District of the African Methodist Episcopal Church, wrote an open letter to Cardinal Spellman, the National Conference of Christians and Jews, and "leading" Protestant clergymen in which he characterized the play "irreligious and stupid" and as damaging to America's spiritual war against the Soviet Union. Nichols further argued that *The Green Pastures* mobilized worn and tired stereotypes of black people, presenting demeaning images of "the Negro church," which, he reminded his readers, had been a powerful force against "all forms of irreligion and communism in particular." Nichols insisted that, as with Roberto Rossellini's *The Miracle*, "any such distortion of things spiritual should be condemned to the scrap heap."[114] He called on his fellow clergymen to participate in a boycott of the production. The revival, directed by Connelly, featured Ossie Davis as Gabriel, Frank H. Wilson as Moses (Wilson had also played Moses in the film version), and William Marshall as De Lawd. Despite the presence of important established actors and promising newcomers, the revival's run on Broadway lasted less than a month. Reviewing the production for the *Daily Worker,* Harold Cruse, a black intellectual and later participant in the Black Arts movement, predicted that audiences in general and black audiences would not be receptive to Connelly's view. Cruse wrote, "For 1951 is not 1930 and it is safe to say that this revival won't be swallowed for too long. The America of 1951 is thinking too deeply about fundamental problems of a very earthly if not earthshaking nature to be long bothered with Marc Connelly's fraudulent message of folk whimsy from heaven." He further emphasized the disjuncture between the green pastures of Connelly's vision and the South of black experience, "red with the blood of Negroes or soaked with Negro sweat."[115] In a photo-editorial about the revival, entitled "No Time for Green Pastures," *Ebony* characterized the production's failure as "one of the most heartening signs of the growing maturity of race relations in America."[116] Connelly was disappointed by the negative response but continued to invest his energies in the production. Eschewing the stage and film screen, he attempted to revive his work on television in 1957 and 1959 for the Hallmark Hall of Fame with William Warfield and Eddie Anderson in the cast and was met with a tepid response.[117]

In the years after the release of the film, a number of participants engaged, directly and indirectly, the questions of authenticity circulating so vigorously around the film. Six years after the completion of the film version of *The Green Pastures* and almost twelve years after the production opened on Broadway, Hall Johnson repudiated the work in an unqualified fashion. Writing to Albert Lewis, an associate producer at MGM who was working on Vincente Minnelli's production of *Cabin in the Sky,* an all-black-cast musical that would be released in 1943, Johnson explained that the black actors involved with the stage and film productions of *The Green Pastures* had taken the parts only as a way of getting work on Broadway and in Hollywood.[118] He argued that, as a result of their presence on the stage and in film and their strong perform- ances, it became impossible for directors to cast white actors in blackface over black actors again. But Johnson saw little that was redeeming in the work, writing,

> The Green Pastures, a third-hand derivation from a second-hand book, was never more than a white-washed burlesque of the religious thought of the Negro. On every program of this entertainment (which, by the way, was not a play but a series of playlets), was to be found a solemn pronouncement by the author that the nonsense it portrayed was actual belief,—the serious reli- gion, of 'thousands of Negroes in the Deep South.' . . . But to this day Negroes have never forgiven the slanderous misrepresentations of the piece, and when, after five successful years on the stage it was finally made into a picture, they did not hesitate to express their true feelings about it.[119]

Even as Johnson felt free to disown the production in a private letter, he neverthe- less capitalized on his association with *The Green Pastures* throughout his career, con- tinuing to provide authentic renderings of Negro spirituals for films such as *Way Down South* (1939), *Tales of Manhattan* (1942), and *Cabin in the Sky* (1943), as well as participating in all of the versions of Connelly's play.

Hall Johnson was not the only participant in Connelly's production who later crit- icized it. Mercedes Gilbert, a veteran stage actress with film credits in two of Oscar Micheaux's race movies, played the part of Zipporah in the original Broadway pro- duction. During the first tour of the Broadway production, she filed reports with the Associated Negro Press about the reception of the cast and the play in a vari- ety of cities, focusing especially on the interactions between the cast and local black communities. Gilbert did not appear in the film, instead turning primarily to the the- ater and writing. By 1938 she had added to her repertoire of monologues and imper- sonations a one-act play she had written called *In Greener Pastures*, which she per- formed at the Harlem YMCA and in Jamaica, New York, where she lived.[120] By 1943, she had expanded this into a three-act farce called *In Greener Fields*. While the play was not a direct parody of *The Green Pastures*, Gilbert did take on broad issues that Connelly's work raised for African Americans, particularly the uses of images of African American religiosity for the entertainment of whites. The play focuses on a black family in Brooklyn and the son who derives a chemical formula to turn them white as a way of dealing with their financial, social, and political frustrations. His parents, sister, and aunt all ingest his concoction with enthusiasm, become white, and move to Riverside Drive on Manhattan's Upper West Side. But the family members soon find that being white does not really make them happy. At a party in their new apartment to which they have invited members of white New York society, two women tell a joke they had recently heard about an "old colored preacher" and his love of flapjacks and chicken. When the women leave the room the daughter comments, "I wonder do they ever have anything interesting or funny happen in their lives. Every time I've been to anything they're having, they always had to tell a story about some colored man."[121]

African American critics of *The Green Pastures* wondered this as well, particularly given the longevity of white Americans' interest in the Broadway production and the success of the film. Connelly's commitment to continuous marketing of the work enabled *The Green Pastures* to secure a firm place in the American imagination, supplanting *Hallelujah* as the standard against which future all-colored-cast films would be judged.

THREE

"A Mighty Epic of Modern Morals"

Black-Audience Religious Films

By 1929, the same year that MGM released *Hallelujah*, thirty-five-year-old Spencer Williams had already begun to make a name for himself in Hollywood and had come to the attention of the black press for his work both as a writer and actor within the white studio system and as an independent director of films for black audiences.[1] The previous year had seen the release of his first film, *Tenderfeet*, and he had begun to work as a sound technician and writer at the white-owned Christie Studios while also beginning work on a second film of his own.[2] In addition, he had appeared as an extra in several films, including *Tarzan and the Golden Lion* (1927), *Ham and Eggs* (1927), *The King of Kings* (1927), *Steamboat Bill, Jr.* (1928), and *Safe in Hell* (1931).[3] At the Christie Studios, Williams was involved in the production of a series of short films based on stories by the white author Octavus Roy Cohen about fictional black detective Florian Slappey: he wrote dialogue and continuity, appeared in them, and, according to some accounts, served as assistant director.[4] In this period, he was at the center of a group of black artists and performers trying to make careers in the film industry, and he devoted particular attention to helping newcomers develop professional skills.[5] In the early 1930s Williams sought to reproduce his success with short films at Christie through his own company, Lincoln Talking Pictures, which he also planned to use in the production of Negro newsreels, but it is unclear whether anything came of these plans.[6] In 1939, Earl J. Morris, motion picture editor for the *Pittsburgh Courier* and actor in black-audience films, hailed Williams as one of the top three actors in black Hollywood and as the year's best film writer, editor, and best "all around Negro film man." In addition, Morris named Williams, along with Clarence Brooks, George Randol, and Ralph Cooper, as the most influential and visionary figures in "sepia films."[7] Indeed, Morris thought so highly of Spencer Williams that he would team with him the same year to attempt to organize a Negro Board of Censorship, in Williams's words, "to help us protect our race."[8]

Although there is relatively little biographical information available about Williams compared with white Hollywood directors, two elements of his personal history stand out as important organizing elements across his body of work in film. First, Williams's commitment to developing himself as an entertainer is the strongest thread through his biography, beginning with his work behind the scenes in the New York theater as a "call boy" (informing actors that the time for their stage entrance is imminent) for the white theater owner and impresario Oscar Hammerstein, then as a student of the black vaudevillian and Broadway performer Bert Williams, and later in various sectors of the film industry.[9] Over more than thirty-five years in film and television, Spencer Williams demonstrated a passion for providing entertainment for African American audiences and a drive to make movies that overcame the racism of the film industry, financial difficulties and meager resources, and lack of access to the kinds of distribution mechanisms available to many white filmmakers.[10] Despite the charge by some black cultural critics like Loren Miller that producers of black-audience films created works with "trite and shopworn plot[s]" that were rife with "technical faults" and failed to present Negro life in America realistically, Williams and others remained committed to the religious, social, and artistic possibilities of film, as well as the business opportunities the medium presented.[11]

Spencer Williams was also clearly moved by the Christian narrative of redemption from sin, and his personal interest in religion figured prominently in many of his films. He took up with vigor the possibility of using the medium to provide religious education and foster religious development, and he saw as much entertainment potential in religious films as in movies that dealt with other subject matter. When Williams teamed up with the white film producer Alfred N. Sack in the 1940s, establishing a relationship that gave him a sustained opportunity to present his own artistic vision, he directed nine films and put what was by then a solid reputation as a filmmaker behind the production of several movies intended to deliver a religious message.

While filmmakers in the race movie industry of the 1930s and 1940s created a range of movies with plots that sometimes involved religious characters, settings, and themes, Spencer Williams, along with a few other African American filmmakers in this period, made and exhibited films with the explicit intention of producing religious affect in their viewers and motivating moral transformation within the context of Christian values.[12] Although the surviving number of such films is small and the record of their production histories and reception meager, these films give some sense of an important mode of engagement between African American Christians and the movies through which filmmakers attempted to shape viewers' religious sensibilities. These religious films took a variety of aesthetic approaches to cultivating Christian character and experience and, examined in the context of broader discourse about the relationship between religion and popular culture, illuminate some of the ways film helped propagate black religious thought and shape black church cultures.

As Christians with interests in art and entertainment, Spencer Williams and the other filmmakers who produced black-audience religious films in the 1930s and 1940s must have thought quite carefully about the often fraught relationship between the film industry and many black religious individuals and institutions. These filmmakers employed a variety of strategies that sought to reconcile the two realms and to show that film could make important contributions to African American religious life. It is difficult to assess the number of black film viewers these movies reached, but their directors and producers marshaled a range of means to distribute and exhibit them and to reach the largest possible audience given the dominance of the industry by Hollywood studios. The creative and business teams of the New York–based Royal Gospel Productions, for example, promoted the company's 1947 release *Going to Glory, Come to Jesus* (see figure 11) by suggesting to churches that it represented a historic occasion for them to be "afforded the privilege to show a Motion Picture BEFORE the Theaters"[13] had access to the film. The company was promoting not just any film but one it insisted was a "momentous Motion Picture Masterpiece which brings out a message for everyone; a message which will reach the hearts of people of all ages," as well as "a magnificent motion picture to add new lustre to the screen!"[14] James and Eloyce Gist, independent filmmakers entirely outside the production and distributions systems of both Hollywood and the race movie industry, made their own arrangements to exhibit their religious films in churches and in secular venues. Spencer Williams, the most influential of the three, had access to the distribution resources of the white Dallas-based exhibitor and producer Alfred N. Sack, who, by the late 1940s, had branches of his operation in Atlanta, Chicago, Los Angeles, and New York.[15] Whatever means of distribution and exhibition these filmmakers employed, each remained committed to charting a path that would make film

FIGURE 11.
Poster for *Going to Glory, Come to Jesus.* Courtesy John Kisch, Separate Cinema Archive.

part of the work of black churches and of the religious experiences of individual viewers.

Little biographical information is available from which to reconstruct the influences on Spencer Williams's art or to gain a sense of what might have motivated him to make religious films along with the other types of films he wrote, produced, or directed during his career. By most accounts, he was born in 1893 in Vidalia, Louisiana, just across the river from Natchez, Mississippi. His mother, Pauline Williams Tatum, was a Baptist, and it is likely that he was raised in this religious context.[16] It is also clear from the images, subject matter, and theology in his religious films that he was influenced by Roman Catholicism, perhaps through contact with members of the thriving community of black Catholics in Natchez and the surrounding area, or perhaps as a result of his later life experiences in New York City, in the military, or in California.[17] In 1910 Williams migrated to New York City, where he studied acting and comedy with Bert Williams of the Williams and Walker comedy team who then had a regular act in the *Ziegfeld Follies*.[18] Spencer Williams served in the U.S. Army during World War I and remained involved in veterans' affairs throughout his life. According to a number of sources, he enlisted in the army in 1914, well before the United States entered the war in Europe, and left the military nine years later in 1923, having worked in military intelligence at some point.[19] It is possible that his interest in military service developed in the context of his mother's commitment to preserving and honoring the memory of black Civil War soldiers through her work as president of the local Woman's Relief Corps, an auxiliary of the Grand Army of the Republic, a Civil War veterans' organization. In their incarnations in Vidalia and Natchez, both the WRC and GAR were dedicated to organizing Memorial Day parades with and for black Civil War veterans.[20] At various points in his life Williams turned his entrepreneurial skills to aiding African American servicemen, and he spent the last years of his life in a veterans' home. Williams turned his attention to black soldiers in World War II in one of the films he directed, and GIs appeared as characters in at least one other.[21]

In the 1930s Williams became a familiar screen presence for black audiences through his appearances in a number of feature-length race films, including a group of popular black-audience musical westerns, *Harlem on the Prairie* (1937), *The Bronze Buckaroo* (1938), *Two Gun Man from Harlem* (1938), and *Harlem Rides the Range* (1939), and a black-audience horror film, *Son of Ingagi* (1940). Williams wrote the screenplay for *Harlem Rides the Range* and provided the story for the horror film.[22] Although he had relatively small acting roles in these films, his participation no doubt helped him advance the technical skills he had been acquiring since his time at the Christie studio.[23] The musical westerns, aimed at a broad audience of young people and adults, engaged and responded to the Hollywood western but, as Julia Leyda argues, reoriented the genre to locate African Americans in American history and geography in new ways. She writes, "The recurring theme and setting of the American west in early African American cinema, most obviously in black westerns, suggests an embrace of the positive values associated with that region, values not typically ascribed to black characters in movies, or for that matter in white-supremacist American culture: freedom, individualism, mobility, masculinity, and a patriotism rooted in a love of the land itself."[24] Though these films worked to situate African Americans in a certain mythic American geography outside the time and space of the slave South, they were also distinctly modern. As Paula J. Massood notes, the use of Harlem in the titles of the black westerns "prompted a chain of signifiers that were already familiar to African American audiences. While the use of Harlem as a motif might have been nothing more than an appeal to urban audiences as a means of making a profit, it also, by calling on the spaciotemporal characteristics of a contemporary urbanscape, confirmed its audience's transformation from rural farmers to urban industrial workers."[25] Williams's later work also addressed the meaning of urbanization for African Americans and often explored the moral implications of this geographic shift. It is likely that he was influenced by the values these black westerns promoted and that his work in the genre helped him envision ways of creating a viable combination of entertainment and serious message in his own films and of addressing questions about the relationship between religious tradition and modernity.

Building on his experiences in Hollywood and in the black-audience film industry, Williams again looked to direct his own film. Around 1940, he began to work with Alfred N. Sack, and the relationship would make it possible for Williams to pursue his own artistic vision and to address topics, including African American Christian experience and identity, that had not been a part of his work up to this time. Sack, who founded Sack Amusement Enterprises with his brother Lester in 1919, had begun distributing "all-colored-cast pictures" in the late 1930s, including two films by the black director Oscar Micheaux, *Underworld* (1937) and his *Lying Lips* (1939), as well as the black westerns and horror film with which Williams had been involved. In 1939, Sack announced his intention to expand this aspect of his work by teaming up with Harry M. Popkin, another white producer and distributor of black-audience films. Popkin and his brother Leo were the founders and executives of the Los Angeles–based Million Dollar Productions and for a number of years had been collaborating with black actor and director George Randol in producing gangster films that starred Ralph Cooper, the host of the Apollo Theater's Amateur Night. Other Million Dollar Productions films featured Lena Horne, Louise Beavers, Mantan Moreland, and Nina Mae McKinney.[26] Many of these films proved popular with black audiences, even while some black film critics noted with disappointment the limited range of stories presented and the focus on crime and gangsters. By the time Popkin and Sack announced their plan for Sack Amusement Enterprises to become the distributor for Million Dollar Productions, Million Dollar had made a public commitment to broadening its scope to produce "stories depicting phases of modern intelligent Negro life."[27] Despite the public pronouncements about the possibilities of this business deal, it seems that the arrangement resulted in the production and distribution of only one film—*Gang War* (1940).[28] It is likely that Cooper's dissatisfaction with working in the gangster film genre and his split with the Popkins after the release of *Gang War* were what ended the collaboration between Sack and Million Dollar.[29] In 1941, Sack began distributing a series of films directed by Spencer Williams, most of which were produced under the auspices of Sack Amusement Enterprises.

According to some sources, Williams financed *The Blood of Jesus* (1941), the first of his films distributed by Sack, with his own money, and others understand Sack to have provided the financial backing.[30] Whatever the case, by all accounts Alfred Sack proved a hands-off producer, willing to provide Williams with the support he needed to make his films. Sack showed confidence in Williams's ability to complete the films within the budgetary limitations of his small company and did not interfere in the creative process.[31] Working with an interracial crew and black on-screen talent, Williams shot his films on location in Dallas, San Antonio, and Fort Worth, Texas, and used various film studios in Dallas, including Jamieson Film Company, for postproduction work.[32] Both cast and crew who worked with Williams recalled the impact of financial constraints on the productions. Many of the actors Williams engaged were local amateurs to whom he could not provide much rehearsal time or the luxury of retakes. Gordon Yoder, who worked at Jamieson and processed the film for *The Blood of Jesus* and was later assistant camera operator on *Dirty Gertie from Harlem U.S.A.* (1946), noted that "Spencer got what he wanted pretty damn quick, without a lot of takes." Robert Orr, who appeared in a number of Williams's films under the name July Jones, said, "There weren't many re-takes. We did a re-take on something, but it didn't take long. Most of the times, we'd get it in one take. The guy that was the sponsor was saving money, you know what I mean? So, everything went fine, and we didn't have any problems."[33] The sound engineer Dick Byers recalled, "Spencer Williams didn't waste any time. When something needed to be done, he got it done without anybody worrying about it."[34] Jack Whitman, camera operator for *The Blood of Jesus*, characterized Williams as "so insightful, so creative, that it was really a pleasure to work with him," and his assessment of the director as "resourceful" and highly professional seems to have been shared by many of his colleagues.

In addition to having to deal with time constraints in filming, Williams lacked access to some of the more expensive film-processing technologies, and he and his crew were forced to use less sophisticated means to achieve their desired ends. Jack Whitman, who was the cameraman for *The Blood of Jesus*, recalled, "[T]here was a lot of trick photography that I was able to do in the camera. I had learned that, it was a lost art really. Even in that time, all those things were done with an optical printer, but [Williams] did not have the money to pay for it, so I used a matte box and double exposures and so forth. . . . There were parts where the soul left the body and went through the walls, and where angels appeared, and the devil appeared, and you know they had to come from nowhere and suddenly be there."[35] Williams edited the films himself, even drawing on the celluloid to create the effect of rifle discharging.[36] As Yoder summed up Williams's approach, "Spencer did anything necessary to make it work, quick, save money, and still get a picture on the screen that people would pay to see."[37] Limited access to funds and to the more advanced film technology of the day resulted in final products that sometimes contain images too dark to see, jump cuts that defy spatial or temporal continuity, and profound discontinuities between the dialogue track and the movements of the actors' mouths.

Despite the degree to which financial constraints helped set the terms for his movies, Williams's religious films provide a strong religious vision that he hoped would have a lasting impact on the lives of his viewers. Unlike the Hollywood black-cast films that measured African American Christianity against a white Christian standard of true religiosity characterized by reserve and propriety, Williams examined universal elements of Christian experience in a particularly African American context. His central theological concerns in *The Blood of Jesus* and *Go Down, Death* (1944), his only surviving religious films, are the possibility and promise of individual transformation through Christian belief in the workings of God's grace, the reality of the divine presence in the lives of individuals, and the assurance of just punishment for those who fail to commit to a life ordered by faith.[38] In both films a man, played by Williams himself, is presented with the opportunity to reform and join the Christian community, and Williams provides viewers a chance to imagine two dramatically different outcomes for him, dramatizing one future in which the character gives himself over to prayer and another in which he suffers just punishment for his intransigence. Although Williams sets the challenge of transformation from a life of sin to one of Christian commitment before the central male characters, the women accomplish much of the religious work of the films, largely through their suffering. At the same time, Williams places all of the characters in his extant religious films in situations where they encounter, both literally and symbolically, the cross and the crossroads. The cross represents his belief in the transformative power of Jesus's redemptive sacrifice for each individual and for humanity as a whole. The crossroads represents an opportunity to exercise agency in one's religious life by choosing the path that will shape one's future in this life and beyond. Here Williams may be drawing on West and Central African notions of the crossroads as a place where past, present, and future meet. As Robert Farris Thompson notes, "The 'turn in the path,' i.e., the crossroads, remains an indelible concept in the Kongo-Atlantic world, as the point of intersection between the ancestors and the living."[39] The conjunction that Williams creates between moments at which his characters find themselves "down at the cross" and at critical crossroads moments is at the center of his theological vision, and he uses the rich visual possibilities of film to convey this vision to audiences.

In *The Blood of Jesus* (see figure 12), Williams gives viewers a positive outcome to the challenge of moral transformation put before the main male character, as well as to the test of moral fortitude for the central female character. The story focuses on the near-death experience of Martha Jackson (Cathryn Caviness), a newly baptized woman whose new husband, Ras (Spencer Williams), refuses to have anything to do with her church. When Ras returns from a day of "hunting" (stealing a neighbor's hogs, as it turns out) on the same Sunday when Martha is baptized, his rifle falls and discharges, sending a bullet through her heart. For the rest of the film Martha's spirit, which has become separated from her body, attempts to find its way back, but it must first withstand various temptations that Satan (Jas. B. Jones) places in its path. Martha's journey back to life requires that she endure travails in the "city," where, in a nightclub, Judas Green (Frank H. McClennan), one of the devil's agents, and Rufus Brown (Eddie DeBase), a businessman, attempt to lure her into prostitution. When she escapes this trap, the devil again attempts to distract her with a dance party and jazz band he has set up at the side of the road. Eventually, Jesus, present in the film in the form of a crucifix from which a voice issues, and a guiding angel (Rogenia Goldthwaite) intervene and come to Martha's aid, permitting her safe return to her body, family, and church community. Williams frames the presentation of the journey of Martha's spirit, the focus of most of the film, with scenes of Ras overcome with emotion and praying for his wife. While we do not see clear evidence of Ras's changed behavior at the film's conclusion, the implication that the experience has

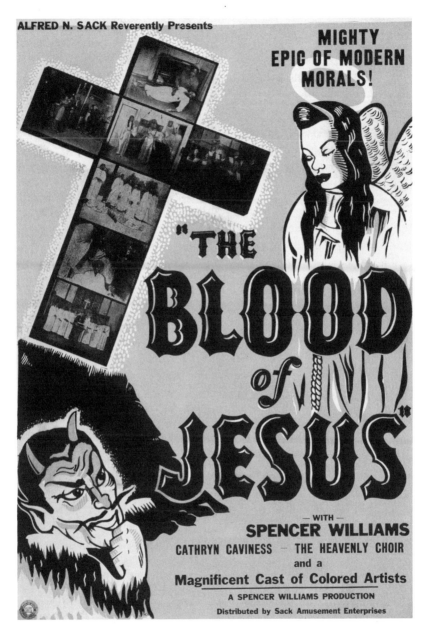

FIGURE 12.
Poster for *The Blood of Jesus*. Courtesy John Kisch, Separate Cinema Archive.

transformed him is strong and indicated by his deep involvement in prayer and the appearance of the angel hovering above Martha and Ras at the film's conclusion. There is no question that Williams intended viewers to leave the theater secure in the knowledge that Martha has withstood temptation and that Ras has come to know the power of God.

The Blood of Jesus sits alongside other early- to mid-twentieth-century stage and screen black folk dramas that sought to help audiences explore individuals' responses to temptation. It is difficult to chart a direct influence on Spencer Williams's work, but *The Blood of Jesus* bears much in common with a number of morality plays that were performed in black churches in the 1930s. *Heaven Bound*, the best known of these, was created in the early 1930s by Lula Byrd Jones and Nellie Davis, both members of Atlanta's Big Bethel AME Church and both members of its Choir Number One.[40] The play, performed in the church's sanctuary, presents a succession of typological characters who must overcome their own weaknesses and Satan's temptations to reach the Gates of Heaven and the welcoming greeting of the Celestial Choir.[41] First performed in February of 1930, the production was critically acclaimed and proved so popular that it generated considerable revenue for the church, even through the Depression, and the congregation still performs it each year. Noting the enthusiastic responses of audiences to the morality play, one white theater critic went so far as to forecast that, through *Heaven Bound*'s reputation, Georgia would become "an American Ober-Ammergau."[42] While this lofty prediction did not come true, *Heaven Bound* became a widely imitated black folk drama in the 1930s, spawning competing productions, some with titles that barely, if at all, disguised their connection to the original, as in the case of the successful *Heavenbound* by Violet Thomas of Shelby, North Carolina.[43] Big Bethel's choirs performed *Heaven Bound* in venues outside the sanctuary on a number of occasions, most notably at the Atlanta Theatre in 1937 in a cooperative production with the Federal Theatre Project of the Works Progress Administration (WPA). *Heaven Bound* and other such black folk dramas drew on long-standing traditions in African American folklore that explore individual and community responses to moral issues. Yvonne Chireau writes that "some of the anecdotes function as thinly disguised morality tales, such as the 'pearly gates' stories—accounts that convey, often in comic format, experiences of persons who have passed away and find themselves knocking upon the doors of the Heavenly City, only to face an angelic messenger who requires that a series of tests or ordeals be passed before the candidate may enter."[44] Thus, regardless of whether Williams saw the Atlanta production of *Heaven Bound* or other similar productions, his work in *The Blood of Jesus* clearly engages established narrative and religious concerns in African American folklore.

Rather than focusing on a single character's attempt to overcome Satan's temptations, as Williams does in *The Blood of Jesus, Heaven Bound* presents a procession to heaven of souls who embody different character types, and the various actors who portray these souls present their stories in pantomime and song.[45] "From eternity comes the sound of many voices, voices of the ransomed hosts of God, the saints and the angels," the narrator begins. "These are they which came out of the great tribulations and have washed their robes and made them white in the blood of the lamb. They come singing—the songs of the sainted!"[46] The audience then watches as a series of pilgrims—including the Wayworn Traveller, the Pilgrim of the Cross, the Striver, the Wayward Girl, the Rich Man, the Pilgrim of Faith, the Pilgrim to the Promised Land, the Pilgrim of Sorrow, the Determined Soul, the Burden Bearer, the Hypocrite, the Gambler, and the Soldier in the Army of the Lord—sing hymns and perform in pantomime as they make their way to the Gates of Heaven, encountering Satan along their journey. Winona Fletcher writes that "the highly stylized, exaggerated action, not unlike that of the Medieval 'bad guys' of the mystery/morality plays, captivated the audience by its visual spectacle, exploited laughter for its instructional purpose, put the sometimes 'unacceptable dramatic realism' into its proper perspective, and generally contributed to the remarkable popularity of *Heaven Bound*."[47] According to accounts from early performances, audiences reacted animatedly when the Wayward Girl, the Gambler, the Hypocrite, and the Rich Man failed to make it to the Gates of Heaven and fell prey to the devil's lures. Had Williams seen *Heaven Bound* or a similar black church morality play and been able to gauge the audience's response, he would probably have come away with an invigorated sense of the possibilities of using a dramatic approach to cultivating an evangelical transformation in his viewers.

While Williams's *The Blood of Jesus* resembles *Heaven Bound*, particularly in the attempt to create dramatic tension around the danger in which Martha finds herself as her soul journeys through the city and in the use of hymns and spirituals to particularly dramatic effect, his work differs from the play in important ways. The most significant of these is his marshaling of the unique possibilities of the medium of film to represent divine interventions in the lives of believers through cinematic special effects. The devil, costumed in a body suit complete with cape and horns, and the angel who guides Martha both move between this world and a spiritual world, appearing fully embodied at times and shadowy or ephemeral at others. Williams uses superimposition not only to represent divine and demonic forces at work in the world but also to locate Martha in a liminal space between life and death. He signals the beginning of her journey with the angel beckoning Martha's soul to rise from her injured body. Martha's soul complies and stands with the angel to regard the body that remains on the bed. Williams also uses superimposition to highlight the spiritual power of certain material objects in Martha's life, particularly an image of the Sacred Heart of Jesus that hangs on the wall above her bed, over which he projects a luminous cross. Indeed, it is in this very image that the bullet that injures Martha lodges after passing through her body.[48] Williams uses the luminous cross again at a further turning point for Martha when she prays before another image of Jesus as she seeks to move from the liminal space between life and death back into her embodied life.[49] At various points in the film, we also see images of people climbing Jacob's ladder and of the gates of heaven. Finally, the transformation of a roadside sign (which points to "Hell," to the left, and to "Zion," to the right) into a crucifix from which Jesus's blood drips enables Martha's return to her body. As with his later film *Go Down Death*, Williams uses the possibilities that film provides to move between earthly and spiritual realms in a way that a stage production like *Heaven Bound* could not.[50]

Williams puts the dramatic and visual possibilities of film in service of an intense focus on the evangelical experience of individual transformation and subsequent commitment to a Christian life. This element of evangelical theology is central to the film's message, but Williams also works hard to locate it in the context of a much more textured religious vision than the "transparent" and "naive" one that some scholars argue the film conveys.[51] Williams does not insist that religious transformation is a straightforward or simple process, and he uses Martha to guide viewers through what he identifies as the dangers faced by even the most committed Christian. The music Williams selected for the film's opening credits signals both joy in finding faith and fear of failing to take full advantage of the benefits that Christians understand the Gospel to provide. Rev. R. L. Robertson and the Heavenly Choir sing:

Good news, the Chariot's coming,
Good news, the Chariot's coming,
Good news, the Chariot's coming,
and I don't want it to leave me behind.
There's a long white robe in the Heaven I know
There's a long white robe in the Heaven I know
There's a long white robe in the Heaven I know
And I don't want it to leave me behind.

In addition, as the members of the congregation process to the river where Martha will be baptized, they sing, "Everybody talking 'bout heaven ain't going there," through which Williams again insists that the life of faith is an ongoing process and that in Christian belief only God can offer the surety of salvation. Adrienne Lanier Seward argues that Martha functions as a liminal figure who, even after her experience of being "born again" and baptized before and into a community of believers, faces moral judgment from her fellow church members.[52] Indeed, at the very moment that Martha is being baptized, Sister Ellerby (Heather Hardeman) and Sister Jenkins (Juanita Riley) stand on the banks of the river and question the depth of her commitment; Sister Ellerby comments, "That gal don't act like she got nothing."[53] Later, when Martha lies gravely injured, Sister Jenkins offers up a prayer emphasizing how new to the faith Martha is and how she has not yet been able to "buckle on the sword and go out in the battlefield and fight" to fulfill her evangelistic responsibilities. As Seward notes, "In the film, baptism is presented as part of a process in which faith is tested and sets of social obligations are met before the individual is truly saved."[54]

While viewers are encouraged to believe that Martha is genuine in her faith and in her plea to Ras to "try to pray and get religion" so that they will be happier, they also see how easily she accepts the gift of a dress and matching shoes that Judas Green offers her in order to lure her to the nightclub in the city that exists between life and death. The experiences of conversion and baptism are not sufficient to protect Martha from temptation or suffering, and the final outcome requires her to choose to give up the material and physical pleasure the city offers. The angel emphasizes the sometimes arduous nature of the journey of faith when she sets Martha along her path. After Martha's soul rises from her body, she stands with the angel before a group of shadowy figures who wander in circles. "This is the end of the trail," the angel tells her. "Here all is silent—save for murmurs of grief and the muffled sobbing of those who have long since departed from among the living." To Martha's query about the reason for their grief and sadness, the angel responds:

They mourn because their efforts are yet unrewarded; because the unjust have struck down the good and the unselfish; because Sin is enthroned in the seat of power.

These were all good people. They came to earth bringing love and truth and were hated in return. They came to teach the Gospel and were treated with scorn. They came bringing redemption and were stoned and crucified. O, that the children of men should be so blind.

Yet, it has ever been so, that the righteous have been treated with contempt and almost driven from the face of the earth. But they have not died in vain. Each succeeding generation has built monuments to their memory.

Despite this vision of the struggles of the righteous, as well as the angel's warnings about temptation, Martha falls prey to Satan's lures. When she finally realizes the danger in which she has placed herself, she prays for mercy before an image of Jesus (placed incongruously on the wall above a bed in the bawdy house), an act that prompts the angel to intervene and encourage Martha to flee the nightclub. While it may seem at the film's start that the positive outcome to Martha's story is inevitable, Williams also emphasizes that Christian conversion is an arduous and ongoing process.

There is an unmistakable gendered element to Williams's story of sin and redemption that elaborates a connection between women and a particular kind of worldliness, an argument found in other black-audience religious films of the period. We know from the outset in *The Blood of Jesus* that Ras is not a church member, and we learn soon after that he has stolen a neighbor's hogs. But his sinfulness is not particularly gendered, and Williams does not associate him with the typical tropes of male sinfulness (e.g., drinking, gambling, womanizing), as he will the character of Jim Bottoms in his later film *Go Down, Death*. Moreover, Ras is contrite about having stolen the hogs and contends that he had no other option to feed his family. Martha's near–moral lapse while in the liminal space between life and death, however, is clearly gendered. It is the lure of beauty and material goods that keeps her from passing directly through the city and on to the crossroads as the angel directs, and Williams and other filmmakers of the period associate women's susceptibility to such lures with a particular openness to demonic address. The temptation of beauty for Martha causes the angel to admonish her about the dangers of materialism, as she does when Judas offers Martha a dress and shoes and invites her to the city. The angel warns, "Be not overanxious for what you will put on. Life is a more beautiful gift than clothing for the body. . . . Sell not your soul for the raiments of a peacock. Seek ye first the kingdom of God and all these things shall be added unto you." Later when Satan tempts her with the money she would earn from prostitution, a voice—presumably that of Jesus—recites a portion of the beatitudes: "Blessed are the poor in spirit; for theirs is the kingdom of Heaven. . . . Blessed are they that mourn; for they shall be comforted. Blessed are the meek; for they shall inherit the earth." Williams's repeated reminders, through various characters in the film, of the value of spiritual rather than material goods can be read as broad messages, but in the context of Martha's particular struggle they can also be understood as an admonishment of women more generally.

FIGURE 13.

Rev. Scott preaches in *Going to Glory, Come to Jesus.* From the author's collection.

The enticement of beauty and material goods for Christian women and the emphasis on their need to overcome such temptation in the context of faithfulness to their conversions is a concern in other extant religious race films from the period. Perhaps the best example is the 1947 feature film *Going to Glory, Come to Jesus,* released by the New York–based Royal Gospel Productions, which sets religious commitment and fashion against one another.[55] Lillie-Mae, the film's main character and daughter of Rev. Scott (see figure 13), is teased by her peers for being ugly, uninteresting, and badly dressed. Bessie, her main tormenter, attributes all of these negative characteristics to Lillie-Mae's religion and tells Lillie-Mae and her friend Ethel, "Religion or no religion—I wouldn't wear clothes like that to a dog's fight. I wouldn't even be caught dead in a dress like that one you have on. . . . You see, I'm hep and you—you little amen-corner-square, you don't know anything but your prayers, catch on? It takes clothes, jewels and plenty of experience to make a woman—you dig—?" (see figure 14).[56] Lillie-Mae begins to covet Bessie's clothes and her beauty, bringing forth the voice of the devil, who seeks to cultivate these desires. "Lillie-Mae, church people don't do anything but work hard, slave and

FIGURE 14.
Lillie-Mae's parents in religious garb in *Going to Glory, Come to Jesus*. From the author's collection.

deprive themselves of pleasures I will give you if you will believe in me," the devil tells her. "Forget your father's teachings. That shouldn't be too hard to do. If you don't you will always be ugly. Believe in me and I will make you beautiful, very beautiful."[57] After the devil tells her that not even her mother loves her because she is so ugly, Lillie-Mae decides that she is willing to lose her soul in order to become beautiful, and the devil accepts the bargain.

The film suggests a connection between a variety of female desires and receptivity to satanic direction, and in Lillie-Mae's case the desire for physical beauty and fashionable clothes leads to other desires. She asks for and gets a handsome man with whom she then drinks and smokes; he spends the money the devil has provided her, and when he leaves her the devil himself appears as "Prince O'Hades." Prince begins to court her, taking her to a nightclub where she drinks and listens to music that lauds drinking and smoking (see figure 15). Prince O'Hades quickly loses interest in Lillie-Mae, takes away the beauty he has bestowed on her, and reduces her to a beggar (see figure 16). Wandering, she finds herself at the bank of a river where she once saw "The Prophet" (costumed to appear as a John the Baptist figure) bap-

FIGURE 15.
Prince O'Hades takes Lillie-Mae to a nightclub in *Going to Glory, Come to Jesus.*
From the author's collection.

tizing people (see figure 17). Lillie-Mae hears the voice of God telling her, "Fear no evil for I am with thee. Follow me my servants for I am your Redeemer," and, committing herself to God, prays for forgiveness. In the end, Lillie-Mae's experience with the devil appears to have been a dream or vision while she was in the throes of the conversion experience (see figure 18). When she emerges from it, she tells her father, "I feel like I want to shout. What is it?" Her father replies, "Shout my child, you've got religion."[58] In this case, as in *The Blood of Jesus,* the caution about materialism is directed at the entire viewing audience, but the emphasis on female characters highlights particular dangers produced by women's desire for material goods. That the films establish the nightclub as the arena to which women are drawn to fulfill many of these desires is also significant and points to a concern with the moral implications of urbanization, an issue that I will address in greater detail in the following chapter.

The cross and the crossroads in *The Blood of Jesus* provide a potent representation of the power that Christians believe Jesus has to transform every individual's life. Williams places images of crosses throughout the film, making it impossible for

FIGURE 16.

Prince O'Hades takes away the beauty he has given Lillie-Mae in *Going to Glory, Come to Jesus*. From the author's collection.

FIGURE 17.

The Prophet's river baptism ceremony in *Going to Glory, Come to Jesus*. From the author's collection.

FIGURE 18.
Satan and The Prophet in a battle for Lillie-Mae's soul in *Going to Glory, Come to Jesus*. From the author's collection.

viewers to forget the work's central theological message—that is, the Christian belief in Jesus's salvific sacrifice on the cross. As noted earlier, Williams uses special effects to project a luminous cross onto the two images of Jesus that hang on a wall in Martha and Ras's bedroom and in the bedroom above Rufus Brown's juke joint. Martha wears a gold cross around her neck, and the members of the church choir wear large crucifixes in early scenes that take place inside the church (see figure 19) and during the procession to the river baptism. The visual power of the choir's crucifixes becomes amplified later when the choir appears at the film's climactic moment at the crossroads.

In the long sequence near the film's end that marks the turning point for Martha, the events of which lead to her return to her body, Williams layers various meanings of the cross and crossroads in both literal and densely symbolic ways. Referring, both visually and through the use of the identical hymn, to the baptism sequence early in the film when Luke Willow (Alva Fuller), another candidate for baptism, runs away from the path to salvation, Williams shows Martha fleeing the juke joint and rushing toward the crossroads where the angel has promised her she will "find

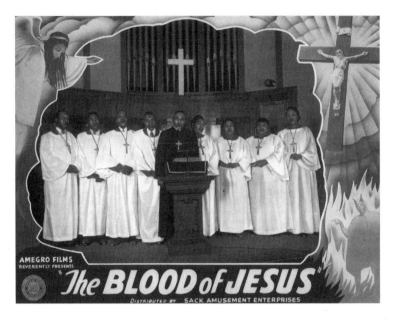

FIGURE 19.
Church choir in *The Blood of Jesus*. Courtesy John Kisch, Separate Cinema
Archive.

what she seeks." Having been followed by a group of men who believe that she has
stolen a wallet, Martha finds herself at the crossroads standing before a sign that
points to "Hell" and "Zion." Satan, who has been waiting nearby, grabs her and
throws her to the ground, only to be sent away by Jesus, whose voice tells him that
he stands on holy ground. Clearly, the presence of the crucifix sanctifies the ground,
but African and African diasporic understandings of the crossroads as marking the
"turn in the path," or the point at which past, present, and future meet, may also
contribute to the place's power. The crossroads, then, becomes the place where
Martha must decide whether to renounce the worldliness the city represents and to
choose Jesus. The men arrive next and, in a recapitulation of the Gospel story of
the adulterous woman, prepare to stone her to death.[59] Here Williams shifts perspective in a way that emphasizes the film's theological concerns. Using a high camera angle that assumes the visual perspective of the crucifix into which the crossroads sign has transformed, Williams underscores Jesus's power and authority as
we hear his voice challenge the men. Indeed, Jesus's authority is so profound in this
realm between life and death that one of the men addresses him as "Lord" as he tries

FIGURE 20.

Martha at the foot of the cross in *The Blood of Jesus*. Courtesy John Kisch, Separate Cinema Archive.

to explain why they believe Martha deserves to be stoned, and the shift in perspective accomplished through the change in camera angle makes this authority clear.

The cross assumes even greater importance in this climactic sequence when Martha lies stretched out and praying at the base of the crucifix (see figure 20). Williams multiplies the image of the crucifix with the appearance of the choir, whose members wear crosses around their necks, and with the choir's singing of the spiritual "Were You There When They Crucified My Lord?" The blood that drips from the crucifix and onto Martha's face as she prays finally effects her return to her body. This sequence is at once powerfully spiritual because of the intensity of her prayer and unmistakably sensual as Martha smears the blood across her face, washing herself "in the blood of the Lamb." In this profound, transformative instant at the cross and crossroads, Williams collapses time, space, and religious sensibilities, placing Martha both at the scene of Jesus's crucifixion so that she can feel the reality of his blood and at the moment of her own rebirth. Martha emerges from her experience with the sense of having died to sin.[60]

Even though Williams focuses intensely on Martha's travails as she attempts to move out of the liminal space between life and death and back into life, and even though his message is clearly gendered, *The Blood of Jesus* engages a set of broader questions beyond one individual's religious experience. What returns Martha to her body is her heartfelt struggle to live as a Christian following her conversion experience, and she is aided by the intervention of the angel and of Jesus, but the responses of Ras and of the members of Martha's church community are also important in Williams's religious vision. In moving beyond the individual stories of Martha and Ras Jackson's religious transformations, Williams addresses a variety of social issues about the nature of religious community and about the relationship between religious tradition and modern life. The film opens with a prefatory sequence that makes a statement about broad social and moral questions. In this sequence Williams presents images of churches, an image of an African American man plowing a field, and other images of rural life along with a sound track by Rev. R. L. Robertson's Heavenly Choir singing "Good News, the Chariot's Coming," and "Go Down, Moses." A voice-over narration introduces the social and moral environment in which Williams wants viewers to locate the characters:

> Almost gone are the days when peace ruled the earth with a firm and gentle hand; when fear of God dwelt in the hearts of men and women and children; when the ten original commandments were the accepted laws of every civilized country and nation on the face of the globe; when those who went to church on Sunday did not go back home to prey on their neighbors the remaining six days of the week; when religion was practiced with unfalse solemnity and honest sincerity and when soul salvation was a heritage from heaven for not merely a few thousand, but for many millions. Those days are almost gone from the earth . . . almost.

On one level, *The Blood of Jesus* may be interpreted as bemoaning how an idyllic rural society characterized by spiritual commitment and fortitude has fallen into moral decay and alienation because of urbanization. The ideal past to which Williams directs us at the film's outset is one in which religious standards grounded in the precepts of the Ten Commandments structured the social order as well as guided people's individual commitments. Moreover, the coupling of the narration with shots of churches and rural scenes works to argue for an association between this ideal state, the local religious community, and the rural context. One of the messages of the film is indeed that, like Martha Jackson, African Americans as a community have been lured from the enveloping safety of the small town and the community church and into the dangerous environment of the city. Williams seems to be telling his audience that it is God's wish, even God's plan, that African Americans reclaim or cling to the rural past. Martha's path is one that, significantly, passes *through* the city and, with the aid of Jesus and the angel, brings her back to her family and community. Yet the proclamation on the lobby cards and posters for the film that this is "a mighty epic of modern morals" contains a key to a more complex interpretation. Williams presents a story of *modern* morals for the community and thus is much more than a plea for a return to an idyllic past. As the tension between the spirituals and the blues—sometimes juxtaposed in the film's sound track in jarring ways—ultimately gave rise to Gospel music, a form that integrates aspects of the two, so too African American Christians are called to bring together seemingly incompatible and disparate elements into an organic whole in order to advance the community.

Although Williams may have been seeking to promote uniquely rural values, he problematizes his characters' social context and refuses to romanticize the South. Williams's work does indeed show some nostalgia for rural life. It seems unlikely, however, that African Americans at the end of the Depression—an era that followed slavery, the failures of Reconstruction, the institution of racial segregation, and a period of urban race riots and lynching—would identify the glorious past that the voice-over describes in the film's opening with any point in their own history. Did any moment in the history of the American South correspond to the narrator's time "when the ten original commandments were the accepted laws for every civilized country and nation on the face of the globe"? While Williams affirms some aspects of rural life by juxtaposing rural images with the opening narrative, the disjuncture between the idyllic fantasy and the realities of sharecropping, perpetual debt, scarce access to education, and the specter of terrorism by whites calls into question an interpretation according to which the film asserts that in this southern setting black folk maintain a pure and authentic traditional life unconcerned with any outside concerns. In this regard, despite Williams's presentation of a self-contained racially segregated world in his films, his message seems substantively different from the untroubled all-black worlds of *Hallelujah* and *The Green Pastures*. In addition, the use of the spiritual "Go Down, Moses," with its refrain of "let my people go," in conjunction with shots of a man engaged in backbreaking agricultural labor suggests a call for rethinking the traditional connection between African Americans and the rural South.

Concern about the nature of religious community and the struggle of believers to evangelize others also moves *The Blood of Jesus* beyond the focus on the experience of Martha as an individual. Williams presents an ambivalent portrait of this religious community through our brief glimpses of some of its members. Early in the film, Luke, who is to be baptized immediately after Martha, runs off before it is accomplished, claiming he sees a snake in the water. Viewers learn later from Sisters Ellerby and Jenkins that he had claimed to see an alligator the previous year. They judge him quickly, agreeing that it was the devil both times and intimating a particular openness to the devil's appearance on Luke's part. Jenkins proves to be a particularly judgmental character who seems to have taken on the responsibility of policing the community's adherence to her religious standard. She takes the opportunity of her prayer for Martha's health to chastise Ras by announcing her belief before those gathered that "[w]e know that you [God] and only you can drive the sin from Brother Ras Jackson's heart." Although Jenkins is clearly at the center of this community's religious life—the minister stands in the background during the community's vigil—Williams also seems to present a critique of her and of those like her who set rigid standards for behavior and admission to the Christian community and at the same time contravene those standards through their own gossiping, jealousy, suspicion, and selfishness.

To ask whether Williams believed, and asked his film's viewers to believe, that this realm between life and death exists in the literal terms in which he conveyed it and that angels and Satan appear in bodily form on the earthly plane is to miss much of the power and appeal of *The Blood of Jesus* for its contemporary audiences. In presenting this tale of a woman's struggle to "die the sinner's death" and become born again, both as an individual and within the context of a broader African American Christian community, as well as her husband's transformation, Spencer Williams drew on and translated for film African American folklore traditions and black Christian approaches to biblical and broader religious narratives.[61] He and his viewers may well have believed in the reality of the workings of evil in the world, and they certainly believed in God's power to transform the lives of believers. However, the goal of such a film, understood in the broader sweep of African American religious culture, was not necessarily to convince viewers of the literal truth of these things as embodied in the film but to promote the moral truths that underlie the film's story and iconography. Of this broader history of conveying such concerns in black religious and folk culture, Yvonne Chireau writes, "Traditionally, African American folklore has manifested a spectrum of forms, embodying practical, explanatory, and narrative discourses. Didactic, biblically based tales and stories, human and animal trickster accounts, apocryphal myths, and supernatural legends have been created and relayed within black communities as sources of wisdom, history and entertainment."[62]

Whereas the action in *The Blood of Jesus* takes place largely in a realm in between life and death, which Williams creates by superimposing figures representing the spiritual world onto the action of characters in this world, *Go Down, Death* (see figure 21) concerns itself primarily with an earthly struggle between "Saturday Sinners and Sunday Saints" who "clash in the battle of good against evil!" as the advertising tells us.[63] Even though some advertising for the film characterizes it as "the story of Jesus and the Devil," these figures are not physically present in the world of the film's characters. As in *The Blood of Jesus*, Williams in *Go Down, Death* is interested in the struggles of Christian believers to remain strong in their faith—that is, to live in light of their belief in Jesus's sacrifice for them on the cross—and in the choices that nonbelievers make when they reach a moral crossroads. Using James Weldon Johnson's poem "Go Down Death" as a starting point, the story involves the attempt of Jim Bottoms (Spencer Williams), a cabaret owner, to discredit Reverend Rhodes, the new pastor of Mount Zion Baptist Church.[64] Jim inaugurates a campaign to counter the minister's public opposition to the "ungodly" activities that go on in the nightclub, particularly on Sundays. Indeed, on the very Sunday that Rev. Rhodes preaches a sermon against the ungodly, one that promotes purity as "the very essence of Christ's message," Jim sends three "fly chicks" to entrap the minister. The women wait for him in his office after the service and pose as potential converts. One of them tells him, "We really do want to be Christians. I just think that one can be a so much better person with religion." The three then walk him home, and he gives them each a New Testament with instructions to read various passages, all of which focus on the possibility of overcoming sin, impurity, and death through prayer and faith in Jesus.[65] Meanwhile, one of Jim's men waits outside the window, and when the women suddenly grab Rev. Rhodes, kiss him, and place a glass of whiskey in his hand, the man snaps a photograph. Sister Caroline, Jim's adoptive mother and a faithful member of the congregation, rescues Rev. Rhodes from the women and from Jim's man, and after the others leave she tells Rev. Rhodes that she will do everything she can to prevent Jim's scheme from working. She is committed to him not only because he is her minister and she respects him but also because he is engaged to her niece, Betty Jean. Caroline eventually finds that Jim has hidden the incriminating photographs in a safe in the apartment he shares with Caroline and Betty Jean.

FIGURE 21.

Poster for *Go Down, Death*. Courtesy John Kisch, Separate Cinema Archive.

Caroline is the character who proves most important in creating access to the spiritual world. In the end, Caroline's faith, which we see make things happen in the film, proves the most powerful force in protecting the minister from Jim's plot and the church from the saloon. Williams's use of film techniques to represent divine intervention in the lives of believers, as in the earlier *The Blood of Jesus*, is especially striking in his depiction of the results of Caroline's faith. In the crucial scene, Caroline stands before a photograph on the wall of her dead husband, Joe, and asks him to tell God that "one of his faithful servants is in trouble and needs his help." Caroline lies down on her bed and looks briefly at a reproduction of Warner Sallman's *Head of Christ* that hangs on another wall and then back at the photograph of her husband, against the sound track of a lone female voice singing "Nobody Knows the Trouble I've Seen."[66] She then sees Joe's spirit emerge from the photograph—as a ghostly superimposition on the frame—and pass through the closed door and out of the room. As the music track shifts to "Ave Maria," Caroline follows the spirit into Jim's room and watches as the spirit opens the safe where Jim has hidden the incriminating photographs of Rev. Rhodes. Despite Joe's intervention on behalf of the minister in response to Caroline's prayer for his intercession with God, the outcome of Caroline's story is not as straightforwardly positive as Martha's in *The Blood of Jesus*. Just as Caroline removes the pictures from the safe, Jim returns and the two struggle. Jim wrests the pictures from her hand and pushes her, causing Caroline to fall and hit her head on the corner of the safe. When Betty Jean rushes in to find out what has happened, Jim tells her that a thief stole his money and injured Caroline. Caroline dies shortly thereafter, surrounded by family and friends, with the final words "I'm going home." Rev. Rhodes comforts Betty Jean, telling her that "God will bring the guilty to justice in his own good time."

Williams's reliance in *Go Down, Death* on melodrama, a genre that focuses on the struggle between good and evil in a particular context and on revealing the virtuous nature of a victimized character, allows him to pursue questions about the moral impact of urban entertainments on family and community, as well as issues stemming from class conflicts within black communities.[67] Of the genre and its appeal to early black filmmakers, Jane Gaines writes, "Melodrama reenacts a moral pattern that coincides with the value system in operation within a community at a particular point in history. In the parallel world constructed by melodrama, it is safe to raise emotionally volatile issues and test traumatic outcomes."[68] In addition, she notes that "the family context serves to intensify" the nature and the implications of conflicts that melodramas explore.[69] In *Go Down, Death*, Jim's betrayal of his surrogate mother sits at the center of the moral conflict and serves as the window onto religious and social issues that extend beyond the family context. In keeping with conventions of melodrama, Williams's work engages questions of community values by both depicting the current state of affairs and using the world of the film to imagine a more morally satisfying one, from the perspective of Christian belief. Christine Gledhill reminds us that "[melodrama's] enactment of the continuing struggle of good and evil forces running through social, political and psychic life draws into a public arena desires, fears, values and identities which lie beneath the surface of the publicly acknowledged world."[70] Family conflict and the struggle between the worlds of the church and the nightclub form the basis for Williams's exploration of community concerns, and in the context of melodrama he uses demonic and heavenly interventions to expose unspoken moral questions and to propose ways for the community to resolve these issues.

Jim's victimization of Sister Caroline forms the core of the film's moral struggle—with Jim representing worldliness and Caroline the church—and Caroline's faith is the basis for the more morally satisfying outcome that Williams proposes. Although the story of *Go Down, Death* turns on the threat that Jim poses to Rev. Rhodes and his ability to function as a leader in the church, the minister is strangely passive and appears at a loss about how to maintain his standing in the community and how to insulate his church community from the incursions of the world of the nightclub. Williams does not position Rev. Rhodes as the character who draws the line against the secularization that the film argues attends the expansion of commercial culture. It is Sister Caroline whose religious commitments seem to anchor the congregation, while the minister appears merely as a moral, if ineffective, figurehead. He does not confront Jim, nor does he take any action to counter the image of himself and his ministry that Jim created through the staged photographs. In fact, Rev. Rhodes decides to resign from the church rather than declare his innocence and is satisfied to "turn it over to the Lord." Caroline is the agent of the minister's rescue, praying to her husband to intercede with Jesus. She is certain that her faith will be able to effect what she needs, and through the use of superimposed images Williams permits us to see the result of Caroline's prayer as her husband's spirit appears to help. Ultimately, it is not the simple retrieval of the incriminating photographs that brings Jim's campaign to an end but Caroline's death.

Caroline's death proves transformative for some of the film's characters, and Williams makes clear, both through these transformations and through the use of James Weldon Johnson's poem as the text of the funeral sermon, that her death can be interpreted as a joyful event because, as Rev. Rhodes tells the congregation, "she is not dead. She is resting in the arms of Jesus."[71] Rev. Rhodes and Bettie Jean, who represent the ideal Christian state of moral fortitude and faith in God, are the least well drawn of the characters. Williams places them both in situations where they need protection rather than redemption, and neither appears as a complex actor in his or her own life. The film, however, does convey the sense that the minister's efficacy as a propagator of the Gospel has been enhanced by his relationship with Caroline and her death. Williams signals this change when, at Caroline's funeral service, we see the three women who worked for Jim and to whom the minister had given Bibles sitting in the pews dressed simply in white and wearing pins from the fraternal organization the Order of the Eastern Star. Their presence at the funeral service, as well as their sartorial transformation, indicates that they have been converted and have dedicated themselves to church and community. The impact of Caroline's death on Jim does not lead to the kind of conversion that Williams provided for Ras in *The Blood of Jesus*. Instead, Williams uses the minister's funeral sermon to amplify Jim's guilt at causing the death of his adoptive mother and to set in motion the events that will eventually lead to his punishment.

In the film's final sequences, Williams integrates events in this world and the next in a single frame and uses voice-overs to represent different modes of intervention of the supernatural in this world. Throughout the funeral sermon (see figure 22) we see images of rays of light streaming through clouds, stained-glass windows, Death riding on a white horse, and finally people marching up a staircase to the gates of heaven, most of these images recycled from Williams's earlier film *The Blood of Jesus*. He edits these sequences into the sermon so that they illustrate moments in the poem and in Sister Caroline's life, death, and afterlife in heaven. After the funeral Jim retreats to his club, which has been the source of his conflict with the minister and Sister Caroline and, for Williams, an arena of commercial culture that threatens to destroy the church community. Jim obviously regrets what he has done, but rather than repenting he simply sits drinking and smoking. Williams ends the film by showing viewers the consequences of Jim's life in the saloon and his disregard for the church. In the film's final sequences we hear a devilish voice torment him that he will be going home, just as Caroline did, but that he will be going not to heaven but to hell—the home he deserves. Williams then shifts the action to show us the vision that the devil has provided in illustration of his anticipated torment of Jim, who, maddened by the voice, runs out of the saloon and then collapses and dies. As is typical of the religious black-audience films that address conflict between the church and the world, the wrongdoers receive their just punishment, and the church community (in this case, through Caroline's sacrifice) protects itself from the incursions of sinful forces.

FIGURE 22.

Funeral service in *Go Down, Death*. From the author's collection.

This final segment of the film is the most distinctive and arresting, as Williams combined images of the devil and of hell from Francesco Bertolini and Adolfo Padovan's *L'Inferno* (1911) with the scenes he filmed of Jim attempting to flee the voice that torments him.[72] Employing techniques similar to those used by directors of exploitation and other low-budget films in the same period, Williams recycled both his own footage from *The Blood of Jesus* and footage from *L'Inferno* and perhaps one other film to save money in the production of *Go Down, Death*.[73] While the subject matter of *Go Down, Death* has little in common with that of exploitation films, both used recycling as part of their modes of production, particularly by including footage from earlier films by the same director, stock footage, and scenes from unrelated narrative films.[74] In fact, according to Eric Schaefer, the 1936 exploitation movie *Hell-A-Vision* "combined new footage with scenes from the 1911 version of *Dante's Inferno*," providing at least one precedent in American film for Williams's approach.[75]

Small budgets and lack of access to the production facilities of the major studios were important factors in the decision to recycle, but Schaefer's work on exploitation films reminds us of the importance of taking seriously the aesthetic goals of low-budget and composite films.[76] It is critical that, rather than seeing Williams's inclusion of scenes from the Bertolini-Padovan *L'Inferno* simply as a means of saving money while giving audiences spectacular versions of hell, we understand his use of this recycled footage as a reasoned artistic and theological choice. Dennis Looney has argued that Williams was "drawn to the structural rigor of Dante's system of moral classification" and that he selected only a small number of scenes from *L'Inferno*, using them in a way that "fit[s] the allegorical purposes of *Go Down, Death* perfectly."[77] Looney notes that Williams emphasizes the portions of *Inferno* that portray the punishment of traitors, gluttons, grafters, and those guilty of simony—all sins the viewers have seen Jim commit in the course of the film. The rich descriptions of the geography of hell in Dante's work may also have appealed to Williams as appropriate for his film vision. In addition, because Bertolini and Padovan's Dante, Virgin, Lucifer, and all those damned to hell are white, Williams's use of *Inferno* inserted whiteness into a film that is otherwise set in an exclusively black world, allowing Williams to present the issues of sin, redemption, and damnation as universally Christian and not racialized in a parochial way.[78] It is difficult to imagine that the majority of African American viewers in the late 1940s would have been familiar with the Bertolini-Padovan film in particular, but the graphic images of the punishment of sinners in hell would certainly have impressed audiences.[79]

The reliance on a sermon, in the form of James Weldon Johnson's poem, to structure the film is noteworthy and helps locate *Go Down, Death* in the broader context of black religious films of the period. A sermon form served as the basis for another black-audience religious film in the period—James and Eloyce King Patrick Gist's *Hell Bound Train*, produced by the couple in the early 1930s along with another film, *Verdict, Not Guilty*. Eloyce was born in 1892 in Hitchcock, Texas, and James was born about the same time in Indianapolis. James, a lifelong Baptist, and Eloyce, a convert to Baha'í, met in Washington, D.C., in the late 1920s or early 1930s and married shortly thereafter. By this time, James had already begun producing silent films, and Eloyce, who was the founder and owner of the Patrick School of Beauty Culture and Personal Improvements, joined him in these projects. Together they rewrote the script to produce a second version of James's *Hell Bound Train* and also made *Verdict, Not Guilty*, which they showed in churches in services that included a short sermon by James and Eloyce's leading of the congregation in hymns.[80] The sensibility of these silent films is distinctly evangelical, and although from all accounts Eloyce was deeply committed to the Baha'í faith the two belief systems would not have been incompatible for her. Baha'í's teaching on the unity of religions and its valuing of the specific teachings of various world religions would have made it possible for Eloyce to participate in and lead such church services.

The Gist films have none of the polish of most race movies or of Hollywood films, nor do they use the conventional narrative structures so central to Hollywood cinema of the 1930s. In general, these silent films are underexposed and often out of focus, but they sometimes provide compelling viewing. In contrast to Spencer Williams's narrative and sometimes humorous approach to projecting his faith, *Verdict*, *Not Guilty* and *Hell Bound Train* are straightforwardly dogmatic and derive their drama largely from promoting fear in viewers. *Hell Bound Train* uses the structure of a sermonic form popular in American and African American Christianity in which the preacher likens the spiritual journey to a journey by train. Train travel as a metaphor for the journey that Christians believe all individuals must take has been common in American preaching and in African American preaching in particular. Indeed, James Weldon Johnson noted in the preface to his collection *God's Trombones* (from which Williams drew the inspiration for *Go Down, Death*) that preachers developed and passed on from generation to generation a set of sermons that included "The Valley of Dry Bones," "The Heavenly March," and the "Train Sermon."[81] Sermons that referred to train journeys were also prominent in African American popular culture in the period in which the Gists made their *Hell Bound Train*, as in the case of "race records" like Rev. J. M. Gates's sermons "Hell Bound Express Train" (1927) and "I'm Going Home on the Heaven Bound Train" (1930) and Rev. F. W. McGee's "The Sure Route Excursion to Hell" (1930).[82] King Vidor and his cast were familiar with the importance of this form in black sermonic culture and used it for the revival scene in *Hallelujah* during which Chick undergoes her conversion experience, with Zeke encouraging his listeners to board the train bound for heaven. In the Gists' *Hell Bound Train*, each train car carries those who have committed a particular type of sin, and the film provides extended descriptions of the activities that will inevitably lead the viewers to hell if they do not repent. The final section of *Hell Bound Train* makes clear that, as in Williams's *Go Down, Death*, a sermon structures the film's presentation of Christian understandings of the consequences of certain behavior. A man stands before a painting of a map that carries the title "Midnight Excursion with no Headlights. It's a hell-bound train." The film's intertitle reads, "Thus I've demonstrated to you this picture which I painted as a vision from hearing a sermon in a revival meeting."[83] It is possible that a comparable opening segment introducing the vision and the map that resulted from it was lost.[84]

As it stands, the opening scene of *Hell Bound Train* establishes the danger facing the unrepentant by presenting the devil—an actor dressed in a body suit with horned hood, pointed tail, and cape similar to the costuming in *Blood of Jesus* and *Going to*

Glory, Come to Jesus—standing behind a ticket window, above which a sign reads: "No Roundtrip Ticket; One Way Only; Free Admission to All; Just Give Your Life and Soul." The words projected in the first title of this silent film announce that "[t]he Hell-bound train is always on duty and the devil is the engineer." A man and woman stand before the window, considering their options, and the next title reads: "Well, we'll take a chance." The film goes on to warn viewers against jazz music, dancing, intemperance, sex, disobedience in children, theft, murder, gambling, Sabbath breaking, dishonesty in business, and backsliding. And in the final dramatic sequence the train speeds toward hell as the title implores, "Get off this train by repenting, believing and being baptized, before it's too late." Death, also a character in the film, stands at the entrance to a tunnel and dances before a sign that reads, "Entrance to Hell, Welcome to All." The titles warn, "The fast, sinful life of the hell-bound train moves on until it's too late." And "Our bible reads, 'The wicked shall be turned into hell; and all nations that forget God.' PSALMS 9:17." The train finally enters hell and we see its passengers burning in agony.

Many of the activities that the film insists will trap viewers on the hell-bound train are aspects of general popular culture and hallmarks of black popular culture in particular. In its critique of these activities, the film warns against certain kinds of display as excessive and un-Christian. For the Gists, chief among these are dancing and listening to jazz. The film warns viewers that "the indecent dance of the day" leads to drunken fighting and other kinds of sin and points to a more general lesson about how activities that may provide pleasure for us during our lifetime can doom us in the next life. Those who dance and listen to jazz are accorded their own cars on the train and receive particular attention in the film, whereas murderers and gamblers share a car, as do "thieves, boot-leggers and law-breakers." In a particularly dramatic sequence, the titles tell the viewers that jazz began as the music of "sporting women" and has now "weaved its way into Christian homes." We see a woman dancing and then suddenly putting her hand on her chest and falling into a chair. The dialogue title in which she calls out, "Mary, Emma come quick. Stop those blues, bring hymn book" is followed by a shot of the pages of the hymnbook and a title telling the viewers, "Too late then." The sequence ends with a shot of the woman's death and of her crying children.

Hell Bound Train explores particularly gendered notions of sin in its approach to proscribing behavior. The majority of the sins that men commit in the film involve failures to devote themselves to their families first and foremost. Thus the film contains a variety of scenes of men squandering their paychecks through drinking and gambling. Women also receive particular attention in the film, but for them almost every activity denoted as sinful also leads to sex and pregnancy. One scene illustrates the consequences of a married woman's attempt to abort a child, showing her dying while her husband looks on. The title reads, "She has taken medicine to avoid become a mother. She'd better get right with God, for it's murder in cold blood." In another scene we are treated to the consequences of "women who don't care what happens before children." Here a mother entertains a man in her living room, and the two kiss, drink liquor, dance, and smoke in front of her small daughter. When the two leave, the little girl imitates them, taking a sip of the drink left on the table, pretending to smoke the cigarette butt, and dancing with and kissing her doll. "Children practice just what they see," the film concludes. The majority of women's sinful activities in the film have a direct, negative impact on children's behavior, whereas men's sins create a general misery for all who come into contact with them.

It is difficult to gauge the efficacy of such films as *Hell Bound Train* for moral education, and audience responses are not preserved in the historical record. One can imagine that the explicit presentation of criminal activities and other behavior marked as sinful might have intrigued and fascinated viewers in ways contrary to the filmmakers' goals. This notion that such representations would motivate young people to engage in similar behavior undergirded the movement in the late 1920s and early 1930s to censor the content of Hollywood movies, an effort that resulted in the adoption of the Production Code in 1930. The general principle behind the code was that a film should not "lower the moral standards of those who see it," so the code required that when filmmakers portrayed characters who engaged in "immoral" behavior those characters would be chastised or punished in keeping with the "rule of compensating moral values."[85] It is also quite possible that the Christian viewers who attended exhibitions of the Gists' films and others like them found a safe arena in which they could imagine what it might be like to engage in taboo behavior. The actors, Gist family and friends, certainly seem to be enjoying themselves in pretending to be criminals, gamblers, and adulterers and in demonstrating lascivious jazz dancing. And given that many, if not most, of the showings of the film took place in churches and were, in effect, "preaching to the converted," it seems important to consider the vicarious thrill that viewing these films made possible for committed Christians.

Neither Williams nor the Gists direct the same critical attention to the medium of film as a threat to the moral well-being of black Christians that they do to other aspects of popular culture. Williams's interest in making the divine present on film through special effects certainly distinguishes his work from that of other directors of black-audience films and provides some sense of why this largely visual art remains exempt from his critique. Though some white Christian critics of the movies saw the use of special effects in early film to simulate miracles and divine interventions as potentially dangerous, Williams's work affirmed the possibility of using the viewing of films to direct and enrich religious experience. In the sequence in which Caroline prays before the photograph of her husband, for example, Williams implies a connection between visual intimacy and religious experience. It is not merely Caroline's prayers but the interaction between her prayers and her gaze upon the images of Joe and of Jesus that gives rise to the appearance of Joe's spirit. Williams makes a similar equation between an intimate gaze and religious experience in a number of important scenes in *The Blood of Jesus* in which Martha prays before an image of the Sacred Heart of Jesus. On the mundane level, Williams's heavy emphasis on the visual aspects of film serves to overcome the severe technical limitations under which he labored, limitations that required him to include inadequately synchronized postproduction sound rather than dialogue recorded at the time of filming. But Williams's production style accomplishes more than simply addressing technical difficulties. In emphasizing the visual experiences of his characters within the frame of the largely visual medium of film, he rejects the notion that to simulate miracles on film demeans the power of the divine. The visual possibilities of the medium of film no doubt contributed to Williams's emphasis on the material-culture aspects of religion, resulting in a unique filmic approach to African American religious culture, but it is also clear that he used film in ways that extended traditional approaches to visual and material culture in American Christianity. As Colleen McDannell's work shows, with the increasing availability of mass-produced commercial items in the nineteenth century, American Protestants and Roman Catholics developed a range of formal and informal practices meant to "establish a relationship with Christ and other religious figures via a material Christianity."[86] Sallman's *Head of Christ* and the detail from Hoffman's *Christ and the Rich Young Ruler* in *The Blood of Jesus* and *Go Down, Death* were two of the most popular images in twentieth-century American Christianity. In addition, the image of the Sacred Heart of Jesus on the wall near Martha and Ras's bed in *Blood of Jesus* is typical of mid-twentieth-century mass-produced Catholic art. McDannell's work reminds us that in the United States the boundaries between Catholic and Protestant visual culture have never been rigid. In choosing items to become part of domestic shrines and in placing religious images on the walls of homes, American Christians integrated images that were meaningful to them and that facilitated religious experience and expression.[87] Understood in this context, the presence of both Protestant and Catholic images in Williams's films is not surprising and would not necessarily have surprised black evangelical viewers.

At various points in his religious black-audience films, Williams moved beyond simply incorporating isolated elements of Catholic visual culture into his movies to a fuller reliance on a Roman Catholic sensibility that lends a unique quality to his films. Williams seems to have been particularly interested in the activities of religious intercessors, populating his films with intermediary beings who act on behalf of humans. In his presentation of the efficacy of Caroline's faith in *Go Down, Death*, for example, Williams presents her dead husband as a figure who delivers Caroline's prayer to Jesus and, through his own prayers and actions, comes to her aid. Similarly, in *The Blood of Jesus*, the angel intercedes on Martha's behalf on several occasions. While there is no evidence that Spencer Williams was Roman Catholic or that he accepted Catholic doctrine regarding intercession, he clearly had a strong interest in the topic of intercession, and the surviving evidence from his 1942 film *Brother Martin, Servant of Jesus* (see figure 23) underscores this attraction.

There is no extant print of *Brother Martin*, but the advertising trailer reveals that the film's subject was Martin de Porres, a sixteenth-century Dominican brother who was the son of an enslaved African woman and a Spanish nobleman in Peru.[88] In 1962 Brother Martin would become the first black saint from the Americas, but in Williams's day he had only been beatified, or declared by the church to be blessed and worthy of veneration.[89] The advertising trailer for *Brother Martin* gives little sense of the film's narrative, focusing instead on introducing the figure of Martin de Porres and the elements of his history that led to beatification. Within the structure of a conversation between Uncle Jed (Spencer Williams) and his young niece, Williams explains that Martin was a healer who worked miraculous cures around the world, even though he never left his home in Peru. It seems likely that, as in medieval miracle plays, *Brother Martin* presents the life story and posthumous miracles of a saint, in this case acting on behalf of Uncle Jed. Jed tells his niece that "even today Brother Martin is called upon to guide people and protect people through dangerous journeys. His medals and relics were carried by soldiers in battle, and the guidance and protection they received was almost unbelievable." In the most elaborated section of dialogue in the trailer, Williams presents a tantalizing and frustrating glimpse of the film's story:

NIECE: Did Brother Martin ever do anything for you?

WILLIAMS: Yes, he saved my life.

NIECE: How, Uncle Jed, and why?

WILLIAMS: How did Blessed Martin save my life? Well, my child, it's quite a story. And just why he saved my life I don't know. Maybe. Maybe it was because I . . .

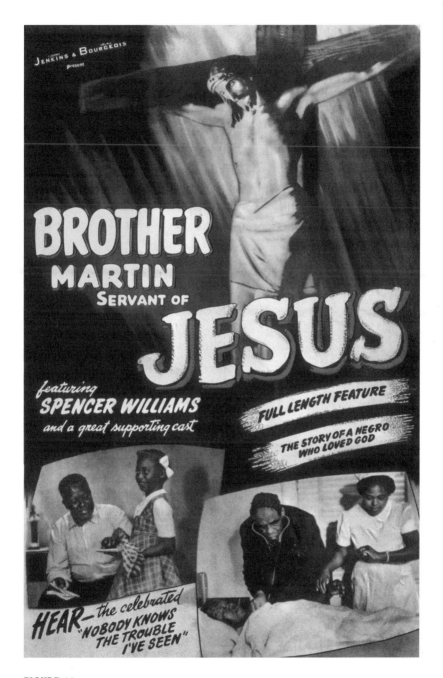

FIGURE 23.
Poster for *Brother Martin, Servant of Jesus.* Courtesy John Kisch, Separate Cinema Archive.

NIECE: Because of what, Uncle Jed?

WILLIAMS: Because I did something for Blessed Martin.

NIECE: You, Uncle Jed? You did something for Brother Martin? When?

WILLIAMS: I believe that is just part of the story.

Through scrolling text on the screen, the remainder of the advertising trailer emphasizes Brother Martin's healing abilities and informs viewers that he found favor with God because he "made personal reparation for the Sins of the World." To see the film and "understand the mysteries of Brother Martin's holy religion" will bless the viewer, the trailer promises. This text scrolls across images of blacks and whites at prayer, some holding rosary beads, and of white Catholic priests and black altar boys, one of whom holds a censer.

The brevity of the trailer and the limited number of images on the film's poster make it difficult to conjecture about the style that Williams adopted for this film, which was produced after *The Blood of Jesus* and before *Go Down, Death*. The images from the poster—of Uncle Jed talking with his niece and of Jed in a hospital bed being attended to by a doctor and nurse—appear realistic, as do most scenes from the trailer. One segment of the trailer, however, provides a glimpse of Williams's characteristic approach to representing the spiritual world in an image of a large cross on a hill with shadowy figures walking nearby.

From these few images and the limited dialogue in the trailer it seems that, in contrast to *The Blood of Jesus* and *Go Down, Death*, which are grounded in an evangelical Protestant sensibility but incorporate some Catholic iconography and theology, *Brother Martin* is explicitly Roman Catholic. The music included in the trailer supports this contention and provides additional evidence. The trailer and the poster promise that viewers will hear the "celebrated spiritual" "Nobody Knows the Trouble I've Seen," but the trailer also includes a "Kyrie Eleison" and other Catholic liturgical music in Latin. It is unfortunate that no print of the film exists at this time, for it seems likely that *Brother Martin, Servant of Jesus* provided audiences with another opportunity to experience the complicated and textured religious vision that Williams put forward in all of his films and with an additional perspective on his interest in the cross, the crossroads, and the intercessory activities of divine and demonic beings.

According to Lester Sack, who worked with his brother Alfred in Sack Amusement Enterprises, Williams's *The Blood of Jesus* "was probably the most successful of all the Negro films and lived the longest . . . and possessed that certain chemistry required by the Negro box office."[90] In fact, Sack released the film for exhibition in 1941, 1944, and 1948, and there is evidence that Williams also traveled with the film, as in the case of his visits to his hometown of Vidalia in the late 1940s. Alma Brown, a friend of Williams's mother, recalled that "the theater was packed" when he showed the westerns in which he was featured and his own religious films in Vidalia.[91] Years later, Lester Sack reported to the film historian Thomas Cripps that the film made more money than all the other Sack Amusement Enterprises releases combined.[92]

But as much as Williams saw *The Blood of Jesus*, *Brother Martin*, and *Go Down, Death* as promoting his own deeply held religious view and hoped to propagate this religious vision, the films were subject to censorship when reviewed by various state censor boards.[93] The majority of the cuts had to do with representations of sexuality in the films, as in the case of the requirement by the Maryland State Board of Censors that parts of the scene from *Go Down, Death* in which the "fly chicks" entrap Rev. Rhodes be eliminated because one of the girls raises her skirt, "showing her bare leg."[94] Maryland also asked that one of the women's exclamations, "Gee, but I could really go to town with that guy!" be cut from the print exhibited in the state. The Motion Picture Division of the State of New York's Education Board, which oversaw film censorship, required that, in the sections set in the club in the city, scenes of a couple "dancing in [an] indecent manner" be eliminated from *The Blood of Jesus*, as well as a sequence in which a man gives a woman money that she puts in her stocking before she leaves with him. The censor deemed this latter sequence "indecent" and "immoral" and argued that it "would tend to corrupt morals."[95] Some sections of the Bertolini-Padovan *Inferno* included in *Go Down, Death* were marked for elimination by the New York censors because they contained images of women with bare breasts, and New York's examiners also felt deeply uncomfortable with references in *The Blood of Jesus* to women's use of bathroom facilities.[96] According to available records, Sack did not object to these relatively minor eliminations, probably because they were typical of the kinds of cuts required by the state censor boards and did not have a serious impact on the films' narrative or on the broad religious message that Williams sought to convey.

However, at least two cases of eliminations by censor boards resulted in major changes to Williams's vision. The Ohio censors insisted that the "entire sequence depicting 'hell,' including scenes of 'devil' chewing man and all scenes of people in 'hell,'" be eliminated before *Go Down, Death* could be shown for a planned 1948 release.[97] Though Williams might have been able to convey his point without the images from *L'Inferno* and without the scenes in which Jim is crazed and running as the devil's voice torments him, the version resulting from the cuts would have been substantially diminished. Even more significant for producers and director was New York State's requirement that the title of *The Blood of Jesus* be changed for release in New York because, in the censors' opinion, its use constituted sacrilege. The reviewer from the censor board wrote, "While the general purport of the picture is to point the way to good rather than evil and while the picture has a religious flavor, there is enough of low comedy and indecency imbedded in the picture to make the use of the words 'THE BLOOD OF JESUS' in the title an irreverent and sacrilegious use. As the picture now stands it should be rejected as 'indecent' and 'sacrilegious.'"[98] Responding for Sack Amusement Enterprises, Vice-President Lester J. Sack insisted that the company and the filmmaker saw this film as "a simple and sincere preachment of faith in God, worthy of the title,"[99] which Williams had drawn from the Negro spiritual "Bathed in the Blood of Jesus." He assured Irwin Esmond, the director of the New York censor board, that the production team had consulted with a group of clergy about both the film's title and the contents of the script before proceeding. "Since the picture's completion," he informed Esmond, "it has been endorsed by numerous ministers."[100] In addition to marshaling the facts of participation by and endorsement from clergy, Sack called attention to the numerous examples of the use of the name of Jesus in films that had received national distribution in recent years, including *Jesus of Nazareth* and *Little Flower of Jesus*.[101]

The dispute over the film's title coalesced around the question of whether a film that contained images of entertainment and was exhibited in commercial theaters could justifiably be considered a religious film. Esmond responded to Sack's insistence that the film was indeed worthy of the title by underscoring his personal objections to the use of the title "in connection with this picture, which is to be exhibited in places of amusement for the purpose of public entertainment. The words: 'THE BLOOD OF JESUS' refer to the most sacred of the symbols of the Christian religion. I cannot view this title, as used in connection with such picture [*sic*], as being otherwise than 'Irreligious' and 'Sacrilegious.'"[102] Hoffberg Productions, Inc., which was serving as the distributor for *The Blood of Jesus* in New York State, eventually agreed to change the film's title to *The Glory Road*, a move that finally secured approval for exhibition. It is difficult to say whether the chastisement concerning perceived misuse of the symbols of Christianity was pointedly directed at the Jewish distributors Sack and Hoffberg or whether it was a reaction to the fact that the entertainment contained within the film came largely from black performance contexts. Whatever the case, it is clear that the censors were deeply uncomfortable with the formula that made *The Blood of Jesus* a successful film and to which Williams had committed himself as a Christian evangelist, namely that entertainment and Christian education were entirely compatible. Spencer Williams, Eloyce and James Gist, and the people involved in Royal Gospel Productions concurred and have left us with a small body of works that demonstrate unique and engaging strategies for combining the two.

FOUR   "Saturday Sinners and
Sunday Saints"

*Urban Commercial Culture and
the Reconstruction of
Black Religious Leadership*

The identification of urban entertainment culture—particularly the nightclub—as
the principal marker of the various dangers that modern life presents to the faith of
individuals is the most striking commonality among the extant black-audience religious films of the 1930s and 1940s. In a most literal presentation of this dynamic in
Spencer Williams's *The Blood of Jesus* (1941), Martha's soul must pass through the
city to return to her body, and it is primarily the lure of a nightclub and its attendant vices that places her soul in jeopardy. Similarly, in the Royal Gospel Productions film *Going to Glory, Come to Jesus* (1947), the minister's daughter Lillie-Mae
accompanies the devil, who has appeared to her in the guise of Prince O'Hades, to
a nightclub where the featured performer sings:

> I'm smokin' my cigarette
> I'm gonna chew my gum
> Just livin' my own life
> And havin' my fun.
> What I do to myself
> Don't concern no one else
> Regardless.[1]

Unlike *The Blood of Jesus*'s Martha, who realizes the danger in which she has placed
her soul by spending time in the nightclub and chooses to leave, Lillie-Mae rejects

the pleasures of the club only after Prince O'Hades has withdrawn the beauty he bestowed upon her in order to lure her away from her family and church. Nevertheless, once she has been cast out by the devil, Lillie-Mae prays, "Oh Lord—please save me. I want to know the right way. I know there is only one God. Even the Devil knows there is but one God," and she forsakes her idolatrous approach to entertainments.[2] With the goal of promoting Christian beliefs and evangelical standards of conduct, these films insist that religious commitment is the key to surviving the temptations and dangers of the modern world. Spencer Williams makes this argument most graphically in *Go Down, Death* (1944) by showing audiences images of tormented souls in hell, indicating that this will be not only Jim's fate for his conduct as a nightclub owner, his scornful attitude toward the church, and his complicity in the death of his adoptive mother but viewers' fate as well should they follow his path.

Explicitly religious race movies constitute only a small portion of the larger body of films produced for exhibition before black audiences from the beginning of the sound era through 1950, and the concern of their directors for what they understood to be the damaging impact of entertainment and commercial culture, usually marked as urban, is palpable in these works. Similar themes about the relationship between religious individuals and modern urban entertainments also appear in the larger group of race movies from the period, even though these filmmakers did not seek to promote a particular form of religious expression or cultivate religious experiences among members of their audiences. Producers and directors of the larger group of race movies located their address of these issues in the context of a range of genres, including dramas, comedies, mysteries, and musicals, and, while the goal of these genre films was primarily to entertain, the ways they engage religious issues are significant. Because race film companies, whether independent black businesses or white-owned businesses with black on-screen talent and sometimes black directors, made these movies for black audiences with no expectation that white Americans would see them, it is reasonable to assume that they explored issues of particular interest to African Americans at the time. Contemporary concerns would certainly have proven timely and topical avenues for entertaining filmgoers. Like the early Hollywood "all-black-cast" films, many of these race movies structured their narratives by setting urban and rural life against one another, but these films also juxtaposed representations of a corrupt and backward church with those of an educated, modern one, exploring the opposition between the ways of the worldly and members of the church (the struggle between "Saturday sinners and Sunday saints," as one advertisement put it). Rather than simply harking back to an imagined idyllic rural past, as was so often the case in Hollywood films, many race movies presented a more nuanced and probing analysis—set in the context of a variety of entertaining genres—of the impact of urbanization and urban commercial culture on black religious life.

A survey of black-audience genre movies that feature religious themes, characters, and institutions reveals a strong connection between anxieties about the urban environment and commercial culture and the films' interrogations of the possibilities and problems of black religious leadership. By the 1930s, African American communities had created a variety of avenues for developing social and political leadership, including electoral politics and the arts, resulting in decreasing reliance on the ministry as the major route to public leadership. The question remained, however, of where to locate the clergy in relation to these other forms of secular leadership, particularly as increasing numbers of African Americans left the rural South and settled in urban areas across the country. There is a strong sense in the world of these films that a modern black community cannot rely exclusively on ministers for direction, particularly when some have not served it well in a variety of ways, and the films provide many representations of uneducated, corrupt, scheming, or ineffectual ministers in order to warn viewers and make the case for needed change.

There is important precedent in African American intellectual culture for the use of film as an avenue to criticize corrupt ministers and put forward a range of more useful models of Christian conduct. The African American filmmaker Oscar Micheaux, whose career as a writer, director, and producer spanned the silent and sound eras and who made more than thirty films between 1919 and 1948, engaged issues about black religious leadership in several of his silent films. The most significant examples of Micheaux's pursuit of these themes are found in *Within Our Gates* (1919) and *Body and Soul* (1925), both of which contain scathing criticism of black clergy.[3]

Body and Soul, in which Paul Robeson made his film debut, portrays the havoc that Isaiah T. Jenkins, a con man preacher, creates in a small southern town. Robeson delivers a chilling performance as Jenkins, and we follow the minister's career as he wins the confidence of the women of the local congregation and proceeds to rape Isabelle, the daughter of Sister Martha Jane, his greatest supporter, and steal her mother's savings. None of the women of the church community know about Jenkins's activities outside the church, and they maintain an unrelentingly positive view of him. Indeed, Martha Jane has saved (and kept hidden inside a large Bible) the money that Jenkins eventually steals in the hopes that he will marry her daughter. Isabelle is the only congregant who suspects that he is a negative force in the community, and when she challenges his position in the community Jenkins rapes her and forces her to leave town. In a critical scene late in the film, "Rev." Jenkins enters the church to preach "Dry Bones in the Valley," which, the intertitles tell us, is "the sermon which is every black preacher's ambition." He begins the service by taking up a large collection and then asks the church members, obviously poor, for more. As the sermon gets underway, the congregants respond positively, jumping up and down out of their chairs. Jenkins drinks liquor from a water glass—looks of jealousy apparent on the faces of the deacons who sit behind him—as he preaches an obviously energetic and commanding sermon. His sermon is so compelling that even the recalcitrant and perpetually napping husband of one of the women begins to move his body to the rhythm of the sermon and leans forward, attentive. Elderly women in elaborate dresses and hats jump up and down, and the intertitles convey their enthusiasm: "Lawdy, Lawdy!" one woman exclaims, "I been washed in the blood of the Lamb and I'se whiter den snow." In the end, Martha Jane's recounting of her daughter's death in Atlanta—with which she interrupts the sermon and, in some sense, makes Isabelle's "bones live"—moves the congregation to turn on Jenkins. He runs, pursued by the congregation, but, with a large lead, is able to make his way to Martha Jane's house. There, on his knees, he begs for her forgiveness, arguing that she ruined him by pampering him. He begs her to pray for him and, following Micheaux's dramatic use of a short intertitle of "Forgiven," is back on the run from the unforgiving mob. Near the film's end he kills a young man in the woods who tries to stop him.[4]

Micheaux's focus on the physicality of Jenkins's sermon in the church scene, rather than on its content, is not merely a consequence of the limits of representing the spoken word in a silent film; it also helps in conveying Micheaux's particular concerns about uneducated black clergy. In presenting Jenkins's sermon, Micheaux does not use intertitles to provide its text to viewers. Instead, he relies on visual evidence of Jenkins's persuasiveness for the members of his congregation. Such evidence includes Jenkins's effective use of his body in relation to both his congregation and the Bible. He holds a large Bible on his left shoulder and pounds it on occasion as he moves back and forth in front of the congregation, punctuating his sermon with his body movements. In making directorial decisions, Micheaux did not generally refrain from including long intertitles to convey information to his audiences. Here, however, he relies on the fact that Rev. Jenkins's text will be familiar to his audience and will help him locate his critique in Jenkins's deployment of the Bible to serve decidedly un-Christian ends. Thus in Micheaux's view it is not religion's inherent characteristics that are dangerous but the way figures like Jenkins use the Bible to deceive their congregants. Moreover, for the filmmaker, the overly emotional approach to worship in some black churches makes black congregations more susceptible to manipulation by unscrupulous clergy. He proposes, instead, a sedate, rational religiosity grounded in knowledge of the Bible as key to the uplift of African American communities.

While neither religious institutions nor religious subjectivity occupies center stage in *Within Our Gates,* this silent film contains a significant digression in which Micheaux considers the economic burden that black church cultures and ministers place on black communities. An exchange between two minor characters—Mrs. Geraldine Stratton, a white southerner, and Mrs. Elena Warwick, a white Bostonian—about charitable giving to black causes serves as Micheaux's vehicle for this discussion. Mrs. Warwick has been approached by Sylvia Landry (Evelyn Preer), a black teacher at a southern school, for a contribution. Sylvia was so moved by the need and sincerity of her students and by the work of Rev. Wilson Jacobs, the school's founder and "an apostle of education for the black race,"[5] that she spent sleepless nights thinking "of nothing but the eternal struggle of her race and how she could uplift it." Sylvia finally announces to Rev. Jacobs, "It is my duty and the duty of each member of our race to help destroy ignorance and superstition. I'm going up north where I'll try to raise the money we need. May God be with us!"

In advising Mrs. Warwick on whether to donate to the school, Mrs. Stratton, the southerner, argues for the impossibility of black uplift, pointing to religious practices as a sign of the backwardness of blacks, and Micheaux uses her tirade about white northerners' naïveté regarding black life to provide a critique of the function of religion for some African Americans. Stratton announces, "Lumber-jacks and field hands. Let me tell you—it is an error to try and educate them. Besides, they don't want an education. Can't you see that thinking would only give them a headache? Their ambition is to belong to a dozen lodges, consume religion without restraint, and, when they die, go straight up to Heaven. Wasting $5000 on a school is plain silly when you could give $100 to old Ned, the best colored preacher in the world who will do more to keep Negroes in their place than all your schools put together." The scene fades and the title introduces "Old Ned as He Is," preaching a sermon on "Abraham and the Fatted Calf." Ned preaches, "Behold, I see that black people will be the first and will be the last. While the white folk, with all their schooling, all their wealth, all their sins, will all fall into the everlasting inferno! While our race, lacking these vices and whose souls are most pure, most all will ascend into Heaven! Hallelujah!" Old Ned jumps and points and shouts, and the congregation becomes increasingly involved in the sermon, some jumping out of their seats and shouting, participating in the sermon. Ned quickly takes advantage of their attention to coerce a large offering from the members of the church. Visually, this scene is remarkably similar to the climactic preaching scene in the later *Body and Soul*, yet Micheaux's critique of the church is textured quite differently. Whereas Rev. Jenkins begs for forgiveness for his actions, he does so only because he believes he is about to die, and Micheaux makes clear the fundamental insincerity of his expression of remorse. Ned, however, understands the personal, political, and religious implications of his biblical illiteracy and his willingness to function as the pawn of local white leaders. After a particularly humiliating encounter with these white men the following morning, Ned meditates on his actions, and we read his thoughts (in the intertitles): "Again I've sold my birthright, all for a miserable 'mess of pottage.' Negroes and whites—all are equal. As for me, miserable sinner, Hell is my destiny." After hearing Mrs. Stratton's tirade, which horrifies her as an illustration of the attitudes of southern whites, Mrs. Warwick decides to help support the school.

Most film scholars who write about Micheaux's body of work remain satisfied to comment on the convincing presence of a critique of the black church and its ministers, particularly in these dramatic examples. Indeed, Micheaux's films often argued that African Americans' investment in the church ultimately turned attention away from what he felt were more significant issues of politics, education, and economics. Moreover, they showed that black engagement with these issues was most productive when kept entirely separate from the sphere of the church. In *Within Our Gates*, Old Ned represents ignorant and manipulative religious leaders, and his delivery of a nonsensical sermon that showcases his biblical illiteracy is central to Micheaux's critique of black religion in ways that he will pursue again in the later film *Body and Soul*. At the same time, however, Micheaux sets Old Ned against Dr. V. Vivian (Charles D. Lucas), the film's primary positive model of black manhood, in a way that reveals a much more complex approach to religion in black communities and to its place in the construction of black male leadership in particular. In setting Dr. V. Vivian, Sylvia's love interest, and Old Ned against one another, Micheaux seems to be charting the most useful combination of body, mind, and spirit for African American uplift work. On several occasions Micheaux shows his viewers what Vivian is reading, and it is striking that each text refers to religious figures or issues. Early in the film, for example, Vivian reads from a race magazine: "Reverend Thurston has begun an active campaign for the education of the black race. He asks that the federal government contribute significantly, so that Negro children in all of the U.S. can receive proper instruction." In another scene almost immediately after Micheaux introduces us to Old Ned, we see that Vivian is reading, "The

Negro is a human being. His nature is not different from other human nature. Thus, we must recognize his rights as a human being. Such is the teaching of Christianity." Micheaux uses Vivian and the texts the character is reading to locate religious institutions and leadership in what the director sees as their proper place as merely one element of a program for racial uplift and thereby to reclaim a place for Christianity in producing black leaders for the struggle against racism.

In addition to concern with religious leadership, many black-audience films reveal anxiety about the possibility that the church's influence will be eclipsed by the world of entertainments. Beginning in the early twentieth century, urban African Americans in particular experienced dramatic expansion in their commercial opportunities as they encountered a growing variety of popular entertainments such as films, theater, nightclubs, professional sports, and radio programs, as well as consumer items like beauty products, records, literature, newspapers, magazines, and toys, all marketed specifically to their communities. While urban African Americans' engagement with commercial culture was in many ways similar to that of other Americans, some aspects of it remained unique to black communities. In his study of black churches in Brooklyn, New York, Clarence Taylor observes that

> [f]or the most part, African Americans embraced mass cultural forms with little resistance. Yet they were not just passive recipients who swallowed mass culture whole. They molded it to suit their needs as African Americans in an urban environment. They made choices in music, clothing, products, movies and other forms of recreation. . . . Although blacks adopted mass cultural forms that were popular in the larger white society, the trend toward mass culture was part of the larger struggle led by African Americans that challenged the racist view of blacks as lazy and incapable of succeeding. African Americans used mass culture to become economically independent and make black communities viable.[6]

During the 1930s and 1940s, a range of race movies that were produced primarily for entertainment purposes and not for specifically religious ends explored how the arenas of church and commercial entertainments would relate to each other in the urban environment.

In the context of exploring the meaning of both urbanization and the rise of secular entertainments for church communities, many race films also addressed the strong presence of women in black churches as a potential problem. In these films, the concern with the present and future of the ministry is directly related to the perception of the church arena as destructively feminized, and the nightclub frequently appears as an arena that allows for the unchecked expression of female sexuality. The perception of a "feminized" church as a problem has not been confined to the history of African American Christians, but because the church is so significant a part of the public sphere in African American communities, taking account of representations of apprehensions about feminization is critical to understanding urban African American life in the early twentieth century.[7] The films associate a potential feminization of the church with the problems that result from African Americans' heavy reliance on the clergy's leadership in realms outside the church. Several films work around these issues and, not surprisingly, use female characters as an argument either for a particular kind of ministerial leadership not tied to women's spiritual agency or for the need to look outside the church for leaders. They are especially concerned with the question of what that new nonchurch leadership might look like and what relationship it would have both to the church and to the increasingly influential arena of the nightclub.

In black-audience films of the early sound period, perhaps the most straightforward critique of the potential dangers of conflating religious and political leadership is found in the 1932 comedy *The Black King*, which was inspired by elements of the life of Marcus Garvey, the Jamaican-born black-nationalist leader of the Universal Negro Improvement Association (UNIA). In the wake of his conviction for mail fraud, his imprisonment in 1925, the subsequent commutation of his sentence, and his deportation in 1927, Garvey's achievements and exploits had begun to make their way into American popular culture. Indeed, Garvey's career had inspired the 1930 Broadway play *Sweet Chariot*, written by the white playwright Robert Wilder. The play opened in October of 1930 and starred a number of well-known and rising African American actors, including Frank Wilson, Vivian Baber, Fredi Washington, and Alex Lovejoy.[8] Wilder's exploration of Garvey's career as the leader of UNIA focused on the possibilities opened up by Garvey's election by his organization's members as the provisional president of Africa and imagined the consequences of the "back to Africa" thrust of the movement. *Sweet Chariot*'s main character, Marius Harvey, is apparently sincere in his intention to assist people of African descent in returning to Africa, but when they finally arrive he finds that his followers are not willing to give up the pleasures of the American urban Saturday night. After his people abandon him to return home on a passing ship, Harvey is left only with the loyal Lola, who he claims is steadfast because of the "white blood in her veins."[9] Even as this generally poorly reviewed production was in the works, theater critics in New York reported on plans for a Broadway production of *The Black King*, a play by the Trinidadian immigrant writer, director, and composer Donald Heywood that was also based on Garvey's life. Although the production apparently never came together for the stage, Heywood's work did become the basis of a film with the same title (Southland Pictures Corp., 1932).[10] Clearly, many people involved in producing entertainment for African Americans felt strongly that stories about Garvey, whose popularity in black communities extended far beyond the official membership rolls of UNIA, would appeal to audiences.

Donald Heywood, in some of his own work for the stage, sought to capitalize on the popularity in the early 1930s of black-cast plays with religious themes on Broadway and to emulate the success of *The Green Pastures*, which had won the Pulitzer Prize for Drama in 1930. Although he was apparently unable to get *The Black King* mounted on Broadway, after many delays his play *Ol' Man Satan* opened at the Forrest Theatre in October of 1932 and ran for almost a month.[11] Heywood's references to Connelly's work and to Roark Bradford's book *Ol' Man Adam and His Chillun*, the source for *The Green Pastures*, are clear in the play's title, in its structure as a black woman's thoughts about Satan, and in various scenes, including one set in God's office in heaven. The *New York Times* theater critic noted the similarities but expressed a clear preference for Connelly's "superlative Negro fable." Heywood's work, he wrote, "misses the point entirely. His play contains neither exultation nor emotional depths. For these qualities he attempts to substitute a show in the manner of those morality plays which were popular before the war. In the manner, specifically, of what was identified by one of the sages in last night's audience as 'Everywoman.'"[12] That post–World War I white theatergoers apparently required a certain kind of emotional approach to black religion in their Broadway productions may account for the difficulties Heywood faced in getting his satirical *The Black King* mounted in New York, although the precise reasons for the production's demise are not clear. Whatever the case, even the prospect that *The Black King* would be directed by Léonide Massine, the famed dancer and former choreographer for the Ballets Russes, could not help the production come to life.[13] It is unclear how Heywood became involved with the white producer and director Bud Pollard, but in the spring of 1932 Pollard directed a screen version of *The Black King* (see figure 24) with a story adaptation by Morris M. Levinson and dialogue by Heywood.[14]

While Marcus Garvey might be most appropriately understood as a political leader with a strong concern for establishing a religious sensibility as part of his nationalist project, Heywood and Pollard's version of the popular leader constructs him as a religious leader first and foremost.[15] Questions about generational issues and reli-

FIGURE 24.
Poster for *The Black King*.
Courtesy John Kisch,
Separate Cinema Archive.

gious leadership set the stage for the film's story as it opens with the congregation of the Rise and Shine Baptist Church of Logan, Mississippi, voting to force elderly Deacon Jones (Harry Gray of *Hallelujah*) to retire and electing Charcoal Johnson (A. B. Comathiere) their new deacon.[16] Deacon Jones, the founder of the church, assures the members of his congregation that his interest lies only in "the furthering of [God's] name" and that he will do whatever they decide is best "for the uplifting of the Gospel to every creature."[17] In contrast, Deacon Johnson's presentation of what he brings to the church relies on a combination of political and religious arguments in which he positions himself as destined to "tote the burden of [his] people on the road that leads to the land of milk and honey and away from that other road that leads to fire and brimstone and everlasting destruction." His ultimate goal, however, is to further not the Gospel but race pride, and this pride will be realized through the political goal of establishing a black nation in Africa. He promises the congregation that he will deliver them from "the shackles of superstition and old-time darkness" to enable "all the black brothers and black sisters

[to] walk with their heads high, proud as peacocks" in front of white folks. The majority of the members of the congregation are invigorated and excited by Johnson's address and vote to follow him and ask Deacon Jones to resign.

Through this conflict between Charcoal Johnson and Deacon Jones, the film reconfigures popular images of the older generation of black religious leadership and the new free-born, modern generation. *The Black King* dismantles the association, frequently articulated in popular culture, between the African American religious past and illiteracy, overly exuberant worship, and the misuse of funds obtained from congregations through questionable strategies. It also complicates the image of the new religious leadership as necessarily articulate, educated, restrained, and focused on racial uplift. Oscar Micheaux's characters of Old Ned and Rev. Jacobs from *Within Our Gates* are emblematic of this stark oppositional mode of representing the generational divide in black religious leadership. Heywood and Pollard's *The Black King* mixes elements of both categories in presenting the conflict between the two deacons. Old Deacon Jones is articulate and reserved (desired characteristics of the new leadership) but entirely otherworldly in his theology (the stereotype of slave religion). Some members of the community value the orientation of Jones's theology. Incredulous that the people could have voted Jones out as leader of the church he worked so hard to build, Mary Lou (Vivianne Baber) tells him that she recognizes his contribution to the community through his work of raising "two generations of Christians." She continues, "You know, you're the one who taught us that the reward for good deeds is not to be expected down here, but in heaven." "That's right, children," Jones replies. "I did teach you that." Charcoal Johnson concerns himself with racial uplift projects, but his moral character is weak, his leadership style is entirely dependent upon charisma, and he lacks the education and refinement that are the desired hallmarks of the new leadership. In claiming to liberate the people from "old-time darkiness and superstition," Charcoal seeks to make black nationalism the focus of African American religion and implies that Deacon Jones's theology entails a commitment to the American project and consequently to "white folks' interests." Indeed, his second public act as the congregation's new deacon (his first having been to perform the funeral of old Deacon Jones, who drops dead on the steps of the church) is to call a meeting to promote his nationalist project. Pollard uses an image of a newspaper clipping of the announcement, which reads, "Notice: I, Deacon Charcoal Johnson, command the presence of all the colored race at the Masonic Hall on Tuesday, May 9th, to organize the BACK TO AFRICA MOVEMENT," to indicate Johnson's aspirations for leadership far beyond his own small congregation.[18]

In ways similar to Marcus Garvey's casting of Africa as the site of the fulfillment of God's ordained destiny for all people of African descent, *The Black King*'s Charcoal Johnson insists that African Americans will have no future as a people unless they go to "the Promised Land."[19] In a speech innocently full of mispronunciations and mangled words, Charcoal emphasizes the need for political organization among people of African descent and the achievement of an independent nation—the United States of Africa—as the means to being "treated with the proper disrespect."[20] Moreover, he tells them, God has provided them with a bountiful land full of "shining 'taters"—diamonds. "The ground over there just naturally grows them. You don't have to sweat or plow or nothing." Near the end of the gathering, Johnson engages the people in a chant that underscores the themes he struck in his address, pointing to the words on a blackboard behind him:

A stands for Adam ([the people add:] the first man made).
F stands for Freedom (the Good Book says).
R stands for Races (whether great or small).
I stands for Insulted (without a cause).
C stands for Carry (which God will do, back to)
A stands for Africa (which belongs to you).

The chant links black nationalist ideology with religious destiny in a way that proves appealing for Charcoal's audience and motivates them to join his movement.

As the film explores Charcoal Johnson's pursuit of rule over an African empire, it incorporates elements of pageantry and display that audiences would have recognized as referring to the public spectacles so central to Marcus Garvey's UNIA. Having been chased out of Logan, Mississippi—the implication is that it is by whites who are hostile to his project—Johnson and his followers head north, passing through Tulsa, Oklahoma, before arriving in Chicago. Johnson has planned a large parade to raise money and garner support from members of the black community. Pollard uses what appears to be newsreel footage of a UNIA parade to invoke the visual power of the organization's marches, and he carries the visual references to Garvey's style into the interior scenes of a grand ball when the group has finally reached New York, the last stop before their departure for Africa on the group's *Black Eagle* ship. Johnson and his officers now wear elaborate uniforms that resemble marching band uniforms, and he and his two vice-emperors carry swords (see figure 25). The pageantry continues as Johnson's vice-emperors oversee the arrival of the guests for the ball, all of whom have been awarded titles in the new empire.

FIGURE 25.
Emperor of Africa, Charcoal Jones, flanked by his vice-emperors in *The Black King*.
Courtesy John Kisch, Separate Cinema Archive.

Indeed, Johnson has commented during the group's stop in Chicago that he has given out so many titles he has run out of towns and been forced to name "two or three sisters queens of the same town in Africa." The ball in New York contains a humorous exchange that seems aimed at highlighting the incongruity between this imagined African empire and the reality of African American life. In the exchange, a woman and her husband attempt to gain entrance to the event, only to be turned away by a guard. "Don't you know who you're talking to?" the woman asks. "I'm the Countess of Zanzibar!"

Incorporating the pageantry of Garvey's movement into the visual style of *The Black King* makes it possible for the film to engage questions about the controversial issue of Garvey's black nationalism, his leadership style, and the relationship of black Americans to Africa. The film participates in the accusation leveled against Garvey by many contemporary critics, most notably W. E. B. Du Bois, who asserted in *The Crisis* in 1924 that "Marcus Garvey is, without doubt, the most dangerous enemy of the Negro race in America and in the world. He is either a lunatic or a traitor. . . . The American Negroes have endured this wretch all too long with fine restraint and every effort at cooperation and understanding. But the end has come. Every man who apologizes for or defends Marcus Garvey from this day forth writes himself down as unworthy of the countenance of decent Americans. As for Garvey himself, this open ally of the Ku Klux Klan should be locked up or sent home."[21] Du Bois and many other critics of Marcus Garvey's charismatic leadership emphasized the embarrassment that his spectacles—which included banners, titles and uniforms for titleholders, parades, and ceremonies at court—caused for all African Americans. Just as the film makes clear that viewers are to understand the pretensions of the Countess of Zanzibar to be humorous, so it ridicules Charcoal Johnson's excessive and performative approach to building the empire he believes has been divinely ordained. One anonymous reviewer saw the filmmaker's willingness to engage what he or she saw as the inherent humor of some aspects of the Garvey movement to be a sign of artistic maturity, writing that the fact that the film "holds the mirror up to nature and ridicules what is laughable, shows that Race art might grow up and develop a sense of humor. That possibility is encouraging."[22]

In the end, two things bring down Johnson's empire—his corrupt business practices and the fact that "Africa" will not receive the emperor and his people. Although Johnson's followers abandon him quickly upon learning of his dishonesty, the film does not redeem the masses of African Americans but indicts Johnson's followers as decisively as it does the charismatic leader himself. Screenwriter Heywood lays the ground for this theme early on in the film. When Mary Lou tells Sug (Knolly Mitchell), Charcoal's most vigorous detractor, that the church voted Deacon Jones out, she describes the scene inside the church, telling him, "And you should have seen the way those hypocrites were making out over Charcoal. You'd have thought he was St. Peter himself the way they were yessing, and him the biggest backsliding sinner in the church." Here the community's support of Johnson's backsliding sinning is as much at issue as Johnson's moral character itself. Near the film's conclusion, as soon as one of Johnson's opponents reveals to the crowd in attendance at the ball that Johnson will be unable to carry out the plan, Johnson's followers immediately turn to this man and make him their new leader, singing, "Lead on brother, lead on," the same song they sang when they elected Johnson deacon of the Rise and Shine Baptist Church.

Moreover, the film insists that it is not just charisma or the force of black nationalism that moves people to follow Johnson. Rather, it is something inherent in African American religiosity that makes the movement possible. It is significant in *The Black King* that when a white Chicago paper attempts to discredit Johnson it focuses primarily on his religious sensibility rather than his political program: "POLICE TO HALT NEGRO PARADE. 'CHARCOAL JOHNSON,' NEGRO RELIGIOUS FANATIC, ELECTS HIMSELF EMPEROR OF UNITED STATES OF AFRICA." Viewers see the power of this fanaticism at work near the film's end when Charcoal's preaching mesmerizes the people until they turn suddenly to the next available leader. *The Black King,* then, presents a very clear message about not only the perils of corrupt black leadership but also leaders' absolute dependence upon the willingness of people to follow blindly. One critic of the film noted that the filmmakers make this case, in part, through deploying traditional Hollywood tropes of black religiosity: "The picture gets off to a bad start. A Negro chorus, unseen moans a weird chant which is unmistakably Negroid, while waving hands and bending figures are shadowed on the screen. This gives the picture the required Negro motif but the scheme is so hackneyed that one immediately recalls previous Negro pictures and plays."[23]

Associations between class, theology, and skin color—which will be important for many of these genre films with religious themes—are also of interest in *The Black King.* As expected, like Marcus Garvey, "Charcoal" Johnson is a dark-skinned black man, and Pollard emphasized the character's skin color with dark makeup on the lighter-skinned actor Comathiere. The film, however, also works to untangle some of the stereotypical associations between dark skin, working-class status, and nationalist politics on the one hand and light skin, middle-class status, and integrationist politics on the other. Charcoal's principal supporters in Chicago, for example, are members of Chicago's black elite—the husband is a newspaper owner—and various servants in their home are opposed to Johnson's back-to-Africa project. While it would be simple to conclude that *The Black King*'s narrative supports the notion that class, politics, theology, and skin color converge to create monolithic social categories based on skin color, the film actually takes a more complicated, if muddled, approach to these questions.

The Black King is merely one of several race films of the 1930s and 1940s that took seriously and evaluated—albeit in a comedic mode—the nature of black religious leadership and raised questions about the appropriate relationship between the church and its leaders and other elements of black civil society. In doing so, the film addressed itself to discussions circulating in black communities across the country about these very issues. In one of his regular columns in the *Chicago Defender,* the actor Salem Tutt Whitney, who played the part of Noah in the Broadway production of *The Green Pastures,* complained about corrupt ministers who sully the reputations of the genuine ones and about the failure of black people to support a variety of important enterprises in their communities:

> We are still slaves of the church. The church has its place and will always keep its place, but that does not mean that it should displace all other Race activities

in our interest. The church is one of our oldest activities, yet in most instances, the business of the church is loosely and sometimes dishonestly handled. The success of the church is the result of the blind or simple unquestioning faith of most of its members, and the zeal with which these members will pour their dollars into the collection box.

There is no record that shows that Christ recommended that His disciples build $500,000 churches for His believers to worship in. . . . It is only fair and sensible that some of our faith and dollars should be invested in the promotion of other Race enterprises as well as the church.[24]

While Whitney was particularly interested in promoting the virtues of the black press in this critique of what he saw as African Americans' slavish devotion to the church, he would also have been acutely aware, as a professional actor, of the role of some black churches in opposing their members' participation in the world of entertainment. The religious race movies directed by Spencer Williams and others present a stark opposition between the church and the nightclub as a means of raising concerns about the moral dangers of worldliness. In the genre films that take up these themes—the comedies and musicals in particular—the exploration of conflict between church and nightclub seems aimed at providing a critique of black clergy and, as Whitney suggested in his column, finding a way to locate the church as one part of a broader set of race enterprises.

In *Dirty Gertie from Harlem U.S.A* (1946), Spencer Williams chose to work with a screenplay by True T. Thompson that pits two Christian missionaries against a nightclub striptease dancer.[25] Although film scholars characterize *Dirty Gertie* as a comedy and generally do not find significant religious themes in the work, it is clear that embedded in the comedic approach is commentary on African American religious life that merits serious attention. In his explicitly religious melodramas, Williams created a great deal of dramatic tension concerning the fate of his characters, but the outcome never seems to have been in doubt, since Williams's belief in the assurance of God's punishment of the wicked and the renewal of the church community is clear. In many ways, the generic choice of comedy with *Dirty Gertie* permits him to take narrative chances and to probe questions about the impact of the nightclub on black life and about the future of the ministry in ways that might have been more difficult within the context of a religious melodrama. The direction of the narrative in *Dirty Gertie* is much less formulaic than in either of his extant religious works, and the film, which includes music and comedy, contains no special effects or scenes depicting divine or satanic intervention in human lives. Despite the obvious differences between *Dirty Gertie* and Williams's religious melodramas, the themes the films take up are quite similar, especially their explorations of tensions between the church and the nightclub and issues of gender and black religious leadership.

Although *Dirty Gertie*'s story is set on the fictional Caribbean island of "Rinidad," it carries a range of issues related to African American urbanization into the context of the island. Harlem is an ever-present referent for the characters in the film and particularly for the members of the performing troupe of Gertie La Rue (Francine Everett), who enumerate the various ways in which Rinidad and Harlem differ. Were Gertie not so selfish and had she not been unfaithful to club owner Al (John King), one of the other performers comments, they would have been able to stay in Harlem. Gertie replies that she would prefer to be in Harlem as well and that once "this thing blows over . . . , then it's Lenox Avenue and 135th Street, here I come." In addition, while it might seem that the missionaries' presence would indicate some intention to interact with residents of the island, Gertie, billed as the greatest performer "this side of Harlem," occupies all their attention (see figure 26), and Jonathan Christian (Alfred Hawkins), the senior of the two missionaries, vows to have the governor "put her and her low-down cohorts off the island. Send them bag and baggage back to Harlem!" Clearly, Christian is interested in ridding the island of the sinful influence of the Harlem troupe, presumably for the benefit of the residents, but the film provides viewers with no evidence of his intention to interact with them. Throughout much of the film, Gertie, the embodiment of the frightening aspects of urbanization and commercial entertainments, engages in an all-out war with these representatives of the church who seek to contain the danger within the confines of Harlem, the trope for all-black urban areas.

In contrast to the presentation of the dedicated and well-meaning, if not particularly forceful, ministers in *The Blood of Jesus* and *Go Down, Death,* the film draws the characters of Jonathan Christian and Ezra Crumm (David Boykin) as morally problematic. Christian, for example, shows himself to be excessively concerned with his comfort as he complains bitterly about his hotel room. Finding that Gertie's troupe has been assigned the best rooms, Christian whines, "Why, I just don't see how I'm going to stand it. And we expect to stay here quite some time. Why, if we're going to teach these people what sin is, we've got to be in more comfortable surroundings." In the course of observing Gertie's behavior with two servicemen stationed on the island and expressing concern to the nightclub owner about the troupe's show, Christian becomes obsessed with Gertie (see figure 27). For her part, Gertie sees Christian as nothing more than a "dirty psalm-singing polecat" who desires her

FIGURE 26.
Jonathan Christian and Ezra Crumm look disapprovingly at Gertie in *Dirty Gertie from Harlem U.S.A.* From the author's collection.

as much as she imagines every other man does. Although Christian does not give in to his desires, his resistance does not seem sufficient to make him an admirable example of the fortitude of ministers. In addition, neither Christian nor Crumm can contain his prurient interest in the show that Gertie's troupe is performing at the club. Crumm sneaks around, peeking in on rehearsals and begging Christian to let him see the show so that he can attest to what a sinful exhibition it truly is. Christian forbids him to go but is able to justify his own attendance as God's will. Putting aside his earlier certainty that God would strike him down if he went to "that den of vice," Christian kneels before the bed in his hotel room and prays:

> Oh God, I beseech thee to show me the way. This woman, this sinner, this temptress of men whose flesh is weak. Please Lord, tell me must I stop this dreadful performance, this horrible exhibition of flesh? You know Lord, I'm loath to witness such a spectacle of filth, but if it is thy will, I will slip into the

FIGURE 27.
Jonathan Christian faces temptation when Gertie faints in *Dirty Gertie from Harlem U.S.A.* From the author's collection.

Diamond Palace tonight, unseen, and watch unnoticed this show of lewdness that I may be better able to judge in thy sight. Tell me, oh Lord, must I go?

Yes, Lord, I'm listening.

You want me to go! Then if it is thy will, I shall not disobey. Thank you, oh Lord, thank you. Amen.

Finally, Christian loses all self-control when he attends the performance, mounting the stage, interrupting the proceedings, and slapping Gertie in the face. He likens his actions to Jesus chasing the money changers out of the temple, and he seems particularly incensed at the religious references, such as "Her spirits shout Hallelujah" in the poem two troupe members recite to introduce Gertie's striptease act. In the end, the missionaries do not play a significant role in the progress of the narrative, and they function, in many ways, as comic relief. Gertie's past comes back to kill her—in the person of Al, her former boyfriend—and the ministers simply observe the course of events, presenting no solutions to the question of how the church can interact with the entertainment world in productive ways.

In addition to exploring the conflict between the church and the nightclub, the film comments on another type of commercial enterprise and religious tradition that True Thompson's story posed as a threat to the moral integrity of black communities. In a scene toward the end of the film, Gertie visits Old Hager (Spencer Williams), a "Voodoo woman," to find out what is in store for her.[26] The Voodoo woman's prediction is bleak—a bloody confrontation with a man who is angry with her—and Gertie leaves even more frightened than she had been before the meeting. Viewers familiar with Williams's work would have expected to find him playing a part in the film (as he did in most others he directed), and his performance here provides an especially lively moment. In addition to providing comic relief, this scene investigates the impact of the African-derived religious traditions of many immigrants from the Caribbean on black churches and black communities. It is also possible that the "voodoo" traditions of Rinidad stand in for the conjure practices that southern migrants brought with them to the urban North. But here what Williams presents as problematic is not simply the form of religious practice but its explicit commercialization in ways that connect it to the commercial realm of the nightclub. Old Hager is not a servant of the community but a businesswoman who is feared by most of the residents of the island and who represents a blending of religious and commercial culture that Williams rejects. Though the missionaries do not prove to be straightforward moral exemplars, the film clearly sides with moral standards of Christianity over against the possible social and religious outlets of the nightclub and the "Voodoo" woman.[27]

Other black-audience films in the period that engaged questions about the relationship between black churches, their leaders, and other spheres of public life used clerical characters to assist in the reconciliation of conflicts between these realms of black life. In *Miracle in Harlem*, released in 1948 by Herald Pictures, Rev. Jackson (Creighton Thompson) serves as a bridge between an old-time church culture, associated with the South, and the modern, urban postwar culture of Harlem, represented by Bert (William Greaves),[28] a veteran who is studying for the ministry.[29] The film focuses on a business struggle over Aunt Hattie's (Hilda Offley) candy business that pits Hattie, her niece Julie (Sheila Guyse), and Bert against a large Harlem candy company. Although the story's drama is meant to derive, in large part, from a murder mystery, the religious conflict between Hattie on the one hand and Julie and Bert on the other frames the story. Infirm and unable to leave her home, Hattie hosts Wednesday evening services in her Harlem brownstone at which Rev. Jackson presides, and, while the film does not identify her as a migrant from the South, she appears to be committed to creating the culture of a small, rural church community in her home. The film opens with one of these services and the congregation singing, "Swing Low, Sweet Chariot."[30] Later, Hattie's parlor becomes the site for another religious service when she reveals that she has had a premonition of her own death and insists that Rev. Jackson hold a rehearsal funeral in her living room. She lies in her casket to monitor the proceedings.

Bert and Julie disapprove of Hattie's capitulation to her age and to her premonition, and Bert argues relentlessly that she should be more modern in her approach to her business, her religion, and the world. Hattie's approach to business is as domestic as her creation of an old-time church community in her living room: she operates her candy business from her own kitchen. Her response, typical of her statements on the issue over the course of the film, is, "Now Bert, I'm an old woman. I haven't much longer to live. You can have your modern ideas . . . just leave me alone with my memories . . . my religion."[31] There's no need for a new approach to religion, she argues, because her "ideas have been good enough . . . all these years."[32] Bert, citing his experience in the army and with the chaplain's religious services, insists that "everything moves fast. Even our religious services had to be speeded up. But basically it's the same. It's still the word of the Lord . . . only it has been modernized."[33] Rev. Jackson attempts to resolve the conflict by interpreting Bert's perspective to Hattie, telling her that "[w]hat Bert means is that old methods have changed. . . . People sure think the same but with more advanced ideas." Bert concurs and connects his interest in a modernized religion to social progress and to his plan to modernize her candy business, continuing, "People want to do things now more than ever and religion comes in for its share." Later, when Hattie can think of little more than her funeral rehearsal, she tells Bert and Julie, "[T]he trouble is that people are too much concerned with this world and not the other." Bert pleads with her, arguing, "We're not put on this earth for useless demonstrations of sadness. . . . Clear thinking . . . knowing what's right to do unto others and what's wrong. . . . Bringing a coffin here to rehearse your funeral is not the way HE wants it. . . . HE wants you to live to stay in this world to spread HIS word."

Rev. Jackson, who plays a minor part in the film's narrative, nevertheless serves as a bridge between Hattie's world and Bert and Julie's aspirations for their life together in Harlem, which include commercial developments, racial uplift, and a modern religious life. The minister serves as a business advisor to Julie when she takes responsibility for the candy business, counsels her when she is wrongly arrested for murder, and, although he is opposed to Hattie's plan to hold a rehearsal funeral, carries out her wishes in order to try to bring the older woman into the culture of the urban North. In the end, when Julie is arrested for murder, Hattie does give up her complacent, otherworldly religion, conceding that "maybe [Bert's] way of religion IS better." Her newfound vigor motivates her to catch the real murderer, which she accomplishes by using the coffin in her living room to pretend to be the ghost of the victim.

The 1940 Jubilee Pictures production *Paradise in Harlem* uses a story by the African American actor Frank Wilson to explore some of the moral challenges faced by black stage actors in the period and, like *Miracle in Harlem*, uses a minister as a bridge between religious cultures and commercial culture, in this case the world of entertainment.[34] Lem Anderson (Frank Wilson), the film's central character, struggles with the moral compromises he makes in his work as a blackface comedian. Longing to play Shakespeare's *Othello*, Lem must put his ambitions on hold after he witnesses a gang murder and is forced to leave Harlem. But, as he tells his nephew, what prevents him from realizing his dream is not simply the murder but producers' reluctance to give him a chance to do dramatic acting. Ultimately, the desire of the pastor of a Harlem church to produce a play to "make better entertainment in the community" and provide spiritual uplift allows Lem to return home.

Although the film does work to reconcile the church and one particular performative arena through the production of *Othello*, it draws a clear distinction between acceptable and unacceptable forms of entertainment culture. The nightclubs and cabarets in which Lem performs when he is away from Harlem and touring in the South are marked as morally dangerous. Lem succumbs to the temptations the cabaret world presents, particularly in his excessive drinking. The Follies, Lem's original performing group, and the boardinghouse where many of the performers from the Follies live appear as positive influences, the latter in large measure because of the presence of Mamie (Mamie Smith), a seasoned performer who looks out for other show people.[35] The interaction between the two realms becomes fraught when the director of the church play casts a cabaret performer in the production along with other cast members from the Follies. However, a final resolution comes with the production of the all-black-cast *Othello*, the performance of which takes place in a theater before an audience that contains representatives both of Harlem's church communities and of the neighborhood's nightclub culture. Both prove hostile to the traditional presentation of Shakespeare's work, so Lem and the other cast members, in response to the audience's heckling, begin to deliver their lines in a style reminiscent of a chanted sermon, and the audience soon joins in, providing an accompanying hum that brings a jazz cast to the performance.[36] Moved by the combination of musical sensibilities, one of the "worldly" hecklers calls out in church vernacular, "Sing it, sister, now we're getting somewhere," and a church heckler implores the performers, "Rock, church, rock."[37] The success of the show leads to an offer for Lem to take it to Broadway and to incorporate the musical combination that emerged spontaneously in the church performance in a formal way with the inclusion of a jazz band and a choir.

The ministers in *Miracle in Harlem* and *Paradise in Harlem* play minor roles in the narratives' explorations of engagements between religion and commercial or entertainment culture, but the films' attempts to find a position for clergy in the context of a broad African American social life differentiate them in important ways from the films that critique and marginalize black ministers. *Sunday Sinners* (1941) (see figure 28),[38] a musical comedy from a story by Frank Wilson, places a minister at the center of a conflict between the church and the nightclub in ways similar to Williams's framing of the issue in *Go Down, Death* and *Dirty Gertie from Harlem U.S.A.* but presents a different outcome in which the minister negotiates a compromise between the two. The film contains elements of a straightforward, sermonizing meditation on the evils of worldliness, but it blurs many of the boundaries between the church and the world and refuses to embrace stark prohibitions against commercial entertainments. Whereas Williams often uses film to promote a particular religious sensibility, *Sunday Sinners'* relationship to Christianity is ambiguous, and religious elements appear alongside stories that include gangsters, cabaret numbers, and comedy routines. The film's reliance on many of the conventions of the musical genre in particular facilitates a conclusion that resolves the tensions between church and secular world and, in this case, provides the space for the minister to be the central agent in the hard-won compromise.

The story in *Sunday Sinners* moves between the Club Harlem and a black church, both located in a small town, and pits different constituencies within the church against one another and the church's members against "the café people." The film opens in the Club Harlem, where Gene Aiken (Norman Astwood), its owner, aligns himself from the outset with the church people, insisting to his wife and business partner, Corinne (Edna Mae Harris), that it is wrong for the town's young people to be in the club on a Sunday night. Corinne, who we later find out is having an affair with her chauffeur, consorting with gangsters, and even considering killing to gain complete control of the club, insists that business is business. In the church world, Rev. Hampton (Earl Sydnor), pastor of a Methodist church, sits with his family in their living room and discusses the problem of the town's young people spending Sunday nights

FIGURE 28.
Poster for *Sunday Sinners*. Courtesy John Kisch, Separate Cinema
Archive.

dancing instead of at the church. Their home is modest but neat, all the family members are dressed conservatively, and the teenage children are attentive to their elders. Rev. Hampton, in formal, staid speech, asserts that he does not oppose dancing in general but simply cannot support the activity on Sunday nights. He concludes that it is not the young people's fault but "the condition itself. As long as these places are open, our youth will be tempted." The family decides that the best approach will be for Rev. Hampton to direct his next sermon to "those café people."

The film includes two long segments set in the church where Hampton preaches, providing some of the most explicit commentary in race movies of the period on the relationship of the church to the commercial arena of the nightclub (see figure 29). The first, and longer of the two, begins with an external shot of a large church and cuts to the interior, where we find the congregation listening to Rev. Hampton and the choir sing. This introduction to the sermon immediately sets *Sunday Sinners* apart from films like Williams's religious melodramas in that the choir sings a musical number written for the film rather than a traditional hymn or spiritual. The minister begins his sermon:

> Today the forces for evil have struck up business at the city gates. And it is our Christian duty to cry out against these sinners. It has been said that without vision the people perish. There can be no greater vision than to fight against the forces that seek to lead our youth astray. They call them nightclubs, cafés. But as they are run in this town they are nothing more than palaces of sin. I ask that we pray that the café people come to the realization that the youth of any community needs religious guidance for good citizenship and that they, the café people, cease in their effort to tempt our youth from their Christian and Sabbath duties.

Rev. Hampton's sermon employs a formula found in many race movies, the contrast between an idyllic rural environment and the sinful influences of urban life. In this case, however, he does not present the city or its commercial culture as inherently evil. His appeal to the proprietors of the cafés to recognize the need to cultivate responsible citizenship in young people marks a significant moment in the film and one that, as we will see shortly, distinguishes Rev. Hampton from some of the fundamentalist members of his church. Thus, while his argument is partly theological, it is also largely sociological, focusing on the political and social needs of the community in the modern world. In contrast to his sociological diagnosis of the city's lures, his discussion of the merits of rural life notably does not, like so many race film discourses, focus on what it offers in terms of forming community. Hampton provides, instead, a theological justification of the inherent worth of the countryside, imploring his congregation to "visit God's café." "Go out into the open country among the birds, the trees and the flowers. Breathe in the good fresh air and come back with your mind refreshed," he tells the congregation.

FIGURE 29.
Rev. Hampton preaches against "the café people" in *Sunday Sinners*. Courtesy John Kisch, Separate Cinema Archive.

Rev. Hampton's second sermon, also directed against "those café people," leads to the film's conclusion and the resolution of the tension between the church and the nightclub. Where his first sermon merely encouraged church members to stay away from the corrupting environment of the nightclub, his second sermon enjoins them to become crusaders in a great holy battle. He emphasizes to the congregation that "at this very moment when our youngsters should be here listening to the word of God, that vile and corrupting gang has got them there in sin and degradation." Rev. Hampton continues, "We've stood just about enough. It's time for us to shed this humble cloak for one of righteous indignation. We should roll up our sleeves and, with the Good Book in one hand, power and might will come to the other. With this hand David killed Goliath; with this hand Samson slew the Philistines; with this hand old Joshua fought the battle of Jericho." The sermon impels the congregation to join Rev. Hampton on a march to the city and directly into the Club Harlem, and in the end Gene and Rev. Hampton strike a deal for a clean, wholesome place of amusement.

The film engages questions of class status and theological orientation as part of the discussion of urban versus rural and of secular entertainments versus the world of the church, and it raises these questions in particularly gendered ways. Rev. Hampton's commitment to confronting "the café people" does not prove sufficient to overcome the criticism and scorn of the board members of his church for his unorthodox approach to his work. Two female board members and a male deacon confront him on a number of occasions, and in the film's presentation of these incidents we see brief discussions of class issues within the church community. The two unnamed "sisters" completely dominate the stuttering deacon in the exchanges. They harangue Rev. Hampton for allowing church members to participate in a range of secular and commercial entertainments, most especially for permitting the men's club to play cards, for allowing a church club to conduct a raffle to raise funds, and for encouraging "devilish youngsters fighting and knocking each other around in their underwear." The minister explains that he supports wholesome exercise and supervised entertainments for the young people, and one of the women counters that the boys should be out working instead. The discussion continues, growing more heated, as Hampton underscores his sense of the relationship between church and citizenship, telling the women that "those youngsters are the very foundation of our church, our race." One sister insists that "Race and Church are going to have a mighty weak foundation," and the other threatens Rev. Hampton, promising, "We're going to take you in charge for your laxitiveness [*sic*]." Here the film associates these women's rigid theological approach to modern entertainments with their class status, marked as below that of Rev. Hampton and his family, because of both their fundamentalism and their lack of education. The film ridicules these women for their beliefs and portrays them as inappropriate representatives of black religiosity because of their theological conservatism.

In addition to the class conflict between the women on the church board and the minister, the film sets out a class conflict between the Club Harlem, an upscale club with mild entertainments—the music is not marked as "black" and the dancing is modest—and the "7–11" club, a small juke joint run by Bootsie (Sydney Easton) and Mamie (Mamie Smith). Eli, Rev. Hampton's brother-in-law, is a regular at the "7–11," drinking to excess and constantly talking about just needing to "get a little capital" in order to get some scheme or other off the ground. Inspired by Rev. Hampton's charge to "visit God's café," Bootsie and Eli go out into the country and discover a type of mud that they eventually use to make an expensive beauty product. Whereas at the film's end the Club Harlem is saved by the elimination of Corinne and her gangster friends from the scene, the "7–11" club and its regulars cannot be redeemed in the context of their own environment. It takes the success of Eli's scheme and newfound money to incorporate the men and their wives, somewhat uncomfortably, into the upscale world of the Club Harlem. Even more problematic is the element within Bootsie and Eli's story that involves Chin (Al Young), a Chinese laundry owner, who enters into their scheme and is, in fact, the one to identify the mud as a potentially valuable commodity. Clearly he is a successful businessman in the town's black community, but the film renders his character in unappealing stereotype, and while the lower-class characters are incorporated into Club Harlem and the church at the film's conclusion Chin remains inassimilable and on the margins of all visible social worlds in the film.

Sunday Sinners stands in contrast to films like Spencer Williams's religious melodramas in its reliance on the structures of the Hollywood musical, and it is this generic location, in part, that enables the reconciliation of the competing realms of church and nightclub. Susan Hayward has noted that the musical is, almost by necessity, a self-referential genre that devotes a great deal of attention to justifying its own existence "as, for example, with the putting-on-a-show musical."[39] *Sunday Sinners* justifies its reliance on the structure of the musical by setting part of the story in a nightclub and, within that venue, focusing on the preparations for an amateur contest to choose the club's new featured act. The film's use of the strategies of the musical genre does not remain confined to the nightclub, however, and musical elements appear as well within the arena of the church. Recall that the song that introduces Rev. Hampton's first sermon is a musical number rather than a church hymn. It is important for the film's conclusion (a rapprochement between church and nightclub) that the musical also inhabit the space of the church. As various theorists of film genres have noted, the musical emphasizes the comparative pairing of different and seemingly irreconcilable opposites, and even while resolving the tensions on which the narrative rests the genre necessarily obscures other elements of social conflict.[40] Having contained the various dangers that Corinne embodies, Rev. Hampton and Gene come to an agreement that permits room for both the church and the Club Harlem to coexist in peace, thus resolving what at first seemed to be an intractable conflict. Other tensions in evidence in this film, including profound gender and class conflicts as well as different approaches to worship style, do not get resolved but are merely masked by the resolution of tension between church and nightclub. Nevertheless, the audience leaves assured that commitment to the church and enjoyment of secular entertainments can be reconciled, and it has been aided in imagining the ways African American clergy could work to effect this new relationship.

One cannot help noticing that the construction and reconstruction of African American religious leadership in relation to urban commercial culture take place in particularly gendered ways in many of the genre race movies that take up religious themes. Certainly, struggles over women's access to religious leadership have not been confined to black Christian contexts; they predate the period in which these films were produced and are indeed ongoing in many religious contexts in the United States. However, the future of the ministry in black communities is of particular concern in these films, and time and again audiences are treated to models of ministers who are useful, productive "race men" or counterexamples of unscrupulous, uneducated, selfish preachers. Although many of these films place black women in central roles in their religious communities and present them as moral exemplars, they also insist on defining the limits of black women's spiritual power. The marking of the church women as ignorant and fundamentalist in *Sunday Sinners* bars them from any kind of leadership in the world of the film. Although countering the relentlessly negative representations of African American religiosity in Hollywood film with a complex range of images, race movies remain invested in the traditional institutional structures of black communities. The films valorize black women's roles in the church in ways never seen in mainstream American popular culture while at the same time recognizing that black churches are not the sole component of the black public sphere. What they do not do is present the possibility of black women as religious leaders within the changing institution of the black church. The message of many of these films concerning the relationship between religion, gender, and black commercial culture positions women either as debilitating in their predominance in the sphere of the church or as representative of an immorality unleashed through participation in commercial culture.

Although it is impossible to chart a straightforward progression in the treatment of the relationships between churches and their ministers and popular and commercial cultures, many films from the 1940s seem to be less interested in exposing the faults of unscrupulous ministers, as in Oscar Micheaux's early films and *The Black King,* than in exploring the place of religious individuals and institutions in the broader field of black social life. The way *Miracle in Harlem* and *Sunday Sinners* position clergy as mediators between churches and the arenas of entertainment and commercial cultures suggests a community interest in establishing a productive relationship between the two realms of black public life. Indeed, these filmic discussions reflect the involvement of some black clergy in the world of movie production and exhibition and their service on local film censorship boards. Spencer Williams, who looms as such an important figure in the engagement of these issues by both religious race films and the various genre films, provided yet another view that highlights this trend in his film *Of One Blood* (1944).[41] Williams wrote the screenplay for this film, which could easily be read as both an engagement of the broad issues of religion and African American social and political life and a reworking of the representational traditions established in the earlier Hollywood all-black-cast films *Hallelujah* and *The Green Pastures*. The film covers a much longer time span and is far more epic in scope than any of his other works, and Williams places his revision of Hollywood representations of African American religion in service of a call for unity among African Americans. In the unified community for which this film makes a plea, Williams presents a broad view of African American social and economic life that cuts across class lines and values the contributions of men and women, as well as of secular and religious activists.

Of One Blood follows the lives of brothers who suffer the poverty of the Depression in their childhoods, become orphaned, and, along with many other African Americans in the period, migrate north and settle in a city. The boys, Zebedee, Zacharia, and Zion, are the children of Zeke and Zenobia Ellis, simple farmers who live in a modest cabin. Although it is impossible to say for certain that Williams intended viewers to draw a connection between his presentation of the Ellis family and the family at the center of King Vidor's story in the 1929 Metro-Goldwyn-Mayer film *Hallelujah*, some of the parallels are striking. That the father in *Of One Blood* and *Hallelujah*'s main character are both named Zeke is noteworthy, as are the similar constitutions of the two families, each consisting of many sons.[42] Williams's visual representation of the family's modest cabin also recalls Vidor's depiction of the home of Zeke's family. Despite such similarities between the two films, the differences are striking, and it is in these differences that one can see Williams's interest in engaging and reorienting the legacy of Hollywood's earlier black-cast films. In contrast to the world that Vidor creates for the family, in which they are happy laborers in the cotton fields who find trouble only when they themselves create it, the Ellises fall victim to a natural disaster: they are made homeless and the children eventually orphaned by a flood. Here Williams emphasizes the impact of external forces on the life possibilities of his characters rather than arguing that African Americans' social status in America is determined by their eternal childlike qualities. In establishing the foundation for the story that follows, the film does not put forward the racism of whites as the primary cause of the family's suffering, but neither does it exclude whites from the frame, as was the case in the Hollywood black-cast films and in many black-audience films. In the world Vidor creates in *Hallelujah*, the family of cotton pickers presumably works land that belongs to a white landowner, but he does not appear in the frame, nor do any other whites. Williams rarely included whites in his films, but in *Of One Blood* the Ellis family have a good relationship with the white local dry goods merchant, who gives them two mules to help them reach higher ground and avoid the flood, and two of the boys, after losing their parents, receive assistance from white nurses from the Red Cross and a white army captain. Thus, in engaging and reworking the representational tradition that Paula Massood refers to as "the antebellum idyll," Williams locates his characters in a social world that is broader than the confining all-black world of the earlier Hollywood films.[43]

Williams uses a framing device in *Of One Blood* that recalls the 1936 Warner Bros. all-black-cast film *The Green Pastures* but, as with his engagement of films like *Hallelujah,* reorients the tradition away from presenting African Americans as a peculiar subculture in American society in favor of a universal vision that provides the basis for a strong argument for full citizenship. The film begins with a shot of a large book with the title "Of One Blood," printed on the cover, recalling the similar shot early on in *The Green Pastures.* With an instrumental version of Stephen Foster's "Old Folks at Home" (Swanee River) in the background, the book opens, revealing a "Foreword," and a male voice reads the text: "Since the beginning, rivers have beckoned to man and especially so in the deep regions of the Southland, where the fascination of the great flood waters has become a heritage among a people who are naturally inclined to deal with the passing hours with a complacent smile even in the face of supreme adversity." Also recalling the context of *The Green Pastures* that focuses on God and angels observing humanity from heaven, the opening sequence in *Of One Blood* takes us to the "Hall of Human Records," where the Keeper of the Books, an ancient black man with a long beard and dressed in a white robe, records the events in the lives of humans. The narration continues: "For, truly, as the ancients have said, 'It is written.' Here in the Hall of Human Records is the Keeper of the Books, eternally aware of the fate of all, to whom the destinies of the humblest of the human race are as engrossing as those of conquerors. Thus it is entirely fitting that we pause to scan a single page in the lives of one of millions of peaceful families which dwell along the river, serene in their enjoyment of simple things daily renewed." Even as Williams identifies an inherent tendency of the black characters in his film to deal with life's difficulties in a dignified way, he continually reminds his viewers of the broader human dimensions of the story.

Having established both the specific contours of the Ellis family's life and the broader context of human struggles against the forces of nature, Williams's story ranges over many years, following Zebedee and Zion, who become orphaned by the flood and separated from their brother Zachariah. The two boys move north, go to school, and find jobs. Twenty-six years after the time of the film's first action, they have taken up careers, Zebedee as a police officer and Zion as a lawyer. Together, they find themselves working to end the reign of a local bootlegger and gangster. The film does not address religious issues directly, but, in a scene in which members of the community gather to formulate a plan to rid the town of bootlegged liquor, Williams presents his vision of a united African American community. Mr. Jordan, publisher and editor of the black newspaper and Zion's father-in-law to be, speaks at the meeting, identifying various people present and describing their contribution to the plan to address the community's problems:

And that, my friends, is exactly why you have been asked to come here.
There is among you a minister of the Gospel; the denomination is not important because there is only one God. President of a woman's club; women must be given consideration in these matters because no race or nation can ever hope to be greater than its women. Then a nurse, whose duty is to administer to our physical ills; a teacher, upon whose shoulders rest the responsibility of educating our children; and a retired businessman who is familiar with all the ramifications of barter and trade. The young, but efficient, attorney-at-law to fight our legal battles; the society leader whose association with culture lends color to our efforts. A domestic worker, whose association and contact with other peoples of other races is a valuable asset. The housewife and mother, the guardian angel of our homes; the laborer who represents the hewers of wood and drawers of water that are so plentiful among us; and last, but not least, a representative of our younger generation upon whose heads will be heaped the fires of racial retribution unless as a people we get together and do something about this crucial situation.

Jordan goes on to emphasize the need for action and not just words.

Although the community meeting is set in 1941, Williams's *Of One Blood* was produced in 1944 and speaks to issues of race and citizenship in light of the nation's experiences in World War II. The film's resolution, in which the city's chief bootlegger is revealed to be Zebedee and Zion's lost brother Zachariah, raises themes that Williams engages in both his religious and his genre films, particularly the just punishment of the sinful. Wesley Hill (Spencer Williams), who met Zebedee and Zion just after their parents died and who helped them begin their journey north before becoming separated from them, reappears as an FBI agent working undercover in Zachariah's organization. When Zachariah, who does not know that the police officer Ellis is his brother, is about to kill him, he is "prevented from slaying unknowingly his brother," as the narrator tells us, by Wesley. As the narrator sums up this portion of the story, "But it is written, 'The wages of sin is death.'" In addition to the religious theme, Williams's conclusion to the brothers' story emphasizes both the ability of the city's African American community to deal with its own problems and avoid "the fires of racial retribution" and the investment of its members in the American project. In the scene in which newspaper editor Jordan calls for unity, the minister rises in support of his call and points to both the problems and the promises of America for African Americans, telling those gathered that he has read a great deal "having to do with miscarriage of justice as far as races are concerned, and I am particularly interested, as I know you are, in having this country of mine go on record—yes, historical record forever—as being a country where all men might receive justice at the law and in the law." Finally, Williams connects the promise of America to a divine plan, as the film ends with the narrator reciting first from Acts 17: "God made the world and all things therein. Seeing that he is Lord of heaven and earth, he dwelleth not in temples made with hands. God made of one blood all nations of man to dwell in all the face of the earth and hath determined the bounds of their habitation."[44] And, with a veiled reference to events in Europe, the narrator's final words are from Acts 20: "wherefore I take you to record this day that I am pure from the blood of all men."[45] Those viewers familiar with the text would have been able to place this verse in the context of Paul's counsel to the leaders of the church at Ephesus to care for and build the church, as well as his warning "For I know this, that after my departing shall grievous wolves enter in among you, not sparing the flock. Also of your own selves shall men arise, speaking perverse things, to draw away disciples after them."[46]

In engaging questions of the place of African American ministers in the broad context of black social life in *Of One Blood*, Williams successfully orients viewers away from the Hollywood tropes of the childish subculture of African American religions. Instead, he presents a vision of a unified and integrated social life in which clergy and businessmen, men and women, working class and middle class all work together, both for the benefit of the community and as citizens of the nation. In the context of the war, African Americans would raise a range of significant questions that moved well beyond the issue of the place of African American ministers in black communities, and media approaches to these issues—in Hollywood studio films, black-audience films, and government propaganda—would prove critical to the discourses about religion, race, and citizenship in the period.

FIVE

"A Long, Long Way"

*Religion and African American
Wartime Morale*

In the winter of 1942, Truman K. Gibson, assistant to the civilian aide to the Secretary of War, enlisted the aid of Clark M. Davis in reviewing the coverage by the major newsreels of issues related to African American soldiers.[1] Davis was responsible for booking films for Abe Lichtman, the white owner of a movie theater chain that catered to black audiences.[2] In March of that year, Davis forwarded to Gibson the continuity sheets provided by the studios for a news item about the Army's 41st Engineering Regiment at Fort Bragg, North Carolina. MGM's "News of the Day" advertised the newsreel with the description, "Crack Colored Engineers Sing at Work! Negro spirituals become marching songs for the 41st Regiment at Fort Bragg, and the unit throws up a bridge in record time just to strut its stuff." Universal's newsreel promoted the segment with the description, "Soldiers Sing as they Work— Negro soldiers of the 41st Engineers indulge in a little 'spiritual' harmony as they build bridge across a river."[3] Davis expressed concern that, of the four national newsreels that covered the story, only Fox Movietone addressed it in a straightforward manner, with the advertising line, "Colored Army Engineers build a bridge in maneuvers at Ft. Bragg."[4] Nevertheless, Davis himself chose to exhibit one of the more problematic newsreels that featured the engineers, prompting a protest from Thomas W. Young, the business manager of the black weekly *Norfolk Journal and Guide*. Young wrote to Davis, "'The Singing Engineers' is a caricature and, in substance, a dishonest job of reporting. These United States soldiers were shown at their job of constructing bridges, all the while purporting to be singing Negro spirituals and work songs. I do not believe that army discipline would permit soldiers on duty to perform in the manner which Paramount, by trick photography and sound effects, purported to show them to the American public. It was an injustice to the United States Army, an insult to the Negro race, and anything but a contribution to the science of reporting."[5] Young urged Davis to lodge a protest with Paramount about the coverage.[6]

This by now entirely predictable and familiar image of happy black laborers singing spirituals appeared in various forms on movie screens even as the War Department and the Office of War Information (OWI) were turning their attention to what many understood to be the problem of "Negro morale."[7] In March of 1942, the same month that the representation of the 41st Engineering Regiment in the newsreels came under fire by some African Americans, Theodore M. Berry, African American liaison officer in the OWI, produced "Blue Print of Program for Strengthening Negro Morale in the War Effort." Berry called attention to the disjuncture for African Americans between the discourse about the war as being "genuinely prosecuted for practical democratic principles" and the reality of second-class citizenship at home and of European colonialism in Africa and Asia.[8] In laying out his blueprint for raising morale, Berry identified a number of "sore spots" for African Americans, including segregation in the army, the relegation of black men in the navy to menial labor, black men's lack of access to service in the marines, discrimination in the workforce at home, and the segregation of blood donations by the Red Cross.[9] Wrapping up the list of grievances, Berry wrote: "*Jim Crow* generally— practices in all phases of civilian and governmental life which embarrass, irritate and remind Negroes of their race and that they are not recognized or treated as American citizens generally."[10] Why, then, those black leaders who considered the question of morale asked themselves, should African American men and women participate in a war effort aimed at achieving the liberty of some while they themselves continued to live under the strictures of segregation and racism? Yet for many there was no more pressing issue than fighting against discrimination at home in the particular context of the war against fascism abroad. To this end, the *Pittsburgh Courier* launched the "Double V" campaign—victory abroad and at home—in February of 1942, inaugurating it with the declaration: "We, as colored Americans, are determined to protect our country, our form of government and the freedoms which we cherish for ourselves and the rest of the world, therefore we have adopted the Double 'V' war cry—victory over our enemies on the battlefields abroad. Thus in our fight for freedom we wage a two-pronged attack against our enslavers at home and those abroad who would enslave us. WE HAVE A STAKE IN THIS FIGHT. . . . WE ARE

AMERICANS TOO!"[11] Other black publications joined in the campaign to stimulate the commitment of African Americans to the war even as they kept attention focused on conditions at home. Charlotta A. Bass, editor of the *California Eagle*, emphasized in an open letter to the National Association for the Advancement of Colored People (NAACP) on the occasion of its thirty-third annual conference in July of 1942 that African Americans should see their goal as "One Victory! One Fight!" "Our full participation in the anti-Hitler war effort must be based upon more than the calculated selection of the lesser of two evils," she wrote. "There is no such choice. In joining the noble hosts which assault the Nazi armies, we do not postpone the battle against our oppressors at home until we have liquidated a common foe. NO! We are engaged in ONE ANTI-FASCIST STRUGGLE. It is an immediate, direct and shattering blow at the very institutions WITHIN AMERICA which have been the source of our misery."[12]

In seeking to address a range of issues that arose in this period, particularly having to do with both the participation of African Americans in the war and their place in the nation's postwar future, some African Americans turned to various forms of mass media to shape and reshape public perceptions of race.[13] African Americans participated in the production of several films in this period, including the army orientation film *The Negro Soldier* (1944) and the black-audience films *Marching On* (1943), *Fighting Americans* (1943), and *We've Come a Long, Long Way* (1944), that were aimed at mobilizing the support of black communities for the war effort and emphasizing to white America that African American loyalty demanded the extension of full citizenship rights.[14] At the same time that black artists and intellectuals were using film in relation to the war effort in particular, they had to contend with ongoing issues in Hollywood with regard to representations of African Americans. Walter White, executive secretary of the NAACP, took on Hollywood in 1942, arguing that "the matter of treatment of the Negro in the motion pictures [is] of such importance that it takes rank over some other phases of our work."[15] Introduced to studio executives and actors by Wendell Wilkie, recently defeated Republican presidential candidate and at that time chairman of the board at Twentieth Century-Fox, White organized both individual meetings and a large gathering in the summer of 1942 in which he called for Hollywood to provide more realistic images of African Americans than those currently presented in the movies.[16]

But this campaign did not meet with approval from many actors who had labored in the Hollywood system and in the race movie industry for many years. Clarence Muse, who had served as the head of the Los Angeles Branch of the NAACP and was a well-known actor, penned a passionate response to White's campaign, emphasizing the lack of consultation with the actors themselves. "We feel that if an organization like the NAACP is sincere in its fight," he wrote, "they should work it out with the moving force of Hollywood, the Actors, through its guild, and that when the meeting with producers becomes necessary, their representatives should be there to protect and advise the true picture from the actors' view."[17] Muse was even more incensed by what he understood to be White's vision for improved representations of blacks in Hollywood film. "Now comes [White's] attitude: Purpose Good, Formula Bad. In order to clean up the matter of wrong done by characters that make the world think that the Negro group is a bunch of careless, illiterate porters, waiters, mammies and share-croppers, they should be done completely without dialect. There should be only a few Black-skinned Negroes, more browns and even more Mulattoes. The boys with their hair straightened will give a better social picture and all the pictures should have the Negro Lawyer, Doctor and Architect and, above all, don't have them too black. This is a reaction that is being broadcast throughout Hollywood circles since the meeting. The Actor must now refuse to play characters other than those mentioned. In other words, this business must be 'whitewashed.'"[18] Muse insisted that dialect delivered by working-class characters could be positive if the characters were "noble." For example, he insisted, "Paul Robeson, who has refused more roles than any other artist in America, when it does not measure up to his ideals, has this advantage, he does not make pictures his business. It is only a side line. Yet he plays a field hand in Tennessee in 'Tales of Manhattan' and is happy to say in dialect, 'I'm goin' to take this money, and buy a tractor. Goin' to buy up all the land' and looking around at hundreds of poor Negroes, he says with great determination, 'we will work together, share alike. There ain't goin' to be no more rich and no more poor.' This is pure ideology, in dialect. Is he to be called 'Uncle Tom' by Walter White?"[19]

Throughout the war years, religion would prove central to the struggle over the morale of African Americans as well as the effort to transform Hollywood representations of black life and culture. With the return of black-cast Hollywood films with religious themes—most notably MGM's *Cabin in the Sky* (1943) but also Twentieth Century-Fox's *Tales of Manhattan* (1944)— the question of the relationship between black religious thought and practice and the demand for full citizenship rights would again come to the fore for black artists, intellectuals, and religious leaders, as well as the general public. Similarly, the inclusion of religious themes in the morale-raising documentaries *The Negro Soldier* and *We've Come a Long, Long Way* moved viewers to imagine military service as a sacred act of black manhood that should rightly result in African Americans' full inclusion as Americans. Although media approaches to these questions during the war years considered a range of issues, representations of religious commitments contributed to discourses about black morale and citizenship in important ways.

What Muse failed to mention in his lauding review of Paul Robeson's performance in the 1942 Twentieth Century-Fox production *Tales of Manhattan* is that the film relied heavily on conventional Hollywood interpretations of the simplicity of black religious thought and on common visual tropes that have traditionally connected religious practice to the social and political subordination of African Americans.[20] Indeed, Robeson himself disavowed the final product shortly before the film's release, concluding that, despite his attempts to change the film during the production phase, "in the end it turned out to be the same old thing—the Negro solving his problem by singing his way to glory. This is very offensive to my people. It makes the Negro child-like and innocent and is in the old plantation tradition."[21] Hollywood's continued reliance on representations of African Americans, in Robeson's words, as "plantation hallelujah shouters" and its capitulation to the box-office interests of the South convinced Robeson to wash his hands of the American film industry.[22] Despite Robeson's public protest against *Tales of Manhattan*'s perpetuation of problematic tropes in representing African American religious thought and culture, pickets at the film's opening in Los Angeles, and many negative reviews in the black press and leftist white papers, it proved both quite popular with white audiences and influential in motivating Hollywood studios to take a similar narrative approach to subsequent films.

Tales of Manhattan follows a men's full-dress tailcoat that is cursed by its fabric cutter upon his learning that he has been fired. The coat's various owners experience dramatic life changes, some positive and some negative, in the course of wearing the coat and then pass it on or discard it. The film received considerable attention for the decisions of the producers, Boris Morros and S. P. Eagle, to connect a series of five unrelated stories through the device of the tailcoat, to sign a large cast of stars that included Paul Robeson, Ethel Waters, Eddie Anderson, Charles Boyer, Charles Laughton, Rita Hayworth, Henry Fonda, Ginger Rogers, Elsa Lanchester, and Cesar Romero, and to engage as many as twenty writers to produce the script.[23] Although Morros had originally imagined using a different director for each segment, he eventually engaged the French director Julien Duvivier as the film's sole director. Critics lauded the stylistic innovation of the "omnibus of short stories"[24] and the producers' daring in signing such a large cast of stars. Coverage in the black press during the production phase was equally positive, indicating a great deal of pride that stars of the caliber of Paul Robeson, Ethel Waters, and Eddie Anderson were involved in this innovative film project.[25]

If the film's conceit of the life of a tailcoat in Manhattan might have led black observers of Hollywood to imagine that the sequence featuring Robeson, Waters, and Anderson would focus on some aspect of black urban life, they were to be sorely disappointed.[26] The final segment of *Tales of Manhattan* in which these actors appear represents a sharp contrast to all that comes before in the film, in terms of both locale and visual sensibility. At this juncture in the narrative, the coat is being worn by Costello (J. Carrol Naish), a white thief who has just robbed a gambling club of $50,000 and who, along with his partner in crime, is on his way to Mexico in a small, open cockpit plane. When sparks from the dash set the coat on fire, Costello flings it from the plane with $43,000 still in the pockets. Luke (Paul Robeson) and Esther (Ethel Waters) are working in the fields in some unnamed locale far south of Manhattan, and they see the coat as it falls from the sky. Esther immediately interprets it as having come from God. "Can't you see the lightning put the mark of the Lord on this thing?"[27] she exclaims, insisting on the money's supernatural rather than mundane origins. The couple decides to bring the coat to Rev. Lazarus (Eddie Anderson) so that he can distribute the money to those in the community who have prayed for specific things (see figure 30). Esther is particularly concerned that they determine that members of their community have actually *prayed* to God rather than simply *wished* for the things for which they desire to use the money. Indeed, even Rev. Lazarus must decline to take some of the money to buy a new horse and buggy after admitting that he did not pray for them as he prayed for money to fix the church's roof. Everyone receives money for the relatively modest things for which they prayed, and the community is left with $41,545.50, which Luke proposes they use to buy the land they currently farm and liberate themselves from what is, presumably, a sharecropping situation. Esther reminds them that they have not consulted "old Christopher" about his prayers, and even though everyone but Esther believes that Christopher is not a praying man Luke goes to visit him. Luke's fear that Christopher will have prayed for something that will deplete the remaining funds is evident. It turns out that Christopher has prayed for something, but only for a scarecrow, and Luke delivers the coat that was once worn by elite white New Yorkers to what is, the film implies, its final home on a scarecrow in old Christopher's field.

This final segment of *Tales of Manhattan* presents a hybrid vision of black life and religious thought, consolidating a range of highly developed and frequently circulated tropes of black religious culture—the source of Robeson's discomfort with the

FIGURE 30.
Esther and Luke discuss the money they found with Rev. Lazarus in *Tales of Manhattan*. From the author's collection.

final product—at the same time that it contains the seeds of a shift in representations of African Americans. In keeping with established Hollywood conventions for presenting African Americans as naturally and often excessively religious, the film contains characters who come to interpret the coat with its pockets filled with money as delivered from heaven in answer to their prayers. Esther's faith is profound, and it is ultimately her religiously grounded vision of how the money should be distributed that determines the community's course of action, even though she is suspicious of the morality of anyone having so much money. Her insistence that they understand the money's arrival as a positive religious event quickly draws in most members of the community and supersedes Rev. Lazarus's initial response that the money might have come from "down there." In recalling the sources of her interest in playing Esther, Ethel Waters indicated that it was, in fact, this religious element that proved most appealing and not the opportunity to work with an all-star cast. She wrote in her memoir that "I became interested only after they told me the story they were using for our episode. Realizing what a large part God plays in our [African Americans'] daily lives, the producers were eager to inject religion in our part of the picture."[28]

FIGURE 31.
Rev. Lazarus, Esther, and Luke distribute the money in *Tales of Manhattan*. From the author's collection.

Luke's interpretation of the significance of the money for this small black community is in accord with Rev. Lazarus's reading, in part. Even after Esther invokes Moses's faith in the manna from heaven to try to convince Rev. Lazarus that the money comes from God, the minister finds it difficult to lend the appropriate religious interpretation to the situation and is even chastised and corrected by a child. Committed to using the money regardless of its origins, Lazarus says casually to those gathered in the church, "Blessed are the poor." The conclusion that the community's members draw about the religious import of the money's arrival remains the most powerful one, despite Rev. Lazarus's attempt to tie it firmly to secular concerns. Nicodemus, a boy who has been helping Rev. Lazarus with the roof, reminds him that the Scripture says "poor in *spirit*." Agitated, Lazarus shouts back, "It all comes to the same thing. When you're poor, you're poor all over." Luke emphasizes that they are poor and that this large amount of money will enable them to leave behind the daily struggles that sharecropping entails and obtain the modest things that would make their lives easier—carpenter's tools, a blanket with no holes, shoes, and a bag of flour, for instance (see figure 31). Luke's vision for the community moves well beyond the

FIGURE 32.
Luke leads the community in song in *Tales of Manhattan*. Courtesy of Photofest.

acquisition of small things, however, and emphasizes the possibility of collective own-
ership of the land and control of the cotton and corn crops they raise. But, probably
to Robeson's dismay, the socialist vision his character puts forward remains firmly
anchored in the otherworldly orientation so common in representations of African
American Christianity. The film ends with Robeson standing on a hill just outside
old Christopher's cabin and, with his arms raised, singing:

> Make way for the glory day,
> No more trouble and woe.
> There'll be angels flying from the sky to the Jubilee
> in our heavenly home.[29]

Esther and Rev. Lazarus stand at the front of the group as they regard and listen to
Luke. Esther appears especially pleased by what seems to be a spiritual transformation on Luke's part as indicated by his adoption of a religious interpretation of events
and acceptance of God's mysterious workings (see figure 32). The community joins

in the song as Luke moves to stand with them. The film's final image is of the scarecrow and a plow shot from below and set against illuminated clouds, thereby emphasizing the community's consensus by this point that recent events have been divinely guided. This sense becomes further underscored by the casting of the Hall Johnson Choir in most of the parts of community members who sing along with Robeson at the film's end. By 1942, the choir had become closely associated with Broadway and Hollywood presentations of African American religious music, having established that reputation largely through its participation in the various productions of *The Green Pastures*. Indeed, the status of Johnson's choir as authoritative and authentic interpreters of black religious music is marked by the billing in *Tales of Manhattan* of the members appearing "as themselves." Robeson's brief exclamations about how the money will facilitate the construction of a community where there are no more rich or poor and where people "get what we shares" are finally drowned out by the song about a far-off heavenly home.[30]

The placement of this segment at the end of *Tales of Manhattan*, the geographic shift from Manhattan, and the stark and dreary set constructed to represent the unidentified southern rural environment all promote an understanding of American national identity in which African Americans exist simply as a soothing appendage to American life. *New York Times* film critic Bosley Crowther found this segment "strangely remote"[31] at best, and extremely hackneyed and undercutting of the film's message (as unsophisticated as it was) at worst. Crowther wrote, "The last episode—or the epilogue—is surprisingly inconsistent with the rest, not only in its locale but in its slippery philosophy. The coat . . . is found by a group of poor Negroes, who turn out, conveniently, to be Paul Robeson, Ethel Waters, 'Rochester,' and most of the Hall Johnson Choir. After a bit of antebellum hallelujahing they split the swag righteously and turn the coat into a scarecrow."[32] *PM*, a white-run leftist paper, also noted how the final segment of *Tales of Manhattan* conformed to established stereotypes in American popular and visual culture, emphasizing the film's "utter failure to visualize Negroes in any realer terms than as a *Green Pastures* flock in a Thomas Hart Benton setting."[33] The black press was even harsher in its criticism, as in the case of a *New York Amsterdam News* headline that charged, "Paul Robeson, Ethel Waters Let Us Down." The review went on to express great disappointment that Robeson seemed to be abandoning the "battle for recognition of the Negro as a true artist" and indicted both Robeson and Waters for accepting the roles in *Tales of Manhattan*. "We have a battle to fight," the unidentified author insisted, "and it's not solely with producers. It's with our Ethel Waters and Paul Robesons who, we believe, can lead the way by refusing roles like the 'Luke' and 'Esther' of 'Tales of Manhattan.'"[34]

Interestingly, in reflecting on the experience some years later, Ethel Waters revised the film's narrative, as well as her own character's part in the story, to bring Esther's perspective more in line with Luke's. Waters recalled that "Hester," as she remembered the character's name, "was the religious stronghold of the whole group, and she says: 'If that money isn't claimed by its legal owner, I think God meant for us to use it to build a hospital, a school, and the other things we needed so badly.'"[35] Although Waters maintained the importance of the religious aspects of this segment of the film, her later reflections emphasized the socially progressive elements of the story that were not actually connected to her character's part in the narrative. In her memoir, Waters was scornful of the leaders of various African American organizations who picketed the exhibitions of *Tales of Manhattan*, insisting that, if these leaders had had real concern for improving the conditions of African Americans, they would not have objected to representations of African Americans as "underprivileged." *Tales of Manhattan*, she felt, showed "colored people as they really are," as complex individuals "with exactly the same faults and virtues as members of the other races."[36] At the same time, she maintained that there was something unique about African American approaches to life and to suffering and that this uniqueness was derived, in part, from an innate religious commitment. "Now and always," she wrote, "I will rest my case for the Negro as he is, gay and game, and with an ability to survive without a parallel in all the history of mankind. Yes, I'll take him with his music and his laughter, his love of God—and all his faults. I am proud of nothing as I am of being his blood sister."[37] Despite Waters's evident pride in *Tales of Manhattan*'s realism in presenting both black social conditions and religious sensibility, it is clear—and most commentators at the time felt similarly—that the film's address of these issues advanced little beyond the conventional traditions established in earlier films like *Hallelujah* and *The Green Pastures*. The longevity of such representations of African American religion that contained black life in ways intended to soothe white audiences clearly indicates the power of such discourse to contribute to limited and limiting understandings of American identity.

Ethel Waters and Eddie Anderson would star in *Cabin in the Sky*, another major Hollywood film released during this period in which many were concerned about the question of the morale of African Americans during the war and about the outcome of Walter White's appeal to Hollywood for more complex screen representations of African Americans. The stage musical *Cabin in the Sky* opened on Broadway in the fall of 1940, with Ethel Waters, Dooley Wilson, Rex Ingram, Todd Duncan, J. Rosamond Johnson, and the dancer Katherine Dunham in the lead roles. Lynn Root wrote the book, Vernon Duke wrote the music and lyrics, and George Balanchine directed the production, which was extremely well received by critics and popular with audiences. The *New York Times* drama critic Brooks Atkinson was effusive about the musical, writing, "Perhaps 'Cabin in the Sky' could be better than it is, but this correspondent cannot imagine how. For the musical fantasy, which opened . . . last evening, is original and joyous in an imaginative vein that suits the theatre's special genius." [38] Using the familiar story of a struggle between representatives of heaven and hell for the soul of an individual, and setting it in an African American context, the stage play follows the efforts of Little Joe (Dooley Wilson) to reform and live the Christian life that his wife, Petunia (Ethel Waters), wants him to live. His love of gambling, the wiles of Georgia Brown (Katherine Dunham), and the machinations of Lucifer, Jr. (Rex Ingram) stand in his way, however.[39] Although Little Joe does reform in the end, his actions lead to his and Petunia's death. The final consolation, however, is that The Lawd's General (Todd Duncan) grants Joe admission to heaven, where he can spend eternity with Petunia.

Black and white critics and observers of American popular culture evaluated the play in the context of the long history of such familiar narratives, particularly as they had been set in African American contexts. Writing for the African American weekly the *California Eagle*, John Kinloch began his review:

> The white brother's favorite story about the colored brother has seldom, if ever, been told with such compelling charm and inoffensive exuberance as it is in Ethel Waters' triumph, "Cabin in the Sky."
>
> Once you accept the fact that this is another story about black folks and their childlike conception of divinity, it becomes a revelation of beauty and joy. The entire production is staged with such apparent good nature and sincerity that the stock figures of de Debbil and de Lawd which have belighted *[sic]* Afro-Americans' theatrical history lose their bad taste and are transformed into beings of unstifled gayety.[40]

Inevitably, many compared *Cabin in the Sky* to Marc Connelly's *The Green Pastures*, with some commentators seeing Connelly's work as superior and others recognizing originality in the more recent production, particularly in light of Balanchine's direction and strong performances of Waters, Ingram, and Dunham. As MGM considered purchasing the rights to make a film of the Broadway musical, *The Green Pastures* loomed large in the studio's evaluations of the work. A report on the production for Metro-Goldwyn-Mayer concluded that it was "[a] colorful extravaganza which brings 'Green Pastures' vaguely to mind . . . although the book is not nearly as original or as sparkling as the Marc Connolly [*sic*] work. It is Faustian in flavor, with many of the most modern musical comedy trimmings, a fair musical score, lavish settings and amusing lyrics. . . . [T]he direction, superb dancing and the excellence of Ethel Waters more than make up for routine deficiencies. A good pattern for a musical film . . . but strictly as an Ethel Waters vehicle. Possibilities."[41] The success on Broadway of DuBose Heyward and George Gershwin's *Porgy and Bess* also contributed to MGM's attraction to *Cabin*, alerting the studio to the box-office potential of black-cast musical productions.[42]

Because *Cabin in the Sky* was another entry in the long tradition of white authors' conceptions of black religious life and thought, it is not surprising that the studio engaged Marc Connelly, who had assumed the status of the premier white interpreter of black religion, to help develop the film script, which had been adapted by Joseph Schrank, with Eustace Cockrell providing additional material.[43] In casting the film, the studio chose the better-known Eddie Anderson for the role played by Dooley Wilson in the Broadway production and Lena Horne for the role originally played by Katherine Dunham.[44] In addition, the studio engaged Hall Johnson as the choral director, replacing J. Rosamond Johnson. The MGM production also featured Louis Armstrong, Duke Ellington, and the dance team Buck and Bubbles.[45] Arthur Freed, whose unit produced musicals at MGM, asked Vincente Minnelli to direct. Freed had enticed Minnelli, a native of the Midwest and a veteran designer of the New York stage, to move from theatrical work into film, bringing him to Los Angeles on a one-year trial basis to see if he would like working at the studio. *Cabin in the Sky* would mark his MGM directorial debut.[46]

Some African Americans and white advocates of black civil rights expressed great disappointment in the continuation of the long trajectory of white visions of black theology that *Cabin in the Sky* represented, even while they recognized the superb performances of Waters and the rest of the cast in the Broadway production. The context of a world war, many felt, demanded a new approach and not the filming of what they saw as tired stereotypes. Following the initial publicity at the start of production, Charlie Sands wrote to the MGM producer Arthur Freed on behalf of what appears to have been a white Motion Picture Study Club, expressing his assurance that the film would be entertaining but also conveying the disappointment he felt as "one who honors the Negro race for its more substantial achievements."[47]

Sands asked, "When is Hollywood going to give us a film in which the Negro is not depicted as a faithful 'Uncle Tom' retainer, a comic of the rudimentary sort, or an exponent of jazz or spirituals? Considering the short time the Negro has been freed from slavery, he has made remarkable strides. They're not all clowns or menials. They have produced great artists, educators, scientists, etc." Sands suggested that Metro-Goldwyn-Mayer produce a biographical film about George Washington Carver and included a page of biographical facts about the scientist. In addition, he placed his request in the context of wartime concerns, emphasizing the disjuncture between American discourse abroad and practices at home.

> Now when we are courting the good-will of peoples all over the world, wouldn't such a film do much to show our willingness to give opportunity to all, regardless of race or color? Wouldn't such a film pay better dividends than mere dollars if shown in Africa and Asia to counteract Axis propaganda? Who could play Dr. Carver? None other than Eddie (forget the "Rochester" for the nonce) Anderson. He has an intelligent and expressive face. . . . I believe he is capable of serious work. Just give him a good script and it would inspire him to make the first Negro film of dignity and distinction.[48]

Some observers were sympathetic to the kinds of concerns that Sands and others expressed about the production, but many also understood the forthcoming film version of the Broadway musical to be a response to Walter White's call for more complex screen representations of African Americans. Upon the release of the film, a piece in the *California Eagle*, for example, noted that "because of the agitation over a period of years for better roles for Negroes in motion pictures by the National Association for the Advancement of Colored People, Negro journals, and Negro welfare agencies, Hollywood has at last given us a classic production in 'Cabin in the Sky.'"[49] The *New York Times* placed the forthcoming production in the context of the government's ongoing interest in raising the morale of African Americans on the home front. The Hollywood correspondent Fred Stanley reported that "two major studios, Metro-Goldwyn-Mayer and Twentieth Century-Fox, in producing pictures with all-Negro casts, are following the desires of Washington in making such films at this time. Decisions to produce the pictures, it is stated, followed official expression that the Administration felt that its program for increased employment of Negro citizens in certain heretofore restricted fields of industry would be helped by a general distribution of important pictures in which Negroes played a major part."[50]

Hall Johnson saw the film's potential to offer a broader vision of religious life than had been presented in earlier black-cast films and, at the same time, cautioned the studio about the dangers of falling into outdated representational patterns. Writing to the associate producer Al Lewis after having read the script for *Cabin*, Johnson railed against Marc Connelly's *The Green Pastures* and bemoaned the play's legacy, characterizing it as "a third-hand derivation from a second-hand book, [which] was never more than a white-washed burlesque of the religious thought of the Negro. On every program of this entertainment (which, by the way, was not a play but a series of playlets), was to be found a solemn pronouncement by the author that the nonsense it portrayed was actual belief,—the serious religion, of 'thousands of Negroes in the Deep South.'"[51] Of course, Johnson himself had been involved in Connelly's production over many years, including arranging and conducting the choral music for the Broadway show and touring productions as well as the 1936 Warner Bros.' film. Reflecting back, Johnson insisted that the black actors in the production had been, in actuality, deeply offended by the play but that they had participated because it provided them with work and with experience in a Broadway production. *Cabin in the Sky,* Johnson argued, moved beyond the *Green Pastures* pattern in that it presented a religious vision that was not narrowly racialized. He wrote to Lewis, "An individual's idea of Heaven and Hell is his own property and, as such, is beyond argument. That individual may be Dante, Mohamet or Billy Sunday. Why not Little Joe Jackson?"[52] Rex Ingram, who, as we noted, would play the role of Lucifer, Jr. in the stage and screen productions of *Cabin in the Sky* and had played De Lawd in *The Green Pastures*, concurred with Johnson's evaluation of *Cabin* but also wanted to recognize the artistic value of the show's connection of universal elements to the particular context of black life and culture. As he noted in an interview, "It is a more grown-up drama than 'Green Pastures,' I think. For one thing, it brings out the power of prayer. Basically, it is the tale of a wayward soul kept on the straight and narrow path by the prayers of his wife. But the treatment is decidedly in the Negro vein of happiness. While good triumphs over bad, there's a lot of fun in the doing of it."[53]

Despite his support of the production of a film version of *Cabin in the Sky,* Hall Johnson found the reliance on dialect in the script to be wrongheaded and characterized the language of the film's script as "a weird but priceless conglomeration of pre–Civil War constructions mixed with up-to-the minute Harlem slang and heavily sprinkled with a type of verb which Amos and Andy purloined from Miller and Lyle, the Negro comedians; all adding up to a lingo which has never been heard nor spoken on land or sea by any human being, and would most certainly be 'more than

Greek' to the ignorant Georgia Negroes in your play."[54] Even with his reservations about the script's language, Johnson signed onto the project, but his participation, which inevitably invoked his past work in *The Green Pastures* and other such productions, would contribute to the hybrid nature of *Cabin in the Sky* as a film that recycled traditional film images of African American religion but also pointed toward new representational possibilities.

Unlike King Vidor and Marc Connelly, both of whose black-cast productions set in religious contexts were their own creations, Minnelli found himself with the opportunity to direct a work written by another white writer. He characterized the play as a "very true and very human . . . a wonderful story."[55] Minnelli brought to it previous experience working with Ethel Waters on the Broadway musical *At Home Abroad*, a professional relationship with Lena Horne as the director of her musical numbers at MGM, and the potential for innovation that his relative outsider status provided.[56] In his memoir, Minnelli recalled having had reservations about the film's story, "which reinforced the naïve, childlike stereotype of blacks." But, he continued, "I knew there were such people as the deeply pious Petunia and Joe, her weak gambler of a husband, and that such wives constantly prayed for the wavering souls of their men. Good and evil, however, usually fought their battle in the man's mind instead of in a vivid fantasy between the devil in black and an angel in white, as we were attempting to portray. If I was going to make a picture about such people, I would approach it with great affection rather than condescension."[57] Minnelli's interest in the project, then, derived not from a desire to present a literalist theology as the very substance of an authentically African American religious sensibility but rather from the work's address of more general human questions. Because of his commitment to this broad vision, Minnelli intervened in the development of the production design to prevent the mobilization of damaging stereotypes of African Americans. In his memoir he recounted his struggles with the members of the studio's art department, who, he felt, were presenting Joe (Eddie Anderson) and Petunia (Ethel Waters) as "slovenly" rather than simply poor, and he was pleased to have succeeded in changing the look of the cabin to make the audience "aware of their simple goodness."[58]

In developing the script, the studio took several approaches to attempt to avoid traditional and, for many observers, problematic representations of African American religious thought. Ironically, it appears to have been Marc Connelly who provided the outline of the version of the final scenes that reveal that Joe's encounter with the representatives of good and evil has taken place in the context of a dream, a revision that deemphasized the literalist and childlike theology of the play and the earlier drafts.[59] The original framing narrative in Joseph Schrank's script began with "Interior of a simple negro home in the deep south. An old negro woman with one of those wonderfully wise, kindly, spiritual faces of the race is seated in a rocker by a sunny window, knitting."[60] When her grandchildren ask her about fighting the devil, she tells them of God's angels and generals and says that "[t]hey lives up in Hebbin. Dat's where yo' Aunt Petunia and yo' Uncle Joe went after dat accident."[61] The script ends with the grandmother concluding, "So yuh see, chillun—yuh always gotta be careful not to let de debbil's imps set yuh to doin' wrong—and dat way you'll get to hebbin'."[62] Schrank was not pleased with Connelly's revisions in which the dialect was toned down and the story made less literal, and he wrote to producer Al Lewis, reviewing problems he saw with the structure of the story and concluding that "[a]ll these faults of story construction and even characterization could be forgiven I suppose—they are not necessarily fatal. But what *is* fatal is the outstanding fact that the screen play has lost much of the flavor, the charm, the excitement, the tenderness, the humor and the deeply spiritual feeling of the original. It is completely uninspired—it never gets off the ground."[63] Nevertheless, the studio remained committed to the new version, which also matched Minnelli's ideas about the appropriate approach to film musicals—that is, that "fantasy should have its physical limits . . . within a canvas of pre-established conventions."[64] In this case, the dream context would provide the plausible explanation for the fantasy elements and discourage the audience from assuming that the film's approach to moral questions was necessarily racialized.

The process of drafting of the film's foreword, which would appear in scrolling words set against clouds and with the Hall Johnson Choir's voices in the background, provides a clear sense of the conflicted position in which *Cabin in the Sky* stood in relation both to traditional representations of African American religious thought and to attempts to present the story as a broadly applicable allegory. Hall Johnson weighed in on the question during the script development phase, writing to Minnelli about the power that such a foreword would have in setting the tone for the film and in shaping public and critical responses to the production. He noted that "[w]hatever appraisal of the picture is indicated in the foreword is going to be taken up and amplified in the press—it saves them the trouble of thinking. I sincerely believe that the studio will get more credit for having produced something definitely solid with a Negro cast (what a novelty!) and I am sure all Negroes themselves will feel much prouder to have participated at last, and so fully, in a picture which really means something and is not ashamed to say so."[65] Johnson also contended that the black-cast film presented an opportunity to make a statement in the context of the war effort: "[H]ow regrettable if it could not be something which would really give an idea of the worth-whileness of the story. Why shy at something a bit serious—now when everybody is thinking of serious things,—even people who have never thought at all before?"[66]

Playwright Elmer Rice provided a draft of the foreword that spoke directly to Johnson's interest in drawing a connection between the film and issues raised by the war. The following is the text he proposed, which was not used in the final version:

> America is a land of many races and many nationalities. Each has woven its own unique thread into the American pattern. The donation of the American Negro has been rich and varied. In lighter moments, he has brought happy gifts of song and rhythm and warm good humor. Today, in the hour of battle, he plays his vital part on the farm, on the assembly-line and on the fighting-fronts. Beyond all this, he contributes to the common life, a sustaining and deeply-needed religious faith: a fervent belief in the power of righteousness and in the ultimate triumph of good over evil.[67]

A version less explicit about the war but still interested in connecting the film to the current social and political moment proposed that the foreword read, "In these times of changing values, man needs not so much a castle in the air as a cabin in the sky,—built of his highest hopes and furnished with his dearest dreams,—from which he can go out every day renewed and strong to make his dreams come true."[68] Other drafts took a similar approach but placed greater emphasis on universal elements of the story.[69] The final version, which was compiled from two different writers' drafts, combined the broad fantasy approach with the sensibility that sought to connect the movie's story to particularly American issues, if not to current events:

> Throughout the ages, powerful and inspiring thoughts have been preserved and handed down by the medium of the legend, the fable, the fantasy.
> The folklore of America has origins in all lands, all races, all colors.
> This story of faith and devotion springs from that source and seeks to capture those values.[70]

In taking up Hall Johnson's caution about the need to be careful with the text of the foreword because of its power to shape the viewers' reading of the entire film, the producers combined text written by James K. McGuinness, a white studio writer, and Philip M. Carter, who was then serving as a special publicity representative to the black press for *Cabin in the Sky*.[71] Carter provided the first and third lines of the final version of the foreword and McGuinness the second, replacing text that referred explicitly to the war.[72] This final version of the foreword would set the stage for the film's narrative by casting the African American setting as a part of the American landscape and the story to follow as a generically American one. At the same time, the text's retreat from the sense in earlier drafts that African American spirituality and values contribute something unique to the nation made impossible the kind of political statement that Hall Johnson hoped the film could make. Indeed, one wonders why the writers, producers, and director saw such a foreword as necessary at all, except to provide a disclaimer to whites for the studio's interest in this black-cast project.

As various scholars have noted, *Cabin in the Sky* moves away from the traditional ethnographic and folkloric approaches to representing black religious life and thought that characterized the earlier black-cast Hollywood films, and the foreword marks this shift through its emphasis on universal elements of legend, fable, and fantasy rather than on specific racial or cultural characteristics. Minnelli's previous work as a set designer for the New York stage led him to express particular concern for the aesthetic values of the production and to be attentive to the art of the various sets, both of which proved important for creating a strong sense of fantasy in the film. In addition, Minnelli became especially concerned with camera work and, in his memoir, noted that "the touches I'm proudest of—though neither audience nor critics took note of them—involved an inquisitive, restless camera."[73] His technique, which also contributes to the feeling of fantasy, is evident in an early scene in which Petunia and Joe attend church, with Joe planning to repent publicly and put aside his gambling ways for church membership. The scene begins with the camera at the front of the church as members of the congregation sing "L'il Black Sheep," clearly a comment on Joe's need to be found and redeemed.[74] The camera draws viewers' attention to a small group of gossipers in the foreground who whisper about Joe's unexpected church attendance, and it then moves to focus on the solo vocalist. As the solo vocal part moves from congregant to congregant, the camera focuses on the next singer who, upon completing the solo, turns to a neighbor for whispered gossiping.[75] As the camera meanders back through the pews, the viewer comes eventually to see Petunia and Joe seated in the last pew, their presence finally arresting the progress of the gossip as well as the camera's movement (see figure 33). In contrast to the staid and formal, yet simplistic and naive, approach to black church worship in *The Green Pastures* and the sexualized and ecstatic rendering in *Hallelujah*, Minnelli's church scene is playful, with those present moving easily between singing

FIGURE 33.

Petunia in church, with Little Joe sitting next to her, in *Cabin in the Sky*. Courtesy of Photofest.

and gossip. Where King Vidor's use of camera movement in the evening revival scene in *Hallelujah*, for example, serves to exoticize the black bodies he displays in religious ecstasy, Minnelli's camera work creates a sense of intimacy within the space and functions to outline the boundaries of the church community. The ultimate effect of this brief scene—the only one that takes place in a church—is to draw the church-goers as human and show that they are just as interested in this world as in the next. Admittedly, the representation of their concern for their lives in this world becomes reduced to the policing of behavior and to the clear demarcation of insiders and outsiders. However, the church community is not exoticized, nor are its members presented as childlike or hypersexual, and Minnelli's playful and loving camera work contributes to this effect.[76]

Although *Cabin in the Sky* employs the well-worn opposition between the rural and the urban and, as Paula Massood notes, establishes Petunia as the embodiment of the domestic and rural and Georgia (Lena Horne) of sensuality and the urban, these spaces are not far from one another in the world of the film. In fact, the char-

FIGURE 34.
The General and Lucifer, Jr. struggle for Little Joe's soul in *Cabin in the Sky*. Courtesy of Photofest.

acters move back and forth between the two quite easily.[77] Club Paradise stands in for the urban and is clearly marked as the site of Little Joe's temptation. Indeed, he leaves the church just as he is expected to respond to the altar call, accompanies a number of gambling buddies to whom he owes money to the club, and is shot in a dispute. As a result of his injuries, he dreams of the struggle between Lucifer, Jr. (Rex Ingram) and The General (Kenneth Spencer) for his soul (see figure 34). But as James Naremore argues, despite the traditional opposition between the rural and urban, "the town is nonetheless an attractive place, and the real story is elsewhere— largely in the photography, the art direction, the costuming, the performances, and the musical numbers. In fact, in order to achieve a satisfying conclusion, *Cabin* finds ways to pull its two worlds into a kind of synthesis."[78] Paula Massood argues against a coherent synthesis between the two realms but notes that the urban world enters the cabin in the form of a washing machine that Joe buys as a birthday gift for Petunia (even though the cabin does not have electricity) and through the appearances of Joe's gambling mates and Georgia at the church and the cabin, respectively.[79] Sim-

FIGURE 35.
Print advertisement for
Cabin in the Sky (back). From
the author's collection.

ilarly, Petunia crosses into the urban space of Club Paradise to move the narrative to its conclusion. The studio's advertising material reflected this emphasis on the film's overarching urban sensibility. For example, one of the print advertisements for the film has a page of artwork by Al Hirschfeld that emphasizes the urban club as the locus of the struggle between heaven and hell by placing dancers, marked as urban by their clothing, at the center (see figure 35). The other page of the advertisement presents an image of the rural that is deeply influenced by jazz and that provides potential viewers of the film with no image of the church environment at all. The cabin is shown in the upper right corner of the front of the picture with brass instruments exploding from it (see figure 36), so that the nightclub atmosphere characterizes even Petunia's home and the heavenly cabin for which she longs.

Despite Minnelli's emphasis on aesthetics and urban modernism in contrast to conventional film representations of African American religious thought, as well as the foreword's attempt to locate the film's story as fundamentally American, *Cabin in the Sky* does not move far beyond traditional images. Many reviewers and critics certainly read the film as decisively in the tradition of *Hallelujah* and *The Green Pastures*. Writing for the *New York Times*, Thomas M. Pryor, for example, character-

FIGURE 36.
Print advertisement for
Cabin in the Sky (front).
From the author's collection.

ized the film as "by turn an inspiring expression of a simple people's faith in the hereafter and a spicy slice of their zest for earthly pleasures," and the *Dallas Morning News*'s reviewer wrote that "[w]hile this is extravagant fun, there is no disrespect for religion, intentional or otherwise. It is all part of the southern Negro's folk tradition."[80] And despite some of the marketing attempts to draw connections to issues surrounding African Americans and the war—one of the suggestions for promotional events at theaters was to have "Negro service men as guests of honor"[81]— for many commentators the disjuncture between the realities of the war and the world of the film fantasy was jarring. The actress Fredi Washington, who was theater editor and columnist for the black weekly the *People's Voice*, wrote, "*Cabin in the Sky*, which had a successful Broadway run and was thought by MGM officials to be good movie material, was unfortunate in-so-much-as its story was one of fantasy about Negroes who are naive and ignorant. The attempt was an honest one by the studio but who, because of their ignorance of the new Negro and what he is fighting for, made a blunder."[82] *The Morning Telegram*'s comment on *Cabin in the Sky*'s release set the film in light of the recent controversies over the political ramifications of film representations of African Americans, reminding readers that

[a] good deal of agitation has been stirred up lately about Hollywood giving proper due to the Negro. Without taking any active part in the controversy, it strikes me that this thing may serve to keep the pot boiling for some time. How Negroes will react to it will be one thing; how the rest of the world will take it another. . . . I don't think, as a matter of fact, it will cement relations to any great extent, but then again neither do I think it will do any more harm than the other pictures that have shown the American Negro in a superstitious, ignorant and accented light."[83]

Other commentators felt that the somewhat more respectful approach to representing African Americans that *Cabin* modeled constituted a significant improvement over past black-cast films and argued that the film's success would open up new opportunities for black performers in Hollywood. The *Hollywood Citizen-News* faulted the production for certain shortcomings, noting in its review that "*Cabin in the Sky* is mainly fantasy and folk lore, with music and comedy liberally interpolated. It does not undertake the forthright and modernly dramatic treatment of the Negro which the Negro has a right to expect in a great democratic medium in a great democracy."[84] The review, however, went on to characterize the film as impressive and "as a valuable contribution, not only to art and entertainment, but also to the national unity that is essential to the winning of the war and the winning of peace."[85] Leo Roa, the Hollywood correspondent for the *California Eagle*, argued forcefully that, should the film prove successful at the box office, "it will start a trend in the making of both all-colored and mixed cast pictures that will give the Negro a strong entertainment and talent outlet in Hollywood."[86]

Despite the hopeful evaluations of the cultural impact of another successful black-cast Hollywood musical production, Walter White of the NAACP, who had expended so much public capital on his attempt to reform Hollywood, was forced to consider *Cabin in the Sky* an exception to what he saw as steady progress in improving representations of African Americans in Hollywood films.[87] The NAACP's own organ, *The Crisis*, had published a piece by the white MGM writer Dalton Trumbo entitled "Blackface, Hollywood Style" a few months prior to White's positive evaluation of the situation in Hollywood. Originally an address before the United Nations Writers Congress, Trumbo's essay insisted that the challenge facing American writers was to recognize the danger of accepting "racial lies" in the face of the fight against fascism. "Our current crop of motion pictures, produced in a moment of national crisis when the President has made a direct appeal for racial understanding and cooperation," he wrote, "reveals many of the vicious old lies dressed up and paraded before us as evidence of our stern devotion to winning the war."[88] *Cabin in the Sky*, he noted, "despite a few minor concessions to Negro dignity . . . contained bad features which far outweigh [its] virtues."[89] Black and white members of the public, it seems, agreed with Trumbo that little progress had been made in representing African Americans on film. In a poll conducted by Wallace Lee of *Negro Digest*, respondents were asked, "Is Hollywood fair to Negroes in its films?" Fifty-three percent of whites and an overwhelming 93 percent of blacks answered "No.".[90] Without question, Hollywood studios struggled to establish modes of representing African Americans in the period that would demonstrate progress in meeting the challenge of Walter White's call for more realistic images and addressing the concerns of many other African Americans that the context of the war demanded new approaches. The industry's recourse to black-cast religious contexts in films like *Tales of Manhattan* and *Cabin in the Sky* made clear the difficulty of satisfying these calls through the use of traditional displays of African American contentedness and simplistic religious sentiment, however aestheticized, urbanized, or placed in the context of tentative socialist beliefs.

Outside the Hollywood studio system, several filmmakers addressed black participation in the war directly and sought, through their art, to intervene in the discussions about the relationship between film representations and African American wartime morale. Two surviving black-audience films of the period raised these questions in largely secular contexts. Toddy Pictures released *Fighting Americans* (1943), for which producer J. Richardson Jones received permission from the War Department to film at the Tuskegee Army Flying School. The film also featured Brigadier General Benjamin O. Davis, the highest-ranking African American military officer, and Truman K. Gibson, assistant to the civilian aide to the Secretary of War.[91] In the 1943 *Marching On*, Spencer Williams also provided a straightforward discussion of what black men could accomplish in the service.[92] The film portrays the transformation of selfish and unpatriotic Rodney Tucker Jr. (Hugh Martin) into a dedicated and courageous soldier fighting for freedom and democracy. Rodney's hesitation to join the service becomes especially highlighted in the film's narrative because not only have his father and grandfather served in the military, but the various women in his life are contributing to the war effort. Rodney's mother (Myra J. Hemmings) sews for the Red Cross, and Martha (Georgia Kelly), his girlfriend who leaves him when he hesitates to join the army but who later reestablishes their relationship, eventually joins the Women's Army Corps (WAC). By the film's end, Rodney is enthusiastic about "showing [that his] blood is red just like every other American." *Marching On* emphasizes that performing one's patriotic duty to support the war effort results in personal fulfillment, and although Rodney concludes that he must fight for "family, home, freedom, and democracy" there is little sense that either racial segregation in the military or African Americans' limited access to freedom and democracy at home is of particular concern to anyone in the film. It is also noteworthy that Williams, who wrote and directed the film, did not attempt to bring together his interests in religion and in black military history in an overt way in this film, choosing to focus more pointedly on a secular vision of African American military service.[93] Such an approach—which sought to make religion central to African American morale and to the representation of black contributions to the war effort—would be taken up in two other films that would eventually come into direct competition with one another.

In 1943 Jack Goldberg, a veteran white producer of black-audience films, formed The Negro Marches On, Inc. film production company to make a documentary film about African Americans' part in the war effort and to emphasize, in the wake of racial violence in Detroit, New York, and other cities, the vital contributions of African Americans to American life.[94] The resulting film, *We've Come a Long, Long Way*, relied heavily on footage that Goldberg had acquired from the U.S. Army Signal Corps. In addition, the film's narrative benefited from his having obtained permission to use material from a pamphlet by the black journalist Chandler Owen, *Negroes and the War*, which had been published by the Office of War Information in January of 1943.[95] Although the pamphlet was in demand and widely circulated, it proved extremely controversial among African Americans for its argument that the primary reason to support the war was that Hitler's victory would bring even worse conditions than those under which African Americans then lived.[96] Despite the focus of the majority of the pamphlet—largely through the inclusion of Farm Security Administration photographs—on "our stake in America," the overall effect was to arouse fear.[97] Mary A. Morton made this point about the pamphlet's reliance on fear and its failure to prove that African Americans had been given the opportunity to advance in America in an article on the government and African American morale for the *Journal of Negro Education*. She wrote, "The fact that, under a fascist regime, Negroes would fare worse than other Americans is not indicative of a new relative position for American Negroes."[98] Although Goldberg did not specifically mention *Negroes and the War* in the promotional material for *We've Come a Long, Long Way*, the influence of the pamphlet on the film's approach to raising morale and to educating white Americans about African American life is clear, even in the title, which amplifies a refrain in the pamphlet of "we've come a long way" (see figure 37).[99]

FIGURE 37.
Poster for *We've Come a Long, Long Way*. Courtesy John Kisch, Separate Cinema Archive.

Perhaps the film's most striking uses of materials from *Negroes and the War* come at the moments when the narrator's voice, heard over footage that Goldberg acquired from the army, outlines the threats that Hitler and fascism pose to African American life. Among these are the outlawing of political and social reform organizations like the NAACP and the Urban League, the banning of African American newspapers, and the suppression of black entertainers. In addition, like the pamphlet *Negroes and the War*, *We've Come a Long, Long Way* focuses on the achievements of African American soldiers, recounting the history of black regiments in World War I, and includes brief profiles of prominent African Americans, such as George Washington Carver, and entertainers including Paul Robeson, Nina Mae McKinney, Cab Calloway, and Lena Horne.

Where the pamphlet could introduce these figures only in text and photographs, the motion picture gave Goldberg an opportunity to allow some of these leaders to speak directly to the audience rather than simply have their achievements described or their speeches quoted. Mary McLeod Bethune, founder of Bethune-Cookman College and president of the National Council of Negro Women, appears in what seems to be a WAC uniform to "speak for the women of our race." She describes the work that women are doing on the home front and insists that "we realize that this is our war too, threatening the Long Long Way that we've come."[100] In the course of her brief address, Goldberg cuts away from Bethune to show footage of African American women in the WAC in training and at work, as well as images of various aspects of their daily life in the military. When the film cuts back to Bethune, she stretches out her arms and speaks encouragingly to female viewers: "March forward, my women. Our trail has been long and hard. But we will continue to march for our country ... for humanity ... for our Race ... SO HELP US GOD!"[101] Major Richard R. Wright, former president of the State College of Industry for Colored Youth and, at the time the film was made, president of the Citizens and Southern Bank and Trust Company, also appears in the film. In his brief speech, Wright tells of his experiences as a soldier in the Spanish-American War, reviews the accomplishments of African American men in the armed services, and emphasizes the danger that Hitler presents to American life, very much in keeping with the sensibility of *Negroes and the War*. "Do not my brothers and sisters play into the hand of these propagandists by believing that the Negro American is a fool to fight," Wright says. "Don't let anyone tell you we have nothing to gain. The hundreds of thousands of our boys who are giving their all to preserve the Glory of this, our United States of America, is living proof of the lie."[102] Bethune's and Wright's appearances in footage shot specifically for *We've Come a Long, Long Way* present a striking contrast to the

Signal Corps footage on which Goldberg relied for the majority of the film, and the speeches they deliver from Goldberg's script implicate them in the film's project in a way that incorporating existing footage of their speeches would not have accomplished. Bethune and Wright speak, for example, the refrain of "we've come a long, long way" several times in their addresses, and Wright specifically refers to the funeral that serves as the framing narrative Goldberg used to tie the compiled footage together.

The film also has in common with the pamphlet *Negroes and the War* the characterization of the war as one to save Christianity, with the narrator asserting:

> Now we know that the Church is the foundation of our race, and the war in which we are engaged would end that very foundation if Hitler and his hate could have their way. He would destroy these beautiful houses of worship. You know what he did to the Churches amongst his own race and in occupied countries.
>
> He desecrated every inch of property where a man could worship his God in his own right and in his own beliefs. Now if he'd do that to his OWN race, what would happen to the Negro whom he considers without a soul? . . . Would he heed the civilized belief that God created all men EQUAL? In the Nazi Code there is no room for both Hitler and God.[103]

Where *Negroes and the War* argued, through its use of a quotation from a speech by Rev. W. H. Jernigan, president of the Fraternal Council of Negro Churches in America, that "our Nation is builded [*sic*] on Christian principles," *We've Come a Long, Long Way* is, if at all possible, even more explicitly Christian in its approach to outlining what is at stake in the war, telling viewers that Hitler would not "agree with the words of a man who dedicated his life to God. . . . Who declared that salvation for the world's condition can be found only in the teachings of Jesus Christ."[104] In addition, Goldberg includes footage of an address by an unidentified Roman Catholic bishop in which he asks, "Are we not members of one another . . . members of the mystical body of Christ?" The bishop continues, "Let us lift up our hearts, for the influences that are to renew the face of the earth must spring from men's hearts. Every baptized Christian, if there is faith in him, should therefore seize the sword of the spirit and be Christ's soldier to win the peace of Christ in the kingdom of Christ. Christ alone can save the world from the despair of war."[105] Near the end of the film Goldberg includes another strong religious message by using footage of the comment of the famed boxer Joe Louis in a speech before the Navy

Relief Society in May of 1942 that "I'm only doing what any red-blooded American would do. We gonna do our part, and we will win because we're on God's side." Audiences would have been familiar with this oft-quoted assertion, which was also reproduced by the government on a striking poster, coupled with an image of Louis in uniform and pointing a rifle with a bayonet. The same image and text appear at the very end of *Negroes and the War*.[106]

The framing structure that Goldberg chose for the film further emphasizes a religious understanding of black participation in the war and promotes a specifically Christian context for interpreting that participation. The film presents its information, culled largely from *Negroes and the War*, in the context of a funeral sermon for the fictional Lieutenant Lester Collins, an educated farmer, churchgoer, and family man who joined the Army Air Corps and was killed in action. Elder Lightfoot Solomon Michaux, radio evangelist and founder of Washington, D.C.'s Temple of Freedom under God, Church of God, plays the part of the minister who conducts the funeral and thereby serves as the film's narrator.[107] The film also features Michaux's "Happy Am I" choir, dressed in robes and wearing mortarboards, singing such songs as "Lift Ev'ry Voice and Sing" and "The Battle Hymn of the Republic" on the sound track.[108] Even as Michaux's presence in the film marked a move away from the mainline, upper-class religious commitments of *Negroes and the War*, his presence nevertheless lent a certain measure of religious authenticity to the production, as well as considerable name recognition for black audiences. Although the majority of his on-screen time consists of medium-close shots of him standing behind the pulpit and delivering the funeral sermon that serves as the film's narration, Michaux is at times passionate and engaging in his delivery and able to overcome the limitations of the direction and production values of the film. At other times, however, his speech is stilted and difficult to understand and the single shot by an unmoving camera becomes tedious. Nevertheless, Michaux's presence as a recognized, politically connected, and successful minister further underscores the film's presentation of the centrality of Christianity to African American and American national identity. In addition, the film's perspective on the role of Christianity in winning the war against fascism conformed to Michaux's own theology and public discourse, with which listeners of his radio program would have been familiar. As Lillian Ashcraft Webb notes of Michaux's theology, "As a Christian missionary, he was committed to principles of the conversion of individuals from sin to holiness. . . . Committed Christians in aggregate would yield a citizenry responsive to eradicating evil and human needs and sufferings. A consequence would be a Christian democracy as opposed to what he then saw as a nation of people merely professing democracy and Christianity."[109] It is unclear what relationship Goldberg had to Christianity, but as a longtime producer and director of race films he had already demonstrated an understanding of the receptivity of black audiences to religiously themed films.

Although the film is firmly in the tradition of many black-audience films of the period in its address to African American audiences, Goldberg sought to move it beyond the traditional audience for such a film. Clearly, he felt strongly that its audience should be as broad as possible, and he marketed the film aggressively to whites. One advertising flyer reproduced the reports by the film review committees of various organizations that were published in the weekly bulletin *Unbiased Opinions of Current Motion Pictures*. Goldberg's promotional campaign featured an evaluation from this bulletin of *We've Come a Long, Long Way* by a film committee of the Daughters of the American Revolution (DAR) that characterized the film as "[a] fine picturization of the American Negro race, covering their opportunities, their achievements, and their contribution to America. . . . The film is strongly recommended for the information it offers on the progress of the Negro race and for the pronouncements on its love for and loyalty to America."[110] In addition, he wrote a letter of appeal to exhibitors, newspaper editors, and community activists introducing the film and arguing that "there are millions of White Americans interested in the progress of Negro Americans, of which you are no doubt aware, and it is for that reason we feel certain that this production will have an enormous appeal in your community."[111] Although the film did not garner much attention at the time of its release for its artistic merit—the *New York Times* reviewer characterized it as "a rambling testimonial"—it would receive considerable press for the struggle in which Goldberg engaged with the representatives of Hollywood over the release of another film.[112]

In April of 1944 Jack Goldberg filed suit in federal court to prevent the U.S. War Activities Committee of the Motion Picture Industry from distributing the U.S. War Department's orientation film *The Negro Soldier*, which the committee planned to make available to movie theaters free of charge.[113] While *The Negro Soldier* had been produced for viewing by African American troops, the War Activities Committee now intended to release it to the general public. In his complaint against the committee, Goldberg insisted that government distribution of a film for which it charged no exhibition fee constituted "unfair competition with private enterprise," and he received a temporary injunction stopping the distribution of *The Negro Soldier*.[114] It was not simply the economic competition posed by the army's film that concerned Goldberg but his apprehension of the similarities between the two movies in their use of a minister as the narrator and a church to set the scene for telling the story of the contributions of African Americans to America, particularly through military service. Similar to *We've Come a Long, Long Way*'s use of Elder Lightfoot Solomon Michaux in the part of the film's narrator, the army's film is set in a Sunday morning church service, with Carlton Moss, the film's writer, playing the role of a minister preaching about the dangers of fascism and the part that African Americans have played in securing democracy.

Although *We've Come a Long, Long Way* had been produced by a leading white figure in the black-audience film industry and featured such high-profile African Americans as Elder Michaux, Mary McLeod Bethune, and Major Richard R. Wright, African American leaders and organizations failed to rally around Goldberg. Many threw their public support behind *The Negro Soldier*, pitting the two films against one another. Prior to either the release of *We've Come a Long, Long Way* or the beginning of public discussions about releasing *The Negro Soldier* to a general audience, the NAACP began a public campaign against Goldberg's film. The *Pittsburgh Courier*, for example, published a brief item reporting that unnamed reviewers connected with the civil rights organization had screened the film and found it "disgusting and insulting."[115] The reviewers' concerns about the film were twofold. Although the pamphlet *Negroes and the War* was not named in the article, the criticism that "the main message of the film seemed to be a warning to American Negroes that they are much better off now than they would be under Hitler"[116] seems a clear reference to the controversy over the pamphlet's argument about the stakes of the war for African Americans. In addition to articulating discomfort with the connection between the film and the pamphlet, the reviewers found the film to be lacking in artistic merit, criticizing it for being "made up of newsreel and documentary film shots put together in a bad sequence" and for faulty "technical execution."[117] The item concluded with the NAACP's assertion that it would not cooperate with The Negro Marches On, Inc. in distributing the film as the company had requested.

The arguments that various individuals and organizations presented against Goldberg's actions to halt the release of *The Negro Soldier* focused on the significance of the government's production of the film and the need for all such accounts of African American achievements to be viewed by the broadest public possible. The black weekly *Norfolk Journal and Guide* telegrammed Michaux and Goldberg to object to the steps that The Negro Marches On, Inc. production company had taken to prevent distribution and exhibition of *The Negro Soldier*. The publishers of the paper warned Goldberg and Michaux that "[t]hese efforts will not be kindly regarded by interested Americans. Interference with distribution of the film will be a blow to morale of soldiers and civilians and a disservice to agencies seeking improvement in race relations."[118] The NAACP also weighed in on the issue, submitting a motion to file an amicus curiae brief on behalf of the War Activities Committee. The brief noted that "during the present war emergency there has been an increase of tension between the races and this has seriously affected the morale of Negro soldiers and members of their families." It concluded that "for these reasons a valid documentary picture such as *The Negro Soldier,* made and sponsored by the Government and offered to motion picture theaters without charge, should be given the widest of circulation in the public interest. Any interference with the freest and widest distribution of this motion picture will seriously hinder the war program."[119] In the end, Goldberg proved no match for the War Activities Committee and its allies, all determined to find an audience for the high-quality orientation film. Ultimately, Goldberg could obtain only a temporary restraining order on new bookings of *The Negro Soldier,* an order that was vacated when he lost the case.[120]

The film historian Thomas Cripps, who has written extensively about *The Negro Soldier,* argues that its makers were bound to win this contest with Goldberg because, although much of the film takes place in a church, the venue serves as "merely the establishing shot from which to spit out his [Moss's] film" and because the film "sets aside" the sermon (and, consequently, religion) in favor of a liberal argument about democracy and inclusion.[121] Cripps contrasts the liberal perspective of *The Negro Soldier* with what he understands to be the old-fashioned religious approach of *We've Come a Long, Long Way,* implying that "liberal democracy" and "religion" remain ever incompatible. Whereas Cripps is correct to emphasize *The Negro Soldier*'s liberal and integrationist sensibility, he misreads the film's uses of religion and ignores the way Carlton Moss imagined that black audiences at the time would probably have understood the film's goals. *The Negro Soldier* proved powerful and persuasive for its viewers not because it renounced religion but because it articulated a vision of an American religion that placed Americanness at its core and defined that Americanness as produced, in part, by African American military sacrifice. Military service, then, became a sacred duty for all who professed the "religion" of Americanness, a religion that included Protestants, Catholics, and Jews.[122] This is, indeed, a different vision from that put forth in *We've Come a Long, Long Way,* which emphasized a particularly Christian understanding of Americanness. The broader conception of the American religion present in *The Negro Soldier* made it possible for the producers of the film and advocates of its integrationist commitment to position African Americans as fundamentally American in their economic, intellectual, and military contributions to the ongoing project of building the nation.

In the context of the period's emerging understanding of American religion as consisting of "Protestant-Catholic-Jew," *The Negro Soldier* attempts to locate African Americans as rightfully representative of the category of Protestant and not simply as "Negro Protestants."

The Negro Soldier came into being through the efforts of the army's Information and Education Division (IED) to raise the morale of black troops by addressing questions that some African American men had raised about military service as well as the discontent that many expressed concerning ongoing discrimination at home. It was one thing for Hollywood studios to attempt to reform their representations of African Americans in narrative feature films for the purpose of aiding wartime morale and for black-audience film companies such as The Negro Marches On, Inc. to engage the question of morale, and quite another for the segregated U.S. Army to do so. Letters from African American servicemen and women to the NAACP described poor conditions in training camps in the United States, lack of medical attention, and instances of general mistreatment by their fellow soldiers and officers.[123] In commissioning a film to address African American morale, the IED walked a fine line between presenting a sanitized and unbelievable version of African American history and giving a more realistic account of black experiences in the military that might inflame discontent among black soldiers.

The film was produced under the auspices of Frank Capra's army film unit, which also produced the well-known documentary series *Why We Fight*, and, as such, benefited from the experience and high production values that the unit provided.[124] As the work got underway, the army engaged Marc Connelly, author of *The Green Pastures*, to write the script but also brought the African American radio and stage writer Carlton Moss, another civilian, into the project. Moss had been involved with the "Double V" campaign—for victory abroad and at home for African Americans—inaugurated by the *Pittsburgh Courier*, and he had already attempted to dramatize the path to "Double V" in his stage review *Salute to the Negro Troops*. In addition, he had considerable experience in the theater, having worked with John Houseman in the WPA's Federal Theater Project (FTP) at the Lafayette Theater in Harlem.[125] Moss traveled with Connelly to collect information on black servicemen and women and, in an interview years later, characterized Connelly as "very gentle" but as unaware of the realities of black life.[126] The army found Connelly's script draft unsuitable for its needs and eventually turned to Moss to write the script, with contributions from Ben Hecht and Jo Swerling, both stalwart Hollywood scriptwriters.[127] To complete the team, Capra selected Stuart Heisler, a relatively new white director. According to many accounts, the army required revisions of Moss's original drafts because, as one general noted, "the more radical leaders of the negro movement are claiming against the United States the exact thoughts expressed." In this, the general was referring to Moss's titling of the film as *Men of Color to Arms*, following on an 1863 speech by Frederick Douglass.[128] In retrospect, Moss found the script that resulted from his exchanges with Hecht and Swerling to be more personal than his original drafts, despite what he took to be ideological rather than artistic comments from the military.[129] In putting the film together, Moss and Heisler relied on a combination of newly shot and archival footage, reenactments, and captured enemy materials, as well as a score composed and compiled by the well-known film composer Dimitri Tiomkin, to create a dramatic and well-paced movie.[130]

The film, which runs approximately forty-five minutes, opens with long shots of churches—a large urban gothic, a smaller urban church, a rural church with children entering, and then the exterior of another large urban church. With the exception of the exterior shot of the rural church in which we see a number of black children, these contextualizing images of Christian institutions are not racialized.[131] Although we know from the film's title that it is about "the Negro soldier," the narrative begins simply with Sunday morning and a range of American Christians gathering for worship. Once inside the last church, we see well-dressed African American men and women taking their seats as a choir sings. The camera cuts to a medium shot of the choir, and we see that the soloist for the hymn, "Since Jesus Came into My Life," is a soldier (Sgt. Clyde Turner).

Carlton Moss, in the part of the minister, rises from his seat to begin the sermon and tells the congregation that, while he prepared a sermon on the text "Make thy name remembered in all generations" (from Psalm 45),[132] he was so moved by the sight of the serviceman singing that he felt called to "depart from [his] prepared sermon." He proceeds to talk about the war and the sacrifice by soldiers in the film's three related sections. First, he outlines the Nazi threat to American democracy, presenting the Joe Louis–Max Schmelling fight as a microcosm of the struggle in which the nation is then engaged. Louis's "American fist" won a victory, Moss tells the congregation, but there is more fighting to do.[133] He then relates Hitler's plans for conquest, in ways similar to *Negroes and the War* and *We've Come a Long, Long Way*, and reads a passage from *Mein Kampf* about the inferiority of the Negro. "The Liberty of the earth depends on this outcome," Moss insists, "and Americans have always defended liberty." In the second section of the sermon, he recounts the history of the American defense of liberty with African American men at the center of the story, beginning with Crispus Attucks and the Boston Massacre and moving through the current conflict, conveniently avoiding the question of the Civil War.

The emphasis on black men's service and sacrifice abroad and their return to industrial service at home appears as a major theme throughout this section. The section concludes with a discussion of living "American monuments," including a black explorer, musicians, surgeons, a school principal, a scholar, and a businessman.[134] In Moss's recounting of this history, African Americans are not merely present but significant and central agents of the American cause.

The final section of the sermon returns to the current conflict and to the various capacities in which American men have responded through military service, with an emphasis on American citizens' willing sacrifice in defense of the nation. The majority of this final section consists of an unusual departure from a typical sermon as Mrs. Bronson (Bertha Wolford), a member of the congregation, interrupts Moss's listing of military units in which there are black soldiers to talk about her son, Robert (Lt. Norman Ford), who is about to begin officer training. She soon turns to read the most recent letter she has received from him, in which he describes his induction into the military and arrival at the army reception center, his transfer to the replacement center, and thirteen weeks of training. The section also includes a portrait of black women in the WAC and their training camp, explicitly including black women in the history of defense of American liberty, as was also the case in *We've Come a Long, Long Way*. At the conclusion of the letter, Robert promises his mother that he will complete officer candidate school and receive a commission. Moss steps in again to talk about the men and women who have followed through on similar promises and, after listing a number of men who have made the supreme sacrifice in war, utters a closing prayer in which he says, "Oh God, we thank you for this land which our fathers have helped to build. Grant that we may, with your help, be worthy of this heritage and in our turn enrich it for our children so that government by the people, for the people shall not perish from the earth." The congregation concludes by singing "Onward Christian Soldiers," which segues into "Joshua Fit the Battle of Jericho" and finally "My Country 'Tis of Thee." Significantly, in "Onward Christian Soldiers" the words "with the flag of freedom" substitute for "with the cross of Jesus."[135] In this section of hymns, the African American congregation presents a black tradition of military service (in the spiritual about fighting the battle of Jericho) as the bridge between the religious commitment they share with many white Americans (as Christian soldiers) and full Americanness (claiming "my country").

In many ways—especially because of Moss's initial retreat from his biblical text—religion does seem to be marginal to the film's romantic narrative of America at war. We may recall that Moss begins by saying that he planned to preach from a biblical text but decided to address the current military conflict instead. This "setting aside," as Cripps terms it, is a common rhetorical move in a variety of Protestant homiletical contexts. Typically the preacher notes that he or she has prepared a text but feels moved by the spirit to take up a different topic, thereby underscoring the role of the preacher as conscientious and thoughtful but also an instrument of God's will. To remind the congregation that the sermon is a divinely guided interpretation of God's word heightens expectations about its content. In the course of the film, however, it becomes clear that the sermon that Moss actually delivers is precisely on the biblical text he prepared: "Make thy name remembered in all generations." The opening reference to the biblical text, with Moss's accentuation of its importance, combines with the closing prayer, which refers to past, present, and future generations, in order to provide a strong and explicitly religious frame that many African American viewers would have found familiar.

Between these two significant framing moments, the film explicitly refers to religion on only a few occasions. In the section of the film that focuses on Robert Bronson's army training, however, we see two military chaplains. The first chaplain, who is white, appears briefly at the reception center where the men are being introduced to army life. The chaplain tells them that conducting religious services is only one part of his work and assures them that that they can feel free to come to him for advice about anything. The second chaplain, who is black, appears in the context of a Sunday religious service on the base.[136] Robert writes to his mother that "after a hard week a good soldier welcomes a Sunday." At the conclusion of a hymn the chaplain begins, not a sermon, but a reading of an official army statement about the high level of education among the men and women in the military and about the unprecedented and, in the reality of the U.S. military in 1944, implausible opportunities for blacks in officer candidate school. Here the army document takes on a religious cast as it substitutes for the sermon, contributing to the film's promotion of military service as sacred duty.

The Negro Soldier's presentation of an "American faith" positions African Americans both as fully American and as representative of the Judeo-Christian tradition. Moss's recitation of the first fallen heroes of the current conflict provides a significant example of the film's sense not merely that military service, American identity, and the American faith are *available* to black people but that African Americans have helped to fashion the meaning of these categories. He lists Colin Kelly and Meyer Levin, who were successful in a bombing raid on a Japanese ship near the Philippines, and Dorie Miller, a black navy mess man aboard the *U.S.S. West Virginia* who saved the life of the ship's captain and took control of an antiaircraft gun and shot down four Japanese planes at Pearl Harbor.[137] Americans and soldiers, these men are also marked as Catholic, Jewish, and (presumably) Protestant. Moss and Heisler felt completely comfortable in allowing Dorie Miller to represent the entirety of the category of Protestant and to set him, as a Protestant, in the broader category of American religion.[138]

In positioning African American servicemen and women fully within the American faith, *The Negro Soldier* also attempts to transform typical popular culture representations of black religion. Moss, who was raised Episcopalian but did not practice in adulthood, recalled years later that he selected a church as the setting for *The Negro Soldier* because he felt that it would provide a familiar, comforting, and inspiring context in which to deliver the message of African American contributions to the nation.[139] Where film historians like Thomas Cripps have understood the choice to have been aimed at comforting whites by mobilizing the "unthreatening image" of the naturally religious Negro, Moss himself saw the religious context as making it possible for him to access a shorthand, insider language—he compared what it provided to the informal conversations of a barbershop—and his use of the church as locating the film's story in the heart of the community.[140] At the same time, Moss chose the high church Episcopalian setting of his childhood and emphasized the minister's formal speech over other possibilities for presenting religious life. While he did not comment on this element of his choice, it is probable that, in an attempt to transform traditional film representations of African Americans, he sought a religious sensibility that spoke clearly of middle-class, integrationist aspirations.[141]

Although *The Negro Soldier* was produced for viewing by black soldiers at U.S. Army replacement centers from which troops would be deployed, the army began investigating the possibility of screening the film before a broader audience. In April of 1944 the army previewed the film before groups of black and white soldiers at Camp Pickett, Virginia, and asked the members of the audience to complete questionnaires after seeing the film. The reaction of the black soldiers was strongly positive, with 55 percent characterizing the film as "one of the best I've ever seen" and 36 percent describing it as a very good film. In addition, 90 percent of the black soldiers responded that all soldiers should view the film and 80 percent thought that civilians should have the opportunity to see it as well. Of the white soldiers who filled out the questionnaire—and there were, apparently, a noticeable number who did not—75 percent characterized the film as very good, and 80 percent thought that it should be viewed by all soldiers. According to the report by the Morale Services Division, "They further agreed with the Negro soldier in stating that civilians should be shown the film because it would create better understanding of the

Negro, would show the part he is playing in the war and in the Army, and would improve relations between the races."[142]

Eventually, the army's film showed in a small number of theaters, moving beyond the initial target audience of newly inducted black troops and later all troops at U.S. replacement centers.[143] The black press took up with vigor the cause of getting theaters to show the film and viewers into the theaters. Herman Hill, the *Pittsburgh Courier*'s Hollywood reporter, for example, castigated film exhibitors for capitulating to pressure by southern politicians and exhibitors to block the showing of the film. Reporting on information obtained from "an unimpeachable source," Hill also expressed his suspicion that Fox West Theatres, which owned four hundred theaters, was refusing to show the film unless the War Activities Committee ordered it to do so.[144] Hill concluded that the claim that there were not enough prints of the film to accommodate the theaters was groundless and argued that "the entire incident smacks of war effort sabotage of the worst type." The *Courier*'s New York entertainment page commentator, who published under the by-line "Izzy," followed up on Hill's charges the following week, explaining that the War Activities Committee could not order theaters to take the film and that the reluctance to show it may have had something to do with its running time—too short to be a feature film and too long to be played as a short film.[145] Over the next two months, the paper published articles that provided readers and potential exhibitors with information about where to obtain prints of the film, as well as free publicity materials, and reported a victory when the Fox West Theatre chain announced that it would screen a shorter version of *The Negro Soldier*.[146]

In addition to the usual print advertisements for the film, the War Activities Committee's distribution campaign benefited from the participation of white artists and producers who took up the film's cause. The Entertainment Industry Emergency Committee, an interracial group of entertainers who had pledged to "work for the full freedom and equality of the Negro here at home," sponsored a preview of *The Negro Soldier* to encourage its members and supporters to promote the film.[147] Radio producers Frank and Anne Hummert, who were among the most influential figures in developing the daytime serial, also aided the War Activities Committee in advertising the film. Anne Hummert, who volunteered as a consultant for the War and Treasury departments, incorporated dialogue about the film in the couple's radio shows *Stella Dallas*, *Second Husband*, *Romance of Helen Trent*, *Lora Lawton*, and *Just Plain Bill*.[148] The advertising spots provide a useful example of the ways the film was reinterpreted for consumption by white audiences. Hummert's dialogue makes a strong case to listeners that the information contained within this film about black soldiers is vital to all Americans, and, indeed, her writing emphasizes the Americanness of black Americans. In the spot aired on *Stella Dallas,* for example, Stella returns to the rooming house in which she lives and tells Minnie Grady, her landlady, about the film she has just seen. Minnie asks her what the film was about, and Stella's reply in the script reads:

> It opened in a church . . . a negro church . . . with the organ playin' and the
> choir singing and the congregation filin' in all in Sunday best. . . . [T]he minister—he picks up a book—*Not* the Bible—which he says is to supply his text
> for the day—Hitler's "Mein Kampf"—Then he looks up at the service flag
> with its stars hanging over the pulpit—each representin' a negro soldier in the
> service of our country. . . . He opens Hitler's book—reads what Hitler wrote
> about the negro *and* us in America . . .—the minister looks slowly over his
> congregation and recalls what *they* and *all* of us here in America are fighting
> for—our freedom and the little things we love.— *Then* he begins to show
> how much the negro soldier and race have contributed to the *building* of
> America—(EMPHASIZE THIS) I learned things I had never known before.[149]

Stella resolves to try to get the manager of the local theater to show the film and to get her co-workers at the defense plant to go see it, concluding, "It would do my heart good to have 130 million Americans see it."

Film critics commented on the importance of the film's refusal to employ stereotypical representations of black religion to its power as propaganda. Black actress Fredi Washington, who wrote an entertainment column for the *People's Voice,* lauded the film, characterizing its portrayal as "the most dignified manner in which Negroes have ever been presented on the screen." She further informed her readers: "You will find that those who have been chosen to represent the Negro civilian population are good, clean, wholesome types. The music is fitting with several choirs singing the most beautiful and stirring of the Spirituals."[150] An op-ed in the *Pittsburgh Courier* characterized the film as "refreshingly free of any condescension or Uncle Tomism and Carlton Moss, technical advisor, will long be remembered for his playing of the role of an intelligent and earnest young Negro minister who tells the story of the Negro's contribution to his congregation."[151] *Time*'s reviewer highlighted the importance of religion, writing, "*The Negro Soldier* opens in a Negro church with the sermon of a Negro preacher (Carlton Moss). From its first moment, it is arresting. For the preacher is no Uncle Tom. He does not talk minstrel-show dialect or advise his flock that, for those who bear their afflictions meekly, there will be watermelon by and by or the Hall Johnson Choir in the sky. He talks sober, unrhetorical English."[152] The reviewer was particularly attentive to the reaction of the audience of black soldiers, writing, "At first the men, who have learned to expect veiled contempt in most Hollywood handling of Negroes, froze into hostile silence. But after 20 minutes they were applauding. For just about the first time in screen history their race was presented with honest respect."[153]

At the same time that many viewers and critics saw this film as an "an inspirational document" and "a brave, important and hopeful event in the history of U.S. race relations,"[154] they could not help noting the degree to which it avoided a range of difficult issues. The *New York Times* film reviewer Bosley Crowther found that "[i]t definitely sugar-coats an issue which is broader than the Negro's part in the war. For this reason, it is questionable whether the purpose which it is intended now to serve publicly may not be defeated by the film's own limitations and lacks."[155] The film's religious frame facilitated taking a strong position on the fundamental Americanness of African Americans, but it also made it impossible to criticize the national project that black Americans had been a part of creating. In the world of *The Negro Soldier,* the Civil War was not an important part of the struggle for liberty, the military was not segregated, and African Americans had unlimited opportunities for military service. Barbara Savage writes of the film that its "narrow narrative identified and defined for black and white Americans an enclosed, contained classless community of African Americans who were themselves the embodiment of worthiness. The focus on black soldiers also protected the film from political charges that it was advocating a more socially, racially equal world at home."[156]

Both in its approach to justifying an integrationist perspective through the promotion of an "American faith" and in the limitations of this vision, *The Negro Soldier* presaged a veritable flood of postwar "message movies," as they were called, in which Hollywood studios sought to help their audiences imagine the shape of a pluralist, postwar nation. Taking up racial discrimination in the military and in civilian life, racial violence, and anti-Semitism, the studios released several major films within a three-year period in which they definitively departed from the black-cast model of *Hallelujah, The Green Pastures, Tales of Manhattan,* and *Cabin in the Sky.* Questions about the relationship between religion, race, and American identity figure significantly in many of the message movies. And in different ways, the producers of each of these films faced the same conundrum that confronted Moss in *The Negro Soldier*—how to argue, in the context of persistent segregation and discrimination, that America's "Judeo-Christian tradition" afforded the nation a privileged position in defending liberty.

SIX

"Why Didn't They Tell Me
I'm a Negro?"
Lost Boundaries *and the Moral Landscape
of Race*

In the December 1947 issue of *Reader's Digest* among the usual condensed books, readers found journalist William L. White's account of the experiences of Albert Johnston Jr., who had learned at age sixteen that he was "colored," that the family had been "passing" as white, and that his father "had had to do it, not because he was ashamed of being colored, but only to make their living."[1] White's portrait of the family explained that Albert C. Johnston Sr., a graduate of Rush Medical School in Chicago, had felt forced to pass as white in order to obtain an internship position and begin his career. Having been turned down by a number of hospitals, Johnston finally hid his racial identity and was selected for a position at a hospital in Maine. Eventually, he and his wife, Thyra, who was also of African descent and able to pass as white, moved to New Hampshire, where he began a practice as a small-town doctor. The Johnstons became well-liked and well-respected members of the community, White wrote, and they felt it necessary to reveal the truth to their children only after the U.S. Navy refused to give a commission to Albert Sr. because it discovered during a routine security check that he "had colored blood" and thus failed to meet the necessary physical requirements[2] *Lost Boundaries,* the title of White's piece in *Reader's Digest* and of the book from which the condensed version was drawn, chronicles the psychological difficulties that Albert Jr. faced in adjusting to the news, as well as the divergent responses of his brother and sister to learning the family's secret. White also notes that the revelation was not a great surprise to the Johnstons' white neighbors. He asks, on behalf of his readers, "How do New Englanders feel about the Johnstons now that a number of people have learned the secret? Well, although the Johnstons didn't know it, there have been rumors for years. 'Do you think it's true they are colored?' people would ask each other."[3] Readers of the excerpt from White's book published in *Reader's Digest* also learned that plans were already under way to transform the Johnston's story into a film that would be made by Louis de Rochemont, producer of *The March of Time* newsreel.

The publication of White's account of the Johnston family's story came barely two months after the President's Committee on Civil Rights submitted its report to President Truman and to the nation and thus first came to readers in the context of a national discussion of civil rights and of the moral obligations of citizens to each other. Established by executive order in December of 1946, the civil rights committee's members were a racially integrated group of fifteen men and women, many of whom represented religious groups and whose religious commitments would influence the group's conclusions.[4] The committee's report, which it titled *To Secure These Rights*, recommended the enactment of civil rights legislation that would protect Americans from discrimination in employment, education, housing, and voting, arguing that "the pervasive gap between our aims and what we actually do is creating a kind of moral dry rot which eats away at the emotional and rational bases of democratic beliefs."[5] The report proposed various practical measures to deal with the persistence of racial discrimination in American civic life, and its language often set the American dilemma in religious terms. Its chair noted the difficult nature of the committee's charge, writing: "We have done our honest best with long-standing and perplexing questions. We ask only a fair hearing and a serious discussion of our proposals in the nation's cities, towns, and hamlets. Action to implement our report can only come with the consent of the people expressed through their leaders. We believe that their decisions will be consistent with the ancient tenets of our faith: All men are brothers; and each man *is* his brother's keeper."[6] The committee located its hope for America's future in the soundness of "our faith," that is, an American religion that emphasized equality under God, and expected that this religion could help the nation reach its full political and social potential. The report presented its case with some urgency, noting, "The United States can no longer countenance these burdens on its common conscience, these inroads on its moral fiber."[7]

Many African American political commentators placed little hope in the potential of white liberals in either political or religious arenas to make significant progress on civil rights through the production of surveys and social studies. A "photo-editorial" published in *Ebony* four months after the release of the Committee on Civil Rights' report castigated committee members like chairman Charles E.

Wilson of General Electric for not already having put into practice in his own company the kinds of employment measures the committee's report recommended. As an illustration of the limited employment opportunities for African Americans, the magazine included on the facing page Gordon Parks's photograph "American Gothic," which featured government office cleaner Ella Watson.[8] The editorial noted, "Negroes like the charwoman on the opposite page have suffered the indignities of the broom and mop brigade long enough without having to undergo the additional humiliation of crocodile tears by do-gooders whose wordy incantations over the Negro's cause is so much bombastic buncombe [bunk]."[9] The magazine saved its most stinging criticism for the liberals among the white representatives of the Roman Catholic Church and of Protestant denominations. "Despite all both church groups have done to wipe out racial segregation," the editorial continued, "there are still hundreds of churches of both faiths which will not allow Negroes inside their doors. Just a year ago a Texas Episcopal diocese passed a resolution praising one of its churches for upholding Jim Crow."[10] "President Truman's project," the editorial concluded, "seems doomed to take its place on the bookshelves besides the dozens of others sponsored by well-intentioned foundations and philanthropists who have devoted millions to studying the so-called 'Negro problem' but accomplished virtually nothing basically to improve the Negro's status in the nation."[11]

Hollywood entered the fray of discussion and debate about civil rights and the relationship of race to national identity in the wake of America's experience in World War II with such vigor that one commentator characterized the industry as being on a crusade.[12] In a range of films released between 1946 and 1950, studios portrayed African Americans dealing with racism in integrated military units (*Home of the Brave,* 1949) and in their professional lives (*No Way Out,* 1950), as well as suffering the terrorism of mob violence and lynching (*Intruder in the Dust,* 1950). Other films engaged the experiences of light-skinned blacks who crossed racial boundaries (*Pinky,* 1949; *Lost Boundaries,* 1949). In exploring civil rights questions, some studios took a broader view of race, focusing on the social exclusion of Jews in America and on anti-Semitic violence (*Crossfire,* 1947; *Gentleman's Agreement,* 1948). Still others explored the concept of prejudice more expansively (*The Boy with Green Hair,* 1948 and *Knock on Any Door,* 1949).[13] In some cases, studio heads made explicit their interest in increasing social awareness through film, particularly given recent events in Europe. Darryl F. Zanuck of Twentieth Century-Fox, for example, produced several message movies in the period, and, when asked by Laura Z. Hobson, author of the novel from which the film *Gentleman's Agreement* was drawn, about his motivation, Zanuck spoke to her of his children. "'If this country ever did go fascist,' he went on, 'and they said to me, "Well, pop, what did *you* do to stop it? You had the studios, the money, the power—what did *you* do to fight it off? "'I want to be able to say to them, well, I made *Wilson*, and then I made *Gentleman's Agreement*, I made *Pinky.'*"[14] A number of white actors who played parts in message movies also expressed confidence in the power of film to help reshape American attitudes and culture. John Garfield, who starred as a boxer with Canada Lee in *Body and Soul* (1947) and also appeared in *Gentleman's Agreement*, wrote a piece for *Negro Digest* in 1947 in which he argued that, although it would be impossible to effect sweeping social change through media representations, significant advances could be made. "We'd be naïve," he wrote, "not to know very well that better film treatment of minorities would result in their greater integration in the life of America. . . . I'm convinced that unless the film medium has something to do with the correction of wrong things, it has no real place in our life."[15] Jeanne Crain, who starred in Twentieth Century-Fox's *Pinky*, told reporter Herman Hill of the *Pittsburgh Courier* that "lots of people talk about doing something to improve race relations but few actually do anything about the problem."[16] She emphasized that she was proud to be involved in a production that might make a contribution to the world.

Other commentators saw the studios' turn to social problem films as aimed less at social change than at increasing box-office returns. The film critic Parker Tyler interpreted the emergence of "problem films" as having to do more with Hollywood's "[indifference] to everything but the personal-professional triumph."[17] The historical moment in which the industry found itself, he argued, made this newfound "Higher Creed" profitable for the studios. It is likely that both a concern for engaging pressing social questions and the desire to increase revenue were of interest to the major studios as their executives sensed some interest among their viewers in something more than escapist films. Gregory Peck, who starred in *Gentleman's Agreement*, endorsed such a combination in a 1948 interview published in *Negro Digest*. Anne Strick described Peck as sinking into a leather chair and sighing, "What a job films could do . . . in helping human relations! This movie industry of ours has got to assume its social responsibility or we'll lose our world leadership."[18] By this Peck meant, not American political leadership, but Hollywood's dominance of the international film industry. For him, taking on important stories rather than "throw[ing] more claptrap into the musicals, more gore into the chillers, more horses into the westerns" would ensure continued audience interest both at home and abroad.[19] The actor, writer, and director Burgess Meredith also saw the commercial possibilities of such films, pointing to the recent success of RKO's *Crossfire* and insisting that "Hollywood has proved that it can make a picture on a budget, and which also does well at the box office."[20] The RKO producer Dore Schary was blunt in his conclusion about the relationship between revenue and representation, writing in *Negro Digest* that "[t]his change in attitude, brought on by the war, toward minority characters in films was not purely altruistic—we found we made more money if we didn't offend so many people."[21] With the release by major studios of a number of successful social problem films in this period, *Variety* could note that "[f]ilm's leading b.o. [box office] star for 1949 wasn't a personality, but a subject matter. And a subject—racial prejudice—that until very recently was tabu [*sic*]."[22] Similarly, a *New York Times* reporter noted in the same year that "[t]he question of the American Negro and the cruelty of society toward him is being faced by the film industry this year with a rush which, to an extraplanetary observer, might suggest that the injustice involved is less than seventy-five years old."[23]

Religious institutions, most notably the Protestant Film Commission, also joined in the use of feature films to address religious and racial discrimination, making a case for "a Christian approach" to these issues. The commission received a great deal of media attention for its aggressive campaign to screen its 1949 film *Prejudice*, which it produced in cooperation with the Anti Defamation League of B'nai B'rith, in theaters, churches, and other public venues.[24] The campaign involved screenings of the film in one hundred venues across the nation on a single day in October of 1949. In New York City, approximately one thousand "clerical and lay representatives of religious faiths and Negro groups" gathered at Town Hall to view the film and discuss its story of a white business executive who becomes consumed by prejudice against blacks, Jews, and foreigners.[25] Herman Hill, the Hollywood reporter for the *Pittsburgh Courier*, singled out James Seay, who played the part of the town's minister. "It is he," Hill wrote, "who encourages his parishioners to make his Sunday sermons a part of their daily lives, rather than once a week preachments."[26] While the response to the film's goals was generally positive, particularly among religious activists, industry insiders found the film unsubtle in its approach. *Variety*'s review argued that it "suffers from punching too hard, too directly, and too repetitiously. The story elements are developed without plausibility, serving only as an obvious peg for several long sermons which are used as a substitute for dramatic situations."[27] The trade magazine envisioned churches and schools making good use of the film but did not imagine that it could compete with Hollywood productions for commercial exhibition, a prediction that proved to be true.

Anti-Semitism most often occupied the attention of the studios in the social problem films immediately following the war. Although the issues involved in the message movies' examinations of religion and race with regard to African Americans and Jews differ considerably in important respects—most significantly in the fact that American Jews have generally come to be understood as racially white—some of the producers, directors, and actors involved articulated a connection between the industry's exploration of anti-Semitism and approaches to addressing discrimination against African Americans.[28] In addition, some argued for an incremental approach to promoting social change in which successful films about one issue would enable the production of films about other issues. Edward Dmytryk, director of RKO's *Crossfire*, for example, commented that "[w]e'll be able to crack Jim Crow in pictures, I hope. If we can crack the producers' fears on anti-Semitism as a movie subject, then we can move on and tackle Jim Crow. Main thing is to show the producers they won't lose money."[29] Along these same lines, Gregory Peck asserted that the best possible film on "the Negro problem" would be one that took a similar approach to that of *Gentleman's Agreement*, in which he starred.[30] The journalist and radio executive George Norford wrote for readers of the Urban League's *Opportunity* magazine that, "[h]aving at last mustered the courage to do films on such a controversial issue, it is but another step for Hollywood to talk about prejudice against the Negro."[31]

Whatever set of motivating factors combined to generate this cycle of films, their appearance on movie screens brought questions of national identity and racial tolerance before viewing audiences in ways that marked a change in Hollywood's approach to representing African Americans. In the broadest sense, the films sought to expose white audiences to "the Negro problem," but the language in the black and white press describing them—ranging from "Negro tolerance" and "pro-Negro" films to "anti-Negro" and "anti-Negro hate" films—betrays a measure of confusion about their goals.[32] Although these films ultimately promoted an understanding of racial categories as natural and fixed, they also attempted to elicit sympathy for black characters to a degree rarely seen prior to this period. In reflecting on the message movies that explored varieties of racism, the novelist and cultural critic Ralph Ellison identified a shift from Hollywood's function of "justifying the widely held myth of Negro unhumanness and inferiority by offering entertaining rituals through which that myth could be reaffirmed" to a presentation of a more complex position on race.[33] Ellison also argued that, while these films did represent an advance over Hollywood's deployment of tropes that had signaled African American inferiority in the past, he did not consider them successful in confronting the most significant aspects of American racism or in asserting the full humanity of African Americans. He wrote, "Obviously these films are not *about* Negroes at all; they are about what whites think and feel about Negroes," but he proposed that they were still valuable, particularly because of what African Americans might learn about whites from the reaction of white audiences to the films.[34] Ellison continued, "And yet, despite the absurdities with which these films are laden, they are all worth seeing, and if seen, capable of involving us emotionally. That they do is testimony to the deep centers of American emotion that they touch. . . . And, naturally enough, one of the most interesting experiences connected with viewing them in predominantly white audiences is the profuse flow of tears and the sighs of profound emotional catharsis heard on all sides. It is as though there were some deep relief to be gained merely from seeing these subjects projected upon the screen."[35] The question would remain whether this cathartic experience would have any practical consequences or whether, as with the numerous studies like *To Secure These Rights*, white liberals would be satisfied with simply presenting the facts of racial discrimination.

African Americans, who knew intimately some of the experiences presented in the films, had a range of reactions, most of which differed considerably from those of white audiences, Ellison reported. Were one to sit in an audience of black viewers, he continued, one would find that at the same moments that white audience members cried, African Americans burst into "derisive laughter" at the "phony" notes struck by the stories, performances, and directing techniques. Although there could be no shock of "discovery" of the humiliation of discrimination on the part of black audience members, as was often the case with many white viewers, some members of black communities came to appreciate the films as important in other ways. In some instances they lauded the achievements of black performers in these films, as when James Edwards, World War II veteran and star of *Home of the Brave*, visited New York City in 1949. Not only was Edwards feted in New York by representatives of the NAACP and the mayor's office, but he also attended a service at Emmanuel AME Church in Harlem in which Bishop Decatur Ward Nichols "preach[ed] on the theme of the play."[36] Despite the interest by black viewers in the African American performers, many African American commentators saw the films themselves as seriously limited in their ability to effect social change. This divergent response to the message movies derived, in large measure, from the thematic approach many of the films took to dealing with racial issues

The act of "passing"—the adoption of an identity, usually racial, to gain access to social privileges otherwise denied—emerged as a prominent theme in the postwar message movies.[37] Treatments of the theme in film engaged and extended coverage in popular black and white media during this period of the phenomenon of "white Negroes." In a lengthy piece in *Ebony*, Roi Ottley bemoaned the volume of attention given to the subject, both in "sober sociologists' articles" and in "scare-headline fiction of True Confession pulp style."[38] He pointed in particular to the publication in 1947 of Sinclair Lewis's novel *Kingsblood Royal* as motivating whites to look "around their circle for the elusive 'mulatto in the woodpile,' so to speak."[39] Ottley and the readers who wrote in to discuss the issue of racial passing expressed some amusement that whites would be shocked that "race measurement" had proven an imprecise endeavor or that failing to legislate "the lust of white men" had resulted in varied skin colors among people of African descent in the United States.[40] The year after publishing Ottley's piece, *Ebony* presented its own experiment on racial passing. "Spectacular to the white community today is the fact that as many as 8,000,000 Negroes are 'passing' as white persons," the piece began. "Newspapers, novels, magazines, and even two forthcoming movies are using 'passing' as a popular theme. Many are the articles warning U.S. whites that their doctor or lawyer, their next-door neighbor might be one of those elusive persons."[41] But, the article asked, could white people identify blacks passing as white? The experiment involved sending "Jane Doe," a light-skinned black woman who regularly passed as white, to various Chicago establishments "that normally bar Negroes" and taking photographs of her. The magazine published images of her at a national bowling alley chain that enforced segregation and at a segregated hotel, beauty salon, nightclub, and stenography class. The magazine also sent a dark-skinned woman to the same establishments and reported that she was turned away. The piece concluded, "With an estimated 12,000 light-skinned Negroes annually joining the army of colored Americans who pass, Jim Crow zealots are having an increasingly difficult time in maintaining race lines in their institutions. . . . The dilemma of Jim Crow advocates is the source of thrills for many Negroes who get a kick out of fooling whites."[42] A significant part of the public discourse among African Americans about racial passing emphasized the ease with which blacks could identify other blacks passing as white, and the *Ebony* piece manifests particular glee at the experiment's success at fooling white people.[43] Some years later, Ralph Ellison wrote that "[m]ost Negroes recognize themselves as themselves despite what others might believe them to be. Thus, although the sociologists tell us that thousands of light-skinned Negroes become white each year undetected, most Negroes can spot a paper-thin 'white Negro' every time."[44] On the morality of such deception, Langston Hughes quipped, "Our white folks are very easily fooled. Being so simple about race, why shouldn't they be? They have no business being prejudiced with so much democracy around. But since they are prejudiced, there's no harm in fooling the devil is there?"[45]

By the time Hollywood studios began releasing passing films, the American public had been exposed to coverage of the practice in a variety of sources. For African

Americans, discussions of the issue helped to indict American racial standards, but much of the coverage in the black press also shows enjoyment in the discomfort of whites about the evidence that racial passing provided concerning the constructed-ness of race. As Ellison implies in his assessment of such Hollywood products, these passing films provided a mechanism for white Americans to attempt to work through guilt about American racism and their own racial privilege. In addition, the responses of white viewers to these films provide evidence of heightened anxiety about the very nature of various categories of identity and, in a number of the films, the relationship of American religion to these categories. One of the fictions that invests whiteness with its social power and its sense of immutability is white Americans' security in their own racial identity and their belief, or at least hope, that they can easily recognize those who are not white. At the same time, the fear of being fooled by those passing for white or seeking access to other aspects of white Protestant privilege emerges as a deep and terrifying possibility in many of the "message movies" of the late 1940s. The passing films reveal white Americans' deep commitment to formulations of identity that involve a sense of natural and justified boundaries, particularly when it comes to race, and anxiety about possible reformulations of American identity in the context of discussions about civil rights.

Although the passing films point to white Americans' fear that their supposed racial "purity" is being endangered by hidden infiltrators, these social problem films ultimately affirm a belief in the natural and immutable essence of racial categories and the justness of the social structures that depend upon race. Eventually, the films' violators of racial boundaries accommodate themselves to their "real" racial identity, a conclusion that reinforces the sense of the reality of racial categories.[46] Of this function of passing fiction and film, Valerie Smith notes that

> [t]he narrative trajectories of classic passing texts are typically predetermined; they so fully naturalize certain givens that they mask a range of contradictions inherent within them. For instance, they presuppose that characters who pass for white are betrayers of the black race, and they depend, almost inevitably, upon the association of blackness with self-denial and suffering, and of whiteness with selfishness and material comfort. The combination of these points— passing as betrayal, blackness as self-denial, whiteness as comfort—has the effect of advocating black accommodationism, since the texts repeatedly punish at least this particular form of upward mobility. These texts thus become sites where antiracist and white supremacist ideologies converge, encouraging their black readers to stay in their places.[47]

Thus, while the viewing experience for audiences of varied backgrounds provides a moment in which the fixity of racial categories can be scrutinized and questioned, and for white audience members opens up the terror of the presence of black interlopers among "pure" whites, it ultimately reaffirms and naturalizes race.[48]

While many scholars have explored issues of racializing and, in particular, the gendering of racial identity and racial passing in these films, the relationship of religious discourse to race in many of these narratives has rarely been addressed. The approach that the message movies took to exploring relationships between religion, race, and American identity differed thematically from that of both early Hollywood films and wartime explorations. Films such as *Hallelujah* and *The Green Pastures* figured African American religious practices as hysterical and sexualized and black religious thought as simplistic and childish in ways that served to marginalize black people from conventional formulations of citizenship. During World War II, other Hollywood interventions in productions like *Cabin in the Sky* attempted, through imagining an African American religious world as merely one manifestation of universal human impulses, to bring African Americans closer to the category of simply American. Nevertheless, the wartime cinematic presentations remained largely in the tradition of earlier Hollywood films. With the postwar message movies, the studios deployed liberal religious rhetoric, rather than representations of religious practices or beliefs marked as particularly African American, to promote a sense of human connectedness and equality. At the same time that the films attempted to broaden the category of American citizenship, through religious arguments, to include African Americans, religion also functioned as a powerful means of reaffirming racial categories and boundaries.

In their focus on the experiences of "white Negroes," films like *Lost Boundaries* and *Pinky* explore and chart the moral landscape of race, arguing that racial boundaries are part of the natural order of things and characterizing contravention of these boundaries as sin. Even as these films make the case that discrimination on the basis of race is not an American value, the solutions they pose to "the Negro problem" are profoundly conservative. In the case of *Lost Boundaries*, that conservative resolution relies entirely on Christian language and on the power of religious authority.

A native of New Hampshire, the white producer Louis de Rochemont had found Albert Johnston Jr.'s story so compelling when he met the young man at a social event[49] that he commissioned William L. White's *Reader's Digest* piece with the intention from the start of producing a film about the family's story.[50] The process of turning the chance encounter into a film script was aided by de Rochemont's having recently entered into a contract to develop films for MGM. According to a Hollywood reporter, the studio had determined to "abandon the ivory tower of escapist drama and . . . decided to come to grips with reality," and it brought de Rochemont on board the project because of his experience with *The March of Time* newsreel and the production of documentary-style films.[51] De Rochemont was to have the freedom to select his own products and to film them where he chose, something of particular interest to the East Coast native. The film's development also benefited from the generally positive critical responses and wide coverage White's book received upon publication. Walter White of the NAACP (who was himself able to pass as racially white) reviewed William White's book for the *New York Times*, pointing out "two or three questionable conclusions," but concluded that the brief book "packs into fewer than 100 pages more sound and accurate observation and comment on the question of 'passing' to escape the burdens of color in a caste-ridden America than many ponderous treatises."[52] *Ebony* characterized the book as "exciting," and sociologist Guy B. Johnson described White's account as "simple but moving."[53] By the late fall of 1948, however, de Rochemont and MGM were parting ways, the studio arguing that it was experiencing budgetary pressures and that, because it had undertaken to produce two other "films dealing with other Negro questions," it would not produce *Lost Boundaries*. One report suggested that the studio had dropped the film "because of the fear of 'overemphasis.'"[54] De Rochemont recovered quickly, forming the RD-DR production company with *Reader's Digest* and getting the film into production in early 1949 with a budget of $600,000 and Alfred L. Werker as director.[55] He engaged Charles Palmer, a New England native and Dartmouth graduate who had been working in Los Angeles as a writer, to adapt the book, and the adaptation was completed by screenwriters Virginia Shaler, de Rochemont's wife, and Eugene Ling. The production team consulted with the novelist Ralph Ellison and with the NAACP's Walter White, who wrote to de Rochemont that he hoped the movie would become "a 'desired yardstick' against which to measure the forthcoming cycle. He even predicted success despite white southern audiences' lingering objection to 'the Negro in other than menial or comic roles.'"[56] De Rochemont arranged to film on location on the New Hampshire sea coast, in Maine, and in Harlem in order to achieve the documentary style for which he was known.[57]

As with all the racial passing films in this period, the question of casting created considerable complications, one of which was the response of black actors to the decision to cast white actors in the main parts. Werker told the press early on that the cast "would be both Negro and white and would be culled from [New York] talent agencies," and both de Rochemont and Werker indicated that a Hollywood actor would likely be cast in the lead role.[58] Werker and de Rochemont eventually cast a group of a relatively unknown white actors in the lead roles, with Mel Ferrer as the father, Beatrice Pearson as the mother, Richard Hylton as the son, and Susan Douglas as the daughter. Ferrer, while not known as an actor in Hollywood at the time, had worked as a theater and radio director, and Pearson had appeared in only one film prior to *Lost Boundaries*, which would, in fact, be her last. The film was Douglas's second, and it marked Hylton's film debut.[59] The two black actors who appeared in significant parts in the film were William Greaves, who might have been known to black audiences for his appearance in the black-audience film *Miracle in Harlem* (1948), and Canada Lee, who was the cast's best-known actor but was beginning to have difficulty finding work in the context of the targeting of Hollywood leftists by the House Committee on Un-American Activities.[60] Despite the addition of Lee to the cast, members of the black press as well as black performers objected to the casting decisions.[61] *Ebony* reported on the black press's opposition to the casting but defended the producers by noting the important inclusion of Canada Lee and a number of other black actors. Most significantly, *Ebony*, in its coverage of the film's imminent release and defense of the casting, went to great pains to draw connections between the white cast members and the lives and concerns of people of color. For example, the article described Mel Ferrer as "of Spanish descent by way of South America" as a means of re-racializing him, and it noted that Richard Hylton was "part Indian and his father, who divorced his mother, re-married to a Negro woman."[62] The article also noted that Ferrer had performed in a stage play of Lillian Smith's *Strange Fruit* and, in the most tenuous connection of all, informed readers that Pearson had appeared as John Garfield's wife in a film. Apparently, readers of the *Ebony* article were supposed to think favorably of Pearson because of her loose association with Garfield's screen work in the social problem film *Gentleman's Agreement* and his appearance with Canada Lee in *Body and Soul*.

When the film was finally released, de Rochemont said that two factors had been at play in his not having cast black actors in the film's main parts. First, as an independent producer, he sought ways to keep production costs down, and casting unknown actors and relying on local talent aided in this, as did "the cooperation of townspeople who heartily responded to appeals" for period costumes and props.[63] He also insisted that he had tried "to get a colored cast" but that because of the time constraints of the shooting schedule he was not able to conduct "a thorough canvass of the country for talent to play the lead roles."[64] He also noted that it had proven difficult to convince white actors to take the parts, as many feared "that rumors would be circulated that they were of mixed blood."[65] In his public comments he expressed pride in the courage of the white actors who had taken on the project.[66] Years after the film had been released, William Greaves spoke of his disappointment at the producers' decision not to hire black actors for the parts, but he also recognized the complicated situation in which the filmmakers found themselves, commenting in an interview:

> You have to decide when you make a movie—and it's a tough decision—how authentic, how pure, how faithful you must be to reality while at the same time making this product so that people will go to see it. This is an extremely tricky, difficult challenge for a filmmaker. And in the climate of an extremely racist society, this was a marketing problem. . . . Mel Ferrer, the star, did a very fine piece of work. It was a very moving film. You say, Jesus, why didn't they have some light-skinned blacks in those roles? You can ask that question very aggressively today, but at the time you had to take into account the very cold temperature of the country.[67]

Fredi Washington, the black actress who had played a black character who passes as white in the 1934 film *Imitation of Life*, was not so charitable toward director Werker at the time, referring to him in correspondence with Carlton Moss as "a bigoted crumb of the first order."[68] Her evaluation came in response to a newspaper interview that Werker gave to the *Los Angeles Daily News* in which he said that he had not cast black actors in the parts of the Johnston family because black actors could not convincingly pass as white and because "the majority of Negro actors are of the Uncle Tom, Minstrel show, shuffling dancer type of performer."[69] In a letter to the paper, Washington railed against Werker, noting that "there are many Negro actors and actresses who are consistently turned down for plays and screen fare on the excuse that they are too fair, too intelligent, too modern looking, etc."[70] In her letter to Moss, she said that she had spoken with Werker during the casting period and she believed that "he resented the very fact that there are intelligent and competent Negro actors."[71] Washington engaged the efforts of the Committee on the Negro in the Arts, in which she was active, to publicize the position of the black artists who opposed the practice of casting white actors as African American characters.[72]

Although the film's story did not violate the Production Code's prohibition against representation of "miscegenation," which the code defined as "sex relationships between the white and black races," the issue of what Susan Courtney calls "spectatorial belief" in the legibility of race was also at stake in the casting of the film.[73] Were de Rochemont and Werker to cast white actors, how would audiences read white actors playing black characters passing as white? Were they to cast black actors, the question of the connection between these actors' racial indeterminacy and the prior acts of "miscegenation" that led to their having light skin would be raised. In at least one case, that of the 1934 film *Imitation of Life*, the Production Code Administration (PCA) had broadened its understanding of "miscegenation" to include the act of blacks passing as white. As Courtney notes, the issue that *Imitation* raised was that "miscegenation" had to have taken place some time in the past for the character to be able to pass as white. The PCA censor Joseph Breen wrote of *Imitation of Life* that, because the film's narrative is "founded upon the results of sex association between the white and black race (miscegenation), it not only violates the Production Code but is very dangerous from the standpoint both of industry and public policy."[74] After protracted discussions with the studio and among the censors themselves, the PCA ultimately approved *Imitation of Life* for production and release. By the time the scenario for *Lost Boundaries* came before Breen, he was less concerned about the film's implications of "miscegenation" than he had been with the earlier film, perhaps because of the clear sense that white actors would be cast in the roles of the characters who engaged in racial passing.[75] He quickly approved *Lost Boundaries* in principle, and although he noted that "some unacceptable details may turn up" in the draft of the script, he was open to working with the studio to ensure that the film met the requirements of the code.[76] The film's story includes dating relationships between white characters and two of the black characters who pass as white, but more than ten years after the controversy over *Imitation of Life* these elements of the script did not seem to trouble the PCA.[77] Certainly the fact that the film clearly reinscribes racial boundaries in its conclusion must have mitigated the potential controversy among whites about the subject matter. In addition, the film's self-presentation as a "document of a New Hampshire family" in its opening titles located the narrative in the experiences of real people whose story had already been publicized.[78] The documentary style of the film's presentation, with its emphasis on the basis in a true story, might also have softened the impact of the racial theme for resistant white viewers. Finally, unlike William L. White's written account of the Johnston family's history, the film version of *Lost Boundaries* does not attempt to address the specific racial calculus of the family in question.

In first introducing Scott Carter (Mel Ferrer), *Lost Boundaries* locates him firmly in a community of elite African Americans. The film's opening scenes signal Scott's security in his identity as a black man in a number of ways. Viewers learn early on in the film that Scott is a member of a black fraternity—the fact that will eventually bring his secret into the open—and it is in the fraternity house, surrounded by a group of visibly black guests, that he and Marcia (Beatrice Pearson) are married by a black Episcopal priest, who is described in the script as "a dignified Negro in surplice and stole."[79] Scott's best man is African American, and the guest of honor at the wedding is Dr. Charles Frederick Howard (Emory Richardson), a black doctor who has been Scott's mentor and who has been helping Scott secure an internship position. Scott is determined to "practice medicine as a Negro doctor" and is willing to work as a red cap at the train station in Boston to keep the family afloat should he not be able to secure an internship. When viewers meet Scott Carter, then, there is no implication in the initial framing of his character that would signal his intention or eagerness to reject his racial identity.

His wife, Marcia, however, appears caught between her devotion to Scott and her own experience as a woman of African descent whose father has insisted that she pass as white. Indeed, Marcia's father, Morris Mitchell (Wendell Holmes), would not attend her wedding because, Marcia's mother (Grace Coppin) explains, "Nowadays, Morris won't admit even to himself that we're Negroes." Later in the film, Mr. Mitchell objects to Marcia accompanying Scott when he visits black friends in Boston, including his mentor, Dr. Howard. At dinner one night he says angrily, "I won't have my daughter seen in the company of Negroes." He insists that Marcia has never been identified as a Negro and has no idea what it is like to live as a black person, but Scott counters that she decided to be a Negro when she married him. Despite Mitchell's attempt to convince them of the benefits of passing as white, even though he himself had to leave his darker-skinned sister behind to achieve his goal, Scott maintains that he wishes to live as a black man. Later in the film when Marcia is pregnant, her father tries to convince her that she should not deliver her baby in a hospital because of the danger of people finding out that they are "colored" should the baby have dark skin. As much as Marcia wishes to resist her father's rejection of black identity, she cannot help scrutinizing family photographs as she contemplates her unborn child's skin color. In the end, however, she relies on Scott's insistence, as a scientist, that the baby will not have dark skin. When the baby is born, Werker provides viewers with a well-lit close-up of the baby, whose skin is white, much to the relief of Marcia and her mother. When Scott first sees his son, he comments that he looks like he could be "anybody's baby."

Throughout the portion of the film leading up to Scott's decision to pass, he never exhibits any anxiety about what it means to "live as a Negro" and remains committed to eventually doing so in his professional life. The film's process of moving Scott to make the decision to pass as white differs from William White's account in ways that undermine de Rochemont's claim of presenting the Johnstons' story. Rather than being motivated by the experience of discrimination at the hands of whites to renounce his identity and pass as white, Scott makes the decision largely on the basis of his experiences with blacks. The rejection by African Americans at a black hospital in Atlanta because he appears to be white makes it impossible for him to intern there, and his black friends in Boston encourage him to pass as white in order to complete his internship and establish a practice.[80] Some of them admit that they would do the same if they were able. Even though he also receives letters of rejection from white hospitals, it is his experience in Atlanta that confuses and shakes Scott. Of this element of the film's narrative, Ralph Ellison wrote, "It just isn't real, since there are thousands of mulattoes living as Negroes in the South, many of them Negro leaders. The only functional purpose served by this fiction is to gain sympathy for Carter by placing part of the blame for his predicament upon black Negroes."[81]

Having blamed discrimination by darker-skinned blacks for placing Scott in the position of having to pass as white and deflected responsibility from the racism of white hegemony, the film attempts to elicit sympathy for the situation in which the Carters' teenage children, Howard and Shelly, find themselves by presenting life in the black world as unsavory and terrifying.[82] Werker effects this through the projection of Harlem as urban nightmare, and Louis Applebaum's score at this juncture uses mournful jazz to lend an air of hopelessness to the film's presentation of Harlem. In a bizarre sequence, Howard flees his small hometown in New Hampshire for Harlem, where he rents a room and sleeps fitfully, dreaming that his family members and girlfriend are replaced by dark-skinned blacks. The following night, he hears terrifying screams for help and finds himself arrested when he intervenes in a fight between two men.[83] Howard is fortunate to meet the kindly Lieutenant Thompson (Canada Lee), to whom he talks about his crisis, explaining, "I'm neither white nor black. I'm both." Thompson tries to help Howard accommodate himself to the facts of American racial calculations, replying, "You're a Negro, and there are plenty of other Negroes light enough to be taken for white."[84] At the same time, Thompson confirms the film's presentation of black life as, in Ralph Ellison's description of the film, "a fate worse than a living death."[85] He explains to Howard that his father "was only trying to buy you and your sister a happy childhood. Free as possible from hatred, fear, and prejudice." When Howard protests that he came to Harlem to try to learn what it means to be black, Thompson replies, "I've been a Negro among Negroes all my life, and more than half of it's been spent here on the police force in Harlem. Even knowing as little as you do about how most Negroes have to live, can you blame anyone for trying to cross the boundary into the white man's world?" Seeing that there is nothing but unhappiness in black life, Howard returns to his family. When the film was completed, Walter White was distressed by the Harlem scene, with "a zoot-suited, shifty looking character paring his finger nails in front of the boarding house."[86] Manny Farber, who reviewed the film in the *Nation*, wrote that this scene underscored the film's tendency to blame African Americans for their subordinated status. "Next to the sticky depiction of the folksy, respectable characters in Keene [*sic*], New Hampshire," he wrote, "these shots tend to make the audience feel that the macabre position of the Negro is due to mysterious factors that have nothing to do with small-town America and probably stems from the fact that the Negro on his own does not know how to live."[87] That Marcia tells Howard, "consolingly,"[88] "You haven't done anything, Howard. It's not your fault"—implying that blackness is inherently shameful—shortly before his experience of black urban squalor frames the viewer's interpretation of life in Harlem as a nightmare in powerful ways (see figure 38).

Lost Boundaries' visual presentation of Harlem in the mode of a horror film, rather than in the realist documentary style that characterizes the rest of the film, foregrounds the film's argument about the shame and terror of blackness, and Werker's visual choices contribute to this project in other ways. Although the characters are clearly meant to come across to viewers as convincingly white, something that Werker had insisted only white actors could accomplish, the director employs a number of strategies to highlight the racial indeterminacy of the Carters and mark them as, in reality, Negroes. Werker pairs Scott and his son, Howard (Richard Hylton), with black male characters who represent who they might have been had they been darker skinned, as well as their "inner" black identity. This pairing becomes the literal representation of their white neighbors' description upon finding out the family's secret that "they're black as coal inside." At Scott's graduation from medical school, his friend Jesse Pridham (Rai Saunders) sits in the row behind him, and Werker creates a shot that prevents the viewer's eye from resting easily on one or the other. Jesse appears as a dark echo of Scott, who is in the foreground of the shot. Werker creates a similar visual pairing between Howard and Arthur Cooper (William Greaves), a college friend, when the two share a piano bench and play together. Shelly (Susan Douglas), the Carters' daughter, appears in the strangest pairing— not with a black character but with the family's dog, whose coat is jet black and who appears as Shelly's almost constant companion after she learns her family's secret. Where her brother and father have available models of what it might be like to "live as a Negro," Shelly has no comparable female model—her mother, Marcia, is the

FIGURE 38.

Print advertisement for *Lost Boundaries*. From the author's collection.

only main character without a black doppelganger—and the bizarre pairing with the family's dog foreshadows Shelly's inability to accept her newly discovered racial status.[89] Near the film's end Shelly separates herself from her family and leaves the Sunday service alone before it ends, and the dog awaits her outside the church. The last shot of the film shows the dog returning to the Carters' home alone. An unseen

FIGURE 39.
Marcia and Scott (right) tell Howard the truth about his racial identity in *Lost Boundaries*. Courtesy of Photofest.

person opens the door to allow the dog to enter, signaling Scott, Marcia, and Howard's acceptance of their racial status but Shelly's likely rejection of it.

In addition to deploying black doppelgangers for the main characters, Werker uses light and shadow to signal Howard's struggle with his father's revelation (see figure 39). In the scene during which Scott tells Howard that he's "part Negro," Howard sits on his bed, with his parents standing and flanking him. He turns his head to look at each of them as he responds, incredulous, to their assertion, and his face moves from shadow to light as he does so. Howard begins to pace the room, and his father stops him and apologizes for not having had the courage to tell him the truth earlier. The two men stand facing one another, and Werker signals Howard's resignation by casting a shadow across his face as he hangs his head in defeat. In another striking use of shadow, shortly after Scott and Marcia have told Howard, and Scott must report to the navy, despite the certainty that he will be rejected, Marcia stands at the top of the stairs, and Werker shoots from below. The railing casts a large shadow on the wall that seems to imprison and lock Marcia into her "true" racial status. The film's overdetermined association of whiteness with light and blackness with darkness and shadow will play a part in *Lost Boundaries'* uses of religion to resolve the Carters' racial conflict as Werker's visual strategies are reflected in the religious discourse of the film's minister.

Lost Boundaries relies, in part, on the authority of the police officer—a black man whom the film presents as fully cognizant of a better life outside blackness, yet who works to contain the unruliness of Harlem because he himself cannot escape it—to help Howard accommodate himself to his racial status. The film also appeals to the much more powerful authorizing structure of religious discourse, largely through the character of the white small-town New Hampshire minister, to draw a moral map of race and to reassert the boundaries that have been temporarily contravened by the Carters. The opening narration frames the story of the Carter family in the context of a small-town Protestant community and foreshadows the centrality of the church and its minister in the ultimate resolution of the multivalent problem of passing in this particular story. As viewers see the town square of a quaint and peaceful small town, the camera takes them to an average Main Street and presents a long shot of a New England church. The voice-over narration begins:

> The town of Keenham, New Hampshire is typical of many small New England communities. Though it is a quiet place, one finds many exciting stories in Keenham's history. Its dignified old houses have sheltered many secrets and a lot of them have been scenes of romance, mystery, and sometimes tragedy. Keenham has its share of legends too—of distinguished ghosts who still haunt some of our old rambling mansions. But stranger than any New England legend is the true story of one Keenham family. The setting for this drama of true life is just a stone's throw from the center of town.[90]

Significantly, the film's introduction to the "true life story" presents and then immediately destabilizes the tranquility of Keenham by pointing to the presence of secrets, mystery, tragedy, and ghosts. The narrator's insistence that these things are typical of a New England town makes it difficult for viewers to assume that such elements of life are necessarily a product of the presence of people of color. The narration also makes clear, however, that the story the film presents will be "stranger" than the typical. The various establishing shots of the town locate that strange story at the center of Keenham's life, and the visual punctuation of the camera's focus on the church indicates that this central institution will play a role in the working out of the story.[91] Similar exterior shots of the church appear throughout the film in ways that make the church the primary symbol of the town.

The first test of the Carters' success at racial passing comes immediately after Scott and Marcia have arrived in Keenham, and the scene functions to introduce Rev. John Taylor (Rev. Robert A. Dunn) and his attitudes about race. Marcia is at home alone with the baby when Rev. Taylor and his wife (Patricia Quinn O'Hara) pay a call. Mrs. Taylor is very excited to see the baby, and when they ask the baby's name Marcia tells them proudly that, although he has not been officially named yet, they will name him after someone who has done a great deal for her husband—Dr. Charles Howard. Marcia's face reveals great anxiety as Mrs. Taylor recalls having met a Dr. Charles Howard in Boston, and she is relieved to have to leave the room to answer the telephone. Rev. Taylor whispers to his wife, "We almost made a bad mistake. The Dr. Charles Howard *we* met was Negro." From this exchange we learn two important things about the minister—that he and his wife have socialized with African Americans and that he understands the workings of the American racial hierarchy well enough to have understood his wife's near "mistake" of associating a white person with a black person.

Rev. Taylor is present at every racially significant moment in the Carters' story as both witness and actor. Three of these occasions stand out as particularly important in setting out the film's understanding of the relationship between race and religion in America. In the first scene, Rev. Taylor witnesses an encounter between Scott and a nurse at the Keenham blood bank at the beginning of the war. The scene opens with a shot of a sign nailed to a tree in the town square that reads: "If you can't go to war— Let your blood fight for you. Keenham blood bank." Inside we see Scott, who is in charge of the blood bank. He tells Rev. Taylor, who himself has just donated blood, that he is considering joining the navy in order to put his medical skills to use in the war effort. A nurse holding a bottle of blood interrupts their conversation to ask Scott what she should do with the blood because she "can't ship it with the others." Scott asks why not and she replies, "It came from somebody's chauffeur and he's as black as your hat. We couldn't refuse him, but we can't mix it with the white." Scott insists that the nurse send the blood, and she becomes increasingly disturbed, arguing that sending "black blood" will create trouble for them all. When Scott replies angrily that it will cause more trouble if she does not, the nurse deliberately drops the bottle on the floor. Looking at the broken glass and blood on the floor, Scott responds coldly, "Some fighting man may lose his life because of this, Miss Richmond."

This scene proves a pivotal one in the film because it marks the first occasion on which Scott must take a public stand on issues of race and racism within the community of Keenham. It also represents an attempt on Scott's part to make an argument that dislocates "race" from "blood," a position that he will take later in the context of Naval Intelligence's investigation of his background. Reviewing Scott's application for a commission as well as the information gathered through the investigation, a naval officer asks him, "Doctor, do you have Negro blood in your veins?" Scott answers, "We all have the same blood in our veins." He pauses briefly and continues, "Yes, I am a Negro," refusing to voice a connection between blood and race and insisting obliquely on the biblical pronouncement that God has "made of one blood all nations of men for to dwell on all the face of the earth."[92] In his conflict with Nurse Richmond, Scott asserts his belief as a scientist that race does not adhere in blood in the most graphic way—by insisting that "white" and "black" blood be mixed—an action that would certainly have been shocking to many white viewers at the time of the film's release.[93] Rev. Taylor witnesses Scott's strong reaction to the nurse's racism and approves of his position by agreeing to write a letter of reference for him for the navy, telling Scott, "I'll write you a humdinger—one that will get you by St. Peter." Of course, Rev. Taylor is not aware at this point of Scott's deception, of which, in the film's logic, St. Peter would presumably disapprove because of its dishonesty.

In another critical sequence that contributes to the film's articulation of religious attitudes about race relations, Rev. Taylor and his wife observe a tense racial situation in the parish house of St. Paul's Church and again provide an example, if not a particularly forceful one, of the sense of religious connection across racial lines. The scene is set up by young Howard's decision to bring Arthur Cooper (William Greaves), a college friend, home with him so that the two can work on some music they have been composing together. Because Arthur is a dark-skinned black man, Howard's parents initially exhibit some anxiety about his presence in Keenham, obviously concerned that associating with him will expose them, but they eventually assent to his visit. It is Howard's sister, Shelley, who has the strongest reaction to the visit. She yells at her parents, with disgust, "But he's colored! What will the gang say? With all the boys in college, my brother's got to bring home a coon." Scott chastises her for using a racial epithet and ends the discussion by asserting, "Arthur Cooper is a Negro and he's a friend of Howard's." Just as Scott works within his own family to assert the importance of friendship over race, Rev. Taylor tries to do the same in the church community when Arthur accompanies Howard and Shelley to a dance at the parish house. As the young people mill about at the dance, the scene shifts to the kitchen of the parish house, where a number of women—members of the parish and perhaps mothers of some of the teenagers at the dance or part of the parish house staff—comment on Arthur's presence. One woman tells the others that the cake that Marcia sent to the dance may be fancy but that she "certainly has the strangest ideas socially. I suppose it wasn't her fault, but nobody with any background invites darkies to their home." Out at the dance, Rev. Taylor demonstrates his comfort with the young black man's presence by shaking his hand and encouraging him to dance, presumably with one of the white girls.[94] The film never provides an instance in which Rev. Taylor directly confronts the openly racist members of their community, however, so while he and his wife remain models of appropriate liberal Christian behavior with regard to race, their impact on their neighbors throughout the majority of the film is unclear.

Rev. Taylor functions in a dual role throughout the film. He is at once the spokesperson for the town of Keenham and a representative of a far more liberal position on race relations than that to which most of the townspeople subscribe. As the liberal voice, Rev. Taylor provides a religious argument that is responsible for the final and most significant turn of events in the film. On the first Sunday after Keenham's residents learn the truth about the Carters, Scott and Marcia decide that the family should attend church as usual, despite how hard the children have taken the news. They find themselves shunned by their neighbors, who have gossiped about their being "black as coal inside," as they walk to the center of town. Their arrival at church creates a spectacle as they walk down the aisle to take their places in a front pew. Rev. Taylor begins his sermon by talking about the Christian imperative to respect each individual as God's creation: "Though the spirit of each of us is a candle of the Lord, many have built around this candle a screen of hate and fear and especially of ignorance—a screen that hides the flame not only from our fellows, but from ourselves. In the light of God and of his son who was himself the light of the world, all men are brothers. But how dim is this light in our time? We know that many small candles must be gathered to make a great light." The sermon builds on the image of illuminated candles marking God's work through humanity by pointing to a contemporary political issue that has direct bearing on the community's recent encounter with race:

> I wonder how many of you saw an article in last Tuesday's papers that
> announced that such a candle had recently begun to shine in Washington,
> D.C. It said that commissions of officers in the U.S. Navy will henceforth
> be extended to all qualified citizens regardless of race or color. I do not know
> whether this candle will burn long or bright, but I do know that we in Keen-
> ham have an opportunity today to cause another such candle to shine into the
> shadows. Should this come to pass, it would be good in the sight of God and

of men, for we are all God's children and bear his heavenly image and one man is the image of all men. I am my brother's keeper.

The service concludes with the minister asking the congregation to sing hymn number 519 in their books, "Once to every man and nation comes the moment to decide." The number 519, which viewers have learned was the town's previous doctor's post office box, telephone, and license plate number and which the community gave to Scott in recognition of his service, is significant, as it connects the hymn's sentiments to Scott's place in Keenham. In asking them to sing the hymn, Rev. Taylor says that the number "is well known to all of you because it belongs to our doctor."

Although the minister's sermon and the hymn he selects both place a challenge of acceptance before Keenham's white residents (as well as before the film audience), Rev. Taylor's theological position also indicts Scott and Marcia Carter for their deception. The film lays the ground for this indictment in the scene in which Scott asks Keenham's postmaster to administer the oath he must take to assume his position as a naval officer. The postmaster holds out a Bible for Scott, who hesitates for a moment before beginning the oath—"I, Scott Carter, do solemnly swear . . . " The quick movement in this scene from Scott's excitement at receiving his commission to the tension of taking an oath to be an officer in a division of the military that, at the time, did not admit black men to the ranks of its officers highlights Scott's agency in the deception. No longer is it a situation of having simply failed to disclose information for the purposes of getting a job; in this instance, in taking an oath before God, Scott moves from a sin of omission to a sin of commission. In his sermon, Rev. Taylor argues that hiding the flame of God's candle from one's self is as contrary to God's will as hiding it from others. In this regard, *Lost Boundaries* makes a similar argument to that made much more forcefully and directly in Elia Kazan's *Pinky*, in which Dicey, Pinky's dark-skinned grandmother, tells her that passing is a sin and insists, "Now you tell the Lord what you done, ask his forgiveness on your immortal soul." Rev. Taylor challenges his congregants "to cause [a] candle to shine into the shadows," a directive that, read in the context of the film's play with light and shadow in racialized terms, appears to be as much about helping the Carters come to terms with their "true" racial identities as about encouraging their white neighbors to overcome their racism. Notably, however, the sermon mentions neither race nor racism. At the same time that the minister's sermon indicts Christians for "hiding their lights," it provides few explicitly religious resources to transform race relations. The film presents an easy solution to Scott's problem of not being able to obtain a commission as a naval medical officer by announcing that the navy has changed its policy.[95] As noted earlier, the narrative includes no scenes of Rev. Taylor confronting the racist whispers of the townspeople after they learn the Carters' secret, so the primary model for revised race relations becomes the military rather than the church.

The complex interplay between the lyrics of the hymn and the action onscreen at the conclusion of the church scene underscores the sense produced in Rev. Taylor's sermon that the Carters have sinned in failing to conform to the American "one drop rule." The hymn, "Once to Every Man and Nation," was, in fact, number 519 in the Episcopal Church *Hymnal* (1940), with lyrics taken from an 1845 antiwar poem by James Russell Lowell and using the tune, "Ebenezer" by Thomas John Williams.[96] It seems clear that the screenwriters sought to call forth the association between the doctor's number and the text of the hymn for those viewers who were familiar with the hymnal. Even for those viewers who may not have known the hymn in the context of the Episcopal Church, this scene helps establish the film's moral map of racial boundaries. The first line of the hymn—"Once to every man and nation comes the moment to decide"—seems to lay out the challenge of acceptance before Keenham's white residents, but the camera rests in a medium shot of Howard and Shelly as they stand in the pew and sing along with the members of the congregation, placing the decision on their shoulders. After a brief shot of Scott and Marcia, the camera returns to Howard and Shelly as the congregation sings the next line, "in the strife of truth with falsehood, for the good or evil side." That Shelly decides to leave the church as her family and neighbors sing of good and evil impresses on the viewers the film's argument that the only "good" choice she can make is to accept her true racial status and that rejection of this truth places her on the side of evil. As the camera cuts back inside after following Shelly outside, viewers see Scott and Marcia again in medium shot as they and the congregation sing that wrong is enthroned and truth is upon a scaffold.[97] Again, the conjunction of the hymn's lyrics describing the struggles of truth against wrong with the image of the Carters who have deceived their neighbors is powerful and compelling. Although Werker follows this shot with a various gestures of acceptance on the part of the white congregants—a man in the pew in front of the Carters shakes Scott's hand, and Andy (Carleton Carpenter), Shelly's boyfriend, winks at Howard—the scene concludes with a message that can also be read as both embracing the Carters as under God's protection, and excluding them from the community of God's own. At the hymn's concluding lines, which profess God's presence "within the shadow, keeping watch above His own," Rev. Taylor and the altar boys continue to recess down the aisle. One of the white congregants runs up to the belfry and is soon joined by a number of other white men, who wait for the hymn's conclusion to begin ringing the church bell. The last images of the church scene appear just following the singing of the phrase "keeping watch above His own," and are of this group of white men ringing the church bell. One could easily draw from this scene the conclusion, particularly given the failure to include Scott or Howard in the group, that God's own is a limited group.

The power of the church scene in making the film's argument for a return to appropriate racial boundaries under the prevailing racial hierarchy is made that much greater by Werker and de Rochemont's casting of Rev. Robert A. Dunn, an Episcopal minister and not a professional actor, for this role. His presence in the film, made clear in the opening credits, enhances the authority of the film's religious discourse.[98] Dunn's performance was singled out and praised by many reviewers, and some drew a connection between the film's message and the authority of his collar. Bosley Crowther wrote, "As a matter of fact, the fine performance which the nonprofessional Mr. Dunn gives as a clergyman in the community who rallies the humanity of the townsfolk at the end is one of the most important and persuasive performances in the film, for upon it depends the credibility of the whole demonstration of the essential theme, which is that the brotherhood of mankind does not draw a color line."[99] As various critics noted, the film's impact relied heavily on its self-presentation as a true story in "re-enactment style," and the casting of an actual minister contributes to the effect. Most reviewers focused on the unexpectedness of Dunn's solid performance, but even more significant is the authority that the presence of an ordained minister lends to the film's conclusion that, while "we are all God's children and bear his heavenly image," racial boundaries are also natural and appropriate. Indeed, the film's title frames its "real life drama" as one that is not about the dissolution of boundaries but about the search to reinstate them. The message of *Lost Boundaries* is not that the "color line" should be erased or that, in light of the possibilities of racial passing, one should question the very nature of race. Finally, the film looks only to redefine the valence of the color line, accepting its existence as natural but presenting a weak case that those unfortunate enough to find themselves on the black side of the line should not be stigmatized. The minister's sermon encourages white Keenham to accept the Carters as *Negro* residents of Keenham, rather than to think about race in a different way after discovering that these white people are "really" black.[100]

This conclusion was, apparently, much milder than the original version of the script, the ending of which sought to reincorporate the Carters into Keenham after they had been explicitly punished for their transgression. Mel Ferrer spoke of the struggle in which he engaged with the film's producer, writers, and director over the film's ending. "The writers originally felt that Dr. Carter should be a bit more humble at the end," he recounted, "that he had made a mistake in trying to pass, that perhaps he should be punished, slapped on the wrists and be allowed to return to his home town but on terms dictated by his white neighbors."[101] After an all-night discussion in which he insisted that he would be ashamed to have participated in the project if the film ended in that way, and that it was essential that the Carters stay in Keenham on their own terms, the writers reworked the script. While there is no explicit punishment of the Carters at the film's conclusion, the implication that they have sinned against nature is strong. Gayle Wald sees such a strategy in both *Pinky* and *Lost Boundaries*, in which "the disciplining of the passer is achieved not through the explicit use of force, but through the character's own, apparently uncoerced internalization of the idea that passing is a form of self-deception."[102] Despite Ferrer's satisfaction with the revisions of the final scene, the implicit punishment of the Carters for their sins in the final version reinforces racial boundaries.

The *Chicago Daily Tribune*'s film reviewer found the film's unwillingness to follow the Carters' story past the end of the church service, with the exception of the voice-over indicating that Scott was still the town's doctor, to be a positive quality. "The film offers no solution to the young Carters' problems," the review declared, "but shows that under the wise guidance of a truly Christian minister, the people of Keenham were willing and able to accept their physician and friend as they had in the past."[103] Brazilian poet and film critic Vinicius de Morae criticized the film's weak conclusion, asserting that "[i]n *Lost Boundaries*, the Negro doctor and his family, who have passed as white, are exposed. Their expulsion from the community is prevented only by the intervention of a pastor who from the pulpit protects them from 'the stain,' basing himself on Biblical text. But the film ends there. The story goes not further. Does the Negro girl, sweetheart of a white boy, continue her romance? Does the doctor, until then an outstanding figure in the city, go on healing white bodies with his 'black hands'?"[104] That the film's black characters exhibit little will or agency in determining the course of their lives underscores the strong sense in the film that whatever shape postwar national identity will take is entirely in the hands of white Americans. In making the case that some "qualified" blacks are denied access to deserved employment, the film presents an array of black characters who not only would prefer to have the economic opportunities that whites have but also desperately long to *be* white. Ralph Ellison, whom de Rochemont consulted on the script, criticized the film's characterization of the Carter family's members as weak.[105] Critic Seymour Peck wrote in *Compass* that he was disturbed that the film "approaches Dr.

Carter with an air of kindly condescension. One might expect him to be a man of fierce pride in his race, its culture . . . yet he goes through the picture feeling ashamed and guilty. . . . When, at the end the townspeople find out he is a Negro, it is as though they are forgiving him for being a Negro, as though they are being generous because he looks so darned white anyway."[106]

Despite the fears of some—most notably among the studio executives at MGM—that the subject matter of *Lost Boundaries* would prove too controversial for audiences, the film received generally positive reviews from black and white critics on its release in the summer of 1949 and also did quite well at the box office. Many of those involved in the production articulated their pride in the social work that they felt the film might accomplish. At the film's Portsmouth, New Hampshire premiere, Canada Lee, who was the cast's most famous actor, declared of the work, "It's about America . . . , our America that I read about in books when I was a boy. Our America that I read about in books but was not so—for me. . . . You see a picture like this and hear all the applause and begin to believe again."[107] The *Hollywood Reporter*, an industry paper, predicted that "[a]t the box office, 'Lost Boundaries' will unquestionably return its $600,000 investment and much more. Its provocative theme assures unusual audience interest. Additionally, the film may expect militant support from church groups and the many other organizations interested in the betterment of race relations in the United States."[108] Bosley Crowther of the *New York Times* commented that "'Lost Boundaries' visualizes emotional experience in terms so plausible and basically revealing that its impact is irresistible."[109] He noted that he felt the limitations of the focus on the experience of a relatively small number of African Americans who could pass as white, as well as the limitations of the New Hampshire setting. "But, for all that," he continued, "its statement of the anguish and the ironies of racial taboo is clear, eloquent and moving. There are tears and there is scripture in this film."[110] Edwin Schallert wrote, "One is conscious of the fact that pictures like 'Lost Boundaries' today stir the attention of audiences. This particular one happens to be unique because it is so splendidly brought to fulfillment."[111] The film won a number of major awards, including Best Screenplay at the Cannes Film Festival and Directorial Achievement for Alfred Werker from the Screen Directors Guild. The *New York Times* and the Protestant Motion Picture Council both placed *Lost Boundaries* on their lists of best films of 1949.

The film ultimately received even more attention as a result of the struggle to have it exhibited in the South than for its address of issues of race in America. In her gossip column in early July of 1949, Hedda Hopper wrote that "[w]e are wait-ing for the Texas reaction to 'Home of the Brave,' the first picture shown there deal-ing with the Negro problem. On its reception will be decided the southern fate of 'Pinky,' 'Intruder in the Dust,' 'Lost Boundaries.'"[112] As it turned out, *Home of the Brave* would not face the kind of opposition that both *Lost Boundaries* and *Pinky* would, with *Lost Boundaries* being banned in Atlanta and Memphis in August of 1949. Christine Smith, Atlanta's movie censor, refused to allow the film to be shown on the grounds that exhibiting it would be "contrary to the public good."[113] The Atlanta city ordinance that empowered her allowed the censor to restrict access to films that were "obscene, lewd, licentious, profane, or will in his opinion adversely affect the peace, health, morals and good order of the city."[114] Lloyd T. Binford, chairman of the Memphis Board of Censors, refused to elaborate on the board's reasoning behind the decision, commenting only that "we don't take that kind of picture here."[115] The following month, when Smith agreed to allow the exhibition of *Pinky* (which opened with a strong police presence at the theater),[116] she commented that "she was sorry that Hollywood had started to make racial pictures. 'The problem is so complicated and many people have devoted a lifetime to it without finding the answers,' she stated." Of *Pinky*, she said, "'I know this picture is going to be painful to a great many Southerners. It will make them squirm, but at the same time it will make them realize how unlovely their attitudes are.' She said she hoped people would view it as entertainment and also learn that 'Negroes are different than they think they are and that Negroes are people and individuals.'"[117] Although Smith was clearly try-ing to extend herself and make her position understood by whites outside the South, her formulation of "people" who would view the film as necessarily white reinforced the degree to which a commitment to southern racial hierarchy framed her approach to the films.

In later comments about the place of censorship in American life and about her own work as a censor, Smith emphasized her role as a guardian of morals. In this case, she underscored the centrality of racial segregation to the moral landscape of her city. In his examination of Atlantans' responses to "pro-Negro films," Gerald Weales interviewed Smith and reported, "Miss Smith resents the continual interest in her treatment of racial pictures, for she feels that a large part of her work, that involving morality, is ignored."[118] While she considered racial violence to be morally objectionable and forbade the exhibition of D. W. Griffith's *The Birth of a Nation* during her years as Atlanta's censor, the only other films she banned in that time were the 1934 *Imitation of Life* and *Lost Boundaries*. In both cases, Weales reported, she understood that the "films present passing favorably."[119] *Pinky*, on the other hand, which also focuses its narrative on racial passing, she permitted to be exhibited because it did not violate the letter of Georgia segregation laws. In that film, the main character Pinky passed as white while living in the North and outside the diegesis of the film. Within the world of the film, she adheres to the requirements of racial segregation and ultimately decides to remain in the South and live as an African American. It is striking that Smith read *Lost Boundaries* as endorsing passing, since the film's conclusion casts as sinful the fact that Scott and Marcia Carter hid their family histories from their children and their neighbors. The challenge for the white characters in the film is to accept them as Negroes, not to imagine that race is not located in blood or to come to understand the socially constructed nature of race. Smith obviously found the continued interaction between the film's black and white characters, even after the revelation that the Carters are black, to be morally offensive.

The rest of the course of the case of the banning of *Lost Boundaries* in Atlanta proceeded in a direction that subordinated the issue of the film's charting of the moral landscape of race to other legal issues. De Rochemont filed suit against the Atlanta censors, charging that the ban violated his constitutional right to free expression, and also arranged for the film to be aired on television in Atlanta and Memphis.[120] The U.S. Supreme Court eventually declined to hear the case, which became focused on the question of whether films fell under the protection of the First Amendment rights to freedom of the press or, as had been the traditional legal position, should be understood as "spectacles" and therefore not protected.[121] In a federal court's review of the case, the judge decided that "[I]n essence that part of the ordinance presently under scrutiny empowers the Censor to determine what is good and what is bad for the community and that without any standard other than the Censor's personal opinion. As here applied it attempts a degree of thought control but unless motion pictures can be afforded the coverage extended the press it is clear that the police power of the State has not been exceeded."[122] Although the central focus of the plaintiffs in the *Lost Boundaries* case was on the question of the protection of film as free speech, some industry watchers interpreted the Supreme Court's refusal to hear the case as a racialized one:

A key reason behind the U.S. Supreme Court's refusal to hear the "Lost Boundaries" censorship appeal case, it was reliably learned today, was a feeling among some of the justices that this could be considered another "racial discrimination" case and that the Court had taken enough action in the controversial anti-discrimination field for the time being. . . . The justices themselves, when they came together to discuss the orders for the following week, had a long and heated debate on the case. Finally, the point was made that the Court had already acted on cases of racial discrimination involving educational facilities, public golf courses, dining cars, and other facilities, and that since the film case might also be interpreted in some areas as another attempt of the Court to lay down rules on discrimination, perhaps the court should call a halt for the time being.[123]

Although, to a certain extent, the legal struggle overshadowed *Lost Boundaries'* approach to issues of race and religion, the controversy also served to keep the film in the public eye long after its period of initial release and, perhaps, added longevity to its moral message. *Lost Boundaries* stands as a powerful representation of the ways in which the passing films in this period charted a moral landscape of racial boundaries that, while marking a change in the representation of the relationship between religion, race, and citizenship, nevertheless leave African Americans in a position in which they are unfortunate and devalued by virtue of their blackness and morally suspect in their desire to be white. Rather than presenting spectacular representations of black religious practices to draw hard racial boundaries, *Lost Boundaries* deployed liberal Christian rhetoric to support and defend conventional understandings of race in equally powerful ways.

Conclusion

I have been concerned in the course of this book with the contexts in which and processes through which filmmakers produced images and discourses about African American religion in the first decades of sound film. As becomes readily apparent from even a cursory survey of the Hollywood films produced in this period that featured black casts and in which African American stories were central, the white writers, producers, and directors of these films saw representations of religious behavior, community, institutions, and leaders as natural and important elements of their work. Religion, many of them understood, was a prominent feature of black public life and culture and as such merited attention and provided appealing material for artistic development. At the same time, the presence in Hollywood films of varied and sometimes conflicting constructions of the "natural" or "authentic" mode of black religious expression reveals the implicit and at times explicit ideological purposes of turning to such representations. It was more than simply the significance of religion in black culture that attracted the attention of white filmmakers. Religion, these Hollywood films argue, helps us make meaning of blackness, and the meanings produced in mainstream films reflect varied understandings of race, the social and moral requirements of American citizenship, and the very nature of American identity.

As tempting as it might be to simply label productions like *Hallelujah*, *The Green Pastures*, *Tales of Manhattan*, and *Cabin in the Sky* as racist and irredeemably problematic in their projections of black religiosity and to leave it at that, the more complex reality of relationships between ideas about black religion and conclusions about the capacity of black people to function as trustworthy moral agents in society requires careful attention. Many of the representations are, undeniably, based in notions that derive from commitment to racial hierarchy and to a belief in natural white supremacy. In some renderings the films present African American religious thought as a fundamentally childish understanding of the workings of divine power, and, in others African American religious expression is inseparable from and compromised by sexual expression. In most, black religion becomes a sign and a symptom of the perpetual backwardness and outsider status of African Americans. Such representations in mainstream Hollywood film are, at the same time, quite complex and often nuanced in how they present such a case, and I have tried to be attentive to this variety, as well as to differences over time in response to changes and events in the culture at large. In addition, consideration of the complicated process of production of Hollywood films, one that involved writers, directors, producers, performers, and censors, reveals much about the implicit and explicit concerns of those involved with regard to the politics of representing African American religiosity. Charting the multiple modes through which mainstream films conveyed information about black religion and constructed ideas about blackness underscores the complex power of cultural productions to speak from and to particular historical moments.

African American cultural critics, politicians, artists, and members of the general public who consumed or monitored mainstream film products engaged in vigorous conversation about the potential social and political ramifications of what, to many white Americans, appeared to be innocuous entertainment. Neither contemporary black observers nor I in my analysis argue that Hollywood films played a determinative role in shaping black civic fortunes. Nevertheless, the vigorous discussions in black communities about these cultural products and the creativity with which black artists, some of whom participated in the production of what they saw as dangerous pieces of art, responded through artistic means give clear indication of the seriousness with which many African American engaged the movies.

For their part, black artists like Spencer Williams and Eloyce and James Gist who produced explicitly religious films situated their work in the context of ongoing discussions among African Americans, both in and outside churches, about the place of church institutions in modern, urban America and the degree to which religious African Americans should engage popular culture. The productions that emerged from companies that catered to black audiences reveal a desire on the part of some filmmakers to incorporate film as a part of the culture of African American Christian life. Other producers and directors saw the inclusion of religious themes and characters as having commercial appeal because of the importance of religious affiliation and expression in the lives of many African Americans. Taking seriously the work of black artists who made religious films and recognizing the enthusiastic responses of audience members to these films underscores the importance of scholarly attentiveness to the existence of alternative spaces for African American religious activity—like the movie theater—and alternative modes of being religious that might derive from these underground or subversive religious spaces. In examining the explicitly religious approaches of independent and semi-independent black films in this period, as well as the projections of black religion in secular race movies, I have endeavored to broaden the scope of the discussion about the complicated interactions between sacred and secular in black religious life and to make possible ways of thinking about unconventional constructions of sacred space.

I have also sought to open up new avenues for research in the increasingly popular area of "religion and film" studies, particularly with regard to scope and methodology. Much of the work from within religious studies on this topic examines recent movies and focuses on uncovering mythic, ritual, or ethical structures encoded in films. Consequently, with the exception of work on biblical and religious epics of the 1950s and scholarship, largely from within film studies, on silent religious films, there has developed little sense of the historical trajectories of filmic imaginings of religion. Critical attention to earlier periods of film history, regardless of whether the representational approaches to religion differ from those taken by recent filmmakers, is crucial to developing a full understanding of the means of, the approaches to, and the reception of popular culture representations of religion in America. Moreover, careful attention to the historical contexts in which these movies were produced and to the ways they resonated in varied communities of viewers only serves to enhance our close readings of film narrative and analysis of aesthetics. It is important to take account of the enduring power of particular films, but it is equally important to examine closely the relationship between specific cultural products and the historical moment of their production, and this concern has been central to my approach to this topic.

The two separate but sometimes intertwining trajectories of filmmaking that I have traced in this book reveal the ways in which representations of African American religious thought, practice, individuals, and institutions have been central to the development of film discourse about race and about the place of African Americans in American life. The trajectories—mainstream Hollywood and independent and semi-independent race movies—have encountered one another at different points in time through the movement of individuals across the various realms of film production and as a result of the filmic conversations and contestations over how to represent black religion in film. Representations of religion remain important to American film's constructions of racialized identities and projections of African Americans in particular, even as the approaches to presenting African American religion have been considerably transformed in both Hollywood and black film. The rise of independent film in the United States and the participation of black filmmakers in this movement have brought to film audiences narrative and visual approaches to representing African American religion that are not necessarily beholden to the requirements of Hollywood story and style. For their part, Hollywood films have used African American religious practices more frequently as a means of situating and developing a movie's white characters than as a way of speaking about black identity or community. The considerable social and cultural changes that have occurred in the years between the production of the early black-cast Hollywood and race films on the one hand and late-twentieth- and early-twenty-first-century movies on the other have necessarily fostered thematic and visual changes in film representations of African American religion. The history of the means by which those changes have taken place and the resulting cultural products is eminently worthy of scholarly investigation. But that is a story for another book.

FILMOGRAPHY

The Black King, dir. Bud Pollard (Southland Pictures Corp., 1932).

The Blood of Jesus, dir. Spencer Williams (Sack Amusement Enterprises, 1941).

Body and Soul, dir. Oscar Micheaux (Micheaux Film Corp., 1925).

Brother Martin, Servant of Jesus, dir. Spencer Williams (Jenkins and Bourgeois, 1942).

Cabin in the Sky, dir. Vincente Minnelli (Metro-Goldwyn-Mayer, 1943).

Clean Pastures, dir. Isadore Freleng (Warner Bros., 1937).

Dirty Gertie from Harlem U.S.A., dir. Spencer Williams (Sack Amusement Enterprises, 1946).

Gentleman's Agreement, dir. Elia Kazan (Twentieth Century-Fox, 1948).

Go Down, Death, dir. Spencer Williams (Sack Amusement Enterprises, 1944).

Going to Glory, Come to Jesus, dir. unknown (Royal Gospel Productions, 1947).

The Green Pastures, dir. Marc Connelly and William Keighley (Warner Bros., 1936).

Hallelujah, dir. King Vidor (Metro-Goldwyn-Mayer, 1929).

Hell Bound Train, dir. Eloyce Gist and James Gist (n.d.).

Lost Boundaries, dir. Alfred L. Werker (RD-DR Corp, 1949).

Marching On (rereleased as *Where's My Man To-Nite?*), dir. Spencer Williams (Sack Amusement Enterprises, 1943).

Midnight Shadow, dir. George Randol (Sack Amusement Enterprises, 1939).

Miracle in Harlem, dir. Jack Kemp (Herald Pictures, 1948).

The Negro Soldier, dir. Stuart Heisler (U.S. War Department, 1944).

Of One Blood, dir. Spencer Williams (Sack Amusement Enterprises, 1944).

Paradise in Harlem, dir. Joseph Seiden (Jubilee Pictures Corp., 1940).

Sunday Sinners, dir. Arthur Dreifuss (Colonnade Pictures Corp., 1941).

Tales of Manhattan, dir. Julien Duvivier (Twentieth Century-Fox, 1942).

We've Come a Long, Long Way, dir. Jack Goldberg (Negro Marches On, Inc., 1944).

Within Our Gates, dir. Oscar Micheaux (Micheaux Film Co., 1919).

Young Man with a Horn, dir. Michael Curtiz (Warner Bros., 1950).

NOTES

The following abbreviations are used throughout:

AFC   Arthur Freed Collection, Performing Arts Archives, Cinema-Television Library, University of Southern California

AMPAS   Margaret Herrick Library, Academy of Motion Picture Arts and Sciences

KVC   King Vidor Collection, Performing Arts Archives, Cinema-Television Library, University of Southern California

MGMC   Metro-Goldwyn-Mayer Collection, Performing Arts Archives, Cinema-Television Library, University of Southern California

MPPDA   Motion Picture Producers and Distributors Association

NACP   National Archives at College Park, College Park, Maryland

NYPL   New York Public Library

NYSA   New York State Archives, Cultural Education Center

UCLA   University of California, Los Angeles

INTRODUCTION

1. *The King of Kings*, dir. Cecil B. DeMille (Pathé, 1927). *Baltimore Afro-American*, December 1, 1928. On movie theaters that catered to black audiences, see Jack Alicoate, ed., *The 1930 Film Daily Yearbook of Motion Pictures* (New York: 1930), 795; Jacqueline Najuma Stewart, *Migrating to the Movies: Cinema and Black Urban Modernity* (Berkeley: University of California Press, 2005), ch. 5.

2. *Baltimore Afro-American*, December 1, 1928.

3. In fact, DeMille prefaced this particular biblical story with intertitles that read: "This is the story of JESUS OF NAZARETH. . . . He, Himself, commanded that His message be carried to the uttermost parts of the earth. May this portrayal play a reverent part in the spirit of that great command." On the possibilities of using film for religious education, see Cecil B. DeMille, "The Screen as a Religious Teacher," *Theatre*, June 1927. His other Bible films included *The Ten Commandments* (Paramount/ Famous Players-Lasky, 1923), *The Sign of the Cross* (Paramount, 1933), *Samson and Delilah* (Paramount, 1949), and *The Ten Commandments* (Paramount, 1956).

4. *California Eagle*, June 9, 1933. *The Sign of the Cross*, dir. Cecil B. DeMille (Paramount, 1933). Both *The King of Kings* and *The Sign of the Cross* generated controversy for DeMille. Many American Jews objected to "malicious and scurrilous caricatures of the Jew" in *The King of Kings*, and the censors found problems with the explicit expressions of sexuality in *The Sign of the Cross*. On *The King of Kings*, see Felicia Herman, "'The Most Dangerous Anti-Semitic Photoplay in Filmdom': American Jews and *The King of Kings* (DeMille, 1927)," *Velvet Light Trap: A Critical Journal of Film and Television* 46 (Fall 2000): 12–25, and "American Jews and the Effort to Reform Motion Pictures, 1933–1935," *American Jewish Archives Journal* 52, nos. 1 and 2 (2001): 11–44.

5. *The Crisis*, November 1934. In 1948 Miller and Thurgood Marshall argued for the plaintiffs in *Shelley v. Kraemer*, in which the U.S. Supreme Court struck down race-based restrictive covenants in housing. In 1951 he bought the *California Eagle*, a black-owned and operated newspaper that had been published since 1874, and he worked with Cyril Briggs, Benjamin J. Davis, and William L. Patterson in editing the Crusader News Agency press releases in the 1930s and 1940s. Miller became a municipal court judge in Los Angeles in 1960. See obituary, *New York Times*, July 16, 1967.

6. Small production companies that made low-budget "B" films.

7. Data compiled by the Bureau of the Census on U.S. religious bodies indicate

that, in 1926, recognized African American religious institutions claimed over 5.2 million adherents, and the Census Bureau noted that many of the churches that responded did not include young people in the membership statistics. U.S. Department of Commerce, Bureau of the Census, *Religious Bodies: 1926* (Washington, DC: Government Printing Office, 1930), 1:69. The 1920 census put the total African American population at approximately 10.5 million.

8. Daniel Bernardi, ed., *The Birth of Whiteness: Race and the Emergence of U.S. Cinema* (New Brunswick: Rutgers University Press, 1996), 7. I use the term *racializing* to insist upon the ongoing process of constructing racial categories and to avoid any implication of races as "natural" entities. Also see Daniel Bernardi, ed., *Classic Hollywood, Classic Whiteness* (Minneapolis: University of Minnesota Press, 2001); Matthew Bernstein and Gaylyn Studlar, eds., *Visions of the East: Orientalism in Film* (New Brunswick: Rutgers University Press, 1997); Lola Young, *Fear of the Dark: "Race," Gender and Sexuality in the Cinema* (New York: Routledge, 1996); James Snead, *White Screens, Black Images: Hollywood from the Dark Side*, ed. Colin MacCabe and Cornel West (New York: Routledge, 1994); Randall M. Miller, ed., *The Kaleidoscopic Lens: How Hollywood Views Ethnic Groups* (Englewood, NJ: Ozer, 1980).

9. On the studio system, see David Bordwell, Janet Staiger, and Kristin Thompson, *The Classical Hollywood Cinema: Film Style and Mode of Production to 1960* (New York: Columbia University Press, 1985), which defines the "classical Hollywood cinema" by both stylistic markers and issues relating to production and exhibition. Bordwell, Staiger, and Thompson argue that the classical Hollywood system was in place from 1917 until 1960 and that it involved a particular style of narrative that emphasized realism through character and motivation, causation, and the creation of a coherent world in the use of space, composition, sound, and editing. In addition, the vertically integrated studio system, in which studios controlled production, distribution, and exhibition of films, prevailed. More recently, Linda Williams has argued against understanding "classical realism" as the single or even dominant form, in favor of highlighting the importance of melodrama, not simply as a genre or subgenre, but as "a central *mode* of American popular culture." Linda Williams, *Playing the Race Card: Melodramas of Black and White from Uncle Tom to O.J. Simpson* (Princeton: Princeton University Press, 2001), xiv.

10. Teresa de Lauretis, *Technologies of Gender: Essays on Theory, Film, and Fiction* (Bloomington: Indiana University Press, 1987), 2. De Lauretis begins with Michel Foucault's understanding of the "technology of sex," but she emphasizes the differential constitution of male and female subjectivity. She does not explore racialized subjectivity here in relation to either sexual difference or the production of gender. I would emphasize the connection between all three but choose to begin with race and understand its connections to religion, gender, and sexuality.

11. Lillian Smith, *Killers of the Dream* (New York: W. W. Norton, 1949), 17.

12. On religion and constructions of race, see Henry Goldschmidt and Elizabeth McAlister, eds., *Race, Nation, and Religion in the Americas* (Oxford: Oxford University Press, 2004).

13. Thomas Doherty, *Pre-Code Hollywood: Sex, Immorality, and Insurrection in American Cinema, 1930–1934* (New York: Columbia University Press, 1999), 5. Indeed, the most comprehensive statement for film writers and reviewers in the period compared the censorship guidelines to the Ten Commandments. Olga J. Martin, *Hollywood's Movie Commandments: A Handbook for Motion Picture Writers and Reviewers* (New York: H. W. Wilson, 1937). Also see Lea Jacobs, *The Wages of Sin: Censorship and the Fallen Woman Film, 1928–1942* (Madison: University of Wisconsin Press, 1991); Gregory D. Black, *Hollywood Censored: Morality Codes, Catholics and the Movies* (Cambridge: Cambridge University Press, 1994), and *The Catholic Crusade against the Movies, 1940–1975* (Cambridge: Cambridge University Press, 1998).

14. Fred Eastman, "What Can We Do about the Movies?" *Christian Century,* June 14, 1933, 781.

15. Martin Quigley, *Decency in Motion Pictures* (New York: Macmillan, 1937), 55. On the hopeful approach of some African American media commentators, see *Baltimore Afro-American,* September 15, 1927, Tuskegee Institute News Clipping File. In applying the prohibition against "miscegenation," the PCA also included most cases of "sex union between the white and yellow races." According to Olga J. Martin, Joseph Breen's secretary, the PCA did not interpret some sexual interactions between whites and people of color as miscegenation. "The union of a member of the Polynesians and allied races of the Island groups with a member of the white race is not ordinarily considered a miscegenetic relationship, however. The union of a half-caste of white and Polynesian parentage with a white member would also be exempt from the rule applying to miscegenation." Martin, *Hollywood's Movie Commandments,* 178.

16. Episcopal Canon William Sheafe Chase of Christ Church in Brooklyn, for example, chaired the New York Civic League and published multiple editions of the *Catechism on Motion Pictures in Inter-State Commerce* in which he argued for federal regulation of the industry, not trusting the studios to censor themselves. "The question," Chase asked, "is, shall the Congress take effective action to prevent the crime-producing pictures being shown in picture houses and shall it authorize an effective method by which a few faithful men, appointed by the Government, and representing the people, shall carry that decision into effect? Or shall the pictures which the children are to see be chosen by Mr. Fox, Mr. Zukor, Mr. Loew, Mr. Laemmle and Mr. Lasky, who control almost the whole of the motion picture business of the United States? Shall no effective control be exercised over these Jews as to prevent their showing such pictures as will bring them the greatest financial returns, irrespective of the moral injury they inflict upon the people?" For Chase, Jews were an unassimilable foreign

element, and he asserted ominously that "[p]atriotic Gentile Americans are wondering whether there is any race purpose in the demoralizing effects of motion pictures or whether it is merely due to the unscrupulous men of that race." William Sheafe Chase, *Catechism on Motion Pictures in Inter-State Commerce* (Albany: New York Civic League, 1922), 13, 116. For a broader treatment of anti-Semitic discourse about movies and moral reform, see Steven Alan Carr, *Hollywood and Anti-Semitism: A Cultural History up to World War II* (New York: Cambridge University Press, 2001).

17. Maude Aldrich of the largely Protestant Federal Motion Picture Council, of which William Sheafe Chase was a founding member, grounded her call for federal censorship in such fears. In 1930 she wrote, "The films that are undermining the ideals of the youth of all lands, causing the colored races of the world to distrust the leadership of the white race, and spreading international misunderstandings, are made in America." Maude M. Aldrich, "The Motion Picture Problem," *Signal*, January 25, 1930, 12, quoted in Alison M. Parker, "Mothering the Movies: Women Reformers and Popular Culture," in *Movie Censorship and American Culture*, ed. Francis G. Couvares (Washington, DC: Smithsonian Institution Press, 1996), 80.

18. The English Methodists R. G. Burnett and E. D. Martell dedicated their work on reforming film to "the ultimate sanity of the White Races," arguing that "the screen could become one of the most useful, educative factors in the modern world" if taken out of the hands of "a few men, mostly Jews, who have deliberately exploited it as a get-rich-quick expedient." R. G. Burnett and E. D. Martell, *The Devil's Camera: Menace of a Film-Ridden World* (London: Epworth Press, 1932), 116.

19. Morris L. Ernst and Pare Lorentz, *Censored: The Private Life of the Movie* (New York: Jonathan Cape and Harrison Smith, 1930), is a useful example of a text that argued that the religious campaign for film censorship was concerned primarily with the protection of white Christian privilege.

20. See Martha Denise Green, "Social Gospels: Class, Race, and Sexuality in Twentieth-Century Biblical Drama" (PhD diss., University of North Carolina at Chapel Hill, 2001), as well as Susan Curtis, *The First Black Actors on the Great White Way* (Columbia: University of Missouri Press, 2001), for treatments of Torrence's work.

21. On the relationship between *Roseanne* and Oscar Micheaux's 1925 film *Body and Soul*, also starring Robeson, see Charles Musser, "To Redream the Dreams of White Playwrights: Reappropriation and Resistance in Oscar Micheaux's *Body and Soul*," *Yale Journal of Criticism* 12 (Fall 1999): 321–56. On *Earth*, see reviews in *New York Sun*, March 10, 1927; *New York Daily News*, March 11, 1927.

22. See reviews in *Columbus Citizen*, September 26, 1930; *Columbus Dispatch*, September 26, 1930; *New York Herald Tribune*, November 26, 1930; *New York Times*, November 26, 1930.

23. *New York Amsterdam News*, December 3, 1930.

24. Langston Hughes, *The Big Sea* (New York: Hill and Wang, 1940). Hughes wrote a humorous one-act play satirizing Barrymore's performance and mocking her for condescending, from her position as the "First Lady of the Stage," to play a Negress. See Langston Hughes, "Scarlet Sister Barry," n.d., ser. 2, box 1, folder 3, Langston Hughes Collection, Camille Billops and James V. Hatch Archives, Special Collections and Archives, Robert W. Woodruff Library, Emory University.

25. Garland Anderson, "A Black Man's Philosophy," *New York Evening Graphic,* January 31, 1925, L. S. Alexander Gumby Collection of Negroiana, Rare Book and Manuscript Library, Columbia University.

26. *New York Amsterdam News,* December 31, 1924.

27. *New York Tribune,* October 14, 1925, L. S. Alexander Gumby Collection of Negroiana.

28. Other productions that followed Anderson's included J. Augustus Smith's *Louisiana* (1933), about a struggle between Christianity and Voodoo, which was also poorly received. Other, more experienced, black artists followed: Donald Heywood's *Ol' Man Satan* (1932) and *How Come, Lawd?* (1937), Hall Johnson's *Run Little Chillun* (1933) and Countee Cullen's *One Way to Heaven* (1936).On *Louisiana*, see *New York Times,* February 28, 1933. On *Ol' Man Satan,* see *New York Times,* October 4, 1932; *California Eagle,* October 14, 1932. On *How Come, Lawd?* see Bernard L. Peterson Jr., *Early American Playwrights and Dramatic Writers: A Biographical Dictionary and Catalogue of Plays, Films, and Broadcasting Scripts* (Westport, CT: Greenwood Press, 1990). On *Run, Little Chillun,* see *Literary Digest,* April 15, 1933; *Amsterdam News,* December 13, 1933. On *One Way to Heaven,* see *New York Times,* September 29, 1936.

29. L. D. Reddick, "Educational Programs for the Improvement of Race Relations: Motion Pictures, Radio, the Press, and Libraries," *Journal of Negro Education* 13 (Summer 1944): 367–89.

30. It is also important to note the ways some white Christians embraced the religious possibilities of motion pictures. See, for example, Vincent T. Rosini, "Sanctuary Cinema: The Rise and Fall of Protestant Churches as Film Exhibition Sites, 1910–1930," (PhD diss., Regent University, 1998); Terry Lindvall, ed., *The Silents of God: Selected Issues and Documents in Silent American Film and Religion, 1908–1925* (Lanham, MD: Scarecrow Press, 2001); and Anne Morey, *Hollywood Outsiders: The Adaptation of the Film Industry, 1913–1934* (Minneapolis: University of Minnesota Press, 2003), ch. 4.

31. Rosini, "Sanctuary Cinema," 2–3.

32. Rev. W. W. Brown, pastor of Metropolitan Baptist Church in New York City, was the director of the Constellation Film Corporation, which made a stock offering in 1921. In the prospectus Brown wrote, "In joining the Constellation Film Corporation organization I did so with a full realization of its importance to our people. The race should have its own picture producing unit, it should have inspiring, clean, up-to-

date productions in which our own performers display their talents and it should have an outlet for its own constantly increasing literature." Constellation Film Corporation stock offering brochure, reel 3, George P. Johnson Negro Film Collection, Department of Special Collections, University Research Library, UCLA.

33. The Investigator, "Is the Church Losing Its Hold on the People?" *Half-Century Magazine,* June 1920. Although the identity of "The Investigator" is not known, the Chicago-based *Half-Century* was edited by two women—Katherine E. Williams and Kathryn M. Johnson—and billed itself at this juncture as "a colored monthly for the home and home maker."

34. Jean Voltaire Smith, "Our Need for More Films," *Half-Century Magazine,* April 1922.

35. "The Church and Recreation," *Georgia Baptist,* April 15, 1936.

36. Ibid.

37. Dennis A. Bethea, "The Era of Leisure," *A.M.E. Church Review,* January 1932, 155. Bethea, a member of the Methodist Episcopal Church, was a 1907 graduate of Chicago Medical College and did additional graduate work at Harvard Medical School. He served as the president of the Gary, Indiana branch of the NAACP, served on the board of the Muncie, Indiana YMCA, and was the health editor for the African Methodist Episcopal Church's *Christian Recorder.* See Joseph J. Boris, ed., *Who's Who in Colored America* (New York: Who's Who in Colored America Corporation, 1927), 13.

38. Bethea, "Era of Leisure," 157.

39. Clarence Taylor, *The Black Churches of Brooklyn* (New York: Columbia University Press, 1994), 88.

40. Langston L. Davis, "Is the Church Fulfilling Its Primary Object?" *Half-Century Magazine,* September–October 1922, 9.

41. Zechariah Johnson to the editor, *Half-Century Magazine,* November–December 1922.

42. *California Eagle,* March 13, 1936, March 19, 1937, and March 3, 1938. On Bilbrew's work on *Hearts in Dixie,* see *California Eagle,* July 12, 1929.

43. Lynne Sachs, dir., *Sermons and Sacred Pictures: The Life and Work of Rev. L. O. Taylor* (First Run/Icarus Films, 1989).

44. See Rev. Michael J. O'Neill, S.S.J., ed., *Some Outstanding Colored People: Interesting Facts in the Lives of Representative Negroes* (Baltimore: n.p., 1943), 149. *The Spirit of Youth,* dir. Harry L. Fraser (Globe Pictures, 1938).

45. Royal Gospel Productions advertising letter, 1947, *Going to Glory, Come to Jesus* file, Motion Picture Case Files, NYSA. I have been unable to locate any company records other than those contained in the New York State Archives and have been unable to determine how many churches may have exhibited this film.

46. William Warley, the first vice president of the club, a Prince Hall Mason, and a member of the A.M.E Church, was the editor of the *Louisville News* and a civil rights

activist. He had led a successful campaign in 1914 against segregated seating in Louisville's National Theater and in 1917 against discriminatory housing laws in the city in *Buchanan v. Warley*, 245 U.S. 60. *Louisville Courier Journal*, December 31, 1999. See also Fitzhugh Lee Styles, *Negroes and the Law in the Race's Battle for Liberty, Equality and Justice under the Constitution of the United States* (Boston: Christopher Publishing House, 1937), 75–77; Thomas Yenser, ed., *Who's Who in Colored America* (Brooklyn: Thomas Yenser, 1930–32), 443.

47. In a call for participation in the project, the club's officers addressed "Mr. Negro," asking: "Have you a drop of real red blood in your veins? Is your spine built up of the bone and cartilage God intended, or have you so far degenerated that there is a fishing worm where your backbone ought to be? We are asking you a plain, unvarnished question. Haven't you been divided against your brother long enough? And has not the immortal Lincoln warned you when he set you free that A HOUSE DIVIDED AGAINST ITSELF CANNOT STAND? Don't you think it is high time that you were waking up and GETTING TOGETHER?" *Louisville News*, April 7, 1917, Tuskegee Institute News Clippings File.

48. On the democratizing character of film, see Garth Jowett, *Film: The Democratic Art* (Boston: Little, Brown, 1976), and Morey, *Hollywood Outsiders*.

49. In the penny-arcade-and-nickelodeon period of movie exhibition, critics of the movies expressed concern about the content of films, exhibition of movies on Sundays, and the culture of the venues in which they were shown. Daniel Czitrom writes that "for critics of the movies, the pictures themselves were only part of a troubling exhibition milieu associated with cheap commercial entertainment: big crowds of unsupervised children, darkened spaces, gaudy advertisements, the large immigrant presence both in the audience and in the ticket office, and the overall fact that movies inhabited the physical and psychic space of cheap commercial urban entertainment." Daniel Czitrom, "The Politics of Performance: Theater Licensing and the Origins of Movie Censorship in New York," in Couvares, *Movie Censorship*, 28. On the urban culture of moviegoing in African American contexts, see Stewart, *Migrating to the Movies*, ch. 4.

50. Emily Bernard, ed., *Remember Me to Harlem: The Letters of Langston Hughes and Carl Van Vechten, 1925–1964* (New York: Knopf, 2001), 58. Hurston reports the visit with Dorothy Harris's parents in a telegram she and Hughes sent to Van Vechten on August 17, 1927. Carla Kaplan, ed., *Zora Neale Hurston: A Life in Letters* (New York: Doubleday, 2002), 105.

1. "'TAIN'T WHAT YOU WAS, IT'S WHAT YOU IS TODAY"

1. *Motion Picture News*, July 14, 1928, quoted in Raymond Durgnat and Scott Simon, *King Vidor, American* (Berkeley: University of California Press, 1988), 95.

2. See, for example, Michael Rogin, *Blackface, White Noise: Jewish Immigrants in the Hollywood Melting Pot* (Berkeley: University of California Press, 1996).

3. King Vidor, *A Tree Is a Tree* (New York: Harcourt, Brace, 1952), 175.

4. Ibid., 176. An undated note handwritten on Metro-Goldwyn-Mayer interoffice stationery and preserved in the King Vidor collection contains items for "a story of the South" and includes some of the same elements that Vidor describes in his recollections on directing, along with others. It is not clear if these are the notes he wrote for *Hallelujah* or for an earlier attempt to convince the studio to allow him to do an "all-colored-cast" film. The note reads:

> A plot expressing the true spirit and traditions of The South;
> With atmosphere and background of—
> Cotton fields in process and in bloom—
> Pickaninnies and bucks dancing and singing in the evenings in the nigger
> quarters—
> Old Black Joe and Mammy Lou a fussing around trying to make like they are
> working in the white folks house. . . .
> A wild religious crazed fanatic negro and a hoodoo woman—.
> KVC

5. Ibid., 176. Vidor deferred receipt of his $100,000 salary until after the film was released and was also to receive 25 percent of the box-office receipts. The MGM production file for the film contains various letters of complaint from Vidor to the studio following the film's release, charging that he was not receiving statements of the monthly receipts. Vidor, who died in 1982, was still attempting to receive his just share of the film's profits beyond his base salary as late as 1981. King Vidor to Metro-Goldwyn-Mayer, February 25, 1930, and Metro-Goldwyn-Mayer Producer/Participant Statement for Hallelujah to August 1, 1981, both in KVC.

6. His power to make this happen was unusual in the context of the Hollywood studio system and of MGM in particular, where Irving G. Thalberg had put in place a production system in which directors did not generally participate in a project from story development through editing. Because Vidor's success in silent films relied heavily on his control over most phases of production, Thalberg permitted him (along with a few other directors at MGM in this period) to work in the way to which he was accustomed. Thomas Schatz, *The Genius of the System: Hollywood Filmmaking in the Studio Era* (New York: Owl Books, 1988), 36–37. Vidor's later directorial credits include *The Champ* (Metro-Goldwyn-Mayer, 1931), *Stella Dallas* (Samuel Goldwyn, 1937), *Duel in the Sun* (Vanguard Films Production and Selznick International Pictures, 1946), and *The Fountainhead* (First National Pictures and Warner Bros., 1949).

7. *Pittsburgh Courier*, September 27, 1929; Jack Alicoate, ed., *The 1930 Film Daily Year Book of Motion Pictures* (New York: J. W. Alicoate, 1930), 21, 53.

8. Interview with Mr. King Vidor, May 1958, transcribed by Oral History Research Office, Butler Library, Columbia University.

9. *Chicago Defender,* June 8, 1929.

10. Frank Davis, "Hallelujah," March 7, 1930, KVC.

11. Nancy Dowd and David Shepard, *King Vidor: A Directors Guild of America Oral History* (Metuchen, NJ: Directors Guild of America, 1988), 107.

12. Thomas Cripps, *Slow Fade to Black: The Negro in American Film, 1900–1942* (1977; reprint, New York: Oxford University Press, 1993), 243. *Opportunity,* April 1929. Rideout had at least one play—*Goin' Home,* the winning play of the Drama League of America's 1927 National Playwriting Contest—staged in New York. It was produced by Brock Pemberton and directed by Antoinette Perry. See Dorothy Peterson's review in *Opportunity,* October 1928, and Brooks Atkinson's review in *New York Times,* August 24, 1928. Tuchock wrote a number of Hollywood continuities, dialogue, and screenplays in the 1930s and 1940s, including *Billy the Kid* (Metro-Goldwyn-Mayer, 1930), *Susan Lenox (Her Fall and Rise)* (Metro-Goldwyn-Mayer, 1931), *Little Orphan Annie* (RKO, 1932), and *Foxes of Harrow* (Twentieth Century-Fox, 1947).

13. Vidor quoted in *King Vidor,* interviewed by Nancy Dowd and David Shepard (Metuchen, NJ: Scarecrow Press, 1988), 107.

In a newspaper account of the production process, musical director Eva Jessye complained about having to wait until all the whites had eaten before she could go to the train's dining car. She also described unequal treatment of the white and black cast and crew members on location and conveyed her outrage that the black cast members were underpaid by industry standards. *Kansas City Call,* July 11, 1930, and *Negro World,* July 26, 1930, in Tuskegee Institute News Clipping File. The location schedule was particularly tight because Vidor wanted to begin while the "white cotton" was still in the fields. To get the cast there in time, the studio chose a route through El Paso on a train with no sleepers (instead of the Kansas City option that would have provided them comfort but would take longer). There was some discussion about how to handle cast members' reactions to the situation. J. J. Cohn to R. A. Golden, Peabody Hotel, Memphis, TN, October 15, 1928, KVC. Garrison continued to work behind the scenes in Hollywood on such films as *The Sea Bat* (Metro-Goldwyn-Mayer, 1930). See *Norfolk Journal and Guide,* March 29, 1930, in Tuskegee Institute News Clipping File.

14. *The Jazz Singer,* dir. Alan Crosland (Warner Bros., 1927). My thanks to Charles Musser for pointing to this connection. On *The Jazz Singer,* see Rogin, *Blackface, White Noise;* Patricia Erens, "Between Two Worlds: Jewish Images in American Film," in *The Kaleidoscopic Lens: How Hollywood Views Ethnic Groups,* ed. Randall M. Miller (Englewood, NJ: Ozer, 1980); Robert L. Carringer, ed., *The Jazz Singer,* Wisconsin/Warner Bros. Screenplay Series (Madison: University of Wisconsin Press, 1979).

15. Quoted in *Pittsburgh Courier,* December 15, 1928. Parsons was referring to Robert Flaherty's *Nanook of the North* (Pathé, 1922), an important work in independ-

ent cinema and one that has been the object of considerable debate about ethnographic film and authenticity. See Fatimah Tobing Rony, *The Third Eye: Race, Cinema, and Ethnographic Spectacle* (Durham: Duke University Press, 1996).

16. *Chicago Defender*, June 8, 1929; *Amsterdam News*, August 21, 1929. In comparing the scale of *Hallelujah* to past films, Vidor was referring especially to *The Big Parade* (Metro-Goldwyn-Mayer, 1925), a six-reel epic about World War I.

17. King Vidor, *King Vidor on Film Making* (New York: David MacKay, 1972), 230, 231.

18. *New York Amsterdam News*, October 17, 1928. On the New York auditions, see *New York Times*, October 6, 1928, October 12, 1928, and August 25, 1929.

19. *New York Amsterdam News*, October 3, 1928. See also *Pittsburgh Courier*, June 9, 1929.

20. *Baltimore Afro-American*, March 2, 1929. Eva Jessye (1895–1992) was born in Coffeyville, Kansas, and attended Kindaro State Normal School in Kansas and Langston University in Oklahoma. She taught in an A.M.E. Church school in Oklahoma before moving to Baltimore in 1919, where she served briefly as the music director at Morgan College. In Baltimore, she joined the Dixie Jubilee Singers, a group that later became the Eva Jessye Choir, and around 1925 the group moved to New York City. In addition to her work on *Hallelujah*, Jessye wrote a number of religious dramas and oratorios, including *The Story of Baltazar, the Black Magus* (1932), *The Chronicle of Job* (ca. 1936), and *Paradise Lost and Regained: A Folk Oratorio* (ca. 1936). She was the choral conductor for the original 1935 production of George Gershwin's *Porgy and Bess* and for Virgil Thomson and Gertrude Stein's opera *Four Saints in Three Acts* in 1934. She published *My Spirituals* (New York: Robbins-Engel, 1927) and *Selected Poems* (Little Balkans Press, 1978). Donald Fisher Black, "The Life and Work of Eva Jessye and Her Contributions to American Music" (PhD diss., University of Michigan, 1986); Judith Weisenfeld, "Truths That Liberate the Soul: Eva Jessye and the Politics of Religious Performance," in *Women and Religion in the African Diaspora*, ed. R. Marie Griffith and Barbara Diane Savage (Johns Hopkins University Press, 2006).

21. *Pittsburgh Courier*, June 9, 1929. On race and sound in early sound films, see Alice Maurice, "'Cinema at Its Source': Synchronizing Race and Sound in the Early Talkies," *Camera Obscura* 17, no. 1 (2002): 31–71.

22. Although Fox's *Hearts in Dixie* was released a few months before Metro-Goldwyn-Mayer's *Hallelujah*, it did not receive the kind of critical or popular attention that Vidor's production did. *Opportunity*, April 1929, 122. See also *Baltimore Afro-American*, March 9, 1929; *Chicago Defender*, March 16, 1929; *Chicago Defender*, July 13, 1929. A reviewer of *Hearts in Dixie* emphasized the importance of sound in the film, writing, "Most of the speaking voices register remarkably well, and the unaffected delivery of these colored folks is a joy after being subjected to the wave of phoney [*sic*] English accent which has been engulfing the talkies. Clarence Muse, who plays a lead-

ing role, is possessor of the best speaking voice I have heard on screen." *New York Life*, n.d., 1929, in Afro-American Actors 2 [Motion Pictures], James Weldon Johnson Collection, Yale Collection of American Literature, Beinecke Rare Book and Manuscript Library, Yale University.

23. See Melvin Patrick Ely, *The Adventures of Amos 'n' Andy: A Social History of an American Phenomenon* (New York: Free Press, 1991).

24. *Pittsburgh Courier*, September 15, 1928.

25. On religious interpretations of and responses to the Great Migration, see Milton C. Sernett, *Bound for the Promised Land: African American Religion and the Great Migration* (Durham: Duke University Press, 1997).

26. On new religious movements among African Americans during the Great Migration, see, for example, Arthur Huff Fauset, *Black Gods of the Metropolis: Negro Religious Cults of the Urban North* (Philadelphia: University of Pennsylvania Press, 1944); C. Eric Lincoln, *The Black Muslims in America* (Boston: Beacon Press, 1961); Randall K. Burkett, *Garveyism as a Religious Movement* (Metuchen, NJ: Scarecrow Press, 1978); Jill Watts, *God, Harlem U.S.A.: The Father Divine Story* (Berkeley: University of California Press, 1992); Hans Baer and Merrill Singer, *African-American Religion in the Twentieth Century: Varieties of Protest and Accommodation* (Knoxville: University of Tennessee Press, 1992).

27. Alain Locke, "Enter the New Negro," *Survey Graphic*, March 1925, 631.

28. Ibid., 631.

29. *Chicago Defender*, December 14, 1929.

30. Martin Quigley, *Decency in Motion Pictures* (New York: Macmillan, 1937), 42.

31. Gregory Black, *Hollywood Censored: Morality Codes, Catholics and the Movies* (New York: Cambridge University Press, 1994), 35.

32. Memo from Colonel Joy, October 4, 1928, *Hallelujah*, MPPDA Production Code Administration Case Files, AMPAS.

33. *Kansas City Call*, July 11, 1930, in Tuskegee Institute News Clipping File.

34. Ibid. See script drafts in KVC and MGMC.

35. Memo from Colonel Joy, February 22, 1929, *Hallelujah*, MPPDA Production Code Administration Case Files, AMPAS.

36. Ibid.

37. Memo from Colonel Joy, October 4, 1928, *Hallelujah*, MPPDA Production Code Administration Case Files, AMPAS.

38. Jason S. Joy to George Kann, Metro-Goldwyn-Mayer, October 6, 1928; Lamar Trotti to Mr. M. McKenzie, October 19, 1928, *Hallelujah*, MPPDA Production Code Administration Case Files, AMPAS. Joy eventually relented on the crap game, convinced that "[b]ecause this form of amusement is indigenous to negro life," the scene could be left in. Memo from Colonel Joy, February 22, 1929, *Hallelujah*, MPPDA Production Code Administration Case Files, AMPAS.

39. Lamar Trotti to Mr. M. McKenzie, October 19, 1928, *Hallelujah*, MPPDA Production Code Administration Case Files, AMPAS. Lamar Trotti (1898–1952), a Georgia native, worked as a journalist before joining the staff of the MPPDA in 1925. He worked there until 1932, when he became head of the story department at the Fox studio. He wrote more than fifty screenplays, including *Judge Priest* (1934), *Young Mr. Lincoln* (1939), *Drums along the Mohawk* (1939), *Brigham Young—Frontiersman* (1940), *The Ox-Bow Incident* (1943), *Wilson* (1944), and *Cheaper by the Dozen* (1950). María Elena de las Carreras-Kuntz, "Trotti, Lamar," *American National Biography Online*, February 2000, retrieved October 1, 2003, from www.anb.org/articles/18/18-03041.html.

40. F. L. Herron, August 22, 1929, *Hallelujah*, MPPDA Production Code Administration Case Files, AMPAS.

41. John V. Wilson to Jason S. Joy, December 12, 1929, *Hallelujah*, MPPDA Production Code Administration Case Files, AMPAS.

42. *Variety*, August 28, 1929.

43. According to the production records, Ransom Rideout supplied the dialogue for this scene. *Hallelujah: Dialogue*, December 19, 1928, 3–4, KVC.

44. Davis, "Hallelujah."

45. Dialogue and bracketed stage directions are taken from my transcription of the film.

46. In a conversation with Adrienne Lanier Seward on May 1, 1981, Vidor claimed that he did not deliberately place the broom in the shot. In response to Seward's reading of the broom's significance in African American history in relation to the film's story, Vidor referred to its presence in the film as "a lucky symbol." The interview was conducted a year before Vidor's death and more than a half-century after the film's release. Vidor's memory about certain elements of the production history is faulty, and it is possible that he is also unreliable on this point. Adrienne Lanier Seward, "Early Black Film and Folk Tradition: An Interpretive Analysis of the Use of Folklore in Selected All-Black Cast Feature Films" (PhD diss., Indiana University, 1985), 259.

47. Jessica Howard argues that music inaugurates all of Zeke's significant transformations from religious to sexual or vice versa. In this case, she argues that it is the act of observing and hearing Rose play the Wedding March that causes him to become "possessed with sexual desire for her." I find the juxtaposition of the wedding that replicates the fall in the Garden of Eden and Zeke's awakening sexual desire much more significant than the music in this particular scene. See Jessica Howard, "Hallelujah! Transformation in Film," *African American Review* 30 (Autumn 1996): 446.

48. See the chapter "Mammies, Matriarchs, and Other Controlling Images," in Patricia Hill Collins, *Black Feminist Thought: Knowledge, Consciousness and the Politics of Empowerment* (Boston: Unwin Hyman, 1991). Although McKinney's character is

marked as "High Yella," Vidor and the studio were obviously uncomfortable with how light-skinned she actually was and used makeup to make her skin appear darker.

49. See Vidor, *King Vidor on Film Making*, 130–31, for his thoughts on the need to use close-up shots sparingly and strategically. An analysis of the frequency of Vidor's use of close-ups in *Hallelujah* contradicts his assertion that he used them infrequently in the film. However, he did not use them in conjunction with dialogue, and this may have had a great deal to do with the technical demands of recording all of the sound after production and in consideration of the difficulty of synchronizing the dialogue under these conditions.

50. King Vidor to Irving G. Thalberg, October 12, 1928, KVC.

51. Irving G. Thalberg to King Vidor, October 22, 1928; King Vidor to Irving G. Thalberg, October 22, 1928, and October 27, 1928; Irving G. Thalberg to King Vidor, October 27, 1928, all in KVC.

52. Irving G. Thalberg to King Vidor, November 1, 1928, KVC. There were rumors in the black press, facilitated by telegrams from a "mystery woman," that the cast change was the result of Honey Brown's unexpected death. She was forced to make a public statement to dispel the rumors, and the police opened an investigation into the telegrams. See unidentified clipping, January 11, 1929, reel 11, George P. Johnson Negro Film Collection, Department of Special Collections, University Research Library, UCLA; *California Eagle*, January 11, 1929.

53. King Vidor and Wanda Tuchock, "*Hallelujah:* Sequence Synopsis of the Continuity of September 25, 1928," KVC. Zeke's proposal follows a scene that is present in an early synopsis and in versions of the script but that did not make it into the final edited version of the film. Chick visits Zeke in the train in which he and the family are traveling, and the two embrace. When Mammy discovers them, she tries to hit Chick with a whip and eventually chases her out. It is likely that the scene was filmed, as the production stills from the movie contain images of the scene. See film stills in MGMC.

54. Rick Altman writes of the folk musical as "project[ing] the audience into a mythicized version of the cultural past" and as especially interested in the family and home. Rick Altman, *The American Film Musical* (Bloomington: Indiana University Press, 1978), 272.

55. *Baltimore Afro-American*, February 16, 1929.

56. *The Crisis*, October 1929.

57. In an editorial in *Opportunity* the year before *Hallelujah*'s release, Charles S. Johnson reported on the absurd assertion by a white neurologist (in a speech before a group of psychiatrists) that Irving Berlin created jazz because his mother had an irregular heart that had unwittingly conditioned him, prenatally, to understand syncopation. Johnson continued, "And so goes another of the preposterous assumptions that Negroes created jazz. There was, not so long ago, a feature article in one of the popular magazines, by a white music hall favorite with the caption: 'How I Created the

Charleston. . . . ' She was naive enough, however, to explain that she had learned the essential steps from her Negro maid, and by transferring them from the servants' quarters to the stage, presumably, supplied the element of creation." *Opportunity*, April 1928.

58. Altman, *American Film Musical*, 272.

59. Here, according to Jessica Howard, "it is not the meaning of the words themselves, but their repetition and treatment, specifically as chanted and chant-sung, that allows the 'true' bodily expression of Mammy to emerge (i.e., piousness, grief)." Howard, "Hallelujah!" 466.

60. Vidor makes use of the song developed from the Largo movement of Antonin Dvôrak's *New World Symphony*.

61. Vidor and Tuchock, "*Hallelujah*," 17.

62. See production stills in MGMC. The decision to cut this and other scenes may simply have been the result of the need to shorten the film's running time.

63. *Chicago Defender*, June 8, 1929.

64. *Pittsburgh Courier*, January 26, 1929. See also *Baltimore Afro-American*, December 28, 1928; *New York Telegram*, February 14, 1929;

65. *Baltimore Afro-American*, July 26, 1930.

66. Ibid. Jessye was disturbed that Vidor said nothing of her contribution to the film in the chapter on *Hallelujah* in his autobiography. Jester Hairston, also a choir conductor, wrote to Jessye, "Yes, I agree with you, Love, that both King Vidor and Virgil Thompson did you a disservice in not mentioning you in their autobiographies. It certainly would not have taken anything away from their own artistic contributions." Jester Hairston to Eva Jessye, January 1, 1967, Eva Jessye Collection, Special Collections, Leonard H. Axe Library, Pittsburg State University. The pages of that chapter have been torn out of her personal copy of Vidor's biography. I am grateful to Randy Roberts for his assistance with Jessye's collection.

67. Haynes would go on to have a productive career in film and on the stage for a number of years, but he declared his ambition to become ordained as a minister from early on in his career. He was ordained a minister in the African Methodist Episcopal Church in 1941 and pastored a number of churches before his death in 1954. *New York Amsterdam News*, November 22, 1941; *New York Times*, July 30, 1954.

68. *New York Amsterdam News*, October 17, 1928; *Baltimore Afro-American*, July 27, 1929. Eva Jessye and Victoria Spivey remained close friends for the rest of their lives. Spivey settled in Brooklyn and, by the late 1940s was singing in her church choir as she became less active as a blues performer. Spivey was raised a Methodist, and there is some evidence that she was a member of Daniel Haynes's church or that she attended Bible study with him. Victoria Spivey Papers, box 12, folder 6; box 13, folder 9; box 14, folder 19, Special Collections and Archives, Robert W. Woodruff Library, Emory University.

69. After the film's release, Eva Jessye wrote of him that he had had particular difficulty with the "illiterate tongue" required of the actors. "Dad Gray had schooled himself in the proper use of the English language for forty years," she wrote, "had so zealously stamped out traces of his one-time slavery speech that he found it impossible to call it back again." She concluded, "I rather believe that he could not bring himself to talk it, that something inside of him rebelled and refused to go back and pick up something he had thrown down in disdain two score years before." *Baltimore Afro-American*, July 26, 1930.

70. *Pittsburgh Courier*, June 15, 1929. Gray died destitute in Harlem in June 1936. A report in the *Amsterdam News* noted that neighbors refused to believe that he was dead, recalling "the fact that, during the winter, he was 'dead' for six hours and he arose again. They crowded the house Thursday waiting for the miracle to happen again, despite the fact that [the doctor] pronounced him dead." *New York Amsterdam News*, June 6, 1936. Gray had joined Father Divine's Peace Mission Movement and, according to press accounts, was close to Father Divine. When no relative or friend could afford to bury him, his body lay unclaimed in the morgue until a number of local businesses, including a funeral home, took financial responsibility for the funeral. Neither Father Divine nor anyone from the Peace Mission Movement attended the funeral because of the group's theology at the time that true faith in Father Divine provided eternal life. One of the members said of Gray, "Daddy was a wonderful brother, but he must have done something wrong why [*sic*] he died, that's all." *New York Amsterdam News*, June 13, 1936. Joining the Peace Mission Movement apparently represented a significant change in belief for Gray. Some time after *Hallelujah*'s release, Eva Jessye wrote about the contrast between Gray's character in the film and her personal beliefs. "How Mr. Gray was able to put over the character of an old parson is a mystery to all who knew his attitude toward religion," she wrote. "He does not believe in God or any of the tenets of Christianity. It was well nigh impossible to get him to put the real feeling into religious scenes, and when called upon to pray, he did so like an automaton." She said that many members of the cast found his attempts at prayer to be humorous. *Baltimore Afro-American*, July 26, 1930.

71. *The Crisis*, October 1929, 355.

72. Ibid.

73. Cripps, *Slow Fade to Black*, 251; *New York Amsterdam News*, November 20, 1929.

74. *New York Amsterdam News*, February 27, 1929.

75. *New York Age*, October 19, 1929.

76. See, for example, Thomas H. Dorsen to the editor, *New York Amsterdam News*, August 28, 1928; *Pittsburgh Courier*, September 7, 1928; *Baltimore Afro-American*, August 31, 1929; *Chicago Defender*, June 8, 1929, January 25, 1930, and February 1, 1920.

77. *Variety*, August 28, 1929.

78. Quoted in *Baltimore Afro-American*, August 31, 1929; quoted in *New York Age*, October 19, 1929.

79. Davis, "Hallelujah."

80. Quoted in *Baltimore Afro-American*, August 31, 1929.

81. Ibid.

82. Thomas H. Dorsen to the editor, *New York Amsterdam News*, August 28, 1929.

83. *Cincinnati Union*, April 3, 1930, in Tuskegee Institute News Clipping File.

84. *Baltimore Afro-American*, July 26, 1930.

85. Ibid.

86. *Pittsburgh Courier*, February 8, 1930; *Baltimore Afro-American*, December 15, 1928.

87. *Baltimore Afro-American*, September 27, 1930.

88. *Variety*, August 28, 1929.

89. Mr. James, *Daily Review and Motion Pictures To-Day*, October 19, 1929, quoted in *New York News*, October 19, 1929.

90. *New York Amsterdam News*, September 4, 1929. Villa Navarra likely refers to Villa Lewaro, the twenty-room mansion that cosmetics producer Madame C. J. Walker built in 1917 in Irvingdale-on-Hudson, New York. See A'Lelia Perry Bundles, *Madame C. J. Walker* (New York: Chelsea House, 1991).

91. *New York Amsterdam News*, October 2, 1929. Exhibitors had raised the same concerns when *Hearts in Dixie* had been released some months earlier. *Billboard* reported: "The main problem faced by the releasing company is the manner in which exhibitors will consider the picture in sections of the North where there is strong racial feeling which might be fanned to dangerous proportions by an intermingling of whites and blacks in their audience. It is regarded as only natural that Negro picture fans will be anxious to witness the picture featuring all members of their race. Whether they will be willing to wait until the picture is shown in their own neighborhood houses, as in the case of other films, is the salient point that is giving film men food for serious thought." Quoted in *Baltimore Afro-American*, April 6, 1929.

2. "'DE LAWD' A NATCHEL MAN"

1. *The Green Pastures*, dir. Marc Connelly and William Keighley (Warner Bros., 1936).

2. *Chicago Defender*, March 14, 1936. The *California Eagle* had begun reporting on the suits in January of 1936, and other black newspapers joined in earnest once the parties in the suit began to meet in court. Ingram would declare bankruptcy in September of 1937, owing almost $10,000 and having only the clothes he was wearing, valued at $20, as assets to declare. *New York Times*, September 10, 1937.

3. Daily production report, February 23, 1936, *Green Pastures* Production Files, WBA.

4. *Chicago Defender*, April 4, 1936. Ingram went on to have a fairly active career in Hollywood (for a black actor in this period), appearing in such films as *The Adventures of Huckleberry Finn* (Metro-Goldwyn-Mayer, 1939), *The Thief of Bagdad* (United Artists, 1940), *Cabin in the Sky* (Metro-Goldwyn-Mayer, 1943), and *A Thousand and One Nights* (Columbia, 1945). After being sentenced to and serving an eighteen-month prison term, beginning in 1949, for admitting to violating the Mann Act and transporting a minor across state lines for immoral purposes, Ingram returned to Hollywood in a number of additional films, including *Anna Lucasta* (United Artists, 1958) and *Elmer Gantry* (United Artists, 1960) and appeared on stage and television. He died in 1969 and is buried in the Forest Lawn-Hollywood Hills Cemetery in Los Angeles under a tombstone that reads: "De Lawd—Remembered Always."

5. In his memoir, Connelly wrote of Rowland Stebbins, the producer, who had made a great deal of money on Wall Street: "Not knowing then that he was as astutely foresighted as he was fortunate, I told him what I would have told anyone not aware of the hazards implicit in *The Green Pastures*. I told him that more than one friendly manager had cautioned me about the enormous risk of disfavor that was likely to arise over a play in which God was depicted as a Negro." Marc Connelly, *Voices Offstage: A Book of Memoirs* (Chicago: Holt, Rinehart and Winston, 1968), 165.

6. Brooks Atkinson, "Lawd New and Old," *New York Times*, March 24, 1935.

7. Marc Connelly to Hal Wallis, November 9, 1935, *The Green Pastures* Production Files, WBA.

8. *Opportunity*, October 1930, 304.

9. Countee Cullen's 1929 poem "The Black Christ" might also have been familiar to audiences of the stage and screen versions of Connelly's play. In this lengthy poem, Cullen draws a parallel between the lynching of a young black man, in part because of his love for a white woman, to the crucifixion of Jesus.

10. Roark Bradford, *Ol' Man Adam an' His Chillun: Being the Tales They Tell about the Time When the Lord Walked the Earth Like a Natural Man* (New York: Harper and Brothers, 1928). There were also a number of important precedents by white writers for Connelly's work in Eugene O'Neill's *The Emperor Jones* (1921) and *All God's Chillun Got Wings* (1924), as well as Ridgley Torrence's *Plays for A Negro Theater* (1917), three one-act plays that take up religious themes. See Martha Denise Green, "Social Gospels: Class, Race, and Sexuality in Twentieth-Century Biblical Drama" (PhD diss., University of North Carolina at Chapel Hill, 2001); Susan Curtis, *The First Black Actors on the Great White Way* (Columbia: University of Missouri Press, 1998).

11. Roark Bradford, "Notes on the Negro," *Forum*, November 1927, 790–91.

12. The group of white writers, artists, and cultural critics who gathered at New

York City's Algonquin Hotel included Robert Benchley, Heywood Broun, Edna Ferber, George S. Kaufman, Harpo Marx, Dorothy Parker, Harold Ross, Robert Sherwood, and Alexander Woollcott. Connelly's collaborations with Kaufman included *Merton of the Movies* (1922), *To the Ladies* (1922), *Helen of Troy, New York* (1923), *Be Yourself* (1924), and *Beggar on Horseback* (1924).

13. "The Reminiscences of Marc Connelly," interview by Louis Shaeffer, 1–9, Oral History Research Office, Butler Library, Columbia University.

14. Connelly, *Voices Offstage*, 148.

15. Ibid., 147.

16. Ibid.

17. Ibid.

18. Ibid., 148.

19. Ibid., 149–50.

20. Ibid., 153.

21. *New York Telegram*, February 28, 1930.

22. *New York World*, February 27, 1930.

23. The play opened on February 26, 1930, at the Mansfield Theatre in New York City and closed on August 29, 1931. The show moved to Chicago for a run of almost five months and then made stops in Milwaukee, Indianapolis, Cincinnati, Columbus, St. Louis, Kansas City, Des Moines, St. Paul, Duluth, Billings, Butte, Spokane, Seattle, Portland, and San Francisco and arrived in Los Angeles in June of 1932 for its one thousandth show. "'Green Pastures' Gives 1000th Show Thursday," *New York Herald Tribune*, July 3, 1932.

24. Emily Bernard, ed., *Remember Me to Harlem: The Letters of Langston Hughes and Carl Van Vechten, 1925–1964* (New York: Knopf, 2001), 95.

25. Hallmark Hall of Fame produced the play twice, in 1957 and in 1958. *Los Angeles Times*, March 23, 1959. On the Swedish production, which reportedly "opened to tremendous receptions of eggs and tomatoes" thrown by the audience, see *The Crisis*, November 1931, and on the Danish production, see *California Eagle*, April 27, 1934. That U.S. Supreme Court Justice Antonin Scalia played the part of Gabriel in a production of *The Green Pastures* at St. Francis Xavier High School in New York City in the early 1950s gives some indication of the play's broad impact and endurance. Margaret Talbot, "Supreme Confidence: The Jurisprudence of Justice Antonin Scalia," *New Yorker*, March 28, 2005, 44.

26. *California Eagle*, October 14, 1932; *New York Times*, October 4, 1932; *Wall Street Journal*, October 5, 1932. Rex Ingram and Ethel Waters starred in a 1959 revival of *Ol' Man Satan*. *New York Times*, July 30, 1959. On *Cabin Echoes*, see *California Eagle*, August 11, 1932, August 25, 1932, and September 8, 1933. This production was promoted by an interracial group of Angelenos that included Protestants and Jews with the goal of "racial betterment and inter-racial understanding."

27. Connelly, *Voices Offstage*, 171–72. On Harrison's background and on his earlier career as a dramatic reader, see Walter C. Daniel, *"De Lawd": Richard B. Harrison and The Green Pastures* (New York: Greenwood Press, 1986).

28. *Opportunity*, May 1930.

29. *California Eagle*, February 12, 1932; *New York Times*, March 3, 1931. Harrison was not the first actor to be awarded the NAACP's Spingarn Medal. Charles Gilpin, a member of Harlem's Lafayette Players who also originated the role of Brutus Jones in the Broadway production of Eugene O'Neill's *The Emperor Jones*, received the award in 1921. *New York Age*, March 26, 1921.

30. *New York Amsterdam News*, March 5, 1930.

31. *California Eagle*, March 22, 1935.

32. *New York Amsterdam News*, March 16, 1935.

33. Marc Connelly, *The Green Pastures: A Fable Suggested by Roark Bradford's Southern Sketches, "Ol' Man Adam an' His Chillun"* (New York: Farrar and Rinehart, 1929), xiv. On Hubbard, see Rosalind Flynn Hinton, "'There Will Be a Grand Concert Tonight': Alma Lillie Hubbard, the New Orleans Years, 1895–1932, Making a Life, Building a Community" (PhD diss., Northwestern University, 2001).

34. Hall Johnson founded the choir in 1925 after having performed with James Reese Europe's band, famous for serving as the band for New York's 15th Regiment (which became the 369th Infantry of the American Expeditionary Forces) during World War I. Daniel, *"De Lawd,"* 61; Thomas Yenser, ed., *Who's Who in Colored America* (Brooklyn: Thomas Yenser, 1940), 280; Karl E. Downs, *Meet the Negro* (Pasadena, CA: Login Press, 1943), 90–91.

35. *Tales of Manhattan*, dir. Julien Duvivier (Twentieth Century-Fox, 1942); *Cabin in the Sky*, dir. Vincente Minnelli (Metro-Goldwyn-Mayer, 1943).

36. Hall Johnson to Al Lewis, July 24, 1942, *Cabin in the Sky* files, AFC.

37. *New York Tribune*, February 23, 1930.

38. *New York Amsterdam News*, January 18, 1936.

39. Howard Bradstreet, "A Negro Miracle Play," *Opportunity*, May 1930, 150; *New York World*, February 27, 1930.

40. Connelly, *Voices Offstage*, 170.

41. Harrison had studied drama at the Detroit Training School of Dramatic Art and had worked for some time with Edward Weitzel, a British drama coach and drama editor for the *Detroit Free Press*. Harrison said that despite Weitzel's attempts to help him break into the Detroit theater, the racism of people in the casts of various productions prevented him from receiving parts. Prior to auditioning for the Broadway production of *The Green Pastures*, he had taught courses in dramatic reading at the Agricultural and Technical College in Greensboro, North Carolina, and had spent a considerable amount of time on the road doing readings of the poetry of his friend Paul Laurence Dunbar. He had also appeared in at least one film, Oscar Micheaux's

Easy Street (1930). Andrea J. Nouryeh, "When the Lord Was a Black Man: A Fresh Look at the Life of Richard Berry Harrison," *Black American Literature Forum* 16 (Winter 1982): 142–46. *Easy Street*, dir. Oscar Micheaux (Micheaux Pictures, 1930).

42. In the same year that the film version of *The Green Pastures* was released, Edna Mae Harris, who played Zeba, also appeared in small parts in *Fury* (with Spencer Tracy and Sylvia Sidney) and *The Garden of Allah* (starring Marlene Dietrich and Charles Boyer). George Randol, who played Pharoah in the play and the High Priest in the film, appeared in Oscar Micheaux's 1931 film *The Exile*. The Hall Johnson Choir also had three other film credits the year that the film *The Green Pastures* was released and would go on to appear in at least nine more. On *In Abraham's Bosom*, see *New York Amsterdam News*, January 5, 1927; *New York Times*, May 3, 1927. Eddie Anderson's credits prior to *The Green Pastures* include *What Price Hollywood?* (RKO Pathé Pictures, 1932), *Behold My Wife* (Paramount, 1934), *His Night Out* (Universal, 1935), and *Transient Lady* (Universal, 1935).

43. *California Eagle*, January 9, 1931.

44. *California Eagle*, August 22, 1932, August 29, 1932, May 6, 1932, July 1, 1932, and October 28, 1932. Many of these reports on the tour were written for the Associated Negro Press by Mercedes Gilbert, who played Zipporah in the original production and who was clearly impressed with the reception the cast received in towns and cities.

45. *Baltimore Afro-American*, October 13, 1934.

46. *Washington Tribune*, February 10, 1933, Tuskegee Institute News Clipping File; Carter G. Woodson, "'Special Performance for Negroes' Gets Rap by Noted Historian," *Pittsburgh Courier*, February 11, 1933, and February 25, 1933. On Richard B. Harrison's support of the segregated performance, see *California Eagle*, February 17, 1933.

47. *California Eagle*, May 6, 1932.

48. Daniel J. Lord to Miss Kelly, June 12, 1930, *The Green Pastures*, MPPDA Production Code Administration Case Files, AMPAS.

49. Ibid.

50. Lamar Trotti memo, February 28, 1930, *The Green Pastures*, MPPDA Production Code Administration Case Files, AMPAS.

51. Jason S. Joy to Miss Julia Kelly, June 21, 1930, *The Green Pastures*, MPPDA Production Code Administration Case Files, AMPAS.

52. Connelly, *Voices Offstage*, 155. Connelly would go on to gain considerably more experience in Hollywood, writing screenplays for a number of films, including *Captains Courageous*, dir. Victor Fleming (Metro-Goldwyn-Mayer, 1937), which starred Spencer Tracy, Lionel Barrymore, Mickey Rooney, and Melvyn Douglas, and *I Married a Witch*, dir. René Clair (United Artists, 1942), starring Fredric March, Veronica Lake, Robert Benchley, and Susan Hayward. His only other directorial effort

was *Rhythm Rodeo* (1938), which he co-directed with George Randol, who played Pharaoh in the Broadway cast and the High Priest in the film version of *The Green Pastures*.

53. Hal Wallis to Henry Blanke, interoffice communication, January 11, 1936, *The Green Pastures* Production Files, WBA.

54. Bob Fellows, a member of the production staff, complained to the studio manager, Tenny Wright, that Connelly took twenty-nine takes of one shot and did not call for a print until the eighteenth or nineteenth take. Fellows apparently printed the eleventh take surreptitiously so that Wallis and Wright could determine whether twenty-nine takes had really been necessary. He continued, "There are daily 101 unnecessary routines that we can handle ourselves, but this condition of Connelly being so particular and wasting so much time on the set I had felt was getting better, is instead getting worse. . . . There is nothing further that I am able to do, and I think Mr. Wallis should step in now and have a show-down with Connelly regarding the above, or this show will take three months to complete at the present rate." Bob Fellows to Tenny Wright, interoffice communication, January 17, 1936, *The Green Pastures* Production Files, WBA.

55. See *California Eagle*, January 17, 1936, and January 24, 1936.

56. Perhaps the best known of Keighley's later films is *The Man Who Came to Dinner* (Warner Bros., 1942), an adaptation of Moss Hart and George S. Kaufman's play. The film starred Bette Davis, Ann Sheridan, Monty Wolley, and Billie Burke.

57. *The Green Pastures*, Daily Production Reports, WBA. Keighley complained to Hal Wallis that he was not receiving due credit for his work on the film and that all public communications about *The Green Pastures* referred only to "Marc Connelly—Marc Connelly—and more Marc Connelly." Wallis instructed the publicity department that Keighley's name should be highlighted. Wallis later ordered that the film's opening titles be reshot because Connelly's name appeared so often that it seemed as if he had been responsible for every aspect of the film. Wallis feared that audiences would find this humorous. The original titles were to have the words "The Green Pastures" in metal with two of God's cleaning women polishing them. Hal Wallis to Selzer, interoffice communication, February 26, 1936; Hal Wallis to Bilson, interoffice communication, March 20, 1936, *The Green Pastures* Production Files, WBA; Marc Connelly, *Green Pastures* script, December 31, 1935, Motion Picture Scripts Collection, AMPAS.

58. See *California Eagle*, January 24, 1936, and January 31, 1936. There had been press reports in 1931 that Jolson was attempting to buy the rights to *The Green Pastures* and intended to produce a film of it in which he would star as "the Lawd." According to the *Chicago Defender* account, Jolson took the main challenge of playing the part to be audiences' expectations that he was a comedian who could not carry off "a straight role of great dignity" and not the potential offense of playing the part in blackface makeup. *Chicago Defender*, June 6, 1931. Rowland Stebbins, the play's producer,

expressed admiration for Jolson but said that he wished to retain the rights because he planned to take the show on a national tour. *Chicago Defender,* June 13, 1931.

59. Elizabeth St. Charles Edwards to Joseph I. Breen, July 29, 1935, *The Green Pastures,* MPPDA Production Code Administration Case Files, AMPAS. The Movie Fan Club was founded "for the purpose of promoting and fostering talent in the theatrical world and to encourage community movements aimed to protect and develop the highest educational and recreational value in pictures." Its first public event was a reception for Louise Beavers, and this was followed by a conference on the movies. *California Eagle,* January 31, 1936.

60. Floyd C. Covington to Joseph I. Breen, August 5, 1935, *The Green Pastures,* MPPDA Production Code Administration Case Files, AMPAS.

61. Joseph I. Breen to J. L. Warner, August 2, 1935, and J. L. Warner to Joseph I. Breen, August 5, 1935, both in *The Green Pastures,* MPPDA Production Code Administration Case Files, AMPAS.

62. Elizabeth St. Charles Edwards to Joseph I. Breen, July 29, 1935, *The Green Pastures,* MPPDA Production Code Administration Case Files, AMPAS. The *California Eagle* reported in its January 24, 1936, issue on the "Goin' to Heaven on a Mule" number from Jolson's *Wonder Bar* (Warner Bros., 1934) as his attempt to compensate for having lost his bid for the rights to *The Green Pastures.* Isadore "Friz" Freleng directed an animated version of "Goin' to Heaven on a Mule" for a Warner Bros. Merrie Melodie cartoon in 1934.

63. Charles Musser, "Passions and the Passion Play: Theater, Film, and Religion in America, 1880–1900," in *Movie Censorship and American Culture,* ed. Francis G. Couvares (Washington, DC: Smithsonian Institution Press, 1996), 64. On the Oberammergau Passion Play, see James Shapiro, *Oberammergau: The Troubling Story of the World's Most Famous Passion Play* (New York: Pantheon Books, 2000).

64. Charles Keil, "*From the Manger to the Cross:* The New Testament Narrative and the Question of Stylistic Retardation," in *Une invention du diable? Cinéma des premiers temps et religion,* ed. Roland Cosandey, André Gaudreault, and Tom Gunning (Sainte-Foy: Les Presses de L'Université Laval, 1990), 113–14.

65. Even the "race movie" *The Birth of a Race,* dir. John W. Noble (The Birth of a Race Photoplay Company, 1919), did not set its telling of the history of the human race through the Bible in a black context but used mostly white actors, including black actors where the filmmakers deemed it historically appropriate. See Judith Weisenfeld, "For the Cause of Mankind: The Bible, Racial Uplift and Early Race Movies," in *African Americans and the Bible: Sacred Text and Social Texture,* ed. Vincent Wimbush (New York: Continuum, 2000); and Thomas Cripps, "The Making of 'The Birth of a Race': The Emerging Politics of Identity in Silent Movies," in *The Birth of Whiteness: Race and the Emergence of U.S. Cinema,* ed. Daniel Bernardi (New Brunswick: Rutgers University Press, 1996).

66. Roark Bradford to Marc Connelly, September 27, 1935, *The Green Pastures* Production Files, WBA.

67. Marc Connelly to Robert Russa Moton, September 24, 1935, *The Green Pastures* Production Files, WBA.

68. Brothers Noble and George Johnson founded the Lincoln Motion Picture Company in 1916.

69. *New York Amsterdam News*, May 2, 1936; *California Eagle*, December 21, 1928, September 14, 1928, and December 27, 1935; *New York Times*, September 20, 1969. Alan Gevinson, ed., *American Film Institute Catalog—Within Our Gates: Ethnicity in American Feature Films, 1911–1960* (Berkeley: University of California Press, 1997), 1013; Bruce Kellner, *The Harlem Renaissance: A Historical Dictionary of the Era* (Westport, CT: Greenwood Press, 1984), 185. Most of the press reports on Ingram's life history, including the obituary in the *New York Times*, indicate that he had undergraduate and medical degrees from Northwestern University. There is no record of his having attended the university under either name. Janet C. Olson, Assistant University Archivist, Northwestern University Archives, e-mail to author, July 2, 2002. Apparently, the story that would become a part of his biography for the rest of his life began taking shape around 1935. Shortly following the end of filming *The Green Pastures*, one newspaper reported that Ingram planned to quit acting, having "played the best role that can be played," and to go to medical school to "be physician to his race." Unidentified clipping, L. S. Alexander Gumby Collection of Negroiana, reel 8, Columbia University Rare Book and Manuscript Library.

70. *New York Amsterdam News*, March 14, 1936.

71. Ibid. Ingram signed a contract to be paid $350 per week for the production (playing three parts in the film). A later budget listed his salary at $550 per week. *The Green Pastures* Production Files, WBA.

72. *New York Amsterdam News*, January 25, 1936.

73. See Thomas Schatz, *The Genius of the System: Hollywood Filmmaking in the Studio Era* (New York: Owl Books, 1988). In a 1978 interview that Thomas Cripps conducted, Connelly complained about the studio's excessive concern for the film's budget and insisted that his ability to be original in transforming the play into a film was hampered by financial concerns. Marc Connelly, *The Green Pastures*, ed. Thomas Cripps (Madison: University of Wisconsin Press, 1979), 28. In media interviews shortly following the end of filming, Connelly claimed that he had had no conflicts with the studio. "It was like being an independent producer," he told one reporter. "No one interfered with me." *New York Sun*, April 1, 1936.

74. In the year before *The Green Pastures* was released, Warner Bros.' film *Bordertown* (1935), directed by Archie Mayo and starring Bette Davis and Paul Muni, was budgeted at $343,000, and its *Captain Blood* (1935), directed by Michael Curtiz and

starring newcomer Errol Flynn and Olivia de Havilland, had a budget of $1.2 million. Flynn made $750 per week on *Captain Blood*. See Schatz, *Genius of the System*, ch. 12.

75. Henry Blanke to Hal Wallis, interoffice communication, December 25, 1935, *The Green Pastures* Production Files, WBA.

76. Connelly, *Voices Offstage*, 144.

77. Connelly, *Green Pastures: A Fable*, xv.

78. For discussions of African American interpretations of the Exodus story in particular, see Eddie S. Glaude Jr., *Exodus! Religion, Race, and Nation in Early Nineteenth-Century Black America* (Chicago: University of Chicago Press, 2000); Albert J. Raboteau, "African Americans, Exodus, and the American Israel," in *African American Christianity: Essays in History*, ed. Paul E. Johnson (Berkeley: University of California Press, 1994); Albert J. Raboteau, *Slave Religion: The "Invisible Institution" in the Antebellum South* (New York: Oxford University Press, 1978).

79. Connelly, *Green Pastures* (ed. Cripps), 191.

80. For example, the opening frame for Cecil B. DeMille's 1956 version of *The Ten Commandments* asserts that the film is "in accordance with the Holy Scriptures" and insists on its historical accuracy by listing Philo and Josephus as providing material to fill in information about Moses not found in the Bible.

81. In Connelly's 1978 interview with Thomas Cripps, he indicated that the studio refused his request to shoot on location "down south," but the production files contain no record of this discussion. Connelly, *Green Pastures* (ed. Cripps), 27.

82. Ibid., 62.

83. Ibid., 60–61.

84. The film script originally included an exchange between "three roustabouts" who smoke and describe their exploits in a barrelhouse in New Orleans the previous evening, behavior that viewers would later connect to the behavior that motivates God to destroy humanity with the Flood. The three men also note that because the river is so high they cannot work that day. While it is not clear why the scene was cut from later versions of the script, it is possible that Connelly and the studio feared the reaction from African American audiences to the three characters. Marc Connelly, *Green Pastures* script, December 31, 1935, AMPAS.

85. Connelly, *Green Pastures* (ed. Cripps), 200.

86. In the author's note in the published version of the play, Connelly wrote, "One need not blame a hazy memory of the Bible for the failure to recall the characters of Hezdrel, Zeba and others in the play. They are the author's apocrypha, but he believes persons much like them have figured in the meditations of some of the old Negro preachers, whose simple faith he has tried to translate into a play." Connelly, *Green Pastures: A Fable*, xvi. Daniel L. Haynes played Adam and Hezdrel in the Broadway production.

87. Connelly, *Green Pastures* (ed. Cripps), 186. Cripps notes that with the move away from the play's emphasis on Hosea as the one who teaches humanity about God's mercy the film "loses conviction" and "God seems merely irresponsible and self-pitying" (202).

88. Green, "Social Gospels," 92.

89. Connelly, *Green Pastures: A Fable*, xv.

90. Quoted in George S. Schuyler, "Mr. Whitney and Mr. Lewis," *Pittsburgh Courier*, October 8, 1930.

91. See Paula J. Massood, *Black City Cinema: African American Urban Experiences in Film* (Philadelphia: Temple University Press, 2003), ch. 1, for a discussion of "the antebellum idyll" in various Hollywood all-black-cast films.

92. *Clean Pastures*, dir. Isadore Freleng (Warner Bros., 1937). Animation by Paul Smith and Phil Monroe and musical direction by Carl W. Stalling. It was a common practice in this period for studios to produce cartoon takeoffs of feature films.

93. Born Lincoln Perry, Stepin Fetchit began his career in vaudeville and moved on to Hollywood in the 1920s, appearing in Fox's 1929 *Hearts in Dixie*. Fox signed him to a long-term contract, and he appeared in some forty films for Fox and other studios. Perry's characters were always slow moving, lazy, and dim witted. See Mel Watkins, *Stepin Fetchit: The Life and Times of Lincoln Perry* (New York: Pantheon Books, 2005).

94. The scene in which the band members lead the people up to heaven is reminiscent of the Marx Brothers' 1937 *A Day at the Races*, which also enlists African American religious culture in its humor but does so in a way that, while making use of stereotypes, presents black culture as authentic and joyful when set against the pretensions of wealthy whites. Near the film's end, Groucho, Chico, and Harpo, inevitably fleeing the authorities, find themselves in the black community of the town in which the film is set. Led by Harpo, the fugitives engage the black folk in a song-and-dance sequence that moves from "Nobody Knows the Trouble I've Seen" to a song that declares (to the tune of "I'm Just Wild about Harry") that "All God's Chillun Got Rhythm, All God's Chillun Got Swing." The scene seamlessly links spirituals, blues, jazz, and jitterbug dancing and the Marx Brothers participate fully and enthusiastically as their characters seem comfortable for the first time in the world of the film. *A Day at the Races*, dir. Sam Wood (Loew's, Inc., 1937). "All God's Children Got Rhythm," music by Bronislau Kaper and Walter Jurmann, lyrics by Gus Kahn. Dorothy Dandridge appears briefly in her film debut.

95. While *The Green Pastures* continues to be exhibited, *Clean Pastures* suffered a different fate. In 1968 United Artists, which had bought the Associated Artists Productions (AAP) library of cartoons, placed *Clean Pastures* on the "censored 11," a list of cartoons it refused to air or to distribute on video because they contained racial stereotypes. Another Freleng cartoon that deals with African American religion, *Sunday Go to Meetin' Time* (Warner Bros., 1936), is also on the list.

96. Benjamin E. Mays, *The Negro's God as Reflected in His Literature* (1938; reprint, New York: Russell and Russell, 1968), n.p.

97. *New York Evening Graphic*, February 27, 1930.

98. *New York Age*, March 5, 1930.

99. *New York Evening Graphic*, February 27, 1930; *New York Age*, March 5, 1930.

100. *New York Telegram*, February 28, 1930.

101. *Motion Picture Herald*, May 30, 1936.

102. *Motion Picture Review*, June 1936; *Commonweal*, June 5, 1936.

103. *California Eagle*, May 22, 1936; *Amsterdam News*, May 30, 1936, June 6, 1936, and June 20, 1936.

104. Will Hays to Joseph Breen, February 14, 1936, *The Green Pastures*, MPPDA Production Code Administration Case Files, AMPAS.

105. See pressbooks in *The Green Pastures* Production Files, WBA; Connelly, *Green Pastures* (ed. Cripps), 29.

106. Connelly, *Voices Offstage*, 196.

107. *Sunday Dispatch*, April 18, 1937.

108. *New York Times*, November 4, 1936.

109. Censor Board Reports, *The Green Pastures*, MPPDA Production Code Administration Case Files, AMPAS.

110. *New York Amsterdam News*, July 18, 1936.

111. Hal Wallis to Jack Warner, interoffice communication, August 6, 1936, *The Green Pastures* Production Files, WBA.

112. *Chicago Defender*, July 4, 1936; *California Eagle*, July 3, 1936; *New York Amsterdam News*, July 18, 1936.

113. Cripps estimated that the film, which he determined ultimately cost about $800,000 to produce, brought in about $2 million. Connelly, *Green Pastures* (ed. Cripps), 35.

114. *New York Times*, March 26, 1951; *Philadelphia Inquirer*, March 28, 1951; *Philadelphia Evening Bulletin*, February 28, 1951. On the controversy over Rossellini's *The Miracle*, which resulted in a decision by the United States Supreme Court protecting film as speech, see Garth Jowett, "'A Significant Medium for the Communication of Ideas': The *Miracle* Decision and the Decline of Motion Picture Censorship, 1952–1968," in Couvares, *Movie Censorship*, 258–76.

115. Harold Cruse, "'Green Pastures' Twenty Years Ago and Today," *Daily Worker*, March 30, 1951, and April 2, 1951, reprinted in Harold Cruse, *Rebellion or Revolution?* (New York: William Morrow, 1968), 42, 44.

116. Connelly, *Green Pastures* (ed. Cripps), 37; *Ebony* (July 1951).

117. Hallmark decided to mount the production a second time in 1959 because the ratings had been extremely low in 1957. Television reporter Cecil Smith noted that the small audience in 1957 had been a result its having been televised against a live broad-

cast of Mike Todd's *Around the World in 80 Days* party at Madison Square Garden celebrating the one-year anniversary of the film's premiere. *Los Angeles Times*, March 23, 1959.

118. In his review of the 1951 revival, Cruse also emphasized the difficult position in which black performers who wanted to work found themselves. Cruse, "'Green Pastures,'" 42–43.

119. Hall Johnson to Al Lewis, July 24, 1942, *Cabin in the Sky*, AFC.

120. Bernard L. Peterson Jr., *Early American Playwrights and Dramatic Writers: A Biographical Dictionary and Catalogue of Plays, Films, and Broadcasting Scripts* (Westport, CT: Greenwood Press, 1990), 90.

121. Mercedes Gilbert, *In Greener Fields* (1943), typescript, box 31, file 3, Negro Actors Guild Collection, Rare Books and Manuscripts, Schomburg Center for Research in Black Culture, NYPL.

3. "A MIGHTY EPIC OF MODERN MORALS"

1. Scholars, including myself in earlier published work, have often used the term *race movies* to refer to the body of films produced and exhibited for black audiences from the mid-1910s through the late 1940s. These films were made in a variety of production contexts, with some produced by black-owned companies using African American casts and crew and others released by white-owned film companies using black on-screen talent. Some scholars have chosen to privilege those films produced by black companies and black directors as the only true "race movies" on the presumption that they reflect authentic black culture in a way that films produced through cooperative endeavors with white-owned companies could not. In examining films from both categories over the next two chapters, I want to emphasize their availability to black audiences as the significant unifying feature, and I therefore use the terms *race movies* and *black-audience films* interchangeably. For a useful discussion of these questions, see Julia Leyda, "Black-Audience Westerns and the Politics of Cultural Identification in the 1930s," *Cinema Journal* 42 (Fall 2002): 46–70.

2. *California Eagle*, September 14, 1928. There are no extant prints of *Tenderfeet* (Midnight Productions, 1928), but according to the *Eagle* article the film was previewed at the Forum Theatre in Los Angeles and subsequently picked up by New York exhibitors for distribution. The cast included Cliff (Rex) Ingram, who would appear the following year in Fox's all-black-cast *Hearts in Dixie* and later as "De Lawd" in the 1936 film version of *The Green Pastures*. The press account does not contain details about Williams's second film. A later press account lists his first film as *Hot Biscuits* (1929). I have been unable to locate any information about this work. Edward T. Clayton, "The Tragedy of Amos 'n' Andy," *Ebony*, October 1961, 68.

3. These appearances are uncredited. See unattributed biographical account in reel 12, George P. Johnson Negro Film Collection, Department of Special Collections,

University Research Library, UCLA. *Tarzan and the Golden Lion*, dir. J. P. McGowan (Film Booking Offices of America, 1927); *Ham and Eggs*, dir. Roy Del Ruth (Warner Bros., 1927), from a story by Darryl F. Zanuck about a black regiment in France during World War I; *The King of Kings*, dir. Cecil B. DeMille (Pathé, 1927); *Steamboat Bill, Jr.*, dir. Charles F. Reisner (Buster Keaton Productions, 1928). On Williams's appearance in *Safe in Hell*, dir. William Wellman (Warner Bros., 1931), which featured Nina Mae McKinney in a major role, see *Chicago Defender*, June 27, 1931.

4. Harry Levette, "'Them Wuz the Days' When the Colored Actors Were Busy," *California Eagle*, March 2, 1924. Williams was involved in the production of *The Melancholy Dame*, *The Framing of the Shrew*, *Oft in the Silly Night*, and *Music Hath Harms*, dir. Arvid E. Gillstrom (Christie, 1929). These films featured members of the New York–based theater company the Lafayette Players, including Edward Thompson and Evelyn Preer. On the Lafayette Players in film, see Sister Francesca Thompson, "From Shadows 'n' Shufflin' to Spotlights and Cinema: The Lafayette Players, 1915–1932," in *Oscar Micheaux and His Circle: African-American Filmmaking and Race Cinema of the Silent Era*, ed. Pearl Bowser, Jane Gaines, and Charles Musser (Bloomington: University of Indiana Press, 2001).

5. Williams founded a club in Hollywood where entertainers would perform for each other, talk about show business, and socialize. Participants included Zach Williams, who would appear in at least one film with Williams, and Madame Sul-Te-Wan, by then a veteran Hollywood actress. Actress Juanita Moore recalled that Williams brought in directors and other professionals to teach participants about the business and to improve their acting skills "so we wouldn't be running around carrying spears all the time." *Spencer Williams: Remembrances of an Early Black Film Pioneer*, dir. Walid Khaldi (Golden Moon Productions, 1995).

6. Williams's proposed company should not be confused with the Lincoln Motion Picture Company, founded by Noble and George P. Johnson in 1916. *Washington Tribune*, May 29, 1931, Tuskegee Institute News Clippings File; *Chicago Defender*, May 2, 1931. Williams's partner in this endeavor was L. Ford, a successful African American auto insurance agent in Los Angeles, who, like Williams, was a native of Louisiana. The films were to be distributed by the white producer Sam Kramer. On Ford, see William Hicks, *History of Louisiana Negro Baptists, 1804–1914* (Nashville, TN: National Baptist Publishing Board, 1918), 231.

7. Earl J. Morris, "1938 Banner Year for Negro Movie Industry," *Pittsburgh Courier*, January 21, 1939.

8. See *Oklahoma City Black Dispatch*, December 16, 1939, and *Kansas City Call*, December 22, 1939, both in Tuskegee Institute News Clippings File.

9. G. William Jones, *Black Cinema Treasures Lost and Found* (Denton: University of North Texas Press, 1991), 32.

10. On Williams's career in television as Andrew Hogg Brown on the CBS show

Amos 'n' Andy (1951–53), see Melvin Patrick Ely, *The Adventures of Amos 'n' Andy: A Social History of an American Phenomenon* (New York: Free Press, 1991).

11. Loren Miller, "Hollywood's New Negro Films," *The Crisis*, January 1938, 8–9.

12. "Race movie" production began in the 1910s and continued through the late 1940s. Over the course of that period production companies released hundreds of films intended for black audiences. Prior to 1929, when sound film began to become the standard, many of the companies that produced race films were black owned. The financial burden of sound production, along with the Great Depression, put many of these companies out of business. During the 1930s and 1940s race movies came from white-owned production companies as well as from joint ventures between black and white producers and directors. The number of race movies declined in the late 1940s as film production became increasingly expensive and as Hollywood began to make greater use of African American actors and actresses. With regard to viewing practices, in her work on Chicago in the silent film era, Jacqueline Stewart has demonstrated that, by the time the race movie industry developed, moviegoing was an accepted part of African American leisure and African Americans were a significant presence in movie theaters. Jacqueline Najuma Stewart, *Migrating to the Movies: Cinema and Black Urban Modernity* (Berkeley: University of California Press, 2005). A 1929 survey of American movie theaters found 461 that catered exclusively to black audiences. Jack Alicoate, ed., *The 1930 Film Daily Year Book of Motion Pictures* (New York: J. W. Alicoate, 1930), 795.

13. Royal Gospel Productions advertising letter, 1947, *Going to Glory, Come to Jesus* file, Motion Picture Case Files, NYSA.

14. Ibid.

15. See, for example, correspondence in *The Glory Road* file, Motion Picture Case Files, NYSA.

16. Telephone interview with Alma Brown, March 25, 2004. Brown, who counted Pauline Tatum as her second mother, recalls that Tatum was a member of Young's Chapel Baptist Church in Vidalia.

17. The strong presence of Roman Catholic imagery and language in some of Williams's religious films made me wonder whether he was raised Roman Catholic, but a search of the sacramental records in the Diocese of Alexandria (LA) and in the Diocese of Jackson (MS) could not confirm this. His mother's Baptist affiliation makes it likely that he was brought up in the Baptist church, but it was not unusual for black Protestants to send their children to Catholic schools. There was an active black Catholic community and school in Natchez, but I have not been able to locate information about Williams's education in order to make a connection. See Richard M. Tristano, "Holy Family Parish: The Genesis of an African-American Catholic Community in Natchez, Mississippi," *Journal of Negro History* 83 (Autumn 1998): 258–83.

18. Jones, *Black Cinema Treasures*, 31–32. According to a number of Williams's

colleagues, he met Bert Williams and musicians James Reese Europe and Noble Sissle in Europe while he was in the service. *Spencer Williams: Remembrances.*

19. See unattributed biographical account in reel 12, George P. Johnson Negro Film Collection; Clayton, "Tragedy of Amos 'n' Andy," 68, 73.

20. The information on Pauline Tatum and the WRC comes from a telephone interview with Alma Brown, March 25, 2004. Vidalia's Post 23 of the GAR and its auxiliary WRC was named after Parson Brownlow, a white West Virginia Methodist minister who remained loyal to the Union. Earnest McBride, "Black Southern Groups Cling to Dying Tradition," *Sacramento Observer,* June 6, 2003.

21. *Marching On* (rereleased as *Where's My Man To-Nite?*), dir. Spencer Williams (Sack Amusement Enterprises, 1943), and *Dirty Gertie from Harlem U.S.A.*, dir. Spencer Williams (Sack Amusement Enterprises, 1946). According to press accounts, Williams moved to Tulsa, Oklahoma, in 1946 to work with Amos T. Hall, a prominent Prince Hall Mason and civil rights attorney, in founding the American Business and Industrial College, "a G.I. school." Williams is interred in the Los Angeles National Cemetery, a cemetery for the burial of residents of the National Home of Disabled Volunteer Soldiers, and his tombstone indicates that he served as a sergeant in the U.S. Army during World War I. On Williams's military service, see Clayton, "Tragedy of Amos 'n' Andy," 61.

22. *Harlem on the Prairie*, dir. Sam Newfield (Associated Features, 1937); *The Bronze Buckaroo*, dir. Richard C. Kahn (Hollywood Productions, 1938); *Two-Gun Man from Harlem*, dir. Richard C. Kahn (Merit Pictures, 1938); *Harlem Rides the Range*, dir., Richard C. Kahn (Hollywood Pictures, 1939); *Son of Ingagi*, dir. Richard C. Kahn (Sack Amusement Enterprises, 1940). Williams's short story "House of Horror" served as the basis for the script for *Son of Ingagi*, and he wrote the screenplay for *Harlem Rides the Range.* John Kisch and Edward Mapp, eds., *A Separate Cinema: Fifty Years of Black Cast Posters* (New York: Noonday Press, 1992), 21.

23. For several years before this, the black press had covered Williams's efforts to acquire the technical skills to produce sound films and even hailed him as a technical innovator. In 1930 the *Chicago Defender* reported that "Spencer Williams, who formerly had an excellent position at Christie Studios, has been working in the technical department of another studio in Hollywood and according to reports has learned all about the science of making the sound strips that have revolutionized the motion picture industry." In 1931 readers learned that "Spencer Williams has completed a sound truck of his own invention and has opened offices here for its promotion." *Chicago Defender*, December 20, 1930, and April 4, 1931.

24. Leyda, "Black-Audience Westerns," 51.

25. Paula J. Massood, *Black City Cinema: African American Urban Experiences in Film* (Philadelphia: Temple University Press, 2003), 76. See also Thomas Cripps, "The Films of Spencer Williams," *Black American Literature Forum* 12 (Winter 1978): 130.

26. The company's films prior to this cooperative arrangement include *Bargain with Bullets*, dir. Harry Fraser (Million Dollar Productions, 1937); *The Duke Is Tops*, dir. William Nolte (Million Dollar Productions, 1938); *Life Goes On*, dir. William Nolte (Million Dollar Productions, 1939); *Straight to Heaven*, dir. Arthur Leonard (Million Dollar Productions, 1939); *Reform School*, dir. Leo C. Popkin (Million Dollar Productions, 1939); *Gang Smashers*, dir. Leo C. Popkin (Million Dollar Productions, 1939).

27. *Nashville Globe*, June 9, 1939, Tuskegee Institute News Clippings File. See also Anna Everett, *Returning the Gaze: A Genealogy of Black Film Criticism, 1909–1949* (Durham: Duke University Press, 2001), 203.

28. *Gang War*, dir. Leo C. Popkin (Million Dollar Productions, 1940).

29. Paula Massood notes that Cooper "had a direct interest in his screen image, a concern that ultimately caused him to break with Randol and Million Dollar Productions in order to move away from gangster films." Massood, *Black City Cinema*, 59.

30. Arthur Terry holds that Williams paid for the film himself, and this could explain the release of the film as "A Spencer Williams Production." Arthur LeMont Terry, "Genre and Divine Causality in the Religious Films of Spencer Williams, Jr." (PhD diss., Regent University, 1995), 214. Thomas Cripps and G. William Jones believe that Sack financed the film. See Cripps, "Films of Spencer Williams."

31. See, for example, the interview with the cameraman John Yoder in Jones, *Black Cinema Treasures*, 174–76.

32. Ibid., 175–76.

33. Ibid., 176, 178. Orr played credited roles in *Dirty Gertie from Harlem U.S.A.* (1946), *Beale Street Mama* (1946), *Juke Joint* (1948), and *The Girl in Room 20* (1949) and said that he played smaller parts in *Of One Blood* (1945) and *Go Down, Death* (1946). Although he emphasized the need for a quick pace on the set, he also insisted that Williams never rushed the actors and gave them the time they needed to prepare for scenes. *Spencer Williams: Remembrances.*

34. *Spencer Williams: Remembrances.*

35. The matte box uses masks to expose only part of the film at any given time. Quoted in Terry, "Genre and Divine Causality," 211.

36. *Spencer Williams: Remembrances.*

37. Ibid.

38. Williams wrote the screenplay for *The Blood of Jesus*. The film's credits indicate that Sam Elljay wrote the screenplay for *Go Down, Death*, based on a story idea by Jean Roddy and a poem by James Weldon Johnson. Some sources list Williams as a writer for *Go Down, Death*, and the promotional materials name only Johnson. Applications for certification by the New York State Education Department, which handled film censorship, indicate that the film was released in 1944 and again in 1948. See Lester J. Sack to Irwin Esmond, Motion Picture Division, State Education Department, April 7, 1941; Jules J. Nayfack, Sack Amusement Enterprises to Ward C. Bowen, Motion

Picture Division, State Education Department, December 10, 1947; *The Glory Road* (a.k.a. *The Blood of Jesus*) file, Motion Picture Case Files, NYSA.

39. Robert Farris Thompson, *Flash of the Spirit: African and Afro-American Art and Philosophy* (New York: Vintage Books, 1983), 109.

40. Adrienne Lanier Seward believes that Spencer Williams may have seen *Heaven Bound* and that he may have been the filmmaker who, according to church oral tradition, attempted to strike an agreement with the congregation to film a performance. The story may be apocryphal, as it exists in the oral tradition of at least one other congregation that performed *Heaven Bound* or a similar morality play. The opera singer Shirley Verrett, who was born in New Orleans in 1931 and was raised Seventh-Day Adventist, recounted a similar story about her church's production of *Heaven Bound*, in which she performed a child. Her father was the church's choir director and also played a major role in the play. Interview with Leonard Lopate, "Survival Kit," National Public Radio, April 30, 2004. Shirley Verrett and Christopher Brooks, *I Never Walked Alone: The Autobiography of an American Singer* (Hoboken, NJ: John Wiley, 2003). On the story of the filmmaker and the Atlanta production, see Adrienne Lanier Seward, "Early Black Film and Folk Tradition: An Interpretive Analysis of the Use of Folklore in Selected All-Black Cast Feature Films" (PhD diss., Indiana University, 1985), 233.

41. The most complete source on the drama is Gregory D. Coleman, *We're Heaven Bound: Portrait of a Black Sacred Drama* (Athens: University of Georgia Press, 1992). See also William H. Wiggins Jr., "Pilgrims, Crosses, and Faith: The Folk Dimensions of Heaven Bound," *Black American Literature Forum* 25 (Spring 1991): 93–100, and Winona L. Fletcher, "Witnessing a 'Miracle': Sixty Years of Heaven Bound at Big Bethel in Atlanta," *Black American Literature Forum* 25 (Spring 1991): 83–92. The authorship of *Heaven Bound* has been surrounded by considerable myth—one white critic claimed that it had come to "a colored laundress in Florida" in an ecstatic dream—as well as a great deal of controversy. In response to local press coverage that gave Davis complete credit for the play, Jones had a text of the drama typed up, registered a copyright, and gave the church notice to cease unauthorized performances. The congregation closed ranks against Jones once she filed suit, with the pastor ejecting her from the choir and many members testifying against her in court. The decision, handed down in district court, found that Jones had only provided the church with the idea, having herself gotten it from a co-worker, and that the play in its current form had been developed through the combined work of Jones, Davis, and the members of the choir. Thus no single person (save Jones's co-worker, who never appeared in court) could claim sole authorship. There was a strong class dimension to the congregation's response to the conflict, with most promoting an image of Jones as insufficiently educated to have created *Heaven Bound*. Davis, by contrast, was a graduate of Clark-Atlanta University and taught in Atlanta University's adult night school. The church's

pastor and many prominent members characterized Jones as a troublemaker in their testimony. From various accounts of the creation of the drama, it seems clear that both Jones and Davis were responsible for developing what would come to be known as "The Scroll Reading," the outline of action and the text of the narration. In addition, the members of Choir Number One, who made up the majority of the performers in the individual parts, selected the hymns that would accompany their characters' stories. Coleman, *We're Heaven Bound*, 47–56.

42. Zelda F. Popkin, "'Heaven Bound': An Authentic Negro Folk Drama Out of Old Savannah," *Theatre Guild Magazine* 11 (August 1931): 14. Other white critics at the time remarked on similarities between *Heaven Bound* and medieval morality plays but insisted that the connection was simply coincidence. One critic wrote in 1931, "[O]f course, this similarity is an unconscious one, as the Negroes developing *Heaven Bound* were absolutely ignorant of theatre history." Gregory Coleman argues that early participants were familiar with literary history and contemporary arts movements. Quoted in Fletcher, "Witnessing a 'Miracle,'" 86.

43. Ida Briggs Henderson, "Shelby's 'Heavenbound' Gets Tempting Offers," *Charlotte, N.C. Observer*, September 16, 1934, in Tuskegee Institute News Clipping File.

44. Yvonne Chireau, "The Bible and African American Folklore," in *African Americans and the Bible: Sacred Texts and Social Textures*, ed. Vincent L. Wimbush (New York: Continuum, 2000), 677.

45. The white dramatists of the Atlanta Theatre Guild who directed the WPA production made a number of changes, the most significant and enduring being the substitution of spirituals for the traditional hymns the choir had originally included. See Coleman, *We're Heaven Bound*, 64–67.

46. Ibid., 4.

47. Fletcher, "Witnessing a 'Miracle,'" 88. The same can be said of Eloyce and James Gist's evangelical films from the early 1930s— *Hell Bound Train* and *Verdict, Not Guilty*. See Judith Weisenfeld, "Teaching Morality in Race Movies," in *Religions of the United States in Practice*, ed. Colleen McDannell (Princeton: Princeton University Press, 2001), 2:131–40.

48. I will return to the question of the strong presence of Roman Catholic iconography, including the image of the Sacred Heart of Jesus, in *The Blood of Jesus* later in this chapter.

49. This is an image of Jesus abstracted from Heinrich Hoffman's *Christ and the Rich Young Ruler* (1889). See Colleen McDannell, *Material Christianity: Religion and Popular Culture in America* (New Haven: Yale University Press, 1995), 26–27, on nineteenth-century mass production of religious paintings for American Protestant consumption.

50. It is possible that Williams did not film these scenes himself but rather incorporated them into his film from elsewhere. This was the case for important sections in *Go Down, Death* (1944), an issue we will return to later. That he may not have been

responsible for filming the segments and that the resulting film may be a composite does not, however, make the final product any less Spencer Williams's artistic and theological vision. Dennis Looney, who has studied *Go Down Death*, believes that Williams did create the Gates of Hell set that appears in both films. Dennis Looney, "Spencer Williams and Dante: An African-American Filmmaker at the Gates of Hell," paper presented at the Dante and Cinema Conference, University of Toronto, March 30, 2001, Webcast retrieved July 5, 2006, from www.utoronto.ca/humanities-centre/archives/activitydetails_dante.html.

51. Thomas Cripps, who did much of the pioneering and invaluable scholarly work on Williams's films, characterized the religious work as "shamelessly literal and fundamentalist." Cripps's reading of all expressions of deeply held religious beliefs in black films as "fundamentalist" obscures the complex theological positions put forward, particularly in Williams's films. Lacking any authenticating evidence about Williams's religious commitments, it is difficult to say whether he adhered to the tenets of fundamentalism as American Christians would have understood the term in the mid—twentieth century—a theological commitment to the inerrancy of the Bible, the Virgin Birth, the divinity of Jesus, Christ's substitutionary atonement, the bodily resurrection of the Christ, and Christ's imminent return. Certainly, some of these elements are present in Williams's work, but it is difficult to determine whether he can be appropriately labeled a fundamentalist. Moreover, Cripps's use of the term seems aimed at ascribing a simplistic character to Williams's religious commitment. He uses similar language to describe the films of James and Eloyce Gist, to be discussed below. For Cripps's view of Williams's work, see Cripps, "Films of Spencer Williams," and Thomas Cripps, *Black Film as Genre* (Bloomington: Indiana University Press, 1978).

52. Seward, "Early Black Film," 217–22.

53. Quotations from the film's dialogue come from my own transcription.

54. Seward, "Early Black Film," 218.

55. To my knowledge, no print of the film exists. I am relying on the dialogue script on deposit at the New York State Archives for my summary of the film's story. Lobby cards, posters, and other advertising materials have survived and provide some sense of production design. Neither the surviving advertising materials nor the promotional materials provide any production information except that it was based on "the successful New York Play by Wesley Wilson and Leola Grant," which I have been unable to identify. The film starred Irene Harper, Lloyd Howlett, Stella Van Derzee, Charles A. Freeman, and John Watts and, according to one poster, was distributed by Toddy Pictures, Inc. Royal Gospel Productions' letterhead characterizes the company as "producing features with all colored casts in 16mm and 35mm" and indicates that, in addition to *Going to Glory*, it had two other films for release—*Go Preach* and *Children of Jesus*. I have been unable to locate information on these films. *Going to Glory, Come to Jesus* file, Motion Picture Case Files, NYSA.

56. "Royal Gospel Productions Presents 'Going to Glory,'" 3, *Going to Glory, Come to Jesus* file, Motion Picture Case Files, NYSA.

57. Ibid., 8.

58. Ibid., 26.

59. John 8:3–11.

60. For accounts of formerly enslaved African Americans and their conversion experiences that make use of similar imagery, see Clifton H. Johnson, ed., *God Struck Me Dead: Religious Conversion Experiences and Autobiographies of Ex-Slaves* (1969; reprint, Cleveland, OH: Pilgrim Press, 1993).

61. Yvonne Chireau notes the interest in African American folklore in the nature of the spiritual world. She writes, "Many of these folklore traditions convey African Americans' preoccupation with the supernatural, making reference to the invisible realm, the world that parallels the material world and is manifest in dreams, visions, and miracles." Chireau, "Bible and African American Folklore," 678.

62. Ibid., 673.

63. Poster for *Go Down, Death,* in Kisch and Mapp, *A Separate Cinema,* 23. *Go Down, Death,* dir. Spencer Williams (Sack Amusement Enterprises, 1944). Some sources list the release date as 1946, but this was probably a rerelease.

64. The credits list the actors' names but do not associate them with their characters. In addition, the sound track is often difficult to decipher, and sources list a variety of names for the minister's character. The dialogue transcription from the New York State Archives lists him as Rev. Rhodes, and I have relied on this source here. James Weldon Johnson's *God's Trombones: Seven Negro Sermons in Verse* (1927; New York: Penguin, 1990).

65. Matthew 5:1–48 (Jesus preaches the Beatitudes to the crowd); Matthew 6:1–24 (Jesus admonishes against praying for the sake of being seen, and instructs people to pray the Lord's Prayer); Matthew 15:1–20 (Jesus talks with the Pharisees and scribes about true purity and impurity); Matthew 7:1–29 (Jesus speaks about judgment and hypocrisy); Romans 6:1–23 (Paul writes about slavery to sin and about Christ's victory over death).

66. On Sallman's religious art, see McDannell, *Material Christianity;* David Morgan, *Icons of American Protestantism: The Art of Warner Sallman* (New Haven: Yale University Press, 1996), and *Visual Piety: A History and Theory of Popular Religious Images* (Berkeley: University of California Press, 1998).

67. On film and melodrama, see Christine Gledhill, ed., *Home Is Where the Heart Is: Studies in Melodrama and the Woman's Film* (London: BFI Books, 1987). On race and melodramatic performance, see Linda Williams, *Playing the Race Card: Melodramas of Black and White from Uncle Tom to O.J. Simpson* (Princeton: Princeton University Press, 2001).

68. Jane Gaines, "*The Scar of Shame:* Skin Color and Caste in Black Silent Melodrama," in *Representing Blackness: Issues in Film and Video,* ed. Valerie Smith (New Brunswick: Rutgers University Press, 1997), 63–64.

69. Ibid., 69.

70. Christine Gledhill, "The Melodramatic Field: An Investigation," in Gledhill, *Home,* 33.

71. The funeral sermon follows the text of Johnson's poem, reading, in part:

Weep not, weep not,
She is not dead;
She's resting in the bosom of Jesus.
Heart-broken husband—weep no more;
Grief-stricken son—weep no more;
Left-lonesome daughter—weep no more;
She's only just gone home.

. . .

And God said: Go down, Death, go down,
Go down to Savannah, Georgia,
Down in Yamacraw,
And find Sister Caroline.
She's borne the burden and heat of the day,
She's labored long in my vineyard,
And she's tired—
She's weary—
Go down, Death, and bring her to me.

72. *L'Inferno* (Milano Films, 1911), dir. Francesco Bertolini and Adolfo Padovan, with Guiseppe de Liguoro. *L'Inferno* is not credited in Williams's film; I am grateful to Dennis Looney for identifying it for me.

73. In his study of exploitation films produced between the 1920 and 1950s, Eric Schaefer identifies a number of common characteristics of these works to distinguish them from general B-movies and other low-budget films of the period. "First, their primary subject was a 'forbidden' topic. The major exploitation topics included sex and sex hygiene, prostitution and vice, drug use, nudity, and any other subject considered at the time to be in bad taste. . . . Second, classical exploitation films were made cheaply, with extremely low production values, by small independent firms. . . . Third, exploitation films were distributed independently. . . . Fourth, the films were generally exhibited in theaters not affiliated with the majors [major studios]. . . . Finally, in comparison to the mainstream motion picture industry, relatively few prints of an exploita-

tion film were in release at any given time. However, unlike most other movies, exploitation films could be in release for ten or twenty years or more." Eric Schaefer, *Bold! Daring! Shocking! True! A History of Exploitation Films, 1919–1950* (Durham: Duke University Press, 1999), 4–6. I am grateful to Charles Musser for encouraging me to consult Schaefer's work in connection with Williams's films.

74. Williams's films also employ what Schaefer calls "padding"—the use of "additional material . . . to expand a film to fifty or more minutes." Padding frequently involved inserting filmed stage acts, and in the exploitation films these floorshows were sometimes erotic. The other two common production strategies of exploitation films, "the square-up" (a prefatory disclaimer or statement about the moral problematic the film addressed) and "hot and cold versions" that contained variable amounts of nudity in order to deal with local or state censorship boards, are not characteristic of Williams's surviving work. The issue of state censor boards' responses to Williams's films will be addressed later. Ibid., 56–75.

75. Ibid., 62. *Hell-A-Vision*, dir. Louis Sonney (Roadshow Attractions, 1936). I have not viewed the film, and Schaefer does not provide any identifying information about the particular Italian film version of the *Inferno* used in *Hell-A-Vision*. It is possible that it was the Bertolini-Padovan version and that Williams saw Sonney's film.

76. Schaefer sees areas of convergence between exploitation films, race films, and Poverty Row movies with regard to the practices of low-budget filmmaking but cautions against conflating the aesthetics of all three because of the unique emphasis on "forbidden spectacle" in exploitation films. It seems to me, however, that there is some overlap in subject matter between some of the black audience films and exploitation films, particularly given the use of *Inferno* scenes in films in both genres. Ibid., 75–76.

77. It is impossible to determine whether Williams had access to the entire Bertolini-Padovan film or used portions of it that had already been recycled in other films like *Hell-A-Vision* (if the Bertolini-Padovan is the one used in *Hell-A-Vision*). Dennis Looney conjectures that Williams may have had access to the entire film through Alfred Sack, who also distributed foreign films. Looney, "Spencer Williams and Dante."

78. Looney describes Williams's work here as an act of racial integration through "literary integration" in bringing together Dante and James Weldon Johnson and "cinematic integration" in cutting together various films. Ibid.

79. There were film precedents available to black viewers in the period in which African American actors appeared in narratives that incorporated Dante's work. The well-known African American actor Noble Johnson had appeared as the devil in *Dante's Inferno*, dir. Harry Lachman (Twentieth Century-Fox, 1935). The film, which starred Spencer Tracy and a young Rita Hayworth (credited as Rita Cansino), includes a staging of *Inferno* as part of the carnival show "Dante's Inferno." *New York Times*, March 24, 1935, and August 1, 1935.

80. Amy Kael Petrine, "Hell Bound, Heaven Bound, the Journey: Black America, 1930s Quest for Personal Advancement Using Motivational Imagery in Dramatic Productions" (n.d., unpublished paper), 11–14, James and Eloyce Gist file, Motion Picture, Broadcasting, and Recorded Sound Division, Library of Congress; Gloria J. Gibson, "Cinematic Foremothers: Zora Neale Hurston and Eloyce King Patrick Gist," in Bowser, Gaines, and Musser, *Oscar Micheaux and His Circle*, 200.

81. Johnson, *God's Trombones*, 1.

82. For advertisements of these records, see *Chicago Defender*, November 15, 1930; November 22, 1930. Rev. J. M. Gates, who was a Baptist minister in Atlanta, recorded many sermons in the late 1920s on a number of record labels, including Victor, Bluebird, and Okeh. See Rev. J. M. Gates, *Complete Recorded Works*, vols. 1–9 (Document Records, 1996–2000). Rev. Ford Washington McGee was a Methodist minister who became a member of the Church of God in Christ in 1918 and founded churches in Oklahoma City and later Chicago. He recorded on Victor Records in the late 1920s. See Rev. F. W. McGee, *Complete Recorded Works*, vol. 1, *1927–1929* (Document Records, 1992) and *Complete Recorded Works*, vol. 2, *1929–1930* (Document Records, 1992). See also John M. Giggie, "'When Jesus Handed Me a Ticket': Images of Railroad Travel and Spiritual Transformations among African Americans, 1865–1917," in *The Visual Culture of American Religions*, ed. David Morgan and Sally M. Promey (Berkeley: University of California Press, 2001), 249–66.

83. Representations in chart and map form of theological concerns have been common in twentieth-century Protestantism. Perhaps the best known and most influential are those by Clarence Larkin, published in his *Dispensational Truth, or God's Plan and Purpose in the Ages* (Philadelphia: C. Larkin, 1918).

84. The Motion Picture, Broadcast, and Recorded Sound Division of the Library of Congress has preserved a video copy of the 16 mm film with the reels out of sequence. Because it is a silent film that uses titles—frames with words that provide the viewer with dialogue, narration, or descriptions of the action—and does not present a narrative of events in a causal sequence, it is particularly difficult to know in what order the filmmakers presented the scenes. My discussion relies on notes in the library's files that record the likely sequence of the original reels, as well as my own sense of the possible order of scenes. The transcription of the film's titles and the descriptions of the action in the scenes are my own.

85. On the principle of "compensating moral values," see Olga J. Martin, *Hollywood's Movie Commandments: A Handbook for Motion Picture Writers and Reviewers* (New York: H. W. Wilson, 1937).

86. McDannell, *Material Christianity*, 28.

87. See also John Davis, "Catholic Envy: The Visual Culture of Protestant Desire," in Morgan and Promey, *Visual Culture*, 105–28.

88. Terry believes that the film may never have been completed because the trailer

contains no clips from the film, but the presence of cast credits and a listing of film's musical selections as well as the surviving poster make it likely that the film was finished. Terry, "Genre and Divine Causality."

89. Martin de Porres was beatified in 1873 and canonized in 1962.

90. Quoted in Cripps, *Black Film as Genre*, 98.

91. Telephone interview with Alma Brown, March 25, 2004. Marjorie Bowman, a friend of the Williams family, said that her aunt would cook a big supper when he came to Vidalia—"fried chicken, mustard greens, cornbread, lemonade, and make a jelly cake." She also noted that "Spencer liked to drink a little too." *Spencer Williams: Remembrances.*

92. *Spencer Williams: Remembrances.* A small notice in the *Pittsburgh Courier* about the upcoming release of Williams's *Go Down, Death* characterizes it as "the successor to his highly successful 'Blood of Jesus.'" *Pittsburgh Courier*, April 15, 1944.

93. The Production Code Administration oversaw the censorship of films released by the major Hollywood studios as part of a system of self-regulation. Films made by production companies outside the Hollywood system were reviewed under state guidelines, where there were such regulations were in place, and the PCA files for these films contain only those cuts required by state or foreign governments' censor boards.

94. Maryland State Board of Censors, Eliminations from *Go Down, Death*, October 27, 1944. *Go Down, Death*, MPPDA Production Code Administration Case Files, AMPAS. A Maryland statute required all films exhibited in the state to be submitted to the board for approval. The law came before the U.S. Supreme Court in the case of *Freedman v. Maryland*, 380 U.S. 51 (1965), in which an exhibitor was convicted of violating the statute. The court found that the Maryland law failed to guard against "unduly suppressing protected expression." Virginia, New York, Pennsylvania, Kansas, and Ohio also had state censor boards in this period, and their activities became circumscribed by the ruling in *Freedman v. Maryland*.

95. Report of Examiner, April 4, 1941, State of New York Education Department, Motion Picture Division, *Go Down, Death* file, Motion Picture Case Files, NYSA.

96. Report of Examiner, April 4, 1941, State of New York Education Department, Motion Picture Division, *The Glory Road* file, Motion Picture Case Files, NYSA.

97. *Go Down, Death*, MPPDA Production Code Administration Case Files, AMPAS.

98. Report of Examiner, April 4, 1941, State of New York Education Department, Motion Picture Division, *The Glory Road* file, Motion Picture Case Files, NYSA.

99. Lester J. Sack to Irwin Esmond, April 7, 1941, *The Glory Road* file, Motion Picture Case Files, NYSA.

100. Sack to Esmond, April 7, 1941, *The Glory Road* file, Motion Picture Case Files, NYSA.

101. *Jesus of Nazareth*, editor-titles, Jean Conover (Ideal Pictures, 1928). I have not

been able to locate any information about *The Little Flower of Jesus*, the film to which Sack referred.

102. Irwin Esmond to Sack Amusement Enterprises, April 8, 1941, *The Glory Road* file, Motion Picture Case Files NYSA.

4. "SATURDAY SINNERS AND SUNDAY SAINTS"

1. "Royal Gospel Productions Presents 'Going to Glory,'" 21, *Going to Glory, Come to Jesus* file, Motion Picture Case Files, NYSA.

2. Ibid., 25.

3. *Within Our Gates*, dir. Oscar Micheaux (Micheaux Film Co., 1919); *Body and Soul*, dir. Oscar Micheaux (Micheaux Film Corp., 1925).

4. The viewers never learn the end of Rev. Jenkins's story, however, as the film shifts back to Martha Jane and positions the events as having taken place in a dream. Charlene Regester has argued that this move on Micheaux's part was a result of the constraints of state-based censorship mechanisms. In response to the objections of censors in a number of states to the representation of a minister engaging in a variety of criminal activities, she argues, Micheaux re-edited the film according to each state's particular objections. The New York State Motion Picture Commission sent an initial review to Micheaux in which it argued, "*Body and Soul* is the story of a man, minister of the gospel, whose habits and manner of life are anything but the life of a good man. . . . The film is of such a character that in the opinion of the Commission it is sacrilegious, immoral, and would tend to incite crime." In Regester's view, Micheaux included the character of Sylvester, an inventor and Isabelle's beau, who is also played by Paul Robeson, and added a closing frame that makes the preceding narrative merely a dream in an attempt to deal with the censors' criticism of the character of Rev. Jenkins. New York State Motion Picture Commission to Micheaux Film Corporation, November 9, 1925, NYSA, quoted in Charlene Regester, "Black Films, White Censors: Oscar Micheaux Confronts Censorship in New York, Virginia, and Chicago," in *Movie Censorship and American Culture*, ed. Francis G. Couvares (Washington, DC: Smithsonian Institution Press, 1996). In contrast, Charles Musser, refusing to see *Body and Soul*'s unusual narrative structure as the result of external interference, instead emphasizes the importance of dreams and flashbacks to Micheaux's narrative style. In addition, he argues for understanding the film as being in conversation with Eugene O'Neill's *The Emperor Jones* and *All God's Chillun' Got Wings* and Nan Bagby Stephens's *Roseanne*. Charles Musser, "To Redream the Dreams of White Playwrights: Reappropriation and Resistance in Oscar Micheaux's *Body and Soul*," in *Oscar Micheaux and His Circle: African-American Filmmaking and Race Cinema of the Silent Era*, ed. Pearl Bowser, Jane Gaines, and Charles Musser (Bloomington: University of Indiana Press, 2001), 97–131.

5. All quotations from *Within Our Gates* are taken from the titles, reconstructed by

Scott Simmon, for the Library of Congress Video Collection edition of the film. The film had been lost until the late 1970s, when Thomas Cripps identified a print of it in Spain under the title *La Negra*. Scott Simmon and the Library of Congress restored the film and reconstructed the titles by translating the Spanish-language titles in the Spanish print, using four surviving English-language titles from the film, using the model of another of Micheaux's extant silent films, and referring to Micheaux's novels. See Scott Simmon's information booklet for the Library of Congress Video Collection, vol. 1: "The African American Cinema I: Oscar Micheaux's *Within Our Gates* (1919)."

6. Clarence Taylor, *The Black Churches of Brooklyn* (New York: Columbia University Press, 1994), 69, 70.

7. On black churches as part of the public sphere, see Evelyn Brooks Higginbotham, *Righteous Discontent: The Women's Movement in the Black Baptist Church, 1880–1920* (Cambridge, MA: Harvard University Press, 1993), 1–18.

8. *New York Times*, August 28, 1930, October 14, 1930, and October 24, 1930. Program for *Sweet Chariot*, Ambassador Theatre, October 23, 1930, Alexander Gumby Collection of Negroiana, Butler Library, Columbia University. *Wall Street Journal*, October 27, 1930. My description of the play's plot is drawn from reviews. I have not been able to locate a published copy of the play. Wilder had one other play produced on Broadway before becoming a journalist, novelist, and screenwriter. His novels *Flamingo Road* (1942) and *Written on the Wind* (1946) were made into successful Hollywood films.

9. *Wall Street Journal*, October 27, 1930; *New York Times*, October 24, 1930.

10. *The Black King*, dir. Bud Pollard (Southland Pictures Corp., 1932). The film was also released under the title *Harlem Big Shot*. *New York Times*, June 4, 1930, August 1, 1930, and March 21, 1931. Heywood's other film credits include an appearance in Oscar Micheaux's *The Exile* (Micheaux Film Corporation, 1931) and a position as music arranger for Micheaux's *Ten Minutes to Live* (Micheaux Film Corporation, 1932). He composed the music for *Moon over Harlem*, dir. Edgar G. Ulmer (1939), *Sunday Sinners*, dir. Arthur Dreifuss (1941), and *Murder on Lenox Avenue*, dir. Arthur Dreifuss (1941). He was the composer and lyricist for a number of Broadway shows, including *Veils* (1928), *Hot Rhythm* (1930), and *Blackberries of 1932* (1932). Of *Blackberries of 1932*, Maud Cuney-Hare wrote, "A number of recent concoctions in the form of Negro revues have been short-lived owing to the fact that they are unfinished, trivial even for that particular medium, and lacking in distinction. Among the plays that received mention we find *Blackberries of 1932*, a revue in two acts and twenty-six scenes by Donald Heywood and Tom Pelusco." Maud Cuney-Hare, *Negro Musicians and Their Music* (Washington, DC: Associated Publishers, 1936), 173. He also wrote the plays *Ol' Man Satan* (1932), *Black Rhythm* (1936), and *How Come, Lawd?* (1937) and was well known as the author, with Will Marion Cook, of the song "I'm Comin' Virginia."

11. There was considerable overlap in the casts of *Ol' Man Satan* and the film *The Black King*, including A. B. Comathiere, Ismay Andrews, Lorenzo Tucker, Knolly Mitchell, and Mary Jane Watkins. *New York Times*, October 4, 1932; *California Eagle*, October 14, 1932. According to an Associated Negro Press item, the production "was almost famous before the public had a chance to look it over. . . . It was perhaps the most postponed play in recent Broadway history. Mr. Heywood's devil threatened to make his appearance half a dozen times only to disappoint at the last moment." *California Eagle*, October 14, 1932.

12. *New York Times*, October 4, 1932. The review, signed "J.B.," was probably by J. Brooks Atkinson.

13. *New York Times*, June 4, 1930, August 1, 1930, and March 21, 1931.

14. Pollard, the first president of the Screen Directors' Guild, was an independent producer whose company was based in New York and who filmed in studios in New Jersey. Michael Pitts characterized his work as having "catered primarily to the exploitation market, occasionally surfacing with minor releases for the general film trade." Michael R. Pitts, *Poverty Row Studios, 1929–1940: An Illustrated History of 53 Independent Film Companies with a Filmography for Each* (Jefferson, NC: McFarland, 1997), 273.

15. See Randall K. Burkett, *Garveyism as a Religious Movement: The Institutionalization of a Black Civil Religion* (Metuchen, NJ: Scarecrow Press, 1978). Burkett demonstrates the importance of religious ritual to Garvey's movement and traces the contours of a theological sensibility within which that ritual was practiced. Burkett writes, "One finds Garvey, for instance, struggling with the problem of theodicy, and endeavoring to define God so as not to make Him responsible for a suffering world (and especially a suffering Black people), yet insisting that God's purposes were being achieved in the world and that His chosen Black people were marked for a special destiny in Africa" (5).

16. Comathiere was an active actor at this point (with additional credits under the name A. B. DeComathiere) in the Lafayette Players in the 1910s and 1920s, on the Broadway stage, and on film in such productions as Oscar Micheaux's *Deceit* (1923), *Thirty Years Later* (1928), and *The Exile* (1931). He became the subject of gossip some years later in an item in Allan McMillan's "Hi Hattin' in Harlem" column in the *Chicago Defender*. McMillan wrote in 1936 that "[I]n 1925 A. B. Comathiere was one of the leading actors in the original cast of the Lafayette Players, an inspiration to the young student of dramatic art. I saw him last Saturday, tottering along Seventh Avenue in a daze. They say that he has lost his nut and out of pity he is awarded a tiny part in the Federal Theatre project's problem play, 'Turpentine,' now current at the Lafayette theatre here." *Chicago Defender*, July 11, 1936.

17. Unless otherwise indicated, the transcriptions of dialogue are my own.

18. The story of *The Black King* bears some similarity to Eugene O'Neill's *The*

Emperor Jones, which opened on Broadway in 1920 with Charles Gilpin as Brutus Jones. The film, with Paul Robeson as Jones, was produced in 1933 and directed by Dudley Murphy (United Artists), with the screenplay by O'Neill and DuBose Heyward. Robeson had played the part in the 1925 Broadway revival of the play.

19. In a piece printed in the *Negro World* in 1922, Garvey wrote, "I have a vision of the future, and I see before me a picture of a redeemed Africa, with her dotted cities, with her beautiful civilization, with her millions of happy children, going to and fro. Why should I lose hope, why should I give up and take a back place in this age of progress? Remember that you are men, that God created you Lords of this creation. Lift up yourselves, men, take yourselves out of the mire and hitch your hopes to the stars; yes, rise as high as the very stars themselves." *Negro World* 12 (March 4, 1922): 1, quoted in Burkett, *Garveyism*, 65.

20. John Louis Clarke, the reviewer for the *Norfolk Journal and Guide*, attributed Charcoal's linguistic style to the white producers' requirements for representing black culture, writing that "[t]he cast is not allowed to use even passable English, although the plantation lingo employed is not agreeable to the ears of the average Negro audience." John Louis Clarke, "'Black King' Not So Hot, Critic Says of Movie," *Norfolk Journal and Guide*, January 23, 1932.

21. W. E. B. Du Bois, "A Lunatic or a Traitor," *The Crisis*, May 1924, 8–9. Garvey met with representatives of the Ku Klux Klan to discuss their mutual interest in racial separatism.

22. *Chicago Defender*, July 16, 1932.

23. Clarke, "'Black King.'" The title sequence features silhouettes of people with their arms raised and bowing while singing the spiritual "Wade in the Water."

24. Salem Tutt Whitney, "Timely Topics," *Chicago Defender*, February 7, 1931. Such discussions were not always confined to black communities. This same period saw a heated exchange in the media over spoken and then written comments by the white magazine editor H. L. Mencken that characterized African Americans as subscribing to "dunghill varieties of Christianity." "Within a half a mile of my home in [Baltimore]," Mencken wrote in the National Urban League's *Opportunity*, "there are dozens of grotesque chapels, each radiating anthropoid superstitions, each supporting an oily go-getter, and each pumping dollars out of poor people." H. L. Mencken, "The Burden of Credulity," *Opportunity*, February 1931, 41. Adam Clayton Powell responded in the following issue of the magazine, lauding the achievements of African Americans in many fields of work and defending the reasonable, intellectual, and progressive stance of many black Baptist and Methodist clergy. A. Clayton Powell, "H. L. Mencken Finds Flowers in a 'Dunghill,'" *Opportunity*, March 1931. Writing for the Associated Negro Press, William Pickens presented an even more vigorous defense of black churches, writing, "The Negro church, under Negro preachers, furnished this race with its first centers of culture and education in Music, Drama, Politics, and Eco-

nomic Organization." Pickens also indirectly accused Mencken of racial prejudice, observing, "Of course, Mencken is a southerner, which is not a crime; but the 'old south' is still deep in his marrow, which is a misfortune. Some Negro preachers, like some white preachers, and like quite a few white editors, have great human faults. But there is also more honest to goodness religion and worth in the average Negro religious leader in America than in the religious leaders of any other race in America." William Pickens, "'Negro Preachers Are Racketeers,'" *California Eagle*, December 26, 1930.

25. *Dirty Gertie from Harlem U.S.A.*, dir. Spencer Williams (Sack Amusement Enterprises, 1946). The credits indicate that Thompson provided both the original story and the screenplay, but it seems likely that *Dirty Gertie*'s story was influenced by Somerset Maugham's 1921 short story "Rain," from *The Trembling of a Leaf: Little Stories of the South Sea Islands* (New York: George H. Doran Company, 1921). The story had already been adapted for the stage as *Rain* and for the screen as *Sadie Thompson* in 1928, with Gloria Swanson and Lionel Barrymore; in 1932 it was adapted for the screen as *Rain*, starring Walter Huston and Joan Crawford. *Sadie Thompson*, dir. Raoul Walsh (Gloria Swanson Pictures Corp., 1928); *Rain*, dir. Lewis Milestone (United Artists, 1932).

Maugham's *Rain* had gained currency in black popular culture through stage productions by black theater companies. The New York–based Lafayette Players included *Rain* in its repertoire in 1928 and had a tremendously successful run in Los Angeles, playing to sold-out audiences at the Lincoln Theatre (which had a capacity of nearly three thousand, according to the *Eagle*). The production starred Evelyn Preer, Lawrence Criner, and Laura Bowman (who appeared in *Son of Ingagi*, for which Spencer Williams wrote the screenplay), among others. The *Eagle* piece read, in part, "Friday, August 24 will be a day that should be indelibly engraved on every man, woman, and child in Los Angeles who has at heart the welfare of the Colored race. On that day or rather that evening at 8:30 sharp the curtain will arise and for the first time in the theatrical history of the colored theatre of the Pacific Coast, there will be presented a truly sensational drama enacted entirely by the world-famous colored artists, i.e. The Famous Lafayette Players." *California Eagle*, August 17, 1928, and August 31, 1928. The company returned to Los Angeles with the production the following year. *California Eagle*, February 1, 1929.

26. According to Robert Orr, who appeared in the film as a dancer under the name July Jones, Williams could not find an actress who could play the part to his satisfaction and so decided to play it himself. Francine Everett recalled that Williams performed the part so well that she saw him only as the Voodoo woman when she filmed the scene with him. G. William Jones, *Black Cinema Treasures Lost and Found* (Denton: University of North Texas Press, 1991), 178; *Spencer Williams: Remembrances of an Early Black Film Pioneer*, dir. Walid Khaldi (Golden Moon Productions, 1995).

27. There are few examples of race films in this period engaging religious traditions other than Christianity. The 1939 film *Midnight Shadow*, produced and directed for Sack Amusement Enterprises by George Randol, features the turbaned Prince Alihabad, who travels across the South and performs as a mind reader. Alihabad courts the daughter in an Oklahoma family that holds the deed to an oil field in East Texas, and although the parents are uncomfortable with his belief in Allah they insist that they want their daughter to be happy. At the film's end, Alihabad is revealed to be a charlatan. *Midnight Shadow*'s story is reminiscent of the opening sequence of William Wellman's *Nothing Sacred* (Selznick International, 1937), in which the sultan of Marzipan, on a visit to New York to raise funds for the Morning Star Temple, turns out to be Ernest Walker, a Harlem bootblack. Randol also seems to have been interested in engaging the film version of *The Green Pastures*, in which he appeared as the High Priest. Using scrolling titles to introduce the story, *Midnight Shadow* begins: "In the southern part of the country lies that great land of romance and sunshine, known as the Old South. Here amid fertile lands, vast areas of timber, oil lands, and rippling rivers live millions of black men and women in the most highly concentrated area of Negro population in America." Unlike *The Green Pastures*, which romanticizes the timelessness of southern black folk life, Randol's film goes on to locate the story in a black middle-class context. The titles continue: "Here in certain communities, the like of which is found nowhere else in the world, these people of darker hue have demonstrated their abilities in self-government by the orderly process of law of which they are capable when unhampered by outside influences. It is in a community such as one of these that the scene of our story is laid, and the events which follow are depicted." In the short musical film *Midnight Menace* (All-American News, 1946), directed by Josh Binney, a "voodoo man" hypnotizes his wife, who is then used in her hypnotized state in a stage show.

28. William Greaves has had a long and distinguished career on stage, film, and television as an actor, producer, and director. His directorial work includes a number of documentaries on aspects of African American history, such as *Ida B. Wells: A Passion for Justice* (1998) and *Ralph Bunche: An American Odyssey* (2001), as well as feature films.

29. *Miracle in Harlem*, dir. Jack Kemp (Herald Pictures, 1948). The film was produced by the white producer Jack Goldberg, a major figure in the production of black-audience movies in the period, who had begun as a vaudeville promoter. Goldberg was married in 1929 to the black blues singer Mamie Smith. William Greaves remembered Jack and his brother Bert as important financial supporters of race films in their heyday. Greaves noted that such partnerships came about because many American Jews in the 1940s, suffering from anti-Semitism and "the exclusion of Jewish businessmen and Jewish political figures throughout the whole length and breadth of this country," identified with African Americans and, in turn, felt accepted as business partners in

film. Jones, *Black Cinema Treasures*, 163. A 1941 *New York Times* profile of Goldberg noted that, with his acquisition of a studio in Florida, he planned to create "a creative center for the development of Negro films and screen talent through a scholarship fund to be raised by local Negro organizations. Working hand in hand with professionals should not only develop native professional technical talents, of which there are practically none, but the studio also would serve as a direct outlet for those talents when they are matured." It is unclear what became of these plans. A. H. Weiler, "Ticket for the Chariot," *New York Times*, August 3, 1941. Jack Goldberg founded Herald Pictures in 1946, and the company specialized in the production of black-audience films. *New York Times*, August 19, 1946.

30. The film's religious music was performed by the Juanita Hall Choir, a well-known choir in the period, particularly famous for interpreting spirituals and other black religious music.

31. Dialogue from *Miracle in Harlem* file, Motion Picture Case Files, NYSA.

32. In a bit of dialogue that was cut from the film, Hattie insists, "I'll never change . . . my prayer meetings . . . good old-fashioned sermons. . . . They're a wonderful consolation to me. . . . [A]fter our services—I am a new person." *Miracle in Harlem* file, Motion Picture Case Files, NYSA.

33. The film also positions Bert as modern by noting his science training in the army as a chemical warfare expert. On the training of African American college students for specialized war work, see, for example, the Office of War Information film *Negro Colleges in Wartime* (ca. 1944), which highlights the work of chemistry students at Hampton Institute. The representation of African American religion in the context of World War II will be taken up in the next chapter.

34. *Paradise in Harlem*, dir. Joseph Seiden (Jubilee Pictures Corp., 1940). Seiden's other directorial efforts included *The Yiddish King Lear* (Lear Pictures, Inc., 1936) as well as other Yiddish-language films. Seiden sometimes filmed in studios in New Jersey and may have encountered *Paradise in Harlem*'s Jack Goldberg, who produced this film, in this context. *Paradise in Harlem* was filmed in Fort Lee, New Jersey. See Weiler, "Ticket for the Chariot." The film's working title was *Othello in Harlem*, perhaps referring to Orson Welles's 1936 Federal Theatre Project production at Harlem's Lafayette Theater of *Macbeth*, which came to be known as "Voodoo Macbeth."

35. Mamie Smith was one of the best-known blues artists of the day, having pioneered in the "race record" industry with her 1920 recording on Okeh Records of "Crazy Blues" and "It's Right Here for You." On Smith and the beginnings of blues recording, see Samuel Charters and Leonard Kunstadt, *Jazz: A History of the New York Scene* (New York: Doubleday, 1961); Daphne Duval Harrison, *Black Pearls: Blues Queens of the 1920s* (New Brunswick: Rutgers University Press, 1988); and Adam Gussow, "'Shoot Myself a Cop': Mamie Smith's 'Crazy Blues' as Social Text," *Callaloo* 25, no. 1 (2002): 8–44. Jack and Bert Goldberg had been vaudeville produc-

ers before getting involved in motion pictures, and Mamie Smith had participated in some of their shows in the 1920s.

36. On the chanted sermon in African American contexts, see Albert J. Raboteau, "The Chanted Sermon," in *A Fire in the Bones: Reflections on African American Religious History* (Boston: Beacon, 1996). The Juanita Hall Singers play the part of the singing audience members and provide the accompanying vocal music.

37. There is a strange juxtaposition in the scene between the audience's mounting excitement and enjoyment of the performance and Othello's murder of Desdemona on stage.

38. *Sunday Sinners*, dir. Arthur Dreifuss (Colonnade Pictures Corp., 1941). Arthur Dreifuss was born in Frankfurt, Germany, in 1905. He directed a number of race movies at the beginning of his career, including *Mystery in Swing* (Aetna, 1940) and *Murder on Lenox Avenue* (Colonnade Pictures Corp., 1941).

39. Susan Hayward, *Key Concepts in Cinema Studies* (London: Routledge, 1996), 241.

40. Rick Altman argues that "cause and effect are fairly tenuous in the musical" and that "it is less a case of chronology or psychological motivation than one of paralleling stories in a comparative mode" (quoted in Hayward, 242). Susan Hayward notes, "The musical therefore functions ideologically to resolve the fear of difference. In this way, it functions as a text which disguises one of society's paradoxes. By extension, of course, this means that it makes invisible the other sets of paradoxes that are inherent in society, thereby ensuring society's stability" (244).

41. *Of One Blood*, dir. Spencer Williams (Sack Amusement Enterprises, 1944).

42. The film's credits list the actors' names but do not associate them with particular characters. Williams appears in the film as the adult Wesley Hill.

43. Paula J. Massood, *Black City Cinema: African American Urban Experiences in Film* (Philadelphia: Temple University Press, 2003).

44. Acts 17:24–26.

45. Acts 20:26.

46. Acts 20:29–30.

5. "A LONG, LONG WAY"

1. Gibson served under William H. Hastie, the civilian aide to Secretary of War Stimson, from 1941 until 1943. Hastie resigned in protest of "reactionary policies and discriminatory practices of the Army Air Forces in matters affecting Negroes." See "Statement of William H. Hastie, Recently Civilian Aide to the Secretary of War," n.d., Records of the Office of the Secretary of War, Records of the Civilian Aide to the Secretary of War, General Subject Files, 1940–1947, box 243, record group 107, NACP. The major newsreels of interest to Gibson and Davis were Fox Movietone News, RKO-Pathé's This Is America, MGM News of the Day, Universal News, and the March of Time.

2. By 1946, when he sold the chain, Lichtman had acquired twenty-nine theaters in Washington, D.C., Virginia, Maryland, and North Carolina. Of Lichtman's 460 employees, more than four hundred were black, including theater managers, projectionists, and stagehands. Robert K. Headley, *Motion Picture Exhibitions in Washington, DC: An Illustrated History of Parlors, Palaces and Multiplexes in the Metropolitan Area, 1894–1997* (Jefferson, NC: McFarland, 1999), 170, 375.

3. Clark M. Davis to Truman K. Gibson, March 24, 1942, Records of the Office of the Secretary of War, Records of the Civilian Aide to the Secretary of War, General Subject Files, 1940–1947, box 225, record group 107, NACP.

4. This particular unit had been profiled in *Time* in July of 1941 as "the first regiment of Negro engineers in the new Army." Although the short piece referred to members of the battalion as "black, grinning engineers" and characterized their trucks as "darky-driven," it also emphasized their ingenuity and efficiency in a mock battle during maneuvers. *Time*, July 21, 1941, 33–34. Gibson had been in contact with Metro-Goldwyn-Mayer about a short subject film about black soldiers and had mentioned both the 41st Engineers and the profile in *Time*. See Truman K. Gibson Jr. to Herbert Morgan, February 13, 1942, Records of the Office of the Secretary of War, Records of the Civilian Aide to the Secretary of War, General Subject Files, 1940–1947, box 225, record group 107, NACP.

5. Thomas W. Young to Clark M. Davis, April 10, 1942, Records of the Office of the Secretary of War, Records of the Civilian Aide to the Secretary of War, General Subject Files, 1940–1947, box 225, record group 107, NACP.

6. Letters from African American soldiers complaining about newsreel coverage often found their way to Gibson's office, as in the case of correspondence from Corporal. J. H. Becton at Fort Huachuca, Arizona, who addressed his letter to the producers of the Army Signal Corps' *Army Navy Magazine* newsreel. Becton wrote, "I am a 'negro soldier' in a combat division and there are more than fifteen thousand 'negro soldiers' in the Division, and we've been preparing for combat for more than twenty months, now the final test is on. We have an 'all negro' Division in action, and we have 'negro soldiers' on every front wearing 'Uncle Sam's Uniform' and fighting for the safety of the country the same as all other 'Soldiers' of 'America.'

"Last night, I saw the film 'This is America' and there was not a single one of 'my people' in the screen, it was a film of 'Whites only,' why don't the armed forces release the 'negroes' and fight their own war, for if this is 'America,' for 'whites' only, we, the 'negroes' have nothing to fight for. Will you please give me an explanation on [*sic*] "This Is America.'" Cpl. J. H. Becton, Fort Huachuca, Arizona, to Army Navy Screen Magazine, August 26, 1944, Records of the Office of the Secretary of War, Records of the Civilian Aide to the Secretary of War, General Subject Files, 1940–1947, box 225, NACP.

7. On the history of the OWI and its production of propaganda about African

Americans and other war-related issues, see Allan M. Winkler, *The Politics of Propaganda: The Office of War Information, 1942–1945* (New Haven: Yale University Press, 1978).

8. T. M. Berry, "Blue Print of Program for Strengthening Negro Morale in War Effort," March 4, 1942, 1, Records of the Office of War Information, Records of the Director, 1942–1945, box 8, record group 208, NACP. Berry was a Cincinnati-based lawyer who had been president of the Cincinnati Branch of the NAACP from 1932 to 1938 and would serve again in this capacity from 1943 to 1946. He would become the first black mayor of Cincinnati in 1972. G. James Fleming and Christian E. Burkel, eds., *Who's Who in Colored America* (Supplement) (Yonkers-on-Hudson, NY: Christian E. Burkel, 1950), 588.

9. Berry, "Blue Print," 1.

10. Ibid., 2. Horace R. Cayton outlined a similar set of concerns in his December 1941 article "Negro Morale" for the National Urban League's *Opportunity*. Cayton placed the complicated issue of African American wartime morale in a longer historical context than did Berry, noting the disappointments of black veterans concerning the failure of their participation in World War I to result in any changes in their social and political status.

11. *Pittsburgh Courier,* February 14, 1942.

12. Charlotta A. Bass, "ONE VICTORY! ONE FIGHT! An Open Letter to the 33rd Annual Conference of the NAACP," *California Eagle,* July 16, 1942.

13. On the complicated uses of radio by African American activists, intellectuals, and artists in this period, see Barbara Dianne Savage, *Broadcasting Freedom: Radio, War, and the Politics of Race, 1938–1948* (Chapel Hill: University of North Carolina Press, 1999).

14. *The Negro Soldier,* dir. Stuart Heisler (U.S. War Department, 1944); *Marching On,* dir. Spencer Williams (Sack Amusement Enterprises, 1943), also released under the title *Where's My Man To-Nite?; Fighting Americans,* dir. Max Dresner (Toddy Pictures, 1943); *We've Come a Long, Long Way,* dir. Jack Goldberg (Negro Marches On, Inc., 1944).

15. Quoted in Kenneth Robert Janken, *White: The Biography of Walter White, Mr. NAACP* (New York: Free Press, 2003), 266.

16. Ibid., 266–68; Thomas Cripps, *Slow Fade to Black: The Negro in American Film, 1900–1942* (1977; reprint, New York: Oxford University Press, 1993), 35–63, 375–76, and *Making Movies Black: The Hollywood Message Movie from World War II to the Civil Rights Era* (New York: Oxford University Press, 1993), 35–63.

17. Clarence Muse, "The Trial of 'Uncle Tom': NAACP and William Pickens Purge As Hollywood Views It," n.d., Afro-American Actors 2 [Motion Pictures], James Weldon Johnson Collection, Yale Collection of American Literature, Bienecke Rare Book and Manuscript Library, Yale University. The piece was published in the

Pittsburgh Courier on September 12, 1942, under the headline "Muse Presents Other Side of Film Picture: Noted Screen Actor Thinks Performers Have Been Ignored." The paper's editorial staff included a disclaimer noting that the paper did not share Muse's opinion, and they did not publish it under the original title. Muse had worked in the race film industry, starring in such films as *Broken Strings*, dir. Bernard B. Ray (Goldport Productions, 1940), and worked regularly playing small parts in Hollywood films.

18. Ibid.

19. Ibid. White never met with Muse or with the other black Hollywood veterans who had criticized his approach, and much of the black press took White's side in what became a heated conflict, characterizing Muse, Hattie McDaniel, Louise Beavers, and other veterans as unable to see beyond the traditional Hollywood stereotypes. See Janken, *White*, 271–72. Lena Horne, who was friends with White, signed a contract with Metro-Goldwyn-Mayer in anticipation of being cast in *Cabin in the Sky* and became a target of many of the veteran black actors. She wrote later that "[o]nly one person among the Negro actors went out of her way to be understanding about the whole situation. That was Hattie McDaniel, who was, I suppose, the original stereotype of the Negro maid in the white public mind. Actually, she was an extremely gracious, intelligent, and gentle lady. . . . She was extremely realistic and had no misconception of the role she was allowed to play in the white movie world. She also told me that she sympathized with my position and that she thought it was the right one if I chose it. I was very confused at the time; the one thing I had not expected was to get into trouble with my own race. Miss McDaniel's act of grace helped tide me over a very awkward and difficult moment, and after that the public tension eased somewhat." Lena Horne and Richard Schickel, "Lena," in *Black Films and Film-Makers: A Comprehensive Anthology from Stereotype to Superhero*, ed. Lindsay Patterson (New York: Dodd, Mead, 1975), 145–46.

20. *Tales of Manhattan*, dir. Julien Duvivier (Twentieth Century-Fox, 1942).

21. *New York Times*, September 23, 1942. In responding to criticism for having taken the part, Robeson defended himself. The *Pittsburgh Courier* reported, "Robeson said that only after he had signed the contract and commenced shooting did he fully realize the import of the scene. It was then that he approached producer Boris Morros and suggested that the script be changed. This was not done and the singer was forced to go through with his deal, since he was not able to buy himself out of the contract. 'If they picket the picture when it opens in New York,' Robeson added, 'I'll join the picket line myself.'" *Pittsburgh Courier*, September 5, 1942. Robeson had also protested the outcome of his involvement with other films, most notably the British-made film *Sanders of the River*, directed by Zoltan Korda (London Film Productions, 1935). Martin Duberman notes that after withdrawing from Hollywood Robeson sought to participate in low-budget independent cinema but ultimately found the theater much more

amenable to his artistic and political goals. See Martin Bauml Duberman, *Paul Robeson* (New York: Knopf, 1988), 178–83, 261–62. See also *Chicago Bee*, March 12, 1939.

22. In a 1945 report on Hollywood in the black journal *Phylon*, William Thomas Smith also emphasized the impact of the concerns of white southerners on Hollywood's representations of African Americans. He wrote, "The censors and the exhibitors of the South do not hesitate to use their shears on any scene in any picture which they consider objectionable. A recent survey showed that those things 'most objectionable' were those in which Negroes were shown 'acting, or talking, or dressing like white folks . . . acting smart alecky and talking back to white folks . . . shooting or striking white folks . . . or in any manner committing any breach of the code which would by implication or otherwise, create an equality between the two races.'" William Thomas Smith, "Hollywood Report," *Phylon* 6, no, 1 (1945): 15–16.

23. *New York Times*, November 2, 1941, and September 6, 1942. Ten writers received credit in the final production, in the following order: Ben Hecht, Ferenc Molnar, Donald Ogden Stewart, Samuel Hoffenstein, Alan Campbell, Ladislas Fodor, L. Vadnai, L. Gorog, Lamar Trotti, and Henry Blankenfort.

24. Bosley Crowther, review of *Tales of Manhattan*, *New York Times*, September 25, 1942. See also Bosley Crowther, "Little By Little: 'Tales of Manhattan' Boosts the Stock of the Short Story in Film," *New York Times*, October 4, 1942. On the influence of the style of *Tales of Manhattan*, see, for example, *New York Times*, February 7, 1943. This was certainly not the first time that a Hollywood film had used such a narrative form, but it was not a common approach and had not been done in a major film since *Grand Hotel*, dir. Edmund Goulding (Metro-Goldwyn-Mayer, 1932) and *If I Had a Million*, dir. Ernst Lubitsch (Paramount, 1932).

25. See, for example, *California Eagle*, November 13, 1941. Anderson, who had many film credits to his name, was listed in the opening titles simply as "Rochester," his character's name on the radio show *The Jack Benny Program*. Clarence Muse appeared in a small part in the film as well.

26. At least one report in the white press during the development stage assumed that Robeson would appear in "a Harlem sequence." See *New York Times*, August 29, 1941.

27. Unless otherwise indicated, transcriptions of dialogue are my own.

28. Ethel Waters with Charles Samuels, *His Eye Is on the Sparrow* (Garden City, NY: Doubleday, 1951), 257.

29. "Glory Day," music and lyrics by Leo Robin and Ralph Rainger.

30. Canada Lee found himself in a similar situation when he was cast in the part of Joe, a ship's steward, in Alfred Hitchcock's *Lifeboat* (Twentieth Century-Fox, 1944). One of Lee's most important scenes in the film required him to recite the Twenty-third Psalm while a group of white men bury a baby at sea. The script contained Joe's dialogue in dialect, and Lee, with the support of lead actress Tallulah Bankhead, refused

to deliver the lines as written. According to Mona Z. Smith, Lee's biographer, although Lee was instructed by the producers and director to speak in dialect, when Hitchcock filmed the scene, Lee performed his lines as he himself wanted. Though Hitchcock had warned him against changing the lines, the director printed the take and used it in the final version. Similarly, at another important moment in the film, when a man's leg is amputated, Lee found himself directed to perform in stereotyped ways. Smith writes, "'What was Joe the steward's contribution? I was supposed to cast my eyes to heaven and wordlessly pray,' Canada said. 'Nobody else prayed.' The actor was livid. Once again, his character—who everyone swore would be treated as an equal—was instead being treated to one of Hollywood's favorite stereotypes: the Negro in crisis, falling to his knees, palms pressed, teeth chattering, crying 'Lawd, save us!'" Lee's approach to the scene was for Joe to reflect quietly. Mona Z. Smith, *Becoming Something: The Story of Canada Lee* (New York: Faber and Faber, 2004), 155–56, 159–60.

31. *New York Times*, September 25, 1942.

32. *New York Times*, October 4, 1942.

33. Quoted in Duberman, *Paul Robeson*, 260. The reference to Benton's work is quite appropriate, as the similarity between the church building in *Tales of Manhattan* and that in Benton's lithograph *Sunday Morning* is striking. Thomas Craven included it in his 1939 collection *A Treasury of American Prints* and wrote of the print: "Benton has often been accused of lack of feeling. It is true that in his great murals sympathy is sometimes submerged by compositional brilliancy and a reporter's instinct, but his lithographs testify to his greatheartedness and his understanding of the underprivileged. 'Edge of Town' and 'Lonesome Road' reflect the hopelessness of barren lives: 'Sunday Morning' strikes a different note, for at least one day a week a thin wedge of hope enters into these lives. The Southern Negro, though naturally optimistic and gay, gets bogged down in the oppressive conditions of daily existence. The little rural church is the answer for the old folk and for some of the younger ones." Thomas Craven, ed., *A Treasury of American Prints: A Selection of One Hundred Etchings and Lithographs by the Foremost Living American Artists* (New York: Simon and Schuster, 1939), plate 10.

34. *New York Amsterdam News*, August 29, 1942.

35. Waters, *His Eye*, 257.

36. Ibid., 258.

37. Ibid.

38. *New York Times*, October 26, 1940.

39. Rex Ingram had become famous in the role of "De Lawd" in the film version of Marc Connelly's *The Green Pastures*. In an interview prior to the release of the film version of *Cabin in the Sky* and published in the *Pittsburgh Courier*, Ingram spoke about his transformation from God into the devil. The actor emphasized the pleasure he took in moving from the older part to this new opportunity because of the particular difficulties associated with assuming the role of the Deity. Making no reference to the great

delight the black press took in his personal difficulties during the filming of *The Green Pastures*, Ingram said, "I was offered the unique opportunity to get away from playing the Lawd when 'Cabin in the Sky' changed me into the devil. Although the earlier part filled me with a feeling of reverence, it brought responsibilities as well. For this reason I tried to keep constantly associated with the finer things. I did a great deal of reading of the Bible to inform myself on how God would act were he on this earth and I really punished myself by not going out and by giving up worldly activities." *Pittsburgh Courier*, May 29, 1943.

40. *California Eagle*, June 12, 1941.

41. Inge, "Report on the Stage Production Directed by George Balanchine," October 28, 1940, *Cabin in the Sky* file, MGMC.

42. Vincente Minnelli with Hector Arce, *I Remember It Well* (Hollywood, CA: Samuel French, 1990), 121. *Porgy and Bess* opened on Broadway in October of 1935 and featured Anne Wiggins Brown and Todd Duncan in the lead roles. Eva Jessye, who served as musical director for King Vidor's *Hallelujah*, was the choral director for the production, and her choir appeared as well. J. Rosamond Johnson, who was in the stage production of *Cabin in the Sky* and directed the choir, also had a role in *Porgy and Bess*. While the original production was not particularly successful, the 1942 Broadway revival, which featured many of the same cast members, did very well.

43. James Naremore, *The Films of Vincente Minnelli* (Cambridge: Cambridge University Press, 1993), 55. Eustace Cockrell was a short story writer who had published "Compliments of R. Smith" in *Collier's* in 1942 and, as a result, was recommended to Arthur Freed by another studio official because "[t]his boy knows how to write negroes better than anybody I've read in a long time and judging from these stories . . . he has a grand sense of humor. He would be worthwhile remembering when you get to CABIN IN THE SKY." Milton Beecher to Arthur Freed, interoffice correspondence, April 30, 1942. *Cabin in the Sky* file, AFC. On Cockrell's contributions to the script, see "Dialect and Line Changes," July 22, 1942, *Cabin in the Sky* file, Motion Picture Scripts Collection, AMPAS.

44. In his memoir, Minnelli wrote that he had wanted to keep Dooley Wilson in the role of Little Joe but was forced to defer to the producers. Minnelli, *I Remember It Well*, 121. Wilson would shortly become quite famous for playing the part of Sam in *Casablanca*, dir. Michael Curtiz (Warner Bros., 1942).

45. The production was clearly prestigious, and various agents lobbied the studio to consider their clients during the casting phase. Canada Lee, Cab Calloway, Oscar Polk, Fats Waller, and Stepin Fetchit all had requests made on their behalf for consideration. Polk was cast as the Deacon, and Albert Lewis, associate producer on the film and producer of the Broadway show of *Cabin*, contacted Cab Calloway and Paul Robeson to gauge their respective interest in the film. *Variety* reported incorrectly on June 3, 1942, that Calloway had been cast as the devil. On Robeson, Lewis reported to

Freed that "I find at this time a certain hesitancy on the part of Robson [*sic*] to make any commitment for this project, and I surmise that he does not relish the idea of doing anything again with Ethel Waters. I don't know what lies behind this, but I will endeavor to make further inquiry next week and keep you advised." Robeson's reasons would become clearer once his dissatisfaction with *Tales of Manhattan* became public. Albert Lewis to Arthur Freed, April 10, 1942. See also Bill Grady to Arthur Freed, interoffice communication, April 27, 1942; Ralph Wonders, General Amusement Corporation, to Arthur Freed, April 30, 1942; Lou Irwin, Lou Irwin Agency, Hollywood, to Lew Sidney, Metro-Goldwyn-Mayer, June 20, 1942; Stepin Fetchit to Lew Brown, Metro-Goldwyn-Mayer, July 16, 1942, all in *Cabin in the Sky* file, AFC.

46. Minnelli, *I Remember It Well*, 111–19.

47. Charlie Sands, Secretary, Motion Picture Study Club, to Arthur Freed, February 12, 1942, *Cabin in the Sky* file, AFC. Motion Picture Study Clubs and Better Motion Picture Committees began to be founded in the 1920s as part of the movement in the period to reform the content of movies. See, for example, *A Plan for Motion Picture Study Clubs* (New York: National Committee for Better Films, 1925); Better Films National Council, *Selected Book Films* (New York: National Board of Review, 1928); Fred Eastman and Edward Ouelette, *Better Motion Pictures: A Discussion Course* (Boston: Pilgrim Press, 1936). Anne Morey has addressed attempts to cultivate "enlightened viewing tastes" among the public in *Hollywood Outsiders: The Adaptation of the Film Industry, 1913–1934* (Minneapolis: University of Minnesota Press, 2003).

48. Carver would die soon after, on July 5, 1943. Metro-Goldwyn-Mayer had made a short film about the scientist, *The Story of Dr. Carver*, dir. Fred Zinneman (Metro-Goldwyn-Mayer, 1938), and Clarence Muse would star as Carver in *The Peanut Man*, dir. Tony Paton (Consolidated Pictures, 1947).

49. *California Eagle*, May 13, 1943.

50. Fred Stanley, "Hollywood Takes a Hint from Washington," *New York Times*, February 7, 1943. Twentieth Century-Fox had *Stormy Weather*, directed by Andrew L. Stone, in production at the time.

51. Hall Johnson to Al Lewis, July 24, 1942, *Cabin in the Sky* file, AFC.

52. Johnson to Lewis, July 24, 1942.

53. *Pittsburgh Courier*, May 29, 1943.

54. Johnson to Lewis, July 24, 1942.

55. Minnelli, *I Remember It Well*, 119.

56. Minnelli was the scenic designer for *At Home Abroad*, which opened on Broadway in 1935 and in which Waters had played a role. Horne and Minnelli had become acquainted in New York and continued their friendship in Hollywood. He wrote in his memoirs of taking Lena Horne to dinner in Hollywood and about telephoning restaurants in advance to make sure that she would not be turned away. Horne, however, recalled that she and Minnelli socialized as "displaced New Yorker(s)" but that they

"did not go out at all," preferring instead to visit each other's homes. Ibid., 115, 121; Horne and Schickel, "Lena," 146.

57. Minnelli, *I Remember It Well*, 121. He had attempted to mount an all-black-cast musical comedy of *Serena Blandish* in New York, with both Ethel Waters and Lena Horne, out of a desire to "do a sophisticated black show because [he] felt uneasy about the conventional stereotype of the Negro as simple, naïve, and childlike" (103).

58. Ibid., 121.

59. "Outline of Final Scenes from Marc Connelly," August 8, 1942, *Cabin in the Sky* file, Motion Picture Scripts Collection, AMPAS.

60. Joseph Schrank, *Cabin in the Sky* script, July 21, 1942. *Cabin in the Sky* file, Motion Picture Scripts Collection, AMPAS. Ethel Waters noted in her autobiography that she had "objected to the manner in which religion was being handled" in the stage production, as well as to the rendering of Petunia as "no more than a punching bag for Little Joe," and recalled that she had demanded a number of changes. She did not indicate what specific elements of the play's presentation of religion offended her, but she recalled that she "objected violently to the way religion was being treated in the screen play." Waters, *His Eye*, 255, 258.

61. Joseph Schrank, *Cabin in the Sky* script, July 21, 1942.

62. Ibid.

63. Joseph Schrank to Al Lewis, August 18, 1942, *Cabin in the Sky* file, Script Notes folder, Vincente Minnelli Collection, AMPAS.

64. Minnelli, *I Remember It Well*, 114.

65. H. Johnson to Vincente Minnelli, November 4, 1942, *Cabin in the Sky* file, Correspondence folder, Vincente Minnelli Collection, AMPAS.

66. Ibid.

67. Elmer Rice, November 4, 1942, *Cabin in the Sky* file, AFC. Rice was known for writing a number of plays that took on social issues, including *Street Scene* (1929), *We, the People* (1932), *Judgement Day* (1934), *Between Two Worlds* (1934), and *American Landscape* (1938).

68. Unattributed and undated drafts, *Cabin in the Sky* file, Foreword folder, Vincente Minnelli Collection, AMPAS.

69. One draft read, "When the world is too much with us, we clear away the underbrush of Actuality and build ourselves a cabin in the sky to house our dreams. But, to live in this cabin, we must approach it by a lane called Unselfish Love and open its door with a key called Tolerance. To all such builders everywhere this picture is dedicated." Another proposed that the foreword read, "The primitive instincts of man are universal. At times, the eternal struggle between good and evil leads us to dream of a haven of refuge, whether it be a castle in the air or a cabin in the sky. To those of us who dream, this picture is dedicated." Unattributed and undated drafts, *Cabin in the Sky* file, Foreword folder, Vincente Minnelli Collection, AMPAS.

70. See *Cabin in the Sky*, Dialogue Cutting Continuity, January 4, 1943, *Cabin in the Sky* file, MGMC.

71. Philip M. Carter had worked as an attorney and a social worker for the New York City Department of Public Welfare from 1933 to 1942. From 1942 to 1943 he served as the public relations representative for African American issues for Metro-Goldwyn-Mayer, and he moved to a similar position at Warner Bros. for the following year before becoming a columnist and editor for a number of newspapers in California. For a brief biography of Carter, see William C. Matney, ed., *Who's Who among Black Americans* (Northbrook, IL: Who's Who among Black Americans, Inc., 1975–76), 104. The Hollywood commentator Earl J. Morris wrote a scathing column on Carter's "jim crow" job at Metro-Goldwyn-Mayer shortly after Carter took the position. Morris wrote that he understood the difficult position in which Carter found himself at the studio, noting that "Carter lurched into his job with the gusto of a highly paid executive publicist and is bombarding the Negro press with blurbs, photos, feature stories and what have you. His job is not easy. Phillip [*sic*] Carter has the task of shoving down our throats during wartime, a picture which will not do much to create morale among his race. The picture was purchased and planned prior to Pearl Harbor, and so maybe [*sic*] regarded as the last of that cycle of films, among which was 'Tales of Manhattan.'" Morris continued to note that the studio had located Carter in a small dressing room half a mile from the publicity building, no doubt, in his opinion, setting him up to fail so that they would no longer need to bother hiring African American publicity staff. *California Eagle*, November 19, 1942.

72. The second line of Carter's draft, not used in the final version, was probably "America has such a story and is fortunate that its warmth and beauty are guarded by a people whose sense of true values is needed in a strife-torn world—the American Negro." Unattributed and undated drafts, *Cabin in the Sky* file, Foreword folder, Vincente Minnelli Collection, AMPAS.

73. Minnelli, *I Remember It Well*, 122.

74. "Li'l Black Sheep," by Harold Arlen and Yip Harburg.

75. Minnelli describes this scene as one of the ones of which he was particularly proud because of the camera work. Minnelli, *I Remember It Well*, 125.

76. The studio received a letter from the African American actress Olive Ball, a bit player in a number of films, including *Tales of Manhattan* and Orson Welles's *The Magnificent Ambersons* (RKO Radio Pictures, 1942), recounting the story of 109 ½-year-old Paralee Priscilla Gray's appearance as an extra in the church scene. Apparently, Hall Johnson and Ball knew Gray, and Johnson arranged for her to be an extra in the film because she was "in dire need of money," her daughter having absconded with all her possessions save her comb and toothbrush. Ball wrote that Gray hesitated before taking the job, telling them, "Well I don't mind workin' in the 'movies,' if they don't want to try and make a fool out of me. I'm not out for being a clown in a circus

or act like a monkey. And I don't believe in making light of the Church doin's." Ball reported that she "explained that there might be persons in the Church scene who would not be sincere; but that, even in real Church scenes, devils creep in and mar religious efforts. However, we assured Grandma Gray that the director and the majority concerned would sincerely desire that the 'Cabin in the Sky' Church scene should be as sacred as it could be humanly possible to make it so." In the end, Ball reported, Gray was moved by Kenneth Spencer's performance as the minister and concluded that "everything was fine, such nice folks, an' oh my what singin'—dey carried me way back yonder." Ball wrote that she imagined that the good deed that those involved had done in casting Grandma Gray in a role in the film would lead to box-office success. It appears that Freed sent along additional money to help Gray return to her native Nashville, Tennessee. Olive Ball, "Cabin in the Sky Should Be a Financial Success," n.d., Olive Ball to Arthur Freed, November 7, 1942, *Cabin in the Sky* file, AFC.

77. Paula J. Massood, *Black City Cinema: African American Urban Experiences in Film* (Philadelphia: Temple University Press, 2003), 33.

78. Naremore, *Films of Vincente Minnelli*, 63.

79. Massood, *Black City Cinema*, 36–37.

80. *New York Times*, May 28, 1943, and *Dallas Morning News*, March 11, 1943, clippings in *Cabin in the Sky* file, AFC.

81. *Cabin in the Sky* pressbook, *Cabin in the Sky* file, AFC.

82. *People's Voice*, December 5, 1934.

83. *Morning Telegram*, May 28, 1943, clipping in *Cabin in the Sky* file, AFC.

84. *Hollywood Citizen-News*, February 10, 1943, clipping in *Cabin in the Sky* file, AFC.

85. Ibid.

86. Leo Roa, "Success of 'Cabin in the Sky' Will Help Negroes in Films," *California Eagle*, February 17, 1943. Roa claimed that Metro-Goldwyn-Mayer had spent $1.5 million on the production, but in actuality the studio spent just over $650,000, making it Freed's lowest-budgeted and least expensive musical. Daily Progress Report, November 25, 1942, *Cabin in the Sky* file, AFC. See also Naremore, *Films of Vincente Minnelli*, 57.

87. *California Eagle*, July 10, 1943.

88. Dalton Trumbo, "Blackface, Hollywood Style," *The Crisis*, December 1943, 366.

89. Ibid., 367.

90. *Negro Digest* poll, reported in *Pittsburgh Courier*, March 7, 1943.

91. *Fighting Americans*, dir. Max Dresner (Toddy Pictures, 1943). See dialogue transcript from *Fighting Americans* file, NYSA. See also J. Richardson Jones to Lt. Fred. J. Driver Sr., February 19, 1943; J. Richardson Jones to Truman K. Gibson, March 18, 1943, and September 20, 1943; Truman K. Gibson to Charles D. Murray, Sr.,

March 29, 1943, all in Records of the Office of the Secretary of War, Records of the Civilian Aide to the Secretary of War, General Subject Files, 1940–1947, box 225, NACP. *Pittsburgh Courier*, April 24, 1943.

92. *Marching On*, dir. Spencer Williams (Sack Amusement Enterprises, 1943). At some point after the film's premiere, the Bourgeois-Jenkins company acquired distribution rights and exhibited the film under the title *Where's My Man To-Nite?* The surviving print contains elements that were inserted for this later release (title cards and, most likely, a musical number). According to the *American Film Institute Catalogue*, a voice-over account of the history of black soldiers was cut from the Bourgeois-Jenkins release. Alan Gevinson, ed., *Within Our Gates: Ethnicity in American Feature Films, 1911–1960* (Berkeley: University of California Press, 1997), 638–39.

93. At a critical juncture in the film, however, when Rodney realizes that he does want to be a good soldier but is uncertain about his prospects in the military, his grandfather (George T. Sutton) implores him to remain committed, "if only for God's sake." Grandpa Tucker continues, "Maybe if we pray to him, he will give you another chance. I'm afraid he's the only one who will give you that chance."

94. Goldberg had made at least one war documentary prior to this, *The Unknown Soldier Speaks*, dir. Jack Goldberg (Lincoln Pictures, 1934). *New York Times*, May 26, 1934.

95. See Cripps, *Making Movies Black*, 137, on Goldberg's negotiations with the Signal Corps and the OWI.

96. Some southern whites interpreted the government's issuing of the pamphlet to be part of a campaign, in the words of Senator John H. Overton of Louisiana, "toward the apotheosis of the negro which gives much concern to the white people of the South where the two races have been living side by side in perfect harmony and mutual workable understanding." Overton characterized the text as "written by some negro out of Chicago" and aimed at placing "the negro on a social equality basis with the Caucasian." With his letter to Elmer Davis, director of the OWI, Overton enclosed a resolution from the Shreveport Chamber of Commerce calling on members of Congress to "use its influence to dissuade the Office of War Information from using its delegated authority for the purpose of promoting so-called social reforms." John H. Overton to Elmer Davis, April 15, 1943, and Resolution, Shreveport Chamber of Commerce, April 8, 1943, both in Records of the Office of War Information, Records of the Director, 1942–1945, box 8, record group 208, NACP.

97. On the FSA images used in the pamphlet, see Colleen McDannell, *Picturing Faith: Photography and the Great Depression* (New Haven: Yale University Press, 2004), 223–29.

98. Mary A. Morton, "The Federal Government and Negro Morale," *Journal of Negro Education* 12 (Summer 1943): 453. See also Savage, *Broadcasting Freedom*, 124–35.

99. Jack Goldberg and Vincent Valentini are credited with adapting the story and

writing the musical score. Valentini had worked as a scenario and screenwriter for a number of black-audience films, including Joseph Seiden's *Paradise in Harlem* (1940), which Goldberg produced, and Arthur Dreifuss's *Murder on Lenox Avenue* (1941) and *Sunday Sinners* (1941). My thanks to J. Fred MacDonald of MacDonald and Associates for providing me with a research copy of the film.

100. Dialogue transcript, "Negro Marches On, Inc. presents We've Come a Long, Long Way," 23. NYSA. Bethune was very involved in recruiting African American women into the Women's Army Auxiliary Corps (WAAC), which later became the Women's Army Corps (WAC). She served as a "special consultant to the Secretary of War" during the selection of WAAC officers. Her status as "special consultant" was presumably established so that she would not be assigned to one of the regional selection boards on which white women sat. See *New York Times*, July 2, 1942.

101. Dialogue transcript, "We've Come a Long, Long Way," 24. The first two sentences of this section do not appear in the transcript, and Bethune may have intentionally changed the lines ("We intend to march ahead. . . . march ahead down through that trail where WE'VE COME A LONG LONG WAY. . . . These things, our women *intend* to do . . . and *WILL* do. . . . ") or simply forgotten them in their original form, as she appears to have recited them from memory.

102. Ibid., 30–31.

103. Ibid., 8. The comparable section in Owen's essay in *Negroes and the War* reads, in part, "Today Negroes own church property valued at nearly 200 million dollars. Baptist, Methodist, Episcopalian—all other denominations—enjoy complete religious freedom. It is easy to foresee what would happen to these churches under Hitler. He has persecuted the churches in his own Germany and in occupied countries. He has murdered or jailed clergymen brave enough to defy him. In the Nazi code there is not room for both Hitler and God. . . . A man who denies the Negro a soul will deny him a church. And in America Hitler would have reason. The Negro churches, before Emancipation, were hotbeds of revolt, meeting places of crusaders for abolition. Today the churches are the strongest organizations of Negroes in the world, and the churchmen are the leaders in the fight for equality. To Hitler, then, they would be dangerous—and, because dangerous, doomed." *Negroes and the War*, Official Publication of the OWI, n.p.

104. Dialogue transcript, *"We've Come a Long, Long Way,"* 9.

105. This segment is not represented in the dialogue transcript on file at the NYSA.

106. On the use of Joe Louis for propaganda purposes during the war, see Lauren Rebecca Sklaroff, "Constructing G. I. Joe Louis: Cultural Solutions to the 'Negro Problem' during World War II," *Journal of American History* 89 (December 2002).

107. Michaux, a native of Newport News, Virginia, became active in the Church of Christ (Holiness) in his adult years and eventually founded his own denomination, the Church of God. He became best known for holding interracial religious gatherings, in

violation of Virginia law, and for his radio broadcasts, beginning in 1929, in Washington, D.C, and on national radio networks as the "Happy Am I" preacher. Michaux was very well known in the 1930s and 1940s and was a supporter of Franklin Delano Roosevelt, whom he considered a political associate and friend. He also had working relationships with Harry Truman and Dwight D. Eisenhower. See Lillian Ashcraft Webb, *About My Father's Business: The Life of Elder Michaux* (Westport, CT: Greenwood Press, 1981); *New York Times*, October 21, 1968.

108. The group was also known as the Cross Choir and often arranged the members in the figure of a cross.

109. Ashcraft Webb, *About My Father's Business*, 37.

110. Advertising brochure, *We've Come a Long, Long Way*, n.d., Records of the Office of the Secretary of War, Records of the Civilian Aide to the Secretary of War, General Subject Files, 1940–1947, box 225, record group 107, NACP.

111. Ibid.

112. *New York Times*, June 26, 1944. *We've Come a Long, Long Way* was included on a preliminary short list of eight films being considered for nomination for an Academy Award in the category of Best Documentary Feature but did not make the final ballot of five films. "The Offical Academy Awards®; Database," retrieved July 5, 2006, from http://awardsdatabase.oscars.org/ampas_awards/DisplayMain.jsp?curTime= 1119100054306.

113. The committee was "a volunteer agency of professionals in the mass media that helped distribute army films to civilian theaters." Cripps, *Making Movies Black*, 113.

114. *New York Times*, April 22, 1944; Telegram, War Department Bureau of Public Relations, April 28, 1944, Records of the Office of the Secretary of War, Records of the Civilian Aide to the Secretary of War, General Subject Files, 1940–1947, box 225, record group 107, NACP. Goldberg also apparently complained that the army had used footage from his own film, but the military's response was that it had originally provided the material to Goldberg and reserved the right to use it as the army saw fit. Memorandum For: Chief, Army Pictorial Services, Office of the Chief Signal Officer, Pentagon, April 1, 1944, Records of the Office of the Chief Signal Office, "Orientation Film" Production Case Files, 1942–1945, box 14, record group 111, NACP.

115. *Pittsburgh Courier*, February 19, 1944.

116. Ibid.

117. Ibid. Perhaps the most striking moment of unexpected use of documentary footage in the film comes when Michaux discusses the execution of men in Velish, Russia, and Goldberg cuts to a British documentary, *The Five Men of Velish*. A different narrator speaks, text titles appear on the screen, and this section of the story is told through still photography rather than moving images. Just as abruptly, Goldberg cuts back to Michaux's funeral sermon.

118. *Norfolk Journal and Guide* to Elder Solomon L. Michaux and Jack Goldberg,

April 24, 1944, Records of the Office of the Secretary of War, Records of the Civilian Aide to the Secretary of War, General Subject Files, 1940–1947, box 225, record group 107, NACP. Truman Gibson made a similar argument in statements to the black press. See *Pittsburgh Courier*, April 29, 1944.

119. U.S. District Court of the Southern District of New York, Negro Marches On, Inc. against War Activities Committee of the Motion Picture Industry, amicus curiae brief, n.d., Records of the Office of the Secretary of War, Records of the Civilian Aide to the Secretary of War, General Subject Files, 1940–1947, box 225, record group 107, NACP.

120. Judge Alfred C. Coxe of the U.S. District Court, Southern District of New York, dismissed the case on May 10, 1944, noting that there were jurisdictional issues and that the complaint was defective in that it was lodged against the WAC, although the U.S. government appeared to be the main target. As such, Coxe noted, it "fails to state any claim against the present defendant. It is alleged in substance that the plaintiff will sustain damage as a result of competition by the government. The government, however, is not a party to the action, and even if it were the allegations would clearly be insufficient." Negro Marches on, Inc. v. War Activities Committee of the Motion Picture Industry, Defendant. Civ. 25–275, May 10, 1944, Copy in Records of the Office of the Secretary of War, Records of the Civilian Aide to the Secretary of War, General Subject Files, 1940–1947, box 225, record group 107, NACP. *Pittsburgh Courier*, May 13, 1944; *New York Times*, June 24, 1944.

121. Cripps, *Making Movies Black*, 135, 137.

122. In her work on the experiences of Jewish GIs in World War II, Deborah Dash Moore writes that many Jews found a way to reconcile their Jewish and American identities "in the Judeo-Christian tradition, especially as mediated through the experience of military service." She argues that "[a]lthough the term 'Judeo-Christian' itself remained largely within the province of intellectuals during the war years and was not standardized until the 1950s, the practice of the concept within the armed forces—its production and performance as standard operating procedure—reached large numbers of officers and enlisted men." Moore's work to historicize the concept of "Judeo-Christian" and understand its place in American experience is especially useful here. Although theirs was necessarily a different struggle over identity issues than that of Jewish GIs, African Americans have historically also contended with the problem of how to reconcile race and religion with Americanness. Deborah Dash Moore, "Jewish GIs and the Creation of the Judeo-Christian Tradition," *Religion and American Culture* 8 (Winter 1998): 34.

123. See Records of the Office of the Secretary of War, Records of the Civilian Aide to the Secretary of War, General Subject Files, 1940–1947, box 222, record group 107, NACP.

124. Capra was the head of the 834th Photo Signal Detachment and was instructed

to produce a set of documentaries to raise morale. The series included *Prelude to War* (1942), *The Nazi Strike* (1943), *Divide and Conquer* (1943), *Battle of Britain* (1943), *Battle of China* (1944), *Battle of Russia* (1944), and *War Comes to America* (1945). Thomas Cripps and David Culbert, "The Negro Soldier (1944): Film Propaganda in Black and White," *American Quarterly* 31, no. 5 (1979): 623; Savage, *Broadcasting Freedom*, 142–43.

125. Moss was a native of Newark and a graduate of Morgan State University who had done additional study at Columbia University. *Pittsburgh Courier*, August 29, 1936; Cripps and Culbert, "The Negro Soldier," 623; Savage, *Broadcasting Freedom*, 110, 143.

126. "An Oral History with Carlton Moss," typescript of interview by Douglas Bell, July 6, 1990–April 20, 1991 (Beverly Hills, CA: Academy of Motion Picture Arts and Sciences Oral History Program, 1995), 36.

127. Cripps, *Making Movies Black*, 108; "Oral History with Carlton Moss," 251. Hecht and Swerling were productive Hollywood writers. Ben Hecht's credits included co-screenwriter for *Gone with the Wind* (1939) and screenwriter for *Spellbound* (1945) and *Notorious* (1946); Jo Swerling's included co-screenwriter for *Gone with the Wind* (1939) and screenwriter for *The Miracle Woman* (1931), *The Pride of the Yankees* (1942), and *Lifeboat* (1944).

128. Another script draft was titled *Right to Fight* and also used the Douglass material. See "'Right to Fight' Comments," n.d., appendix to "An Oral History with Carlton Moss." In his autobiography, Capra characterized Moss as someone who "wore his blackness as conspicuously as a bandaged head" and noted that he had to do considerable work to tone down "the angry fervor" of Moss's early script drafts. In an interview years later, however, Moss insisted that Capra had had nothing to do with the process of producing the script. Frank Capra, *The Name above the Title: An Autobiography* (New York: Vintage, 1971), 358; "Oral History with Carlton Moss," 103.

129. "Oral History with Carlton Moss," 253, 308.

130. Tiomkin's scoring credits up to this point included *Mad Love* (1935), *You Can't Take It with You* (1938), *Mr. Smith Goes to Washington* (1939), and *Meet John Doe* (1941). The majority of musical selections in the film, although copyrighted by Tiomkin, were adaptations of existing songs, particularly spirituals and hymns. See Dimitri Tiomkin memo, January 25, 1944, Records of the Office of the Chief Signal Office, "Orientation Film" Production Case Files, 1942–1945, box 14, record group 111, NACP.

131. The shot list indicates that Moss and Heisler used footage of the exterior of St. James Presbyterian Church in Harlem, the Beverly Hills Catholic Church, and of a "southern Negro church." "*The Negro Soldier* Legend," December 31, 1943, Records of the Office of the Chief Signal Office, "Orientation Film" Production Case Files, 1942–1945, box 14, record group 111, NACP.

132. "I will cause your name to be celebrated in all generations; therefore the peoples will praise you forever and ever." Psalm 45:17.

133. The Louis-Schmelling bout took place at Yankee Stadium on June 22, 1936.

134. None of the figures shown in this section are identified, but they include Matthew Henson, W. C. Handy, Gertrude Elsie Johnson MacDougald, and Marian Anderson. Handy hesitated before signing the release to have his image included in the film, asking for a revised version of the document that would protect against unauthorized uses of the image. He wrote to the Signal Corps' representative, "I do not have to tell you that I am a Negro citizen of the United States whose right to vote even is questioned by other citizens, and in giving rights in this picture I have the same patriotic feelings and interests as any other citizen and I want these rights respected as if I were a member of any other racial group. There are those who would deny me." Despite his reservations, Handy was pleased with the final product, writing that his son saw the film and applauded it, prompting Handy to see it twice himself. W. C. Handy to Mr. Lehman Katz, April 20, 1944, and April 24, 1944, Records of the Office of the Chief Signal Office, "Orientation Film" Production Case Files, 1942–1945, box 14, record group 111, NACP.

135. The film's choir was directed by the African American choral conductor, composer, and arranger Jester Hairston. "'The Negro Soldier' Press Materials," Records of the Office of the Secretary of War, Records of the Civilian Aide to the Secretary of War, General Subject Files, 1940–1947, box 225, record group 107, NACP.

136. The part of the chaplain is played by well-known actor Clarence Brooks, who had appeared in many of the black-audience westerns and other race movies, as well as in Hollywood films such as *Arrowsmith*, dir. John Ford (Howard Productions, 1931). "'The Negro Soldier' Press Materials."

137. Miller was awarded the Navy Cross and was later assigned to the *U.S.S. Indianapolis*, the *U.S.S. Enterprise*, and, finally, the *U.S.S. Liscome Bay* as cook, third class. He died in 1943 when a Japanese submarine sank the *Liscome Bay*. Jack Salzman, David Lionel Smith, and Cornel West, eds., *Encyclopedia of African-American Culture and History* (New York: Macmillan, 1996), 4:1797. Captain Colin Kelly was a B-17 bomber pilot who in 1941, along with his crewmate Sergeant Meyer Levin, attacked a Japanese ship in the Philippines. Kelly died when his plane was hit. Levin died on another mission in 1943.

138. In a radio interview that Orson Welles conducted upon the dedication of the Doris Miller Theater, Miller's father Connery Miller, a sharecropper in Waco, Texas, told Welles that Doris preferred not to speak of his war experiences because of the sadness of remembering those of his colleagues who had already died in battle. Connery Miller insisted that the war had done nothing to improve the situation of African Americans. Welles attempted to get him to concede that black and white men fighting and dying together decreased prejudice, but Miller maintained his position. Miller concluded that, if given the choice between a meaningful death for his son (as Welles had characterized Doris's sacrifice) and having his son back, he would prefer to have his

son with him. Orson Welles, "Doris Miller Tribute," radio broadcast, December 9, 1945, transcribed in Kim Scarborough, "The Mercury Theatre on the Air Project," www.mercurytheatre.info (accessed September 4, 2006). I am grateful to MacDonald Moore for bringing this interview to my attention.

139. "Oral History with Carlton Moss," 119, 205.

140. Thomas Cripps, *Black Film as Genre* (Bloomington: Indiana University Press, 1978), 109; "Oral History with Carlton Moss," 205.

141. "Oral History with Carlton Moss," 188.

142. Karl W. Marks, "Reactions of Negro and White Soldiers to the Film, 'The Negro Soldier,'" April 17, 1944, Report B-102, Records of the Secretary of Defense, box 992, record group 330, NACP.

143. According to Cripps and Culbert, *The Negro Soldier* played in 1,819 theaters, far fewer bookings than most OWI shorts, which played in more than 13,000 theaters, or the Air Corps combat film *Memphis Belle* (in Technicolor), which was seen in over 12,000 theaters the same year. Cripps and Culbert, "The Negro Soldier," 632. The United Auto Workers later used the film "to prepare its members for an integrated work force." *New York Times*, August 15, 1997.

144. Herman Hill, "Claims Exhibitors Refuse to Show Racial Unity Film," *Pittsburgh Courier*, April 8, 1944.

145. *Pittsburgh Courier*, April 15, 1944.

146. *Pittsburgh Courier*, May 6, 1944, and June 24, 1944.

147. Members included Helen Hayes, Canada Lee, Paul Robeson, Bette Davis, and Paul Muni. *Pittsburgh Courier*, May 27, 1944.

148. Frank and Anne Hummert, Hummert Radio Features, to Major Monroe Greenthal, Chief, Motion Picture Branch, Industrial Services Division, April 24, 1944, Records of the Office of the Secretary of War, Records of the Civilian Aide to the Secretary of War, General Subject Files, 1940–1947, box 222, record group 107, NACP. The Hummerts produced these radio programs for the NBC radio network. On Anne Hummert's work as a consultant and on the couple's other contributions to the war effort through their radio programs, see Jim Cox, *Frank and Anne Hummert's Radio Factory: The Programs and Personalities of Broadcasting's Most Prolific Producers* (Jefferson, NC: McFarland, 2003), 120–21.

149. "Stella Dallas Dialogue on Motion Picture—'The Negro Soldier,'" Records of the Office of the Secretary of War, Records of the Civilian Aide to the Secretary of War, General Subject Files, 1940–1947, box 222, record group 107, NACP.

150. *People's Voice*, February 19, 1944.

151. *Pittsburgh Courier*, February 26, 1944.

152. *Time*, March 27, 1944.

153. Ibid.

154. *New York Times*, April 22, 1944; *Time*, March 27, 1944.

155. *New York Times,* April 22, 1944.

156. Savage, *Broadcasting Freedom,* 147.

6. "WHY DIDN'T THEY TELL ME I'M A NEGRO?"

1. W. L. White, "Lost Boundaries," *Reader's Digest,* December 1947, 137.

2. This evaluation of Johnston's racial location took place in the context of a U.S. definition of blackness that requires people with any African ancestry to define themselves as black. Although different states codified this definition in varied ways, the general system of classification became known the "one drop rule." Published accounts relate the racial backgrounds of Albert Sr. and Thyra in various ways. White described Thyra's grandfather as a German who married "a colored woman" and Albert Sr. as descended from a line of northern, light-skinned blacks on his father's side and from former slaves in Mississippi on his mother's side. An obituary for Albert Sr., who died in 1995, claims that "he was listed on his birth certificate as white." W. L. White, *Lost Boundaries* (New York: Harcourt, Brace, 1947, 1948), 11, 15; *New York Times,* November 29, 1995.

3. White, *Lost Boundaries,* 86.

4. Committee members included, among others, two African American laypeople (Sadie T. Alexander, assistant city solicitor of Philadelphia and a prominent figure in the National Council of Negro Women, and Channing Tobias, former senior secretary of the National Council of the YMCA and director of the Phelps-Stokes Fund); a rabbi (Ronald B. Gittelsohn, former marine chaplain and a rabbi in Rockville Center, Long Island); a lay Catholic and a Catholic bishop (Francis P. Matthews, a Nebraska attorney and former Supreme Knight of the Knights of Columbus, and Francis J. Haas, bishop of Grand Rapids); an Episcopal bishop (Henry Knox Sherrill, presiding bishop of the Protestant Episcopal Church); and a lay representative of the Methodist Church (Dorothy Tilly, secretary, Department of Social Relations, Woman's Society of Christian Services, the Methodist Church).

5. Charles E. Wilson, Chairman, introduction to *To Secure These Rights: The Report of the President's Committee on Civil Rights* (New York: Simon and Schuster, 1947), 139. In addition to outlining "the moral reason" for reexamining the state of civil rights in America, the committee presented economic and international reasons.

6. Ibid., n.p.

7. Ibid., 141.

8. Parks took photographs of Watson for the Farm Security Administration in 1942. On this series and on Watson's religious life in particular, see Colleen McDannell, *Picturing Faith: Photography and the Great Depression* (New Haven: Yale University Press, 2004).

9. "Photo-Editorial," *Ebony,* March 1948.

10. Ibid.

11. Ibid.

12. *New York Times*, March 6, 1949. The forces that ended this crusade lie outside the scope of this work, but the impact of the 1947 and 1951 House Un-American Activities Committee hearings on communism in Hollywood certainly made it difficult for studios to produce what they saw as advocacy films.

13. *Home of the Brave* (Screen Plays II Corp., 1949); *No Way Out*, dir. Joseph L. Mankiewicz (Twentieth Century-Fox, 1950); *Intruder in the Dust*, dir. Clarence Brown (Metro-Goldwyn-Mayer, 1950); *Lost Boundaries*, dir. Alfred L. Werker (RD-DR Corp., 1949); *Pinky*, dir. Elia Kazan (Twentieth Century-Fox, 1949); *Crossfire*, dir. Edward Dmytryk (RKO Radio Pictures, 1947); *Gentleman's Agreement*, dir., Elia Kazan (Twentieth Century-Fox, 1948); *The Boy with Green Hair*, dir. Joseph Losey (RKO Radio Pictures, 1948); *Knock on Any Door*, dir. Nicholas Ray (Columbia Pictures, 1949). The latter film was based on a novel by the African American author Willard Motley.

14. Laura Z. Hobson, *Laura Z: The Early Years and Years of Fulfillment* (New York: Primus, 1986), 434. At the same time, in personal correspondence, Zanuck presented a more narrow interpretation of the potential social impact of *Pinky*. He wrote, "This is not a story about how to solve the Negro problem in the South or anywhere else. This is not a story particularly about race problems, segregation or discrimination. This is a story about one particular Negro girl who could easily pass as white and did pass for a while. This is the story of how and why she, as an individual, finally decided to be herself—a Negress." Darryl F. Zanuck to Dudley Nichols, November 1, 1948, in Rudy Behlmer, ed., *Memo from Darryl F. Zanuck: The Golden Years at Twentieth Century-Fox* (New York: Grove Press, 1993), 162.

15. John Garfield, "How Hollywood Can Better Race Relations," *Negro Digest*, November 1947, 7. *Body and Soul*, dir. Robert Rossen (Enterprise Productions, 1947). Garfield would refuse to name colleagues as communists or communist sympathizers when asked to do so by the House of Un-American Activities Committee, and his career would suffer as a result.

16. *Pittsburgh Courier*, May 21, 1949.

17. Parker Tyler, "Hollywood as a Universal Church," *American Quarterly* 2 (Summer 1950): 165.

18. Anne Strick, "Peck on Prejudice," *Negro Digest*, July 1948, 18.

19. Ibid.

20. Peggy Weil, "Race Tolerance: Newest Box Office Hit," *Negro Digest*, August 1948, 46.

21. Dore Schary, "Minorities and Movies," *Negro Digest*, February 1948, 23.

22. "$20,000,000 Box Office Payoff for H'Wood Negro-Tolerance Pix," *Variety*, November 30, 1949, 1, 18, quoted in John Nickel, "Disabling African American Men: Liberalism and Race Message Films," *Cinema Journal* 44, no. 1 (2004): 25.

23. *New York Times,* March 6, 1949.

24. *Prejudice,* dir. Edward L. Cahn (Protestant Film Commission, 1949). The film featured Barbara Billingsly, who would go on to television fame playing the part of June Cleaver. Director Cahn had worked on *Our Gang* shorts and had a long career directing B movies, particularly science fiction films.

25. *New York Times,* October 18, 1949.

26. *Pittsburgh Courier,* May 28, 1949.

27. *Variety,* February 23, 1949.

28. There is a large body of literature on Jewishness and American constructions of race, although little of it seeks to incorporate religion as an element of racial identity. See, for example, Matthew Frye Jacobson, *Whiteness of a Different Color: European Immigrants and the Alchemy of Race* (Cambridge, MA: Harvard University Press, 1998); Karen Brodkin, *How Jews Became White Folks and What That Says about Race in America* (New Brunswick: Rutgers University Press, 1998); Jonathan Boyarin and Daniel Boyarin, *Jews and Other Differences: The New Jewish Cultural Studies* (Minneapolis: University of Minnesota Press, 1997); Michael Rogin, *Blackface, White Noise: Jewish Immigrants in the Hollywood Melting Pot* (Berkeley: University of California Press, 1996).

29. Robert Jones, "How Hollywood Feels about Negroes," *Negro Digest,* August 1947, 8.

30. Strick, "Peck on Prejudice," 18.

31. Quoted in Thomas Cripps, *Making Movies Black: The Hollywood Message Movie from World War II to the Civil Rights Era* (New York: Oxford University Press, 1993), 218.

32. See, for example, reviews of *Lost Boundaries* in *Variety,* November 30, 1949, and June 24, 1949, and in *New York Amsterdam News,* May 7, 1949.

33. Ralph Ellison, "The Shadow and the Act," in *Shadow and Act* (New York: Vintage Books, 1964), 277, originally published in the *Reporter,* December 6, 1949.

34. Ibid., 277.

35. Ibid., 280.

36. *New York Times,* June 4, 1949. The screenwriter Carl Forman transformed the Jewish main character in Arthur Laurents's play on which the film is based into a black character whom director Stanley Kramer named after Carlton Moss, the writer and actor in *The Negro Soldier.* Rogin, *Blackface, White Noise,* 288, 234.

37. On racial and sexual passing in literature and film, see, for example, Gayle Wald, *Crossing the Line: Racial Passing in Twentieth-Century U.S. Literature and Culture* (Durham: Duke University Press, 2000); Elaine K. Ginsberg, ed., *Passing and the Fictions of Identity* (Durham: Duke University Press, 1996).

38. Roi Ottley, "5 Million U.S. White Negroes," *Ebony,* March 1948, 22. The sociological study to which Ottley referred is probably E. W. Eckard's "How Many

Negroes Pass?" *American Journal of Sociology* 52 (1947): 498–500. In addition to *Ebony*'s contributions to the genre, *Negro Digest* published many original pieces dealing with racial passing and with scientific understandings of the nature of race, and it reprinted already published articles, including Ralph Linton, "Will U.S. Negroes Vanish in 200 Years?" August 1947, 33–39, reprinted from *American Mercury*, February 1947; M. F. Ashley Montague, "What Will the Negro Look Like 1000 Years from Today?" (November 1947), 9–11; Bergan Evans, "Do Negroes Have a Racial Odor?" January 1948, 4–8; Leo Swaim, "How a Negro Minister Passed in Dixie," February 1948, 4–6, condensed from the *St. Louis Post-Dispatch;* Robert Lucas, "Is the U.S. Negro Becoming Lighter?" February 1949, 29–33; David W. Evans, "My Son Is a Blonde Negro," March 1949, 30–35; John Hewlett, "Four Who Are Passing," April 1949, 8–13, condensed from *Pageant;* Langston Hughes, "Fooling Our White Folks," April 1950, 38–41; Janice Kingslow, "I Refuse to Pass," May 1950, 22–31; Pearl W., "I Passed for a Negro," June 1950, 35–43. For a useful discussion of the course of this literature in the popular media, see Wald, *Crossing the Line*, ch, 5.

39. Ottley, "5 Million," 24.

40. Ottley contrasted the subjection of black women to "the lust of white men" with "the profitable affairs Negro women have had with wealthy white men" ("5 Million," 24, 28). He pointed to the sensational New York annulment trial in November of 1924 of Leonard "Kip" Rhinelander and Alice Jones Rhinelander, who had been married one month earlier. Leonard, wealthy and white, claimed in his suit (filed at his father's urging) that Alice, who hailed from a working-class family, had deceived him and that she was a black woman passing as white. Alice's lawyer claimed that she had "colored blood" and that Kip knew this when he married her. Her lawyer had her expose her partially naked body to the judge in his chambers, particularly her breasts, to provide evidence that her husband must have known that she was black. See Earl Lewis and Heidi Ardizzone, *Love on Trial: An American Scandal in Black and White* (New York: W. W. Norton, 2001); Miriam Thaggert, "Racial Etiquette: Nella Larsen's *Passing* and the *Rhinelander* Case," *Meridians: Feminism, Race, Transnationalism* 5, no. 2 (2005): 1–29.

41. "Passing," *Ebony*, May 1949, 27.

42. Ibid., 30.

43. Gayle Wald confirms this impression in her more extensive survey of passing narratives in popular black magazines. She writes, "In contrast to these postwar books and Hollywood films, popular black magazines provided a context in which passing stories could be produced explicitly for consumption by African American audiences, who had longstanding awareness of racial passing and who, by most contemporary accounts, tended to see its practice in comic rather than tragic terms." Gayle Wald, "Crossing the Line: Racial Passing in Twentieth-Century American Literature and Culture" (PhD diss., Princeton University, 1995), 214.

44. Ralph Ellison, "The World and the Jug," in *Shadow and Act*, 124. For a broader discussion of this question, see Amy Robinson, "It Takes One to Know One: Passing and Communities of Common Interest," *Critical Inquiry* 20 (Summer 1994): 715–36.

45. Hughes, "Fooling Our White Folks," 41.

46. The reverse-passing narrative, in which whites assume identities of cultural blackness, sometimes presents an exception to the requirement to return to one's true identity. *Young Man with a Horn* (Warner Bros., 1950), directed by Michael Curtiz, is a useful example of a white man's passage into cultural blackness through jazz and in which African American religious practices play a part in enabling that passage. The film, which stars Kirk Douglas, Doris Day, and Lauren Bacall, was based on the 1938 novel by Dorothy Baker and was inspired by the life of jazz trumpeter Bix Beider-becke. Producer Jerry Wald tried for many years to have the film made after the studio purchased the rights to the book. Wald's superiors resisted, probably because the majority of the book's characters were black, and the various treatments that studio writers provided did not successfully solve what Wald referred to jokingly as "the col-ored problem." Eventually, all but one of the black characters were transformed into white characters in the final screenplay. The film tells the story of the rise, fall, and res-urrection of a white trumpeter, Rick Martin (Kirk Douglas), and tracks his increasing frustration with his career as an orchestra musician because of his deep attraction to black jazz. The scene in which the film makes its clearest argument that Rick is not a white hipster simply trying on black identity but a black man with white skin comes at the funeral of his black mentor, Art Hazzard (Juano Hernandez). Rick is the only white person in a church full of black mourners, and he sits at the back, seemingly dis-tanced and uncomfortable. However, as his mentor's band prepares to play a hymn, Rick walks to the front of the church, picks up Art's trumpet from on top of the cas-ket and joins in with the band, and they play, "Nobody Knows the Trouble I've Seen." On the perception that the story presented a "colored problem" for the studio, see Jerry Wald to Steve Trilling, September 19, 1946, WBA. On the production history of the film, see *Young Man with a Horn*, Warner Bros. Production Files, WBA.

47. Valerie Smith, "Reading the Intersection of Race and Gender in Narratives of Passing," *Diacritics* 24 (Summer–Autumn 1994): 43–44.

48. Susan Courtney notes that the racializing function of Hollywood film was solidified by the Production Code. She writes, "Hollywood cinema has contributed to the cultural production and dissemination not only of particular racial fictions—the wide array of types and stereotypes—but of an entire racial epistemology, a system of knowledge that deems 'race' to be a visible fact." The effect of the passing films and the "miscegenation" films in which "black" female characters appear to be "white" was to "shift . . . the location of racial meaning from invisible discourses of 'blood' and ancestry to visual discourses anchored increasingly by the properties of classical cin-ema itself." Susan Courtney, *Hollywood Fantasies of Miscegenation: Spectacular*

Narratives of Gender and Race, 1903–1967 (Princeton: Princeton University Press, 2005), 143.

49. There are various stories about where this meeting took place and under what circumstances. Some accounts indicate that the two met in California and others in New Hampshire. Paul Johnston, the youngest of the Johnston children, said that his brother met de Rochemont in New Hampshire when Albert and a friend from college visited de Rochemont to pitch a film about George Washington Carver. *Concord Monitor*, December 28, 2003.

50. Cripps, *Making Movies Black*, 227. The Johnston family revealed after the film has been released that they had received $10,000 for the rights to the story. *Baltimore Afro-American*, July 16, 1949.

51. Thomas F. Brady, "Old Order Changes: Metro Adopts Topical Films and Signs de Rochemont," *New York Times*, February 8, 1948.

52. Walter White, "On the Tragedy of the Color Line," *New York Times*, March 28, 1948. White had published an article in *Negro Digest* the month before entitled "Why I Remain a Negro."

53. "Lost Boundaries: Exciting New Book Tells Case History of a Family That Passed for 20 Years," *Ebony*, May 1948, 45; Guy B. Johnson, review of *Lost Boundaries*, *Social Forces* 27, no. 3 (1948–49): 332.

54. *New York Times*, November 14, 1948, and November 10, 1948.

55. *New York Times*, November 14, 1948. Werker had been a longtime studio director at Twentieth Century-Fox, perhaps best known for directing *The Adventures of Sherlock Holmes* (1939). De Rochemont reported later that filming took nine weeks, one week more than planned, and that the final cost was $620,000. *New York Times*, May 15, 1949.

56. Cripps, *Making Movies Black*, 228.

57. *New York Times*, January 30, 1949, and June 26, 1949.

58. *New York Times*, January 30, 1949, and May 15, 1948.

59. In a newspaper profile that was published shortly after the film premiered, Ferrer declared his hatred for acting, although he would go on to have a long career as actor, producer, and director. The article's author quipped, "He is a man in rebellion against a fate which has played such a dirty trick on him as to make him a movie star." Helen Colton, "Reluctant Star: Mel Ferrèr, Noted for His Performance in 'Lost Boundaries,' Hates Acting," *New York Times*, September 4, 1949.

60. Mona Z. Smith, *Becoming Something: The Story of Canada Lee* (New York: Faber and Faber, 2004), 243. A number of other black actors appeared in smaller roles, including Leigh Whipper, Maurice Ellis, and Emory Richardson.

61. See *Chicago Defender*, March 19, 1949; *Amsterdam News*, August 6, 1949.

62. "Lost Boundaries: New Film Records Chronicle of Negro Doctor Who 'Passed,'" *Ebony*, July 1949, 53.

63. *New York Times,* June 26, 1949.

64. *Baltimore Afro-American,* July 16, 1949.

65. Some years after the film's release, Mel Ferrer told of "having achieved true and complete identity with the role" and of experiences of having been assumed to be black. He said that his response to people's inquiries about whether he "really is a Negro" was to say, "Yes, I have about a 16th Negro blood in me, but it's not very noticeable." Gayle Wald reads this as an admission on Ferrer's part, but it seems more likely, when read in the broader context of the article, that Ferrer was interested in revealing the questioner's prejudices. Al Weisman, "He Passed as a Negro," *Negro Digest,* October 1951, 16–20; Wald, "Crossing the Line," 181.

66. *Baltimore Afro-American,* July 16, 1949.

67. Adam Knee and Charles Musser, "William Greaves: Documentary Filmmaking, and the African-American Experience," *Film Quarterly* 45 (Spring 1992): 15. Greaves had worked in the American Negro Theatre, in radio, and on television, and he went on to direct a number of well-received documentaries on aspects of African American history, such as *Ida B. Wells: A Passion for Justice* (1998) and *Ralph Bunche: An American Odyssey* (2001), as well as feature films.

68. Fredi Washington to Carlton Moss, July 28, 1949. Fredi Washington Papers, Amistad Research Center Microfilm Collection. *Imitation of Life,* dir. John Stahl (Universal, 1934). The film starred Fredi Washington, Louise Beavers, and Claudette Colbert.

69. Quoted in Fredi Washington to Darr Smith, *Los Angeles Daily News,* August 2, 1949, Fredi Washington Papers, Amistad Research Center Microfilm Collection.

70. Washington to Smith, August 2, 1949.

71. Washington to Moss, July 28, 1949.

72. Ibid.; *Amsterdam News,* August 6, 1949.

73. Courtney, *Hollywood Fantasies,* 170.

74. Quoted in ibid., 143.

75. Gayle Wald notes, "More practically, the selection of Crain, Ferrer and others made it possible for the studios to advocate racial integration in the postwar period without having to confront their own discriminatory hiring practices. As a result of the studios' refusal to use black actors (a practice which recalls Griffith's use of whites in blackface for many of the black roles in *Birth of a Nation*), Hollywood made its first tentative forays into the 'realistic' representation of racism without ever depicting 'real' black people as the objects of racial violence of discrimination—or, for that matter, as visible political subjects who could advocate on behalf of 'Negro rights.'" Wald, "Crossing the Line," 178.

76. Joseph I. Breen to Louis B. Mayer, May 19, 1948, *Lost Boundaries,* MPPDA Production Code Administration Case Files, AMPAS. At this point, the production was still under Metro-Goldwyn-Mayer's jurisdiction.

77. When the production moved to RD-DR, Breen wrote to screenwriter Eugene Ling, informing him that the PCA had again approved the story, this time noting that they should be careful about the costuming of the female characters. "The Production Code makes it mandatory that the intimate parts of the body—specifically, the breasts of women—be fully covered at all times. Any compromise with this regulation will compel us to withhold approval of your picture." Such a caution had become routine for Breen by this time, and there is no evidence that Ling's script included any scenes that involved revealing costumes. Breen also cautioned about scenes that included drinking of alcohol and noted that the scene of the marriage ceremony should be "played with dignity. Above all, there should be no suggestion of any comedy about it." This last admonition had to do with the code's requirements that "the sanctity of the institution of marriage and the home shall be upheld" and that "ceremonies of any definite religion should be carefully and respectfully handled." Joseph I. Breen to Eugene Ling, January 17, 1949, *Lost Boundaries*, MPPDA Production Code Administration Case Files, AMPAS.

78. In her work on the disparate responses by the PCA to the *Imitation of the Life* (1934) and to *Pinky* (1949), Susan Courtney argues that the workings of the cinema as medium enabled the shift in attitude on the part of the censors. She writes, "Indeed, whereas racial epistemologies organized around discourses of blood and skin were only becoming increasingly vulnerable to dilution (through growing resistance to segregation, scientific research, etc.), cinema could counter the evident 'facts' with fabrications of fantasy, and with the medium's particular knack for wedding fantasy to the impression of encounters with 'real' phenomena (skin, voice, space, etc.)." Courtney, *Hollywood Fantasies*, 190.

79. Virginia Shaler and Eugene Ling, *Lost Boundaries*, shooting script, Schomburg Center for Research in Black Culture, NYPL. Unless otherwise indicated, dialogue and stage directions have been taken from the shooting script.

80. In White's account, Johnston had a choice of only four black hospitals at which to intern, none of which proved acceptable to Rush Medical College. He was then turned down by a number of white hospitals that had been interested in him initially but that declined to offer him a position after finding out that he was black. White, *Lost Boundaries*, 17–18.

81. Ellison, "Shadow and the Act," 279.

82. Miriam J. Petty argues, in her analysis of *Pinky*, that the conventions of horror films are employed across all of the racial passing films of the period. Miriam J. Petty, "Passing for Horror: Race, Fear, and Elia Kazan's *Pinky*," *Genders* 40 (2004), retrieved July 5, 2006, from www.genders.org/g40/g40_petty.html.

83. Actress and columnist Fredi Washington was outraged about the film's portrayal of Harlem. She wrote, singling out Werker's contributions to the production, "[P]erhaps his New Hampshire scenes may be documentary, but his Harlem scenes are

a gross exaggeration. I live in Harlem, and I think I am a better judge of that area than Werker." Washington to Smith, August 2, 1949.

84. The actor Canada Lee faced a similar situation in his own life of counseling a forlorn teenager when Jack Geiger, a young middle-class Jewish man whom he had met a few times, ran away from home and went to live with Lee in Harlem for a year. The two had met when Geiger attended a performance of *Native Son* and was moved by Lee's performance. Lee, who had himself run away from home at a young age, took the young man in and paid for his college education. Geiger became a civil rights activist and a physician with a specialty in community medicine. Geiger related the story of his relationship with Lee in an episode of the radio program *This American Life*, Episode 75, September 12, 1997.

85. Ellison, "Shadow and the Act," 279.

86. Walter White to Louis de Rochemont, May 23, 1949, quoted in Cripps, *Making Movies Black*, 228.

87. *Nation*, July 30, 1949, 114.

88. This is the stage direction as written in the script. Shaler and Ling, *Lost Boundaries*, shooting script.

89. The dog first appears sitting outside the gate in an establishing shot of the Carter's home. Scott and Marcia have told Howard their story, but Shelly does not yet know.

90. De Rochemont created a composite town from the Johnstons' experiences in Gorham and Keene, New Hampshire.

91. White's written account of the family's story, locates the Congregational church at the center of the typical New England town and writes that the Johnstons joined when the minister in Gorham asked if they would enroll the children in Sunday school. White wrote, "He didn't ask their religion any more than he had asked their color, so the doctor and his wife said, why not? Neither had given much thought to religion; this seemed to be the church to which almost everybody belonged, and why shouldn't their children grow up with the others?" White, *Lost Boundaries*, 23.

92. Acts 17:26.

93. During the war, the NAACP charged that the Army and Navy had asked the Red Cross to provide them with blood only from white donors, a policy to which the Red Cross objected. Rear Admiral Ross T. McIntyre, Surgeon General, denied that blood donations from African Americans were being rejected. After discussions with William Hastie, civilian aide to the Secretary of War, the military's public policy was to accept donations of blood from African Americans, but it required the Red Cross to segregate donations according to race. Phillip McGuire, "Judge Hastie, World War II, and Army Racism," *Journal of Negro History* 62 (October 1977): 355–56; *New York Times*, January 18, 1942.

94. A little later, Arthur becomes a strange spectacle of black pathos as he and

Howard perform a song they wrote together and Arthur sings the lyrics "Nobody loves me now." The song, "Guess I'm Through with Love," was written by Albert C. Johnston Jr., the "real" Howard. Joseph I. Breen to Eugene Ling, June 1, 1949, *Lost Boundaries*, MPPDA Production Code Administration Case Files, AMPAS.

95. Until 1942, African American men in the navy served in noncombat assignments as stewards, cooks, and mess men. The U.S. Navy began accepting African American men to the ranks of noncommissioned officers in the reserve in April of 1942, with plans to place them in segregated units. African American women were accepted into the WAVES beginning in 1944. The navy did not commission its first African American officer until 1947. *New York Times*, April 8, 1942, October 20, 1944, and October 29, 1947.

96. This scene uses the first and last verses of the hymn:

Once to every man and nation, comes the moment to decide
In the strife of truth with falsehood, for the good or evil side;
Some great cause, God's new Messiah, offering each the bloom or blight,
And the choice goes by forever, 'twixt that darkness and that light.

Though the cause of evil prosper, yet the truth alone is strong;
Though her portion be the scaffold, and upon the throne be wrong;
Yet that scaffold sways the future, and behind the dim unknown,
Standeth God within the shadow, keeping watch above His own.

97. The shooting script indicates that, at this juncture, Mrs. Adams, who stands next to Marcia, "puts her arm around Marcia's shoulders. Together they continue singing." In the final version of the film, she does not touch Marcia but merely continues to stand next to her, singing. Shaler and Ling, *Lost Boundaries*, shooting script, 96.

98. De Rochemont cast Dunn in two other films, *The Whistle at Eaton Falls* (1951), dir. Robert Siodmak, and *Walk East on Beacon!* (1952), dir. Alfred Werker. In the former film Dunn played a minister and in the latter he played a doctor.

99. *New York Times*, July 1, 1949. Edwin Schallert wrote in the *Los Angeles Times* that "Rev. Dunn gives an astonishingly competent portrayal." *Los Angeles Times*, August 6, 1949.

100. This conclusion is the mirror image of that reached in *Gentleman's Agreement*, about which screenwriter Ring Lardner Jr. quipped, "The movie's moral is that you should never be mean to a Jew, because he might turn out to be a gentile." Otto Friedrich, *City of Nets: A Portrait of Hollywood in the 1940s* (New York: Harper Perennial, 1987), 366.

101. Weisman, "He Passed," 20.

102. Wald, "Crossing the Line," 185.

103. *Chicago Daily Tribune*, September 3, 1949.

104. Vinicius de Morae, "The Making of a Document: 'The Quiet One'" *Hollywood Quarterly* 4 (Summer 1950): 376.

105. Cripps, *Making Movies Black*, 227.

106. Quoted in Mike Waldman, "Critics Hail Powerful 'Lost Boundaries,'" *Pittsburgh Courier*, July 9, 1949. The Johnston family's public statements following the publication of White's book and the release of the film also told a story of the moral consequences of passing. At the end of White's account, Dr. Albert Johnston Sr. appears as a fearful man who is uncomfortable with African Americans, completely opposed to living in the political and social environment of the segregated regions of the country, and unable to socialize easily among whites as he had before his story became known. "I guess I've become morose," Johnston concluded. He later charged that Elliot Community Hospital in Keene, New Hampshire, at which he worked part time as a radiologist, had fired him because the film "revealed him as a Negro." The family eventually moved to Hawaii, which they felt "was more of an ethnic melting pot." White, *Lost Boundaries*, 83; *New York World Telegram and Sun*, June 14, 1953; *Concord Monitor*, December 28, 2003.

107. Quoted in M. Smith, *Becoming Something*, 288.

108. *Hollywood Reporter*, July 20, 1949.

109. *New York Times*, July 1, 1949.

110. Ibid.

111. *Los Angeles Times*, August 6, 1949.

112. *Chicago Daily Tribune*, July 5, 1949.

113. *New York Times*, August 21, 1949.

114. *RD-DR Corporation et al. v. Christine Smith et al.*, 89 F. Supp. 596 (1950).

115. *New York Times*, August 21, 1949.

116. *Pinky* was banned in Taladega and Sylacauga, Alabama, as well as in Marshall, Texas. In the latter case, a theater manager was arrested and convicted of violating a city ordinance, revived specifically for the case of *Pinky*, that allowed the censors to bar a film "of such character as to be prejudicial to the best interests of the people of the city." The case made it to the U.S. Supreme Court in 1952, which struck down the ban on the grounds of the vague and indefinite nature of the statute. The court had struck down a New York State ban, on the grounds of sacrilege, of the exhibition of Roberto Rossellini's *The Miracle* the week before issuing the ruling on *Pinky*. *New York Times*, June 3, 1952; *Motion Picture Daily*, June 3, 1952.

117. *Motion Picture Daily*, October 31, 1949.

118. Gerald Weales, "Pro-Negro Films in Atlanta," *Phylon* 13, no. 4 (1952): 299.

119. Ibid.

120. *New York Times*, August 22, 1949, and November 19, 1949; *Motion Picture Daily*, August 29, 1949; *Variety*, August 29, 1949; *Motion Picture Daily*, November 22, 1949.

121. The courts reached this conclusion in the case of *Mutual Film Corporation v. Industrial Commission of Ohio* 236 U.S. 242 (1915), in which the unanimous decision declared, "It cannot be put out of view that the exhibition of moving pictures is a business, pure and simple, originated and conducted for profit, like other spectacles, not to be regarded, nor intended to be regarded by the Ohio Constitution, we think, as part of the press of the country, or as organs of public opinion. They are mere representations of events, of ideas and sentiments published and known; vivid, useful, and entertaining, no doubt, but, as we have said, capable of evil, having power for it, the greater because of their attractiveness and manner of exhibition. It was this capability and power, and it may be in experience of them, that induced the state of Ohio, in addition to prescribing penalties for immoral exhibitions, as it does in its Criminal Code, to require censorship before exhibition, as it does by the act under review. We cannot regard this as beyond the power of government."

122. *RD-DR Corporation et al. v. Christine Smith et al.*, 89 F. Supp. 596 (1950). After this decision by the U.S. District Court for the Northern District of Georgia, de Rochemont appealed the case, but the original decision was upheld by the Fifth Circuit Court of Appeals in *RD-DR Corporation et al. v. Christine Smith et al.*, 183 F.2d 562 (1950). Of the Supreme Court justices, only Justice William O. Douglas felt the case should be heard. *RD-DR Corporation et al. v. Christine Smith et al.*, 340 U.S. 853 (1950).

123. *Motion Picture Daily,* November 9, 1950. The U.S. Supreme Court would hear a case involving film as free speech two years later in *Burstyn v. Wilson,* which dealt with New York State's banning of Roberto Rossellini's *The Miracle* on the grounds of sacrilege. The opinion held that "[i]t cannot be doubted that motion pictures are a significant medium for the communication of ideas. Their importance as an organ of public opinion is not lessened by the fact that they are designed to entertain as well as to inform." *Joseph Burstyn, Inc. v. Wilson, Commissioner of Education of New York, et al.* 343 U.S. 495 (1952).

SELECT BIBLIOGRAPHY

The bibliography does not include periodical sources (such as the *New York Amsterdam News*, *Chicago Defender*, *Pittsburgh Courier*, and *California Eagle*) that have been cited in the notes.

ARCHIVES AND SPECIAL COLLECTIONS

Camille Billops and James V. Hatch Archives. Special Collections and Archives. Robert W. Woodruff Library, Emory University.

Arthur Freed Collection. Performing Arts Archives. Cinema-Television Library, University of Southern California.

L. S. Alexander Gumby Collection of Negroiana. Rare Book and Manuscript Library, Columbia University.

Eva Jessye Collection. Special Collections. Leonard H. Axe Library, Pittsburg State University.

George P. Johnson Negro Film Collection. Department of Special Collections. University Research Library, University of California at Los Angeles.

James Weldon Johnson Collection. Yale Collection of American Literature. Beinecke Rare Book and Manuscript Library, Yale University.

Vincente Minnelli Collection. Margaret Herrick Library, Academy of Motion Picture Arts and Sciences.

Motion Picture, Broadcasting, and Recorded Sound Division. Library of Congress.

Motion Picture Case Files. New York State Archives. Cultural Education Center.

Motion Picture Producers and Distributors of America. Production Code Administration Case Files. Margaret Herrick Library, Academy of Motion Picture Arts and Sciences.

Motion Picture Scripts Collection. Margaret Herrick Library, Academy of Motion Picture Arts and Sciences.

Negro Actors Guild Collection. Rare Books and Manuscripts. Schomburg Center for Research in Black Culture. New York Public Library.

Oral History Research Office. Butler Library, Columbia University.

Victoria Spivey Papers. Special Collections and Archives. Robert W. Woodruff Library, Emory University.

USC Warner Bros. Archives. Performing Arts Archives. Cinema-Television Library, University of Southern California.

United States, National Archives and Records Administration. National Archives at College Park, College Park, Maryland.

King Vidor Collection. Performing Arts Archives. Cinema-Television Library, University of Southern California.

BOOKS, DISSERTATIONS, AND ARTICLES

Affron, Charles, and Mirella Jona Affron. *Sets in Motion: Art Direction and Film Narrative*. New Brunswick: Rutgers University Press, 1995.

Altman, Rick. *The American Film Musical*. Bloomington: Indiana University Press, 1978.

Baer, Hans, and Merrill Singer. *African-American Religion in the Twentieth Century: Varieties of Protest and Accommodation*. Knoxville: University of Tennessee Press, 1992.

Behlmer, Rudy, ed. *Memo from Darryl F. Zanuck: The Golden Years at Twentieth Century-Fox*. New York: Grove Press, 1993.

Belton, John, ed. *Movies and Mass Culture*. New Brunswick: Rutgers University Press, 1996.

Bernard, Emily, ed. *Remember Me to Harlem: The Letters of Langston Hughes and Carl Van Vechten, 1925–1964*. New York: Knopf, 2001.

Bernardi, Daniel, ed. *The Birth of Whiteness: Race and the Emergence of U.S. Cinema*. New Brunswick: Rutgers University Press, 1996.

———. *Classic Hollywood, Classic Whiteness*. Minneapolis: University of Minnesota Press, 2001.

Bernstein, Matthew, and Gaylyn Studlar, eds. *Visions of the East: Orientalism in Film*. New Brunswick: Rutgers University Press, 1997.

Black, Donald Fisher. "The Life and Work of Eva Jessye and Her Contributions to American Music." PhD diss., University of Michigan, 1986.

Black, Gregory D. *The Catholic Crusade against the Movies, 1940–1975*. Cambridge: Cambridge University Press, 1998.

———. *Hollywood Censored: Morality Codes, Catholics and the Movies*. Cambridge: Cambridge University Press, 1994.

Bogle, Donald. *Toms, Coons, Mulattoes, Mammies, and Bucks: An Interpretive History of Blacks in American Films*. New York: Viking Press, 1973.

Bordwell, David, Janet Staiger, and Kristin Thompson. *The Classical Hollywood Cinema: Film Style and Mode of Production to 1960*. New York: Columbia University Press, 1985.

Bowser, Pearl, Jane Gaines, and Charles Musser, eds. *Oscar Micheaux and His Circle: African-American Filmmaking and Race Cinema of the Silent Era*. Bloomington: University of Indiana Press, 2001.

Bowser, Pearl, and Louise Spence. *Writing Himself into History: Oscar Micheaux, His Silent Films, and His Audiences*. New Brunswick: Rutgers University Press, 2000.

Boyarin, Jonathan, and Daniel Boyarin. *Jews and Other Differences: The New Jewish Cultural Studies*. Minneapolis: University of Minnesota Press, 1997.

Boyd, Malcolm. *Christ and Celebrity Gods: The Church and Mass Culture*. Greenwich, CT: Seabury Press, 1958.

Bradford, Roark. *Ol' Man Adam an' His Chillun: Being the Tales They Tell about the Time When the Lord Walked the Earth Like a Natural Man*. New York: Harper and Brothers, 1928.

Brodkin, Karen. *How Jews Became White Folks and What That Says about Race in America*. New Brunswick: Rutgers University Press, 1998.

Burkett, Randall K. *Garveyism as a Religious Movement: The Institutionalization of a Black Civil Religion*. Metuchen, NJ: Scarecrow Press, 1978.

Capra, Frank. *The Name above the Title: An Autobiography*. New York: Vintage, 1971.

Carr, Steven Alan. *Hollywood and Anti-Semitism: A Cultural History up to World War II*. New York: Cambridge University Press, 2001.

Chase, William Sheafe. *Catechism on Motion Pictures in Inter-State Commerce*. Albany: New York Civic League, 1922.

Coleman, Gregory D. *We're Heaven Bound: Portrait of a Black Sacred Drama*. Athens: University of Georgia Press, 1992.

Collins, Patricia Hill. *Black Feminist Thought: Knowledge, Consciousness and the Politics of Empowerment*. Boston: Unwin Hyman, 1991.

Connelly, Marc. *The Green Pastures*. Edited by Thomas Cripps. Madison: University of Wisconsin Press, 1979.

———. *The Green Pastures: A Fable Suggested by Roark Bradford's Southern Sketches, "Ol' Man Adam an' His Chillun."* New York: Farrar and Rinehart, 1929.

———. *Voices Offstage: A Book of Memoirs*. Chicago: Holt, Rinehart and Winston, 1968.

Cosandey, Roland, André Gaudreault, and Tom Gunning, eds. *Une invention du diable? Cinéma des premiers temps et religion*. Sainte-Foy: Les Presses de L'Université Laval, 1990.

Courtney, Susan. *Hollywood Fantasies of Miscegenation: Spectacular Narratives of Gender and Race, 1903–1967*. Princeton: Princeton University Press, 2005.

Couvares, Francis G., ed. *Movie Censorship and American Culture*. Washington, DC: Smithsonian Institution Press, 1996.

Cox, Jim. *Frank and Anne Hummert's Radio Factory: The Programs and Personalities of Broadcasting's Most Prolific Producers*. Jefferson, NC: McFarland, 2003.

Cripps, Thomas. *Black Film as Genre*. Bloomington: Indiana University Press, 1978.

———. "The Films of Spencer Williams." *Black American Literature Forum* 12 (Winter, 1978): 128–34.

———. *Making Movies Black: The Hollywood Message Movie from World War II to the Civil Rights Era*. New York: Oxford University Press, 1993.

———. *Slow Fade to Black: The Negro in American Film, 1900–1942*. 1977. Reprint, New York: Oxford University Press, 1993.

Cripps, Thomas, and David Culbert. "The Negro Soldier (1944): Film Propaganda in Black and White." *American Quarterly* 31, no. 5 (1979): 616–40.

Cruse, Harold. *Rebellion or Revolution?* New York: William Morrow, 1968.

Curtis, Susan. *The First Black Actors on the Great White Way*. Columbia: University of Missouri Press, 2001.

Custen, George Frederick. *Twentieth Century's Fox: Darryl F. Zanuck and the Culture of Hollywood*. New York: Basic Books, 1997.

Daniel, Walter C. *"De Lawd": Richard B. Harrison and The Green Pastures*. New York: Greenwood Press, 1986.

De Lauretis, Teresa. *Technologies of Gender: Essays on Theory, Film, and Fiction*. Bloomington: Indiana University Press, 1987.

Diawara, Manthia, ed. *Black American Cinema: Aesthetics and Spectatorship*. New York: Routledge, 1993.

Doherty, Thomas. *Pre-Code Hollywood: Sex, Immorality, and Insurrection in American Cinema, 1930–1934.* New York: Columbia University Press, 1999.

Dowd, Nancy, and David Shepard. *King Vidor: A Directors Guild of America Oral History.* Metuchen, NJ: Directors Guild of America and Scarecrow Press, 1988.

Durgnat, Raymond, and Scott Simon. *King Vidor, American.* Berkeley: University of California Press, 1988.

Dyer, Richard. *White.* London: Routledge, 1997.

Eastman, Fred, and Edward Ouelette. *Better Motion Pictures: A Discussion Course.* Boston: Pilgrim Press, 1936.

Ellison, Ralph. *Shadow and Act.* New York: Vintage Books, 1964.

Ely, Melvin Patrick. *The Adventures of Amos 'n' Andy: A Social History of an American Phenomenon.* New York: Free Press, 1991.

Erens, Patricia. "Between Two Worlds: Jewish Images in American Film." In *The Kaleidoscopic Lens: How Hollywood Views Ethnic Groups,* edited by Randall M. Miller. Englewood, NJ: Ozer, 1980.

Ernst, Morris L., and Pare Lorentz. *Censored: The Private Life of the Movie.* New York: Jonathan Cape and Harrison Smith, 1930.

Everett, Anna. *Returning the Gaze: A Genealogy of Black Film Criticism, 1909–1949.* Durham: Duke University Press, 2001.

Fauset, Arthur Huff. *Black Gods of the Metropolis: Negro Religious Cults of the Urban North.* Philadelphia: University of Pennsylvania Press, 1944.

Fletcher, Winona L. "Witnessing a 'Miracle': Sixty Years of Heaven Bound at Big Bethel in Atlanta." *Black American Literature Forum* 25 (Spring 1991): 83–92.

Friedrich, Otto. *City of Nets: A Portrait of Hollywood in the 1940s.* New York: Harper Perennial, 1987.

Gaines, Jane M. *Fire and Desire: Mixed-Race Movies in the Silent Era.* Chicago: University of Chicago Press, 2001.

Gevinson, Alan, ed. *American Film Institute Catalog—Within Our Gates: Ethnicity in American Feature Films, 1911–1960.* Berkeley: University of California Press, 1997.

Ginsberg, Elaine K., ed. *Passing and the Fictions of Identity.* Durham: Duke University Press, 1996.

Gledhill, Christine, ed. *Home Is Where the Heart Is: Studies in Melodrama and the Woman's Film.* London: BFI Books, 1987.

Goldschmidt, Henry, and Elizabeth McAlister, eds. *Race, Nation, and Religion in the Americas.* Oxford: Oxford University Press, 2004.

Green, J. Ronald. *Straight Lick: The Cinema of Oscar Micheaux*. Bloomington: Indiana University Press, 2000.

Green, Martha Denise. "Social Gospels: Class, Race, and Sexuality in Twentieth-Century Biblical Drama." PhD diss., University of North Carolina at Chapel Hill, 2001.

Guerrero, Ed. *Framing Blackness: The African American Image in Film*. Philadelphia: Temple University Press, 1993.

Hayward, Susan. *Key Concepts in Cinema Studies*. New York: Routledge, 1996.

Headley, Robert K. *Motion Picture Exhibitions in Washington, DC: An Illustrated History of Parlors, Palaces and Multiplexes in the Metropolitan Area, 1894–1997*. Jefferson, NC: McFarland, 1999.

Herman, Felicia. "American Jews and the Effort to Reform Motion Pictures, 1933–1935." *American Jewish Archives Journal 52*, nos. 1 and 2 (2001): 11–44.

———. "'The Most Dangerous Anti-Semitic Photoplay in Filmdom': American Jews and *The King of Kings* (DeMille, 1927)." *Velvet Light Trap: A Critical Journal of Film and Television* 46 (Fall 2000): 12–25.

Hicks, Heather J. "Hoodoo Economics: White Men's Work and Black Men's Magic in Contemporary American Film." *Camera Obscura* 18, no. 2 (2003): 27–55.

Hicks, William. *History of Louisiana Negro Baptists, 1804–1914*. Nashville, TN: National Baptist Publishing Board, 1918.

Howard, Jessica. "Hallelujah! Transformation in Film." *African American Review* 30 (Autumn 1996): 441–51.

Jacobs, Lea. *The Wages of Sin: Censorship and the Fallen Woman Film, 1928–1942*. Madison: University of Wisconsin Press, 1991.

Jacobson, Matthew Frye. *Whiteness of a Different Color: European Immigrants and the Alchemy of Race*. Cambridge, MA: Harvard University Press, 1998.

Janken, Kenneth Robert. *White: The Biography of Walter White, Mr. NAACP*. New York: Free Press, 2003.

Johnson, Clifton H., ed. *God Struck Me Dead: Religious Conversion Experiences and Autobiographies of Ex-Slaves*. 1969. Reprint, Cleveland, OH: Pilgrim Press, 1993.

Johnson, James Weldon. *God's Trombones: Seven Negro Sermons in Verse*. 1927. Reprint, New York: Penguin, 1990.

Jones, G. William. *Black Cinema Treasures Lost and Found*. Denton: University of North Texas Press, 1991.

Jowett, Garth. *Film: The Democratic Art*. Boston: Little, Brown, 1976.

Kellner, Bruce. *The Harlem Renaissance: A Historical Dictionary of the Era*. Westport, CT: Greenwood Press, 1984.

Kisch, John, and Edward Mapp, eds. *A Separate Cinema: Fifty Years of Black Cast Posters*. New York: Noonday Press, 1992.

Knee, Adam, and Charles Musser. "William Greaves: Documentary Filmmaking, and the African-American Experience." *Film Quarterly* 45 (Spring 1992): 13–25.

Leab, Daniel J. *From Sambo to Superspade: The Black Experience in Motion Pictures*. Boston: Houghton Mifflin, 1975.

Lewis, Earl, and Heidi Ardizzone. *Love on Trial: An American Scandal in Black and White*. New York: W. W. Norton, 2001.

Lincoln, C. Eric. *The Black Muslims in America*. Boston: Beacon Press, 1961.

Lindvall, Terry, ed. *The Silents of God: Selected Issues and Documents in Silent American Film and Religion, 1908–1925*. Lanham, MD: Scarecrow Press, 2001.

MacCann, Richard Dyer. *The People's Films: A Political History of U.S. Government Motion Pictures*. New York: Hastings House, 1973.

Marchetti, Gina. *Romance and the "Yellow Peril": Race, Sex, and Discursive Strategies in Hollywood Fiction*. Berkeley: University of California Press, 1993.

Martin, Joel, and Conrad Ostwalt Jr. *Screening the Sacred: Religion, Myth, and Ideology in Popular American Film*. Boulder, CO: Westview Press, 1995.

Martin, Olga J. *Hollywood's Movie Commandments: A Handbook for Motion Picture Writers and Reviewers*. New York: H. W. Wilson, 1937.

Massood, Paula J. *Black City Cinema: African American Urban Experiences in Film*. Philadelphia: Temple University Press, 2003.

Maurice, Alice. "'Cinema at Its Source': Synchronizing Race and Sound in the Early Talkies." *Camera Obscura* 17, no. 1 (2002): 31–71.

Mays, Benjamin E. *The Negro's God as Reflected in His Literature*. 1938. New York: Russell and Russell, 1968.

McDannell, Colleen. *Material Christianity: Religion and Popular Culture in America*. New Haven: Yale University Press, 1995.

———. *Picturing Faith: Photography and the Great Depression*. New Haven: Yale University Press, 2004.

———, ed. *Religions of the United States in Practice*. Vol. 2. Princeton: Princeton University Press, 2001.

McGuire, Phillip. "Judge Hastie, World War II, and Army Racism." *Journal of Negro History* 62 (October 1977): 351–62.

Miles, Margaret R. *Seeing and Believing: Religion and Values in the Movies*. Boston: Beacon Press, 1996.

Miller, Randall M., ed. *The Kaleidoscopic Lens: How Hollywood Views Ethnic Groups*. Englewood, NJ: Ozer, 1980.

Minnelli, Vincente, with Hector Arce. *I Remember It Well.* Hollywood, CA: Samuel French, 1990.

Moore, Deborah Dash. "Jewish GIs and the Creation of the Judeo-Christian Tradition." *Religion and American Culture* 8 (Winter 1998): 31–53.

Morey, Anne. *Hollywood Outsiders: The Adaptation of the Film Industry, 1913–1934.* Minneapolis: University of Minnesota Press, 2003.

Morgan, David. *Icons of American Protestantism: The Art of Warner Sallman.* New Haven: Yale University Press, 1996.

———. *Visual Piety: A History and Theory of Popular Religious Images.* Berkeley: University of California Press, 1998.

Morgan, David, and Sally M. Promey, eds. *The Visual Culture of American Religions.* Berkeley: University of California Press, 2001.

Morrison, Toni. *Playing in the Dark: Whiteness and the Literary Imagination.* New York: Vintage Books, 1992.

Naremore, James. *The Films of Vincente Minnelli.* Cambridge: Cambridge University Press, 1993.

Nouryeh, Andrea J. "When the Lord Was a Black Man: A Fresh Look at the Life of Richard Berry Harrison." *Black American Literature Forum* 16 (Winter 1982): 142–46.

Null, Gary. *Black Hollywood: The Negro in Motion Pictures.* Secaucus, NJ: Citadel Press, 1975.

Patterson, Lindsay. *Black Films and Film-Makers: A Comprehensive Anthology from Stereotype to Superhero.* New York: Dodd, Mead, 1975.

Peterson, Bernard L., Jr. *Early American Playwrights and Dramatic Writers: A Biographical Dictionary and Catalogue of Plays, Films, and Broadcasting Scripts.* Westport, CT: Greenwood Press, 1990.

Plate, S. Brent, ed. *Representing Religion in World Cinema: Filmmaking, Mythmaking, Culture Making.* New York: Palgrave, 2003.

Pollard, Deborah Smith. "The Phenomenon Known as the Gospel Musical Stage Play." *CEA Critic* 62 (Summer 2000): 1–17.

Powers, Stephen, David J. Rothman, and Stanley Rothman. *Hollywood's America: Social and Political Themes in Motion Pictures.* Boulder, CO: Westview Press, 1996.

Quigley, Martin. *Decency in Motion Pictures.* New York: Macmillan, 1937.

Richards, Larry. *African American Films through 1959: A Comprehensive, Illustrated Filmography.* Jefferson, NC: McFarland, 1998.

Rogin, Michael. *Blackface, White Noise: Jewish Immigrants in the Hollywood Melting Pot.* Berkeley: University of California Press, 1996.

Rony, Fatimah Tobing. *The Third Eye: Race, Cinema, and Ethnographic Spectacle*. Durham: Duke University Press, 1996.

Rosini, Vincent T. "Sanctuary Cinema: The Rise and Fall of Protestant Churches as Film Exhibition Sites, 1910–1930." PhD diss., Regent University, 1998.

Sampson, Henry T. *Blacks in Black and White: A Sourcebook on Black Films*. Metuchen, NJ: Scarecrow Press, 1977.

———. *That's Enough Folks: Black Images in Animated Cartoons, 1900–1960*. Lanham, MD: Scarecrow Press, 1998.

Savage, Barbara Dianne. *Broadcasting Freedom: Radio, War, and the Politics of Race, 1938–1948*. Chapel Hill: University of North Carolina Press, 1999.

Schaefer, Eric. *Bold! Daring! Shocking! True! A History of Exploitation Films, 1919–1950*. Durham: Duke University Press, 1999.

Schatz, Thomas. *The Genius of the System: Hollywood Filmmaking in the Studio Era*. New York: Owl Books, 1988.

Sernett, Milton C. *Bound for the Promised Land: African American Religion and the Great Migration*. Durham: Duke University Press, 1997.

Seward, Adrienne Lanier. "Early Black Film and Folk Tradition: An Interpretive Analysis of the Use of Folklore in Selected All-Black Cast Feature Films." PhD diss., Indiana University, 1985.

Shapiro, James. *Oberammergau: The Troubling Story of the World's Most Famous Passion Play*. New York: Pantheon Books, 2000.

Smith, Mona Z. *Becoming Something: The Story of Canada Lee*. New York: Faber and Faber, 2004.

Smith, Valerie. *Not Just Race, Not Just Gender: Black Feminist Readings*. New York: Routledge, 1998.

———. "Reading the Intersection of Race and Gender in Narratives of Passing." *Diacritics* 24 (Summer–Autumn 1994): 43–57.

———, ed. *Representing Blackness: Issues in Film and Video*. New Brunswick: Rutgers University Press, 1997.

Snead, James. *White Screens, Black Images: Hollywood from the Dark Side*. Edited by Colin MacCabe and Cornel West. New York: Routledge, 1994.

Sobel, Mechal. *Trabelin' On: The Slave's Journey to an Afro-Baptist Faith*. Westport, CT: Greenwood Press, 1979.

Stewart, Jacqueline Najuma. *Migrating to the Movies: Cinema and Black Urban Modernity*. Berkeley: University of California Press, 2005.

Taylor, Clarence. *The Black Churches of Brooklyn*. New York: Columbia University Press, 1994.

Terry, Arthur LeMont. "Genre and Divine Causality in the Religious Films of Spencer Williams, Jr." PhD diss., Regent University, 1995.

Thaggert, Miriam. "Racial Etiquette: Nella Larsen's *Passing* and the *Rhinelander* Case." *Meridians: Feminism, Race, Transnationalism* 5, no. 2 (2005): 1–29.

Thompson, Robert Farris. *Flash of the Spirit: African and Afro-American Art and Philosophy.* New York: Vintage Books, 1983.

Tristano, Richard. M. "Holy Family Parish: The Genesis of an African-American Catholic Community in Natchez, Mississippi." *Journal of Negro History* 83 (Autumn 1998): 258–83.

Vaughan, Stephen. "Morality and Entertainment: The Origins of the Motion Picture Production Code." *Journal of American History* 77: 1 (June 1990): 39–65.

Verrett, Shirley, and Christopher Brooks. *I Never Walked Alone: The Autobiography of an American Singer.* Hoboken, NJ: John Wiley, 2003.

Vidor, King. *King Vidor on Film Making.* New York: David MacKay, 1972.

———. *A Tree Is a Tree.* New York: Harcourt, Brace, 1952.

Wald, Gayle. "Crossing the Line: Racial Passing in Twentieth-Century American Literature and Culture." PhD diss., Princeton University, 1995.

———. *Crossing the Line: Racial Passing in U.S. Literature and Culture.* Durham: Duke University Press, 2000.

Walsh, Frank. *Sin and Censorship: The Catholic Church and the Motion Picture Industry.* New Haven: Yale University Press, 1996.

Watts, Jill. *God, Harlem U.S.A.: The Father Divine Story.* Berkeley: University of California Press, 1992.

Webb, Lillian Ashcraft. *About My Father's Business: The Life of Elder Michaux.* Westport, CT: Greenwood Press, 1981.

Weisenfeld, Judith. "For Rent: 'Cabin in the Sky': Race, Religion, and Representational Quagmires in American Film." *Semeia* 74 (1996): 147–65.

———. "For the Cause of Mankind: The Bible, Racial Uplift, and Early Race Movies." In *African Americans and the Bible: Sacred Texts and Social Textures,* edited by Vincent Wimbush. New York: Continuum, 2000.

———. "Saturday Sinners and Sunday Saints: The Nightclub as Urban Menace in 1940s Race Movies." In *Faith in the Market: Religion and The Rise of Urban Commercial Culture,* edited by John Giggie and Diane Winston. New Brunswick: Rutgers University Press, 2002.

———. "Teaching Morality in Race Movies." In *Religions of the United States in Practice,* edited by Colleen McDannell, vol. 2. Princeton University Press, 2001.

———. "Truths That Liberate the Soul: Eva Jessye and the Politics of Religious

Performance." In *Women and Religion in the African Diaspora*, edited by R. Marie Griffith and Barbara Diane Savage. Baltimore: Johns Hopkins University Press, 2006.

Wiggins, William H., Jr. "Pilgrims, Crosses, and Faith: The Folk Dimensions of Heaven Bound." *Black American Literature Forum* 25 (Spring 1991): 93–100.

Williams, Linda. *Playing the Race Card: Melodramas of Black and White from Uncle Tom to O.J. Simpson*. Princeton: Princeton University Press, 2001.

Wimbush, Vincent, ed. *African Americans and the Bible: Sacred Texts and Social Textures*. New York: Continuum, 2000.

Winkler, Allan M. *The Politics of Propaganda: The Office of War Information, 1942–1945*. New Haven: Yale University Press, 1978.

Young, Lola. *Fear of the Dark: "Race," Gender and Sexuality in the Cinema*. New York: Routledge, 1996.

INDEX

Edwards, James, 210

Ellington, Duke, 175

Ellison, Ralph: Hollywood message movies and, 209–210, 212; *Lost Boundaries* and, 214, 219, 230; passing and, 211

Emperor Jones, The, 258n10, 281n4, 283n18

Entertainment Industry Emergency Committee, 201

Esmond, Irwin, 128

Everett, Francine, 146

Farber, Manny, 220

Fellows, Bob, 262n54

Fentress, J. Cullen, 82

Ferrer, Mel, 215, 217, 229–230, 311n59, 312n65

Fetchit, Stepin (Lincoln Perry), 80, 266n93

Fighting Americans, 187. *See also* black audience films

Flagg, James Montgomery, 79, 80

Fletcher, T. Thomas, 59–60

Fletcher, Winona, 99

Fonda, Henry, 167

Ford, Norman, 198

Freed, Arthur, 175

Freleng, Isadore "Friz," 79, 263n62

Fuller, Alva, 107

Gaines, Jane, 115

Garfield, John, 207, 215, 307n15

Garrison, Harold, 21, 63

Garvey, Marcus, 284n21; black God and, 54, 55; *The Black King* and, 137, 138, 141, 283n15, 284n19

Gates, J. M., 120, 279n82

Gentleman's Agreement, 206, 207, 209, 215, 315n100. *See also* Hollywood

Gibson, Truman K., 163, 187, 288n1, 289n4

Gilbert, Mercedes, 86, 261n44. See also *In Greener Fields*

Gilpin, Charles, 44, 260n29

Gist, Eloyce and James, 90, 129, 236; *Hell Bound Train* and, 119, 121, 122

Gledhill, Christine, 116

Go Down, Death, 100, 102, 272n38; *The Blood of Jesus* and, 117, 118; censorship and, 127–129, 280n94; divine intervention and, 95–95, 113, 115; *L'Inferno* and 118–119, 127, 278n77; melodrama and, 115–116; popular Christian images and, 123; urban entertainment and, 131. *See also* black audience films; Williams, Spencer

Going to Glory, Come to Jesus, 90, 91, 103–104, 130

Goldberg, Jack, 286–287n29; *We've Come a Long, Long Way*, 188, 190–193, 299–300n99; *The Negro Soldier* and, 193–194, 301n114

Goldthwaite, Rogenia, 96

Goodwin, Ruby Berkley, 23, 45

Gracia, Jack, 68–69

Gray, Harry, 23, 31, 44, 139, 256nn69–70. See also *Hallelujah*

Gray, Paralee Priscilla, 297–298n76

Greaves, William, 149, 215, 216, 286n28, 311n67

Green, Marthan Denise, 77

Green Pastures, The, 235, 265n84, 267–268n117; African American actors and, 59, 62, 65–66, 67–68; artifice of, 71–72, 265n8; the Bible and, 53, 54, 55, 67, 70–81; *Clean Pastures* and, 79–81, 266n95; composition of, 57–58; critical response and, 53, 54–55, 62, 63, 68, 78, 59, 80, 81–82, 87; depiction of God and, 53–55, 65–66, 75–78, 265n86; *In Greener Fields* and, 86; international reaction and, 83–84; music and, 60–61; segregation and, 63–64; stage production of, 10, 53–54, 55, 56, 58–59, 138, 259n23, 259n25; theology of, 57–58, 70, 75–58, 213;

Text: 10.25/14 Fournier

Display: Fournier

Compositor: BookMatters, Berkeley

Printer and binder: Thomson-Shore, Inc.